Shamans of the *Foye* Tree

Shamans of the *Foye* Tree

Gender, Power, and Healing among Chilean Mapuche

ANA MARIELLA BACIGALUPO

University of Texas Press ⟡ *Austin*

Requests for permission to reproduce material from this work should be sent to:
    Permissions
    University of Texas Press
    P.O. Box 7819
    Austin, TX 78713-7819
    www.utexas.edu/utpress/about/bpermission.html

⊗ The paper used in this book meets the minimum requirements of ANSI/NISO
Z39.48-1992 (R1997) (Permanence of Paper).

Library of Congress Cataloging-in-Publication Data
Bacigalupo, Ana Mariella.
Shamans of the foye tree : gender, power, and healing among Chilean Mapuche /
Ana Mariella Bacigalupo. — 1st ed.
p. cm.
Includes bibliographical references and index.
ISBN-13: 978-0-292-71658-2 (cloth : alk. paper)
ISBN-10: 0-292-71658-3 (cloth : alk. paper)
ISBN-13: 978-0-292-71659-9 (pbk. : alk. paper)
ISBN-10: 0-292-71659-1 (pbk. : alk. paper)
1. Mapuche Indians—Rites and ceremonies. 2. Mapuche Indians—Government
relations. 3. Mapuche Indians—Ecology. 4. Shamans—Chile. 5. Trees—Chile—
Religious aspects. 6. Chile—Social life and customs. I. Title.
F3126.B33 2007
299.8′872—dc22
2006029141

To my parents

Contents

Acknowledgments

The support of various institutions, friends, and colleagues made this work possible. I conceived this project during a Harvard Women's Studies in Religion Fellowship in 1998–1999. I am thankful to Ann Braude, director of the program, for her backing and encouragement and for the insightful comments by Fellows that year: Janet Gallagher, Eveline Goodman-Thau, Lynn Lyerly, and Alison Weber. William Merrill and Phillip Rothwell helped me think through the initial stages of this project. A Rockefeller Residential Fellowship at the Institute for Research on Women, Rutgers University; a John Simon Guggenheim Fellowship for Writing and Artistic Creation at the Latin American Center at Princeton University; and a Rockefeller Bellagio Center Residential Fellowship, Bellagio, Italy, provided the financial support which enabled me to complete the manuscript. I am thankful for comments by fellow scholars in the research seminars at these institutions, particularly to Ethel Brooks, Angela Dalle Vacche, Robin Greeley, Shuchi Kapilas, Negar Mottahedeh, and Bonnie Smith. The University at Buffalo was generous to grant me a Nuala McGann Drescher Leave Award to complete the revisions of the book and prepare the illustrations and a Julian Park Publication Fund award to help defray the costs of publication.

Many colleagues were kind to comment on individual chapters, including Ana Alarcón, Kiran Asher, Warren Barbour, Erika Bourguignon, Michael Brown, Tom Dillehay, Greg Dimitriadis, Jeffrey Ehrenreich, Louis Faron, Rolf Foerster, Suzanne Zhang Gottschang, Juan Carlos Gumucio, Matthew Guttmann, Jonathan Hill, Don Joralemon, Lisa Lucero, Sylvia Marcos, José Marimán, Pedro Mege, David Myhre, Juan Ñanculef, Don Pollock, Patricia Richards, Steven Rubenstein, Louisa Schein, Pamela Stewart, Andrew Strathern, Lawrence Straus, Barbara Tedlock,

Peter van Deer Ver, Aldo Vidal, and Neil Whitehead. Students in my seminar "Gender and Healing in Latin America" provided insightful comments on drafts of several chapters. I am especially indebted to those who assessed drafts of the entire book. Many thanks to Gustavo Geirola, Laurel Kendall, and two anonymous reviewers.

I would like to thank Carolina Schiolla for researching ethnohistorical sources for this project at the Biblioteca Nacional in Chile and to Sylvia Galindo and Miriam González for help finding other library resources. Clara Antinao, Armando Marileo, Doris Millalen, and José Ñanko provided careful translations of narratives and prayers from Mapudungu, the Mapuche language, into Spanish. I translated narratives in Spanish into English. Helmut Schindler generously allowed me to use one of his photographs. My deepest thanks to Jane Kepp and Kathy Bork for careful editing and to all the staff at the University of Texas at Austin, especially Theresa May for her support and wise council.

Special thanks to all the Mapuche who generously allowed me into their homes and lives and discussed shamanism, gender, sexuality, and politics with me. I am particularly thankful to the shamans who trusted me to participate in their rituals and everyday lives and who told me about their experiences. This work would have been impossible without the generous help of many Mapuche friends, chiefs, intellectuals, factory workers, musicians, weavers, housewives, domestic workers, schoolchildren, and farmers who shared their perspectives and time with me. I have chosen to use pseudonyms to represent all my Mapuche interlocutors in order to protect their privacy and prevent potential embarrassment to those who might regret certain confidences when they see them in print. Although I cannot name them here, I trust that my gratitude for their openness and my admiration for them and their work is evident in the pages that follow. I have used real names for those Mapuche who have chosen to enter the public academic discussion as authors of texts, speakers at conferences, translators, or researchers who collect ethnographic materials and record other Mapuche narratives and rituals.

Permissions

Preliminary versions of Chapters 3, 4, 5, and 6 have appeared as journal articles. Permission to republish my article "Gendered Rituals for Cosmic Order: Mapuche Shamanic Rituals for Healing and Fertility" (*Journal of Ritual Studies* 19[2] [2005]:53–69) was granted by the co-editors,

Dr. Pamela J. Stewart and Prof. Andrew Strathern. Lawrence Strauss, journal editor and professor, and the University of New Mexico Press granted me permission to republish "Ritual Gendered Relationships: Kinship, Marriage, Mastery, and Machi Modes of Personhood" (*Journal of Anthropological Research* 60[2] [2004]:203–229). Permission to republish "The Struggle for *Machi* Masculinities: Colonial Politics of Gender, Sexuality and Power in Chile" (*Ethnohistory* 51[3] [2004]:489–533) was granted by the editor, Prof. Neil Whitehead. Elaine Inverso, permissions coordinator for the Taylor & Francis Group, LLC, granted me permission to republish "Shamans' Pragmatic Gendered Negotiations with Mapuche Resistance Movements and Chilean Political Authorities" (*Identities: Global Studies in Culture and Power* 11[4] [2004]:1–41).

I am grateful to Helmut Schindler for allowing me to use two photographs published in his book *Bauern und Reiterkrieger: Die Mapuche-Indianer im Süden Amerikas* (Munich: Hirmer Verlag, 1990). Many thanks to Helen Hughes and to the Consorcio Periodístico de Chile for allowing me to use one of their photographs.

Shamans of the *Foye* Tree

CHAPTER I

Introduction:
The Gendered Realm of the *Foye* Tree

Foye *tree, I am calling your path to the high sky, your path beside the*
transparent earth. I am invoking you, Father God Foye; I am giving you
signs, Mother God Foye. Put yourself in front of his heart, of his head, Old
Man Foye of the eastern lands from above. Old Woman Foye of the high sky,
of the earth, of the four directions. Old Man Foye of the four dawns, warrior
of the four wars. Send us from above water from waterfalls; lighten up the
powers of the original earth.
—ROGATION BY MACHI JOSÉ, DECEMBER 21, 2001
    (ALL TRANSLATIONS INTO ENGLISH ARE MINE)

Since 1991, when I first began working with Mapuche shamans in the
Bio-Bío, Araucanía, and Los Lagos regions of southern Chile, I have been
intrigued by the myriad meanings of the *foye* tree, also known as *canelo*
(*Drimys winteri*), and its connection with the many gendered dimensions
of shamanic powers, identities, and practices (Figs. 1.1 and 1.2). *Foye* trees
are sacred trees of life that connect the natural, human, and spirit worlds
and allow Mapuche shamans, or *machi,* to participate in the forces that
permeate the cosmos. They are symbols of *machi* medicine, and *machi* use
the bitter leaves and bark to exorcise evil spirits, as an antibacterial for
treating wounds, and to treat colds, rheumatism, stomach infections, and
ringworm. *Foye* trees also serve a political purpose. During colonial times
Mapuche used them as symbols of peace during parleys and for deceptive
purposes in setting up ambushes.[1]

Today, *machi* use *foye* trees to bind ritual congregations together in collective *ngillatun* rituals and as symbols of Mapuche identity and resistance
to national ideologies and practices. *Foye* trees also express spirits' perceptions of *machi*'s gender identities. The masculine and feminine aspects

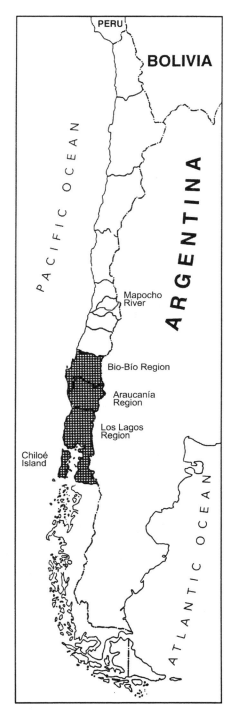

Figure I.I. Chile, showing the research area.

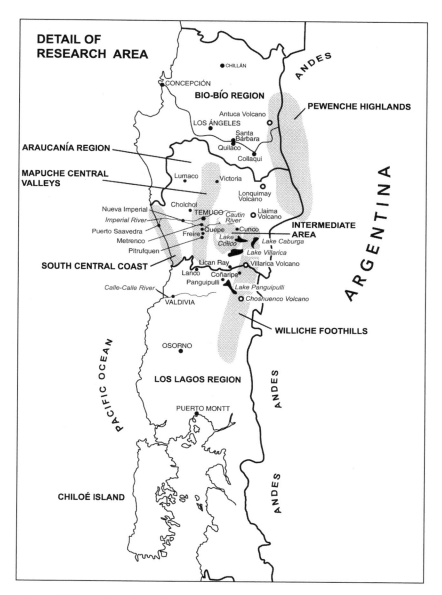

Figure I.2. The southern Mapuche regions of Chile.

of the *foye* tree and its white, hermaphroditic flowers legitimate *machi*'s ritual transvestism, their sexual variance, and their co-gendered ritual identities (during rituals they move between masculine and feminine gender polarities or combine the two), which mark *machi* as different from ordinary women and men.[2] Chilean national discourses construe *machi* as sexual deviants who voluntarily engage in gender crossing. Mapuche believe *machi* gender identities are determined by spirits who subject *machi* to a series of hierarchical gendered relationships which sometimes result in sexual variance among *machi* (Fig. 1.3).

The night before he said the prayer quoted in the epigraph to this chapter, Machi José had performed a healing ritual at his home in which he mounted his step-notched *foye* tree altar and pounded his painted drum (*kultrun*) to propitiate ancestral and nature spirits, as well as Catholic and national figures, to help him divine and heal. He wore women's clothes to seduce the spirits. José donned a purple head scarf and a black shawl pinned by a silver brooch. He flattered the spirits with stories of power and begged them for spiritual knowledge: "You have all the power . . . You have power of the heart. You have power of the head . . . Look at me. I am not a *machi* because of my own choice. I am your bud, your child, your humble servant . . . I kneel before you. I beg you to blow me your healing knowledge, your remedies. Have pity on me."

José rocked from side to side as he beat his drum. His head rolled loosely as he entered into trance. Once the spirits were present, José assumed masculine, feminine, and co-gendered identities for purposes of healing. When he mounted his step-notched axis mundi, or tree of life (*rewe*), which connects the human and spirit worlds, he traveled in ecstatic flight to other worlds as a masculine master of animals and a mounted warrior. José called on male ancestral warriors, Chilean generals, and Jesus to help him exorcise illness and misfortune from his patient's body. He placed crossed knives behind his patient's head and sprinkled firewater first around the patient's bed and then around the outside of the house.

José also became a feminine bride possessed by spirits, embodying Old Moon Woman, the morning star, and the Virgin Mary, in order to reintegrate patients into their communities. He rubbed this patient's body with soothing laurel leaves and told his parents they had to be kinder to the boy: "He wandered around and lost his soul because he doesn't feel supported. He will find a job and will help you, but you have to embrace him or the evil spirits will get him."

José's ability to move between genders also enabled him to embody the four aspects—male, female, young, and old—of the Mapuche deity

Figure I.3. *Machi* praying with *foye* leaves at the *rewe*, which is flanked by branches of the *foye* and *triwe* trees (photo bought at the market in Temuco).

Ngünechen in order to become whole, create new order in the world, and transform sickness into health and unhappiness into well-being: "Father God of the sky, Mother God of the sky, Young Man and Young Woman of the sky. You exist in the transparent earth above and you are looking from there . . . you take hold of me, my breath and body . . . You powerful people who know the destiny of the universe, help me heal." José's hierarchical, gendered relationships with spirits, deities, other *machi,* and animals, expressed through spiritual kinship, marriage, and mastery, reflected historical ethnic and national relationships, social and gender dynamics, and complex understandings of personhood.

In his everyday life, in contrast, José dressed in jeans and a sweater and responded to the heterosexual normative gender model of Chilean society by reinventing himself as a celibate Catholic priest, a heterosexual spiritual doctor, a man of politics, and a masculine spiritual warrior. Female *machi,* in turn, often present themselves as Mary-worshiping mother figures, moon priestesses, chaste nuns, apolitical housewives, and moral angels. Since colonial times, *machi* have been women or partially transvestite men who assume co-gendered roles, but today they respond to the gender expectations of Chile's male-dominated Catholic society and of the country's biomedical discourses. They carefully negotiate the political practices considered acceptable for men and women, trying not to endanger their spiritual roles, which Mapuche view as antithetical to roles of political authority. José and other male *machi* masculinize themselves by drawing on the image of the spiritual warrior, through which they synthesize their spiritual authority and their political practices. Female *machi* develop nonpartisan, shamanic reinterpretations of political authorities for their own pragmatic ends, offering a new understanding of the workings of power.

Machi, Gender, and Sex

I initially became interested in the gendered dimensions of *machi* practice because I wanted to understand why women and partially transvestite men predominated as shamans and held spiritual power in Mapuche society, whereas descent, succession, and inheritance were traced through men, and men held positions of political authority. I was interested in the cultural assumptions that motivated *machi* and in the meaning of their practices for both Mapuche and Chileans—among whom the legality and legitimacy of *machi* medicine is disputed. I supposed that I would find

Figure I.4. *Machi*, regardless of their sex, wear head scarves, necklaces of *kopiwe* flowers, and shawls during rituals to seduce the spirits (photo by Ana Mariella Bacigalupo).

significant differences in the healing therapies and practices of male and female *machi* that expressed men's and women's roles in everyday life, as well as their goals, concerns, and authority within the family, the community, and Chilean society at large. I assumed that male and female *machi*'s negotiations with the spirits echoed the types of social relationships they had in their everyday lives and that accusations of witchcraft reflected conflict and jealousy.

Although these assumptions held true in certain contexts, I discovered that *machi*'s experiences and practices were also shaped by gendered relationships that had little to do with their sex or their roles as women or men in everyday life. The spirits were interested in *machi*'s gendered discourses and performances, not in the sex under the *machi*'s clothes (Fig. 1.4).

In this book, I show how *machi* use paradoxical discourses about gender, as well as notions of spirituality, health, politics, and power, to legitimate themselves as prestigious, co-gendered shamans and as either modern, masculine men or traditional, feminine women. Gender is one of the metaphors *machi* use to mark boundaries and connections between local and national ideologies, to link ordinary worlds with spiritual realities, and to facilitate health and healing. I argue that *machi*'s bodies, their desires and gendered performances, and their possession by or control over spirits become sites for local conflicts and expressions of identity and difference between Mapuche and non-Mapuche people—the places where power, hierarchy, and healing are played out.

Shamans of the Foye *Tree* is about the cultural construction of gender and sexuality through the lives and healing practices of *machi* and the contested understanding of their gendered powers and practices. It is also about how *machi* engage their marginality, relative to the gendered discourses of the state, by protesting, reinterpreting, and parodying those discourses for their own ends. I argue that gender—the assortment of attributes and predispositions considered either feminine or masculine— takes precedence over biological sex in constructing the *machi* self in ritual contexts and in shaping *machi*'s erotic relationships with spirits.[3] In everyday contexts, however, *machi*'s identities are further complicated by the more biologically oriented hegemonic discourses of Chilean society, in which sex is "naturally" associated with gender and male sexuality is determined by who penetrates whom. *Machi*'s sexualities—the ways in which *their* genital acts with other humans are viewed—are interpreted from various perspectives and are often contested and contradictory.

The Chilean state stigmatizes *machi* as witches and sexual deviants regardless of the sexual acts they perform, and it constructs them as exotic folk practitioners in spite of their hybrid healing practices. *Machi,* in turn, reinterpret and contest these images and draw on national prestigious gendered positions to legitimate themselves. They shape their gendered occupations, healing practices, and political activities according to the expectations Mapuche and Chileans hold of women and men. I am concerned with the dialectic between gendered meanings, knowledge, and power as filtered through these various lenses. I analyze the ways in which the dynamics of gender and power explains the complex gendered relationships between *machi* and the spirit world, their communities, and the Chilean state.

In this ethnography of the shifting gender identities and sexualities of *machi* in a variety of ritual, everyday, and political contexts, I address a crucial aspect of the anthropology of shamanism and studies of gender, sexuality, and personhood that to date remains unexplored and undertheorized. The idea that gender is culturally constructed, performed, and enmeshed in relations of power is generally accepted in anthropology, but the ways in which gender and sexuality relate to spiritual experiences and change in different contexts are often ignored. Although anthropologists have long recognized the existence of different cultural representations of selfhood (Appadurai 1990; Desjarlais 2000; Ewing 1990; Geertz 1973, 1983; Langness 1987), rigid notions of "permanent" personhood persist where gender or sexuality is concerned. I believe anthropologists' preoccupation with anatomical sex as the guiding component of gender and sexuality has clouded other issues central to the gendered construction of sexuality and personhood and the discontinuities in shamans' gendered and sexual identities. I want to question received wisdom about the gendered and sexual nature of shamanism and personhood and offer new ways of thinking about the relationship of gender, genitals, sexual acts, and sexualities in the context of everyday, spiritual, and ethnic-national power relations.

Judith Butler, in *Gender Trouble: Feminism and the Subversion of Identity* (1990), argues that gender slippage is limited to that between "normative gender behavior" and its re-creation in performance. She maintains that few possibilities exist for subverting gender. I hope to demonstrate that *machi* subvert various gendered ideologies as they move among three notions of "normative gender behavior" and perform different gender identities in everyday, ritual, and political contexts.

The three gendered binaries that shape the way *machi* see themselves and the way others view them are structured by different principles. First is the male-female binary of the majority discourse, defined by biological sex and associated with men and women; second is the binary defined by the sexual-penetration paradigm, in which penetrating men are opposed to receptive nonmen and women; and third is the binary defined by *machi*'s ritual performances of the feminine and the masculine. These polarized gender referents are not antagonistic to gender fluidity. Indeed, the polarization of the masculine and the feminine is precisely what allows *machi* to move between the two or to collapse them. *Machi*'s juggling of different genders adds an important dimension to the ways in which national and Mapuche discourses conflict, overlap, are transformed, and are appropriated. My goal is to offer a new perspective on current discussions of personhood, gender, and sexuality and on the connection between gendered social relationships, altered states of consciousness, and shamanic performances.

The Making of an Experiential Ethnography

The shifting gendered practices and subjectivities of *machi* are the most controversial aspects of Mapuche shamanism. Anthropologists have widely misread them, and the Chilean majority has shunned them as the practice of homosexuals and witches. Mapuche see *machi* practice as both sacred and gender deviant, and *machi* themselves have reacted to Chilean national and Mapuche prejudices against gender variance by shrouding their shifting gender identities and sexualities in silence. I learned about the ways in which *machi* complicate notions of personhood, gender, and sexuality gradually over the span of fifteen years (1991–2006) as my friendships with *machi* grew and I participated in discussions and rituals. I shared my life stories, preoccupations, and ideas with *machi,* and they reciprocated. Like Jill Dubisch (1995:47), I believe that, by revealing myself to my consultants, I participated in relationships that were more equal and allowed for the emergence of a more authentic other.

I became a patient of several *machi,* who treated me holistically for hormone imbalances; melanoma; "thin blood"; depression; bad luck; the stress of academic life; the emotional upheaval of a marriage, a divorce, and a new partnership; and the uncertainty created by multiple moves in Chile, the United States, and Canada. I learned much about *machi* practice through my apprenticeship to Machi Pamela and Machi José and through my experiences as their ritual assistant. I did not seek to become initiated as a *machi* because I did not desire shamanic power and because my dream experiences were those of a ritual assistant, not of a shaman. Nor did I try to develop shamanic power through drum-induced trances and visions. I felt it would be unethical for me to assume a spiritual role and be unable to fulfill the commitments that *machi* make to their patients, community, and ritual congregation.

I met most of the Mapuche I knew through Eugenio, a community chief (*longko;* the word also means the head of a body) who owned first a butcher shop and then a liquor store on the outskirts of the town of Quilmawe, near Temuco, the capital of the Araucanía region. I met Eugenio through his brother Vladimiro, a Chilean Mapuche who moved to work with my Hungarian maternal grandfather and Anglo-Indo-Argentine grandmother on a farm in Neuquén, Argentina, to earn better wages and benefits. Vladimiro knew me and my family well. I spent all my summers in Neuquén until 1988, when I graduated with my *licenciatura* in history from the Catholic University in Chile and left for the United States to begin doctoral studies in anthropology at the University of California, Los Angeles. When I returned to Chile in 1991 to begin my fieldwork, Eugenio and his family invited me to community events and rituals and introduced me to a number of *machi* and other Mapuche. I met other Mapuche through Mapuche and non-Mapuche friends and colleagues.

My experience as a Peruvian woman of paternal Quechua and Italian descent who had lived in Chile as a student (1978–1988) and as a professor and nationalized Chilean citizen (1991–1996), and, later, my experience as a Chilean feminist anthropologist living in the United States since 1996 shaped my interactions with *machi*. As a woman, I had easy access to the world of shamanism, which is dominated by women and celibate men and which dealt with household crises: conflicts within families and between neighbors; ungrateful children; unfaithful spouses; and issues of fertility and childbirth. As a single woman, however, I could only attend the public ritual performances of *machi* accompanied by a Mapuche man. My divorce in 1997 granted me some of the relative freedom accorded to separated women and widows. At the same time, I was unwillingly incorporated into the local web of *machi* alliances and accusations of witchcraft; my friendships with some *machi* barred me from developing close relationships with their enemies.

As a Chilean woman, I was familiar with the dominant national gender ideologies with which *machi* struggled every day. I was aware of the traditional expectations for proper behavior on the part of unmarried women, and I behaved accordingly. My aversion to the Chilean national patriarchal and homophobic discourses that discriminated against Mapuche women and marginalized male *machi* who did not meet national standards of masculinity facilitated my relationships with *machi*. Yet, in other ways, I was always a different kind of woman. And as a non-Mapuche Chilean anthropologist living in the United States, I was an outsider who stood apart from the Mapuche I worked with because of my education, ethnicity, economic status, and the power I had to represent them once the fieldwork was completed. My curly hair and Jeep were a constant reminder of what my rural Mapuche friends were not and did not have. I possessed the car-driving, place-finding, literate knowledge of Spanish and the physical presence that helped my Mapuche friends gain entrance to banks and administrative offices. My status also allowed me to negotiate with policemen to help my Mapuche friends avoid fines for selling grains and vegetables without permits.

In the homes and communities of my Mapuche friends, this power relationship was reversed. I was at their mercy, and they determined whom I could talk with and when, what they would tell me, what our relationship would be like, which rituals I could go to, what and when I could record and photograph, and how and when I was to learn certain types of knowledge. Machi Pamela, for example, demanded that I learn about *machi* lore through experience as her ritual helper. She highlighted what she thought was important: "Bring your recorder; I have something important to say." *Machi* had local knowledge and prestige and the ability to see spirits, perform rituals, and heal. I depended on my Mapuche friends to guide me.

My friendships with *machi* reflected the unequal power relationships between us and combined disinterested generosity with what we hoped to gain from each other. *Machi* were generous in helping me with my project and sought to gain small benefits by working with me. Machi José boasted: "I have an anthropologist, so I'm better than all other *machi*." Machi Pamela asserted her power by claiming: "Mariella comes to see me because I am the only real *machi*. When I become angry with her, she clings to me." I drove my Mapuche friends to the hospital, to the local pension office, to the crowded farmer's market, and to visit patients, friends, and family. I gave them clothing, household items, medicine, farm implements, and food, which made their lives somewhat more comfortable. I did not give my Mapuche friends money, because other Mapuche would have construed it as my friends' selling knowledge and would have associated it with witchcraft. But I often paid for repairs in the Mapuche homes where I stayed, gave donations for collective rituals, and, like other Mapuche, paid for healing services by *machi*.

My ethnographic work, based on my friendships with *machi* and other Mapuche, was not entirely disinterested either, but was for the purpose of understanding *machi*'s gender identities and practices and their multiple, contextual representations. My worldview expanded and I was transformed by my experiences with *machi*, but I was also an anthropologist who documented and analyzed other people's lives. In the process, I learned as much about *machi* as I did about myself and my own culture, which was both similar to and different from theirs.

Machi sometimes felt that I understood their predicament and asked me to write a book that would legitimate their gender identities, lives, and practices in the eyes of the Chilean majority. At other times Mapuche and *machi* themselves appropriated Chilean patriarchal and homophobic discourses to slander *machi* they disliked or feared. They attributed my resistance to these accusations to my "being too much like a gringa." As Kirin Narayan points out (1993:672), the loci along which we are aligned with or set apart from those whom we study are always multiple and in flux.

In this experiential ethnography I combine the empirical doing of ethnographic research—observing what went on in front of me—with my subjective experience of the research—participating in and heeding what was happening to me.[4] Barbara Tedlock calls this intersubjective methodology "the observation of participation," in which ethnographers combine the historical, political, and personal in a single account (2000:455, 459). I try to combine detachment and engagement in what Nancy Scheper-Hughes labels a "highly disciplined subjectivity" that accounts for the understanding produced by the encounter between different worlds (2001:318). Like Don Kulick and Margaret Wilson (1995) and Karla Poewe (1996:179–200), I believe this methodology is epistemologically productive because it brings up the question of how we know what we know. It encourages anthropologists to examine their assumptions, methods, and theories and to formulate hypotheses that can later be disproved. I explore the epistemological productiveness of experiences and social action as well as their representation through various discourses of power. I include my experiences and interactions with Mapuche to the extent that they contribute to a deeper understanding of *machi*'s gendered identities and practices. But this is not an autobiographical, confessional ethnography, and my subjects of study are *machi*, not myself.

Shamans of the Foye Tree weaves together the different voices through which *machi*'s gender identities have been experienced and represented. I combine the accounts and experiences of three male *machi* and three female *machi*, in particular, with those of their patients, families, and communities, in order to explore how *machi* negotiate their gendered identities and practices in a variety of ritual, everyday, and political contexts. I also include the testimonies and ritual practices of other male and female *machi* that illustrate specific *machi* gender ideologies and practices, and I quote from conversations with a variety of other urban and rural Mapuche: ordinary women and men, community chiefs, weavers, farmers, professionals, intellectuals, and Mapuche who work in nongovernmental organizations (NGOs). I combine these readings with ethnohistorical documents about *machi*, reports by anthropologists, reports from the Chilean media, and my own experiences. I am interested in what Lila Abu-Lughod (1991) calls the "anthropology of the particular," seeing context as an ongoing construction. I draw on the methodologies of narrative and dialogical anthropology (Bakhtin 1981; Tedlock and Manheim 1995), and, like Anna Tsing (1993), Ruth Behar (1993, 1996), and others, I include my role as ethnographer in the text.

Because of the highly controversial nature of *machi*'s gender identities and practices in Chile, I have, as mentioned earlier, used pseudonyms for all the people and communities mentioned in this book, to protect their privacy. I have included the real names of important geographic referents for Chileans and Mapuche and the cities of Temuco and Santiago (the capital of Chile), and the city of Neuquén in Argentina. Several *machi* asked to be identified by their real names in order to gain additional prestige and clients. Machi Sergio wanted me to include his name and that of his community, as well as his cellular phone number. Machi José asked me to take a color photograph of him facing the camera and publish it in my book. I chose to retain pseudonyms for all Mapuche interlocutors and not to publish photographs in which the faces of individual *machi* are easily identifiable, because I am weary of the way *machi*'s multiple, shifting gender identities and special sexualities can be misinterpreted and misused by others and with the unforeseen consequences this can have on *machi*'s lives. I have combined the life histories of two *machi* to make them more difficult to identify.

The Organization of the Book

In the following chapters I unravel the dynamics of gender, healing, and power in southern Chile in different contexts and through various lenses and experiences. In Chapter 2 I draw on my experiences as Machi Pamela's ritual assistant and my relationship with Machi Jorge to illustrate how *machi* conceive of witchcraft and its relationship to colonization, non-Mapuche people, and modernization. In addition, the testimonies of other *machi* and Mapuche aid in exploring the ambiguous powers of *machi,* the ways in which they are called to healing, and how they diagnose natural and spiritual illnesses.

Chapters 3 and 4 unravel *machi* ritual gender identities and their relationships to cosmic powers, colonization, and contemporary social contexts. Chapter 3 explores the relationship between the gender and generational aspects of Mapuche persons, the cosmos, the Mapuche deity, and *machi* symbols. I analyze the various bodily and performative dimensions of holistic personhood in a sample of *machi* divination, healing, and collective fertility rituals officiated over by Machi José, Machi Ana, and Machi Pamela. I analyze the implications of these diverse expressions of ritual wholeness for Mapuche identity politics and for theories about gender and embodiment. Chapter 4 examines *machi* spiritual kinship ties, spiritual marriages, and relationships of mastery between *machi,* animals and spirits in initiation, healing, and death rituals. I show that *machi* spiritual experiences of becoming spirit brides through possession, or becoming masters of animals and mounted warriors who travel in ecstatic flight to other worlds, are gendered according to hierarchical historical and sociopolitical power dynamics rather than a *machi*'s biological sex or everyday gender identity. I show how *machi* ritual relationships contribute to current discussions on the gendering of shamanic experiences as well as to theories on embodiment, "ensoulment," and personhood.

Chapters 5 and 6 discuss how *machi* gender identities and sexualities are represented in colonial and national discourses of power and how *machi* respond to these discourses by resisting, reinterpreting, and transforming them. In Chapter 5 I analyze the gender identities of male and female *machi* in the colonial period by considering ethnic, gender, and power dynamics. I contrast colonial Mapuche perceptions of *machi* as co-gender specialists having alternative sexualities with the discourses of sodomy, sorcery, and effeminacy used by Spanish and criollo soldiers and Jesuit priests. I explore the process by which the categories of the two groups gradually merge and how they shape contemporary Mapuche and Chilean majority discourses about *machi* as well as *machi* perceptions about themselves. In Chapter 6 I look at the ways gendered national discourses and the discourses of Mapuche resistance movements coerce and construct *machi* and the ways *machi* appropriate, transform, and contest these images. I explore the contradictions between the hybrid practices of *machi* and their traditional representations of self, and why they choose to represent themselves as they do.

Chapters 7 and 8 explore how male and female *machi* negotiate the gendered expectations of the spirits with those of Mapuche and dominant Chilean society in their everyday lives, healing, and political practices. I organize these chapters around particular issues in the gendered practice of *machi* and compare and contrast different *machi* experiences and perceptions on these particular questions. In Chapter 7 I explore how three male *machi* (Jorge, Sergio, and José) have either fulfilled or challenged the gendered expectations of their spirits, the public roles assigned to males in Chilean society, and Mapuche notions of gender and sexuality. I explore the different ways in which they have reconciled their ritual co-gendered identities, partial transvestism, and special sexualities with the need to masculinize themselves in their everyday lives. I look at how these three *machi* have reinvented themselves as celibate priests, spiritual doctors, and politically active spiritual warriors in order to deflect accusations of homosexuality or witchcraft. I show how these newfound roles also allow male *machi* to legitimate their spiritual and healing practices and regain their political roles. In Chapter 8, through the lives and practices of Machi Nora, Ana, Tegualda, Hortensia, Javiera, María Cecilia, and, particularly, Rocío, Pamela, and Fresia, I analyze how female *machi* sometimes fulfill and sometimes challenge gender roles, Catholic norms, and perceptions of Mapuche tradition. I begin with the intimate realm of sexuality, marriage, motherhood, and paradoxical gender roles before moving to healing practice and the national arena of New Age practitioners, national and Mapuche political figures. I show how female *machi* are continually faced with balancing their ritual practices against their roles as daughters, mothers, and wives. They must cope with the ever-present tension between the social legitimacy they gain through marriage and motherhood and the opposing demands of spirit husbands and spiritual power. Female *machi* resort to diverse strategies to reinforce their image as representatives of tradition, yet equally engage with the modern political world. I show that the nonideological political practices of female *machi* can contribute to current discussions of power and resistance, agency and structure, and the practice of power itself.

Finally, Chapter 9 discusses the politics, paradoxes, and conflicts of representing *machi* gendered identities. I include my discussions with *machi* and other Mapuche on "witchcraft" and "homosexuality," foregrounding the difficulty of generalizing between *machi* and the stakes of different *machi* in presenting themselves and being represented by clients, anthropologists, the Chilean nation, and the New Age audience.

CHAPTER 2

The Ambiguous Powers of *Machi:* Illness, *Awingkamiento,* and the Modernization of Witchcraft

"That place is charged with witchcraft," Machi Pamela said as I drove her through the lush green countryside to the lakeside tourist town of Rukalikan, where the paved road ended. It was February 1995, and we were on our way to the home of Segundo and his family, whom Pamela believed had been hexed by a *kalku,* or witch. "The old *kalku* from the top of the hill envies them because Segundo got more land," she explained. She catalogued the family's afflictions for me:

> The house creaks and the dogs bark because of the witchcraft. They have bad luck. They saw evil *cherrufe* spirits [fireballs] dancing on the path. A *bruja* [witch] put a small coffin full of feathers in the outhouse and earth from the cemetery on their threshold so that they would die. Segundo's wife died. The witch made Segundo deaf. He cries all the time . . . The *kalku* threw putrid dogs' legs on the wheat fields to make them barren. Anita [Segundo's younger daughter] is hexed. She runs to the woods like an animal and rubs her hands together. No one will marry her. Carmen [the elder daughter] cannot think, because the evil has possessed her head. Her urine is black with evil. Joaquín [the youngest son] . . . wants to be like a *wingka* [a non-Mapuche Chilean], and he is ill. The *bruja* wants them all to die so that she can get the land.

Mapuche people call on *machi* to heal them of many forms of illness, both natural and spiritual in origin, and they believe witchcraft to be a prime cause of illness and misfortune. In modern Chile, where Mapuche feel increasingly alienated and experience conflicts and jealousy over growing economic inequalities, accusations of witchcraft are on the rise. *Machi* are in unprecedented demand to heal witchcraft-related illnesses. As another *machi,* Rocío, explained: "Some Mapuche are wealthy and others are poor. The envy and gossip are so great that all I do is cure people of witchcraft."

Mapuche hire *machi* such as Rocío and Pamela to counteract *kalku-tun* (witchcraft by *kalku*) or *wekufetun* (witchcraft by evil spirits known as *wekufe*) and regain control over their lives. *Machi* conduct all-night *datun* healing rituals to cure patients of a variety of witchcraft-related and other kinds of illnesses. They usually induce trance through the auditory stimulation of rhythmic drumming, and they gain knowledge from spirits and deities. They pray, give their patients massages and enemas, perform smoke exorcisms, prescribe herbal remedies for the patient to drink or use as poultices, and give advice about social relationships.

The roots of these rituals are ancient, but *machi* today thrive as they engage with contemporary concerns and incorporate into their spiritual practices the knowledge and symbols of Catholicism and the national medical and political systems, transforming and resignifying them in the process. Besides curing the effects of witchcraft, they cure soul loss and evil-spirit possession, abate divine punishments, and provide antibiotics. They treat insomnia, stress, and depression, and they legitimate the Mapuche's political struggles for land recovery and sovereignty. Shamans mediate between the human and spirit worlds, female and male gender identities, and discourses about good and evil, tradition, and modernity.

In this chapter I begin and end with witchcraft, not only because *machi* find it such an important part of their healing work but also because, as we will see, Mapuche view *machi* and witches as not entirely different from each other. The powers of both arise from complementary forces of good and evil in a dual universe, and *machi* are thought to be capable of using their powers for ill as well as for good. Along the way, I describe how spirits call certain people to vocations as *machi* healers and how *machi* diagnose natural and spiritual illnesses.

A *Datun* for Witchcraft

From Rukalikan, Pamela and I continued along narrow dirt roads to the Mapuche community of Tren-tren filu, where the dirt road ended, too. Before the trip Pamela had surprised me by saying about Segundo's family: "I am going to heal them, and I need you to come as my ritual assistant."

I was hesitant to accept. I had grown close to Pamela since our first meeting in 1991; she referred to me as her granddaughter, and I often stayed at her house and traveled with her to healing rituals, where I prepared herbal remedies, shook tree branches, and played sleigh bells and rattles for her. But Pamela's daughter Beatriz had always been her main ritual assistant. I was afraid I might confuse the herbal remedies in the dark of the night or fail to recognize when the skin of the *machi*'s drum needed to be heated over the fire to change its tonality. I wondered what the patient's family would think about having a *wingka,* a non-Mapuche, as a ritual helper, because accusations of witchcraft among Mapuche are often related to *awingkamiento*—any action, practice, or belief associated with becoming like a *wingka*.

"What will they say if they see a *wingka* healing? What if I make mistakes?" I asked. Pamela was adamant: "I taught you many things, now you have to help me. If you do things badly, I will correct you." Referring to my mixed ethnic background and to her fictive kinship with me, she argued that I was not a *wingka:* "You are *champurrea* [mestizo], like me. You are my granddaughter." Shortly afterward I had a dream in which I became Pamela's *metawe* (a ceramic vessel used in rituals), which she interpreted as a sign that her *machi* spirit approved of our healing partnership.

Now I was about to be tested, assisting Pamela as she conducted a *datun* healing ritual for Segundo and his children. She prayed as we continued across a river she believed was riddled with evil spirits. I parked my Jeep at the bottom of a hill, and we made the steep ascent to Segundo's house in a cart pulled by oxen.

Segundo and his family had already taken several measures to protect themselves against evil spirits. For four consecutive days before our arrival they had drunk Pamela's emetic medicine to expel the witchcraft. For counterhexes, they had tied red yarn around their wrists, painted white crosses on their doors, and drawn a circle of ashes around the temporary altar they had made for Pamela. Now, speaking to the spirits, she summarized the witchcraft experienced by the family:

> Here I have a family that suffers. They deserve to live well, to be united and healthy . . . They are asking for tranquillity . . . But the witchcraft makes you fight among yourselves. You insult and hurt each other. You treat each other like dogs instead of like brothers . . . Someone has tried to cause you harm . . . Now we shall clean these bodies and do good remedies so that the witchcraft leaves . . . These ill people feel headaches and heartaches. They feel dizzy, forgetful, and desperate. They don't

know what to do. They are afraid . . . I am praying so that you will be
well. I am looking for the best remedies, because my ancient ones have
sent me here to return you to life, to health and happiness.

Segundo lay on a sheepskin on the floor with a potted *foye* tree at his
head and a laurel tree at his feet, which pointed toward the door on the
east. Pamela prayed and drummed softly over him while her *dungumachife,* or ritual interpreter, engaged in a highly stylized conversation with
her. I alternated between playing sleigh bells and massaging the patient's
body with a mixture of crushed laurel leaves and water. Segundo's children took their own turns at being the patient (Fig. 2.1).

Then, Pamela drummed loudly and signaled for me to rub all the
patients' arms with another potion made with firewater and crushed *foye*
leaves while she prayed to expel the evil spirits:

Leave my patients alone. We don't want you here. You are bad for people's health. Leave now. You wander around transforming yourself into
anything, dog, cat . . . Go somewhere else where we won't see you again,
you putrid dog. This time you will not win . . . Why do you give people
away as if they were things? Why don't you value their life? . . . If you
come again we shall confront you. We shall not admit you in this house.
You will have to leave humiliated and despised by this family. We shall
shoot you. We shall burn you. We have more strength than you.

We followed Pamela as she circled inside and outside the house, playing
the drum loudly over her head. I sprinkled a "strong" remedy made from
firewater, ammonia, and chile peppers in the corners while the others
screamed and pounded the walls with canes and knives. Outside, Carmen and Anita prepared a *sahumerio* (smoke exorcism) made from *wilkawe, foye,* rue, absinthe, chile peppers, salt, and sulfur, and Joaquín fired
gunshots from the roof (Fig. 2.2). The smoke snaked down the path,
back to the alleged witch's house, which Pamela interpreted as proof of
the witch's culpability. During the night we heard footsteps outside the
house. Anita shot the revolver through the window, and the noise subsided. A few hours later I had a nightmare about a huge dog that barked
at the head of my bed. I screamed. Anita shot through the window again.
Segundo dreamed that the witch said: "I am screwed now; they all know
who I am," and left. Pamela saw this as a sign that healing had begun.

Mapuche believe that people who practice *kalkutun,* or *brujería* (witchcraft), introduce evil, unhappiness, and illness into bodies, both physical

Figure 2.1. *Machi* drumming over patient during ritual to divine the patient's illness and heal him. The laurel leaves on the patient's chest and forehead calm his symptoms and thoughts (photo by Ana Mariella Bacigalupo).

and political, instead of extirpating evil from the body and soul, as *machi* do. Witchcraft has a physical, emotional, and spiritual effect on the victim who fears the witch. As Adam Ashforth (2000:247) comments with reference to Sowetans in South Africa: "The witch's power works on and through that fear of the witch."

Kalku can intentionally direct illness and misfortune toward a victim, or they may manipulate the victim's will and actions. They use ritual manipulations as well as powers they inherit from their families in order to separate a person's soul from his body and transform him into an evil *wekufe* spirit or do him harm.[1] According to Mapuche logic, *kalku* send witchcraft, illness, and death to their victims by linking anything that contains the essence, image, or bodily humors of the victim to an evil spirit (*wekufe*), a dead person, or the underworld (*munche mapu*). They achieve this through ritual incantations in which they invoke evil spirits; by poisoning (*illeluwün*) the victim by introducing into her food or drink a substance called *fuñapue*, composed of nails; hair; pieces of lizards, frogs, or worms; earth from the cemetery; poisonous herbs;[2] or parts of the decomposing cadavers of animals; by taking the victim's hair, nails, clothing, photograph, or belongings and contaminating them (*infitun*)

Figure 2.2. A smoke exorcism from *wilkawe, foye, ruda, ajenjo,* chile peppers, salt, and sulfur expels the evil spirits (photo by Ana Mariella Bacigalupo).

with one or more of the elements in the *fuñapue;* by putting earth from the cemetery in the places where a person walks or sits; or by hexing scrapings taken from the victim's footsteps or a place where she has sat (*punon-namun*).

Kalku also have contracts with evil *wekufe* spirits who offer them wealth and prestige in exchange for Mapuche souls and bodily humors. *Kalku* send these evil spirit helpers to seduce victims, attack them, and suck their blood, breath, flesh, or semen. *Wekufe* may have direct encounters with their victims or appear to them in dreams or visions. *Kalku* manipulate evil spirits such as the *chon-chon* (evil bird or flying *kalku*'s head), the *piwichen* (winged serpent), the manta ray (*cuero*), the cow-sheep (*wallipen*), fireballs, the *witranalwe* (a mounted conquistador spirit), the *anchümalleñ* (the conquistador's wife), and whirlwinds (*meulen*) to invade a person's homestead and land. These magical penetrations jeopardize the normal functioning of the body and household, as well as the victim's emotions and soul, by lodging in the victim's head, stomach, and chest. They create conflict and loss of self. *Wekufe* spirits can also act independently from *kalku* to seduce, attack, trick, and trap the souls of living humans and cause illness or death. Anita described an attack by an independent fireball spirit: "A *cherrufe* pursued me and landed on my shoulder and then the bone from my shoulder poked out."

Any Mapuche who has knowledge of witchcraft techniques can be a *kalku,* but the most powerful *kalku* are *machi* who are thought to have succumbed to evil spirits while fighting them. Mapuche can hire a *kalku* to do a *trabajo,* or witchcraft job, to harm others—often neighbors or family members with whom they have conflicts over money, land, belongings, or social obligations. This was what Pamela diagnosed as having happened to Segundo's family.

Mapuche use diverse methods to combat the power of witches. Sometimes they embrace the witchcraft paradigm, accuse someone of witchcraft, and hire a *machi* to reverse it through ritual treatment. Sometimes they adopt a rational, Western approach by refusing to acknowledge the existence of witches altogether, effectively denying them the power to act. A third approach is to embrace the witchcraft paradigm but to distinguish between those one believes to be witches and those who are falsely accused of witchcraft. Machi Ana took this last perspective in April 1995 when she healed both Machi Pamela and Machi Jorge, who had been labeled dangerous witches in the nearby communities. Ana chuckled: "Now I have healed two *brujos.*"

"If they are *brujos,*" I asked, "why did you heal them?" She replied: "People say they are *brujos.* But they don't know their real selves. Really, they are good people."

In conducting her healing ritual for Segundo and his family, Pamela called on spiritual powers that were cosmologically linked to those of *kalku* themselves. In order to understand the powers of *machi* and *kalku,* one must understand the way Mapuche perceive the relationships between cosmology, life force, and soul.

Ambiguous *Machi* Powers

Mapuche believe that humans, animals, and natural phenomena all possess a body (*trawa*) and a spiritual essence separate from that body, which may be captured and manipulated by *kalku, wekufe* spirits, and other spirit beings. *Ngen*—owners of various ecosystems—grant Mapuche power if they are propitiated correctly, but they capture and possess people's spirits or punish them with illness if they fail to ask permission to enter the *ngen*'s realm. Horses, chickens, and sheep are each believed to possess a *püllü* (living soul), and *machi* initiates share spiritual essences with them to protect themselves from evil spirits. Dogs and pigs, in contrast, share spiritual essences with *kalku* and *wekufe*. Humans have both a *püllü* and an *am,* the soul that remains after death.

Machi are exceptional in that they embody and travel with a spirit that is referred to as either the *machi püllü* (the specific spirit that guides a *machi*'s actions) or the *filew* (the generic ancestral spirit of all *machi*). They also obtain powers to heal, divine, and help others from a variety of nature, ancestral, and astral spirits, as well as from the Mapuche deity Ngünechen, also referred to as Chaw Dios (Old Man God) and Ñuke Dios (Old Woman God). In different ways, both *machi* and *kalku* share in the life essences of animals, natural phenomena, and spirits. In doing so, they participate in different worlds and direct the flow of energy between them. *Machi* and *kalku* together play important roles in balancing the conflicting forces of the universe. Machi Pamela argued that the Mapuche God "made *machi* as well as *kalku,* because there has to be equilibrium of good and bad powers in the world."

Mapuche view the world as divided into three vertical planes constituted by different forces in conflict with each other. The *wenu mapu,* or spiritual dimension of good, purity, and creation, located in the sky, is where deities and ancestral spirits are believed to live. It is associated with the colors white, yellow, and blue. The sun, the moon, and the stars are associated with the powers of life and generation and are also located in the *wenu mapu.* The *munche mapu,* or the dimension of evil, death, destruction, and pollution, where the *wekufe* spirits are believed to reside, is the reverse of the *wenu mapu* and is located under the earth. This dimension is associated with the colors bright red and opaque black, volcanic eruptions, cemeteries, and whirlwinds. The *mapu,* or earth, is the everyday dimension, where the Mapuche live and work. It is where conflicting powers encounter each other and where the struggle between good and evil, life and death, health and illness takes place (Bacigalupo 2001b; Dillehay 1990:89; Grebe, Pacheco, and Segura 1972; Marileo 1995). The *mapu* is populated by different *ngen* spirits of the environment, to whom the Mapuche pray, and is associated with the colors of nature, blood red and green.

Machi combine older Mapuche notions of good and evil that are relational and contextual with a Christian dualistic morality. According to traditional Mapuche logic, all deities and spirits have a good and a bad side. They punish Mapuche with illness, scarcity, and infertility if they fail to perform rituals or make offerings and animal sacrifices or if they transgress traditional religious or social norms called *admapu*. But if humans perform these functions, spirits and deities will reciprocate by granting them good harvests, wealth, fertility, and well-being. Even *wekufe* can be benevolent or malevolent, depending on who enters into contact with them (Kuramochi 1990:45; Schindler 1989). Alberto, a Mapuche *ngen-pin* (ritual orator), explained: "Good and evil are relative things that have nothing to do with God and hell. You can make *wekufe* and use them for good or evil." Yet most Mapuche refer to the *wekufe*'s negative dimension and merge it with the Christian concept of the devil. *Machi* speak interchangeably of "chasing the *wekufe*" and "chasing the devil."

The distinction between witches and shamans among the Mapuche is a matter of perspective. Like the Sowetans described by Ashforth (2000), Mapuche believe that numinous powers make their presence felt only through signs, visible or invisible, that must be interpreted if one is to understand the meaning of life. The signs are ambiguous, and the powers behind them, uncertain. Mapuche continually interpret and reinterpret the meaning of such signs and those who control such powers. They view individual *machi* along a continuum from good to bad, a phenomenon that is common in other Latin American shamanic traditions as well (Mentore 2004; Taussig 1987; Vidal and Whitehead 2004; Whitehead and Wright 2004; Wilbert 2004). There are no self-acknowledged *kalku*, but *machi* who are perceived as transgressing social norms and who acquire unprecedented wealth and prestige may be believed by others to use their powers for evil. The paradoxes and ambiguities of human nature imply an absence of clear-cut characteristics in evildoers (Langdon 2004: 311). Mapuche fear that their friends and families will perform witchcraft against them for emotional, social, or economic gain and that *machi* might use their numinous powers to do them harm. All *machi* instruments, symbols, and herbal remedies can be used to cure visible symptoms, combat evil forces, cure shamanic illnesses, or perform witchcraft. Evil spirits can be warded off but never eliminated, so extirpating evil from one body or household inevitably means that it will wander to another one. Some *machi* practice ritual revenge, sending evil spirits back to the household they came from; in those cases, healing one person always involves harming another.

Machi cannot help other people unless they have power, and they have power only if they are recognized as *machi* by spirits and their ritual congregation. As Steven Rubenstein (2002:243) points out, in such a context it is impossible to distinguish between helping oneself and helping others. In order to heal, *machi* must promote themselves to gain individual prestige. The thin line between shamanism and sorcery is defined by the way *machi* balance their call to help others with their desire for power and money. Those who are too selfless lose power, and those who are too selfish are accused of being witches. To defend their authority as powerful but selfless defenders of health, life, fertility, and good, *machi* combat the negative forces of evil, death, and witchcraft in *datun* healing rituals. At the same time, they acknowledge the ambiguity of their practice. Machi Pamela explained this in a prayer to the ancestral *filew* spirit: "Ancient *machi,* you know that sometimes they speak badly about us and call us witches. It is true that we know the effects that plants produce and that we can manipulate them to do good, although on some occasions we do the contrary."

The same spirits that give *machi* their powers to heal are those that demand that people become *machi* in the first place. The call to *machi*-hood may come in any of several ways, and the person called (the *machil*) may resist, for the vocation is not an easy one. But the spirits are insistent, and a true calling can seldom be ignored.

Initiation through Divine Coercion

> Eeeeeeeh! I am going to be a *machi*. I'm going to be a *machi* that heals with herbal remedies, they told me. Many different types of medicinal plants came together. They frothed and flowered. Suddenly they gave me my instruments that would accompany me. "You will pass through all places on earth. You will ride on a horse. You will go everywhere," they said. They conquered me because I was going to be a *machi*. I supplicated the *filew,* the *machi* from above. My mother *machi* with the spirit of *püllomeñ* [green fly], my grandmother *machi* with the spirit of *püllomeñ*. For so long I felt embarrassed, I felt impotent. I cried so much. For so long I felt alone. "Because you demanded it, now I am *machi,* now I am *filew.* But you should help me always. Do not leave me alone. Do not leave me in the dark. Illuminate my path. Give me your light. Look at me . . . superior beings from above, wise people from above."
> —*PILLAMTUN,* OR ROGATION TO THE SPIRITS,
> BY MACHI HORTENSIA[3]

Mapuche individuals are called to *machi* practice through dreams (*pewma*) and visions (*perimontun*) in which spirits reveal the medicinal and spiritual qualities of herbs and give the future *machi* ritual tools for healing: a shamanic drum, an axis mundi, and spirit animals such as snakes, a horse, a bull, a sheep, or a chicken. Machi Rocío told me: "I dreamed about the horse they gave me to ride. I dreamed about my *rewe* with a face on it, the flags blue, white, and black. They showed me how to play *kultrun,* to pray, all of this in dreams . . . They gave me two knives to scare away evil and told me to ride the horse."

Neophytes become *machi* against their will and experience great suffering in the process. *Machi püllü* and *filew* emulate colonial authorities such as masters, kings, and queens and use systems of dominance, hierarchy, and punishment to force neophytes to become initiated and service them. They conquer and coerce neophytes through spiritual illness until they become initiated in a *machiluwün* ritual. If *machi* fail to renew their powers periodically in *ngeykurewen* rituals, they will become ill again. The neophyte's suffering is what convinces the ritual congregation—a group of four communities that jointly hold collective *ngillatun* rituals—that he or she is a legitimate *machi*. Machi Ana said: "I almost died to become a *machi*. I suffered so much. I did not want to become a *machi*. I am not a *machi* by my own will. Taita Dios made me a *machi*. That is why I am powerful. I am not like those *machi* that just take money from people." Neophytes experience a variety of trance states (*küymi*)—states of hyperlucidity provoked by sensory overstimulation through rhythmic drumming or deprivation. They learn to control their dreams, visions, and encounters with spirits during rituals or in places of power.

Machi obtain their powers in different ways. Some inherit their *machi* spirit from a deceased *machi* on the mother's side of the family and are thought to possess the qualities of the dead *machi*. Machi Hortensia, for example, inherited the spirit of the green fly; Machi Pablo, the spirit of the jumping *luam* (guanaco); Machi Rocío, the spirit of the *lican* (precious stone or remedy); and Machi Fresia, the spirit of *lefun rayen kalfu newelme* (fields of flowers and blue sky). Others are initiated directly by natural phenomena such as earthquakes and lightning. Machi Pamela described her initiation during the 1960 earthquake as follows:

> My stomach fell as if they had cut it off. I ripped off my sweater and my shoes. I was like crazy. I was with my head drunk. The sky opened. They brought me down my *kultrun*. Then I looked upward and they gave me all the remedies I should use for different things. They got my right arm and gave it power. It tells me things. I went up to the sky, up the stairs, and there were wheat, potatoes, herbal remedies up there. There was a man with a long mustache there who looked at me. There was a stone,

my *licancura*. He told me to go and get it. Now it is Chaw Dios who bosses me, I cannot decide things on my own.

Other *machi* are initiated through a particular type of vision known as *perimontun,* in which a spirit shows itself. *Machi* often experience visions of snakes, horses, or bulls playing shamanic instruments such as the drum, trumpet, or flute, wearing *machi* ribbons or headdresses, or dancing on the altar. They may also see visions of wild nature spirits, *ngen,* who offer them their powers (Bacigalupo 1996a, 1996c). Machi Marta told me: "I saw a bull in the water. He had huge horns and small little legs. Afterward, I saw a big fat snake dancing on top of a *canelo* [*foye*]; it had ribbons on its head [like those used by *machi* in rituals]. And then I saw a rainbow."

Machi's prestige is influenced by the way in which they obtain their powers, as well as by age and ability. *Machi* who inherit their spirits from deceased *machi* relatives tend to seek additional legitimacy by going through a formal training process with other *machi,* who support them for life. They cluster in *machi* schools of practice and share similar powers, ritual paraphernalia, and healing methods. Machi María Cecilia's parents equated her *machi* training with going to university. *Machi* who inherit their spirits often experience shamanic illnesses and become *machi* early in life, "when there is no doubt that they were chosen by God," explained Longko Daniel.

Machi who receive their powers directly through visions or during catastrophic natural events are often considered more powerful and ambiguous than other *machi*. They are not legitimated by any particular *machi* ancestral spirit or school of practice. Because their powers are unknown and some of them are willing to practice ritual revenge, they are often accused of witchcraft. These *machi* are initiated later in life and occasionally experience initiatory illnesses. They act individually and often incorporate non-Mapuche practices such as love magic and divination through tarot cards (Bacigalupo 1994b).

Each *machi* "type" encompasses a wide variety of experiences. Some *machi* experience *machikutran* (*machi* illness), *machi-pewma* (*machi* dreams), and visions; others have *machi* illnesses and dreams but no visions. Although there is some overlap between some *machi* specializations, each type remains conceptually differentiated in ways that *machi* themselves recognize discursively. *Machi* with different specializations are rivals and often accuse each other of witchcraft. Catholicized, moralistic *machi* often find themselves in conflict with *machi* who practice ritual revenge; *machi* who inherited their spirits conflict with those who met their spirits solely through visions or who were initiated suddenly during a natural catastrophe; and *machi* who claim to adhere to "ancient, traditional" shamanic practices often criticize *machi* who divine with tarot cards, perform love magic, or incorporate elements of Chilean popular medicine (Bacigalupo 1994a). *Machi's* individual qualities, however, supersede any rankings based on types of power or specialization. *Machi* who are able to classify and diagnose illness correctly, who are charismatic performers, and who are empathetic, effective healers are popular with patients regardless of the origin of their powers.

Illness and Wellness

For Mapuche, wellness means physical, spiritual, and emotional balance as well as good social relationships. This balance is disrupted by illness, soul loss, social conflict, or witchcraft, which *machi* must heal. Mapuche conceive of illness holistically: emotions affect the flow of blood in the heart, stomach, liver, and kidneys; sadness and family conflicts affect the functioning of the organs; and evil-spirit possession makes a person depressed, anguished, and unmotivated, with physical symptoms related to the type of evil spirit that is acting. Alberto, for example, experienced asthma, nausea, and weight loss because he believed his mother-in-law had attacked him using an evil whirlwind *meulen* as her spirit helper. As Don Pollock (1996:334) puts it: "Illness reveals a moral dimension to personhood in which individuals become the victims of social disorders and the locus of illness that social disorder provokes. In addition, practices that cause illness can be transformed into practices that cure social disorders or metaphorical illness."

Mapuche classify illnesses (*kutran*) according to their causes, intensity, duration, and localization (Grebe 1975; Oyarce 1988). Mapuche illnesses can have natural causes (*rekutran*), spiritual causes (*wenumapukutran* or *wedakutran*), or mental causes (*wesalongko*). They can be less intense, minor illnesses (*pichikutran*) or major illnesses (*fütakutran*), and they may be recent ailments (*lefkutran*) or long-duration or chronic illnesses (*kuifikutran*). Mapuche also classify illnesses according to their site in the body: head illnesses (*kutranlongko*); heart illnesses (*kutranpiuke*); tooth and bone illnesses (*kutranforro*); stomach illnesses (*kutranputra*); foot illnesses (*kutrannamun*). The most difficult illnesses to heal are chronic spiritual illnesses that affect the heart (*piuke*), the locus of emotion (*nün-*

kün), and illnesses of the head (*longko*), the locus of consciousness (*zuam*) and thought (*rakiduam*). Machi Fresia described her stress over being a *machi* as an "excess of thought." Machi José described one of his patient's illnesses as "illness of the head," which deformed his heart: "He had bad thoughts that are doing him in. His thoughts are very accelerated . . . His heart is stretched like the pod of a bean . . . his heart is about to burst. They have sent him an evil so that he will never be well. Keep his heart company with herbal remedies. Keep his head company with remedies. Any evil thing that has been done should be expelled, father, mother, and ancient spirits" (prayer, March 17, 1995).

A *machi*'s ability to diagnose the correct cause of an illness is central to its cure. Natural illnesses remain localized in the body and can be cured by a variety of Mapuche and non-Mapuche traditional healers. They are produced by an excess of work, sadness, or negligence, by digestive or nutritional problems, and by the malfunction of organs. The most common types of natural illnesses cured by *machi* are *empacho* (indigestion); *nervios* (nerves), related to distress and a feeling of being out of control; *la sangre que sube* ("rising blood," postpartum or from menstruation), which is believed to generate tumors, cysts, cancer, and hematomas; *enfriamiento* (chills), related to rheumatism, arthritis, pain in the bones, swelling, or inability to move; *la orina atrapada* (trapped urine), which is produced by the cold and causes urinary tract infections, fever, and pain in the sides; and various kinds of epidemics that produce fever and diarrhea (see Oyarce 1989:53). *Machi* compete with a variety of other health practitioners, including *meicas* (traditional healers), *yerbateras* (herbalists), *hueseros* (bonesetters), and *suerteros* (diviners), in healing natural illnesses (Bacigalupo 2001b:109–117).

When the balance between the society of humans and the spiritual and natural world is broken, Mapuche experience different types of spiritual illness. *Wenumapukutran* (often shortened to *wenukutran*) is caused by good spirits as punishment for transgressions or as a sign of spiritual calling. *Wedakutran* is caused by evil spirits, or *kalku*, with the purpose of harming the victim via physical symptoms, whereas *wesalongko*, or mental illness, has no physical symptoms (Bacigalupo 2001b). Spiritual illnesses are classified according to the social and spiritual contexts in which they take place. The differentiation of "positive" spiritual illnesses from "negative" ones is crucial for diagnosis and treatment, but the classification may change as the illness and treatment progress or as circumstances surrounding the illness change. Spiritual illnesses move around the body and can be healed only by *machi*. Machi Pamela explained this to the family of one of her patients: "The patient has been in *wingka* hands and has got tired of so many remedies, so many lies and false promises. The *wingka* do not know about these illnesses. Only *machi* know about them."

The most common types of *wenukutran* are *kastikutran* (punishment illness) and *machikutran* (shamanic illness). The term *kastikutran* is a neologism derived from the Spanish word *castigo* (punishment) and the Mapuche word *kutran* (illness). Spirits punish Mapuche with *kastikutran* if they fail to use their knowledge adequately, stray from what spirits consider to be traditional norms, or fail to fulfill ritual obligations. Machi Pamela experienced *kastikutran* when she allowed a television program to film her playing her *kultrun*. The spirits exhorted her to speak only Mapudungu, to eat traditional Mapuche foods, and to avoid contact with modern technologies. When Machi María Cecilia gathered herbal remedies, she sang to the *ngen* spirits and left them offerings of maize to avoid *kastikutran*.

Mapuche with spiritual gifts become ill with *machikutran*. Their symptoms include fevers, boils, foaming at the mouth, insomnia, partial paralysis, and partial blindness. Once neophytes heal themselves, they can become initiated and heal others (Bacigalupo 2001b). Machi Rocío described her *machikutran* this way: "I could not get out of bed. I could not move my tongue, my legs. I could not hear. They took me to the hospital in Chamico. They washed me and gave me pills, but I knew that they would not make me better. At the hospital they told me I would not hear anymore, but in dreams they said that if I became a *machi*, then I would hear again."

Machi who ignore their shamanic visions (*perimontun*) experience *perimontukutran*, another type of *machikutran*, with symptoms such as fever, dizziness, convulsions, sores, bleeding, bruises, and a feeling of unreality. Machi Marta told me about her *perimontukutran*: "After I saw the snake with ribbons dancing on the *rewe*, I began to feel ill. I had fever and I didn't know what was happening. I only saw shadows. I had purple sores all over my body. I couldn't move my fingers. My body was very heavy and the spirits attacked me. I screamed and my mouth frothed. They thought I had gone crazy."

The most common types of *wedakutran* are *kalkutun* and *wekufetun*. *Machi* perceive people who experience *wedakutran* as "animals whose mind has become disorganized and disoriented." They perceive the illness itself as frogs, insects, snakes, worms, balls of coagulated blood, or feathers lodged in the victim's body. Like healers in northern Peru (Joralemon and Sharon 1993:249–250), *machi* use metaphors of con-

Figure 2.3. *Machi* divining a patient's illness and future by looking at her urine sample (photo by Ana Mariella Bacigalupo).

Figure 2.4. *Machi* divining a patient's illness by drumming over her apron, a one thousand peso note, and a *foye* branch (photo by Ana Mariella Bacigalupo).

tamination and entrapment when they speak about evil-spirit possession. Machi Pamela exhorted her spirits to expel "la cochinada" (the filth). Machi Sergio spoke about the evil lodged in a woman's ovary as a "bola de sangre podrida" (a ball of putrid blood). Machi Rocío claimed that her patient "lo agarró el *wekufe*" (was trapped by a *wekufe*), and Machi Marta told me that Machi Patricia "tiene todo amarrado con el *wekufe*" (is all tied up with the *wekufe*).

Machi use a holistic and practical approach to healing illness. During consultations, they seek the natural or spiritual causes of the illness, analyze its social context, and schedule ritual treatments. They diagnose illness by looking at urine samples (*willentun*), by drumming over the patient's used clothing (*pewuntun*), or by looking into the patient's eyes (Figs. 2.3 and 2.4). They also perform the *ulutun*, a diagnostic ritual without trance but including prayers, massage, and the playing of rattles and sleigh bells. *Machi* need information about patients—their social relationships, and the incidents that preceded the illness—as well as the family's participation in order to effect a cure. In the case of spiritual illnesses, *machi* must find out which *kalku*, *wekufe*, deity, or spirit is responsible; whether the illness is a positive or a negative one; and how to treat it. In the case of a negative spiritual illness, the *machi* must locate the victim's soul, cleanse and release it, alleviate the victim's symptoms, reintegrate the victim back into everyday life, and provide a *contra*, or counterhex, as protection against future attacks.

Patients must pay *machi* to ensure that the diagnosis will be effective, to allow the *machi* to recover the money she spent for training and initiation, and to assure the *machi* that her knowledge, powers, and services are valued. The *machi* places the patient's money on the divination table or beside the patient's head during the healing ritual. Some *machi* have set fees; others ask the patient to give whatever she thinks is appropriate. Pamela prayed for Segundo: "The patient shall pay for his recovery with money. He is not asking for a free favor. So please help me heal him, strengthen his spirit and his heart."

The Witchcraft of Colonization and *Wingka* Culture

Machi Pamela's prayer for Segundo brings us back to the prominent role that curing the effects of witchcraft plays in *machi* practice. Mapuche witchcraft is tied closely to the history of Spanish colonialism, missionizing by Catholic priests, resistance to Chilean national projects of assimilation and development, and Mapuche people's incorporation and resignification of Chilean majority discourses. The Mapuche were accomplished guerilla warriors who resisted the Incas and the Spaniards and expanded into the Argentine province of Neuquén in the eighteenth century. Before colonization, the lush Mapuche region in Chile stretched from the Andean foothills to the Pacific coast between the Mapocho River and the southern island of Chiloe. These varied environments allowed the Mapuche to develop economic activities ranging from hunting, fishing, and gathering to incipient agriculture.

The Mapuche were finally defeated by the Chilean army in 1883, after Chile's independence from Spain. The Chilean army seized Mapuche territories and massacred the people. The survivors were missionized and given small plots of eroded land on reservations in the Mapuche heartland between the Bio-Bío and the Calle-Calle rivers, between latitudes 37 and 40 degrees south.[4] The state sold the Mapuche's fertile land to settlers and, more recently, forestry companies. The landless Mapuche must now work as wage laborers for farmers or forestry companies or migrate to the cities, where they become impoverished secondary citizens working as bakers, construction workers, truck drivers, or domestic servants. More than a million Mapuche live in Chile today, making up 6.25 percent of the population. Eighty percent of them are *wariache,* or city dwellers, and 50 percent of *wariache* live in the capital, Santiago.

The destructive powers of colonization are still expressed through the Mapuche's belief in several evil *wekufe* spirits who suck Mapuche blood and identity dry and bring illness, misfortune, and death. The *sumpall,* a beautiful blonde mermaid, seduces and kills young Mapuche men in the river and steals their souls. She represents the destructive powers of unbridled sexuality and non-Mapuche women and the loss of identity that ensues when Mapuche are mesmerized by *wingka* culture.

The *witranalwe* is a spirit in the form of a tall, thin Spanish man mounted on a horse. He is the image of the feudal criollo landlord who took Mapuche land, exploited his Mapuche workers, and raped Mapuche women. His wife is the *añchümalleñ,* a small, white, luminescent being with iridescent eyes, who is often associated with urban models of femininity. Her lips are red from sucking her victims' blood; she cries like a baby, not like an adult; and her blonde hair marks the devouring power of foreignness. Machi Pamela described the *añchümalleñ* as "a little light that walks around doing evil. The people take care of it like a baby, then the *añchümalleñ* helps them and gives them everything and sends evil to the people that person wants to send evil to." She chided the *añchümalleñ* that possessed Carmen: "Why have you done this? . . . You are *wingka* woman, you pretend to be people's friend, but you only do them harm.

Other times you pretend to be a family member, but you are nobody's family. You have no friends, no family. You cannot continue seeding evil in the fields and hills . . . we know you wish to harm people. That's why we are here together to clean you, to make you lose all your power."

Other human-style *wekufe* include Punkure and Punfüta, nocturnal *wingka* spouses who seduce their victims in their dreams, take their life energy, and render them infertile, impotent, or unable to establish romantic and sexual relationships with human partners. Machi Ana explained: "The affected person gets accustomed to this new power, which transforms itself into a man at night and tries to conquer and seduce the *machi* by sleeping with her."

Mapuche believe that their loss of identity and their incorporation of what they view as deviant sexualities and the lax moral values of the dominant society in Chile are attributable to the attacks of evil colonial spirits. Machi Pamela believed such spirits had caused the witchcraft experienced by Segundo's family:

> I see people wandering in the forest without any destination, like animals without an owner. They want to take a young woman to harm her, but if it doesn't work with her, they will take a young man, because they don't care whether it is female or male. There is a woman who appears to this young man in bed at night as if she were his lover [Punkure]. When this young man drinks some wine, he becomes another being, a nonperson. At this moment, he believes that this woman is his wife, but he feels as if he is tied by his hands and his feet. This is the illness that will do him harm. He says that his hip, his heart, his chest, his back, and his heart hurt. Many times he thinks that he is going crazy and that he forgets everything. My son, I also have to say that the *witranalwe* and *añchümallen* follow this young man.

Colonial spirits have become increasingly dangerous to Mapuche as they incorporate *wingka* values. The Mapuche were disappointed when the advent of democracy in Chile in 1990 and passage of the Indigenous Law in 1993 did not improve their socioeconomic situation or allow them to participate in new systems of capitalist gain or the nation's power structure. Rural Mapuche communities are threatened by the building of highways and hydroelectric dams and the rapid exploitation of forests by the logging industry. The social disruption caused by loss of native land, job uncertainty, and impoverishment has intensified the frequency of accusations of witchcraft linked to *awingkamiento,* which is often cited as the root of illness, evil, and alienation. In a prayer she performed on January 17, 1995, Machi Pamela voiced her dismay over the changes wrought by *awingkamiento:*

> The sons and daughters have changed a lot. They have become *chileni-zados* ["Chileanized"], *awingkados.* Everything has changed. Before we had people who gave good advice. Today we no longer have those old people. Now we are all like *wingka.* Everyone wears pants. Men no longer use the *chiripa* [woolen breeches] as they did traditionally, women don't wear the *chamal* [black woolen wrap]. Chaw Dios, give us strength to recover what we were before. When we speak in Mapudungu, every-thing comes out so nicely, my heart is happy. Now the young people don't speak Mapudungu anymore. This is not good for us. We cannot think like *wingka.*

Mapudungu is gradually disappearing as a secular means of commu-nication among Mapuche. The Chilean majority discriminate against Mapuche, who must speak fluent Spanish, the official language of Chile, in order to be hired for wage labor. *Machi* pray mostly in Mapudungu but alternate between Spanish and Mapudungu during other parts of rituals and in their everyday conversations. Mapuche have also introduced many words such as *kawello* (from the Spanish word *caballo*) that are Spanish in origin and Mapuche in form (Robertson–De Carbo 1977:76).

Mapuche view *wingka*—outsiders by definition—as witches because they in effect manipulate the powers of Catholicism, the military, and the state for their own benefit. *Wingka* are wealthier than Mapuche and higher in socioeconomic status, and they are perceived as valuing indi-vidual gain over communal well-being—all proof of their pact with the devil. Furthermore, the state consumes Mapuche land, selling it to forestry companies, and wealthy *wingka* exploit Mapuche who work as maids, bakers, and construction workers. Mapuche who ally themselves with such forces can be seen as having succumbed to *awingkamiento* and, by extension, as having become witches. Mapuche resistance to *awingka-miento* is expressed in the tension between local community norms and those of modernization.

Local Mechanisms of Power and the Modernity of Witchcraft

Anthropologists have long debated the relationship between witchcraft, traditional community norms, and modernization. Authors of earlier anthropological studies viewed witchcraft as a conservative mechanism of social control (e.g., Douglas 1970; Gluckman 1955; Whiting 1950). The threat of being a victim of witchcraft or of being accused of witchcraft pressured people into behaving in "traditional," socially approved, ways. Contemporary anthropologists have furthered these notions by showing that "traditional" cultural norms are always dynamic and that beliefs and practices surrounding witchcraft both respond to and engender cultural change.

Some anthropologists argue that discourses of the occult involve colonizers' and natives' mutual appropriation of images (Taussig 1987). They have characterized witches as embodying the "evils of modernization," becoming like outsiders, and causing transformation in their communities (Santo-Granero 2004:298–300). Others have found, in contrast, that witches sometimes portray themselves as hypertraditional symbols of the past for purposes of identity politics. They reject Christianity and modernity and hex those who step outside the cultural system. Witches can become potent symbols of an indigenous society capable of defending itself from depredation by outsiders or the nation-state (N. Whitehead 1999:176, 204). For Mapuche, the traditionalizing of witchcraft operates simultaneously with its modernization.

Mapuche notions of witchcraft associated with outsiders have changed over time. In the 1950s Mapuche located the source of evil in Mapuche women from outside the community who had married local men but did not belong to the local patrilineages (Faron 1964). Contemporary Mapuche more often associate witchcraft with differences in prestige and wealth created by relationships with the *wingka* world. Witches are men and women from the same community or ritual congregation as their accusers. Regardless of whether these witches belong to a local patrilineage or married in, they are not seen as external to the ritual congregation but are thought to destroy communal solidarity from within. Accusations of witchcraft flare up most often among people who share communal responsibilities and have conflicts over communal obligations or property. Local witches have a vested interest in attacking specific persons and households in a way that *wingka* or Mapuche from other ritual congregations do not.

A good example is that of Machi Jorge, forty-eight at the time I met him in 1991. We will become better acquainted with Jorge in Chapter 7, but for now his case illustrates the way local notions of witchcraft are closely tied to modernity and the social, political, and economic changes it brings to local communities (Bacigalupo 2005). Mapuche nowadays see witches as people who draw on older Mapuche notions of ambivalent shamanic powers rather than on Catholic morality; who challenge local sociopolitical hierarchies and communal egalitarian ideals; who accumulate wealth and prestige through engagement with modern beliefs and practices, capitalism, and foreign influences; who are excessively poor or wealthy; who challenge dominant Chilean gender norms and are suspected of being sexually variant; who challenge Mapuche norms of sociality through aggression, individualism, and amorality; and who commodify indigenous knowledge for their own benefit rather than that of the community.[5]

Jorge lived in a poor, rural, predominantly Catholic community that construed itself as traditionally Mapuche in order to distance itself from the nearby city of Temuco and resist its modernizing influence. Most community members lived off the land or worked for wages on nearby farms or for forestry companies. The community held an egalitarian ideology in which decisions were taken by consensus, but it also had a traditional system of sociopolitical hierarchy in which a few prestigious families held positions of authority as community chiefs, orators, and shamans.

The community's vision of itself changed, however, after Chile's return to democracy in 1990, as a result of fractures that developed when community members took different positions in relation to foreign influences. Some increased their economic status by marketing Mapuche traditions through ethnotourism, artisanship, and the commodification of shamanism; Jorge was one of these. Some urban Mapuche returned to the community with modern ideas and commodities such as cars and cellular phones that locals could not afford.

The new ways of accumulating wealth and power through interaction with non-Mapuche challenged the local sociopolitical hierarchy and ideology of egalitarianism, creating great uncertainty. Community members who lacked access to the new systems of power were envious of those, such as Jorge, who did and accused them of using witchcraft to gain their status and of undermining Mapuche identity and communal solidarity. The new elites, in turn, accused ordinary people in the community of using traditional witchcraft against them. As Peter Geschiere (1997:5) found in Cameroon, witchcraft can work as "a leveling force which opposes new inequalities and relations of domination or [it can] emphasize the role of these forces in the accumulation of wealth and power."

Jorge had been born into a poor family at the bottom of the local sociopolitical hierarchy, and he had not legitimated his shamanic calling through a training process. Yet, he had become wealthy by local standards, both through his *machi* practice and by promoting himself in the *wingka* world. For example, he agreed to have his initiation ritual filmed by anthropologists for a fee, and he sold his old *rewe* to a museum in the United States instead of leaving it in the river to rot, as is traditional. In 1998 he performed in an annual folklore festival held in the town of Villarica for an audience consisting mostly of American and European tourists. An urban Mapuche woman videotaped the event, in which Jorge staged a renewal ritual with herbal remedies, musicians, and dancers. He climbed a *rewe* that had been rigged with microphones covered with *foye* branches. He shook the branches violently and began to quiver. Two musicians from another group argued over whether Jorge was in trance or was faking it for the benefit of the tourists. Jorge himself called the event a performance: "It was not a *machi purun* [initiation or renewal ritual]. It was a celebration, a dance . . . Gringos came to see ancient traditions that they don't have in their land." Like other *machi* who perform at festivals, he claimed legitimacy by distinguishing between rituals conducted for patients and communities and paid performances that are adapted to suit tourists' images of the exotic and teach them something about Mapuche culture.

Many members of Jorge's community believed he was a witch. Accusations of witchcraft against him were linked to the different positions members of his community took in relation to modernization, capitalism, and foreign influence. Certain factions believed that modernization would not benefit them and that they should remain traditional; others embraced capitalism, change, and the commodification of Mapuche knowledge. Jorge's community coveted the commodities of capitalism but could not participate equally with him in long-distance relations with *wingka,* nor did community members benefit from the web of exchange in which he took part. His fellow community members lacked the shamanic knowledge that Jorge had to share with outsiders for a fee.

Jorge was not alone in being thought a witch for such reasons. *Machi*'s wealth is a sign of their prestige and popularity among patients, but if they charge too much for their services or do not share the benefits they gain from cultural exchanges, other Mapuche accuse them of witchcraft. Machi Javiera's husband, for example, in an interview on December 18, 2001, criticized the moneymaking healing practices of Machi Lisa and Machi Abel and the consumer goods they had accumulated: "Lisa is a little witch. She knows nothing about herbal remedies, she knows only how to charge, and she charges huge amounts of money. That's the worst thing. She charges 140,000 pesos for a basic treatment . . . She has a car, she has a huge number of things . . . Abel has an extended-cab truck. He got money through research projects and abroad. He became a *machi* overnight with no preparation, and although he has many clients he doesn't have a lot of herbal remedies. He gives all his patients the same ones. He is a rich *kalku*."

An increasing number of *machi* of both sexes argue that the less secretive aspects of their knowledge and practices can be commodified and adapted to the needs of museums, anthropologists, and tourists, as long as *machi* reap the benefits. Machi José, for instance, taught a course in Mapuche medicine and beliefs at the intercultural hospital at Antumalal and sold his *kultrun* to a museum in Chile.

Mapuche believe that female *machi* are more traditional than male *machi* and therefore less willing to commodify their culture, but this does not hold true in practice. Machi Javiera charged a fee to have herself videotaped by a national film crew, and Machi María Cecilia sold her life story to an American writer for US$2,000.[6] "If I am giving part of my identity, my word, then they have to pay lots of money," María Cecilia explained by telephone in January 2002.

"Won't the spirit be angry with you?" I asked.

"No," she said, "because if I am paid well, then . . . the spirit is happy because of that. Of course, most things I will keep secret to keep the *machi* strong. I will tell her [the writer] superficial things to keep her happy."

Such engagements on the part of *machi* with anthropologists, journalists, and tourists draw heavy criticism from many Mapuche and even the spirits themselves. The Mapuche feminist Isolde Reuque (2002:73) tells of a *machi* whose *machi* spirit punished her with an illness and facial paralysis for neglecting to renew her powers in a *ngeykurewen* ritual, for speaking publicly on the radio, for accepting an interview, and for allowing her grandson to videotape her. Many Mapuche blamed the death of Machi Carmen on her having made an ethnographic video with anthropologists. "Nothing happened to Machi Carmen straight away, but many years later she died . . . She was going to die anyway because she had cancer, but people said she was sick because of the video. She was almost a paraplegic sitting in a wheelchair," said Machi Javiera in December 2001.

Some Mapuche view anthropologists as evil beings who suck the knowledge and identity from Mapuche, write and sell books, and become wealthy. Machi Abel couched my ethnographic research for *La voz del kultrun en la modernidad* in such terms. Some of the Mapuche who participated in that project argued that, because the book royalties went to their ritual congregation, my ethnography was not an instance of *wingka* witchcraft. Some Mapuche believed Abel was jealous because he regretted his decision not to be part of the project, which he later thought might have brought him fame. Others said he was resentful because he was not part of the ritual congregation that benefited from the book project, but they claimed that ethnographies were dangerous anyway.

Scholars of postcolonial Africa have focused on the ways in which witchcraft has become intertwined with the changes produced by modernization in politics, economics, and social hierarchies (Geschiere 1997). The African occult economy has been shown to be paradoxical: it provides new, magical means by which people can obtain otherwise unattainable ends, but it also offers a means for eradicating people who are considered to have enriched themselves by those very means (Comaroff and Comaroff 1999). Similarly, Jorge's community saw him as a witch who used magical means to gain contacts with foreigners to gain wealth and social ascendancy. But he also used these powers against *wingka* anthropologists who represented his knowledge and practices to the outside world.

Witchcraft against *Wingka* and Witchcraft by *Awingkamiento*

Paradoxically, Jorge's neighbors believed that, being *awingkado,* he possessed the secrets of *wingka* witchcraft, and therefore he could conduct Mapuche witchcraft against *wingka* and their powers. My relationship with Jorge and his relationships with other anthropologists demonstrate his personal hostility toward *wingka,* in contrast to his profitable accommodation of them.

My relationship with Jorge was unusual in that, after only five visits in late 1991, I was barred from seeing him by six other *machi* who believed he was a dangerous *kalku* because he sought and found legitimacy outside his immediate community. I was unwillingly incorporated into the local web of accusations of sorcery because I had close relationships with Machi Pamela and with my host father, Longko Eugenio, who were Jorge's enemies. But although I stopped visiting Jorge, whom I had found difficult to work with in any case, I remained interested in other Mapuche's opinions of him.

Jorge was known in his community for his mercurial moods and often aggressive behavior, traits that clashed with Mapuche ideals of egalitarianism and hospitality and contributed to people's perception of him as a witch. I observed such behavior myself in December 1991, when I visited

Jorge's house and talked to Sandro, an anthropologist and old friend of Jorge's who was staying there with a group of students taking a fieldwork class. Jorge returned tipsy from a *ngillatun* and began to berate me for his past experiences with American women. "I hate gringas. Once a gringa came here to watch a ceremony and said I had stolen her camera."

"I'm not a gringa, I'm Chilean," I reminded him, but to little effect.

Jorge then reversed the unequal power relationship between *wingka* anthropologists and Mapuche interlocutors by asking his sister to bring some tripe for "the anthropologists" and insisting that Sandro and I eat it. The tripe was difficult to swallow. My stomach churned. Jorge became angry. "Eat it all. You anthropologists always want information. You have to do what I say and you have to pay me." Jorge turned to Sandro and said: "That student of yours. You have to flunk her in the course. I gave her horse meat and she didn't eat it, that dirty *wingka* bitch." Then he turned to me and grabbed my hands. "So small and so cold," he said as he drew closer. "Bonita wingkita [pretty little non-Mapuche]," he chanted and threw his arms around me. I pulled back and stood up. "Such nice legs," Jorge commented. "Don't wear those jeans. Wear a dress to show them off."

As I was leaving I was unable to get my Jeep out of four-wheel drive, and it made a loud grinding noise as I drove back to the apartment I rented with a journalist in Temuco. I wondered if my stomachache and the grinding noise were related. But I refused to attribute a simple stomachache to *illeluwün,* as many Mapuche did, nor would I interpret a mechanical failure as *kalkutun.* The next day my stomachache was gone, and the mechanic was unable to find anything wrong with my Jeep. The mysterious grinding noise never reappeared.

It was after this incident, which other *machi* considered not only an egregious breach of Mapuche etiquette but also downright dangerous, that I stopped visiting Jorge. Machi Pamela said: "I heard that you went to Jorge's house and I was angry. He's a *brujo.* People who go and see him do not come and see me. He treats you badly. He gives you evil . . . When he is pleasant, then everything is all right. But if he gets angry with you, he can kill you . . . You must never go there again." Pamela also feared that if I visited Jorge I might give him photographs or recordings of her, which he might use to hex her. Pamela and I resumed our close friendship only when I promised that I would not return to Jorge's house.

Machi Jorge illustrates the many contradictory ways in which Mapuche engage with *wingka* and *awingkamiento.* He had access to some *wingka* structures of wealth and prestige and used them to reject the power of gringos, anthropologists, and *wingka* and to challenge the Mapuche's unequal positions in national power relationships. But he also gained power through these contacts and outside systems and used them to challenge local sociopolitical structures in order to impose his own.

All *machi* must find ways to resolve the relationship between local politics and *wingka* ideologies, tradition and modernization, shamanism and witchcraft, spirituality and politics. These negotiations become far more complex and dynamic when we explore them through the lens of *machi*'s gendered identities and practices and how these are viewed by others. I begin unraveling the dynamics of gender, healing, and power in southern Chile by exploring *machi*'s diverse holistic and shifting gender identities during rituals. As we will see in the next two chapters, these gender identities are central to the balance of cosmic powers and social order as well as to the maintenance of complex, gendered relationships among humans, animals, and the spirit world.

CHAPTER 3

Gendered Rituals for Cosmic Order: Shamanic Struggles for Wholeness

*I ask you to support me, take pity on me, do me a favor, Old Woman of the
Morning, Old Man of the Morning. I ask you to lift my heart . . . Because
my kin are not well, Father of the Sky, Mother of the Sky, I ask you to help me.
Look at me, Young Father of the Sky, Young Mother of the Sky, Old Woman
Who Lives in the Sky, who lives in the transparent earth, help me. Send me the
help I need from the young earth, the transparent earth, the old earth.*
— EXCERPT FROM A DIVINATION BY MACHI JOSÉ,
DECEMBER 21, 2001

The struggle for wholeness—the melding of all the world's experience and
knowledge—is central to the practice of *machi* in Chile today. Mapuche
people, marginalized by the Chilean state socially, economically, and politically, link individual and social order with cosmological order. Both
social and cosmological relations affect individual health and illness. A
healthy person and body offer a model of social harmony and cosmic
wholeness. Disruptions or transgressions of social or moral norms and
failure to fulfill commitments to kin, ancestor spirits, and the Mapuche
deity Ngünechen produce individual and social illnesses as well as cosmological chaos.[1]

To help prevent or repair such disruptions, *machi* use gender and generational categories to link the human world with spiritual realities. By
mimicking and manipulating the gender and generational categories inherent in the fourfold deity Ngünechen, *machi* unleash cosmic powers in
an effort to convert illness into health, disorder into order, and scarcity
into abundance.

Theorists of "embodiment" have explored the symbiosis of mind and
body in the person, the cultural meanings and concepts inscribed onto

bodies, and the interdependence of bodies and persons with social, cosmological, and political processes. Nancy Scheper-Hughes and Margaret Lock (1987) distinguish between different dimensions of embodiment: the individual body as the lived experience of body as self; the social body, or the representational uses of the body as a symbol of nature, society, and culture; and the body politic as the regulation and control of bodies. Maurice Merleau-Ponty (1962) and Thomas Csordas (1990) both view embodiment as the existential condition of the possibility of culture and self, whereas Michel Foucault (1977, 1980) is concerned with the body as a readable text upon which social reality is inscribed. Some researchers have viewed the body as a passive reflector of social and cultural values; others have focused on its active role in shaping personal agency. Pamela Stewart and Andrew Strathern (2001) explore the way in which the body-mind complex becomes a vehicle for the expression of values and relationships in the social and cosmological realm. People are both individual and separate from other creatures and consubstantial with or linked to these others in the realm of sociality and the cosmos. Bodies, bodily humors, and souls share the substances and qualities of social processes (Pollock 1996:320), are important in the physical and moral constitution of persons, and are linked to the cosmos.

In this chapter I explore the ways in which the gender and generational aspects of Mapuche persons are extended to the sociocosmological order, to Mapuche ritual practice and the symbolic items used in it, and to the creation of a holistic *machi* personhood. After outlining Mapuche cosmology, I describe the ways in which its gender and generational attributes are symbolized in the drums, *rewes,* plants, and other items *machi* use as tools in healing rituals. Then I turn to three kinds of Mapuche rituals to illustrate the ways in which *machi* perform the holistic personhood that is intrinsic to Mapuche cosmology. First, in divination rituals, gender difference is enacted by *machi* and *dungumachife* (ritual interpreters for *machi*), and wholeness is expressed through their ritual partnership. A divination ritual performed by Machi José and his sister demonstrates how ecstatic and formal discourses are gendered independently of the sex of the actors.

Second, in communitywide *ngillatun* rituals, difference is impersonated by diverse actors, and wholeness is enacted collectively to integrate the ritual community. A collective *ngillatun* ritual led by Machi José and Machi Norma demonstrates that both sex-based and performative dimensions of gender and generation are crucial for collective renditions of wholeness.

Third, in individual healing rituals, difference is subsumed by the *machi,* who enacts wholeness as wellness, and the performative dimension of gender prevails over the notion of gender as linked to sex. A complex healing ritual performed by Machi Ana for Machi Pamela demonstrates how *machi,* both male and female, assume masculine, feminine, and co-gendered identities—moving between masculine and feminine gender polarities or combining them—for the purpose of healing.[2]

Cosmic Ordering through Age and Gender: Myth, Spirits, and Deity

The big spirit lived with a number of little spirits [children], who wanted power and rebelled, so the big spirit spat on them, and their bodies turned to stone. They fell to the earth and became mountains. Some spirits stayed trapped inside the earth . . . and turned the mountains into smoking and erupting volcanoes. They were the big spirit's sons, who became the first male warrior spirits in the form of thunder, lightning, volcanoes, and stones. Our ancestors came from these spirits, called *pülliam.* Other spirits were loyal to the big spirit and cried copiously over the mountains and ashes. These were the big spirit's daughters, who were transformed into stars that mourned their brothers. Their tears formed lakes and rivers. The earth was created from the mixture of water [daughters' tears] and ash from the volcanoes [brothers' anger] and was therefore both male and female. The big spirit then became Elchen or Chaw Elchefe, the creator of humankind, and divided itself into male sun and husband/father [*antü*] and female moon and wife/mother [*küyen*] . . . The moon and the sun took turns looking over their children, thereby creating the balanced relationship between day and night.[3]
— EDITED EXCERPT FROM ARMANDO MARILEO'S NARRATION
OF THE MAPUCHE CREATION MYTH, JANUARY 5, 1995

In the Mapuche creation myth (*epeu*), the initial ordering of the world is followed by a deluge in which most of humanity drowns or is transformed into sea creatures. Some humans survive on the mountains, but they re-sort to cannibalism, producing further cosmic disorder. When only one couple is left, a *machi* reveals that the two must pray and sacrifice their only child by throwing him into the waters to appease the divine anger. The couple performs the sacrifice, and order is restored in the world.

This myth explains the symbiotic relationship of humans, animals, nature, and the divine and *machi*'s role in restoring cosmic and social order through ritual. It also explains the need for Mapuche periodically to offer animal sacrifices and prayers in collective *ngillatun* rituals in order to maintain balance among cosmic forces and avoid catastrophes (Carrasco 1986; Mege 1997). The myth was enacted literally by a *machi* from Isla Huapi in 1960 during a massive earthquake and a series of tidal waves, which she thought would bring an end to the world. The *machi* had a young boy thrown into the water to save the world.

The Mapuche creation and deluge myths are maps of reality that Mapuche use "to think about and act upon the world" (Lakoff and Johnson 1980), as well as models for the relationships between *machi*, the spirit world, and the world of humans. The interdependence of these cosmological realms is reinforced by the way the stories attribute the creation of nature and culture to beings of both genders and the way they make both old age (wisdom) and youth (sexuality) crucial for Mapuche survival. The Mapuche organizing principle is a quadripartite one in which the masculine and the feminine, youth and old age are complementary and are equally needed to obtain wholeness (Bacigalupo 1998a). These four principles are often represented as a family in which Old Man and Old Woman play the role of parents and spouses who possess knowledge and wisdom. Young Man and Young Woman are their son and daughter; they possess life force and sexuality and relate to each other either as brother and sister or as husband and wife. This four-part gendered principle organizes the Mapuche cosmos and *machi* rituals, and it is the basis for the Mapuche deity Ngünechen. Mapuche historian Antonio Painecura describes Ngünechen's dualities this way: "Ngünechen is dual, *epu*, woman and man. It never dies because even though we die he can continue birthing Mapuche . . . Old Man and Old Woman concentrate wisdom and experience because they are still able to procreate through Young Man and Young Woman. Those four people create our world, and all Mapuche are created from these four people. For the Christians it is Adam and Eve. But we have four people instead of two."

Mapuche themselves debate the relationships among *machi*, the physical world, and the world of spirits. Some argue that natural and supernatural phenomena are one and the same, or have equal value. According to this perspective, Mapuche pray to a variety of nature, ancestral, and astral spirits but not to gods (Quidel 1998:30–31). Meli Küyen (the four moon spirits) and Meli Wangülen (the four spirits of the stars) grant *machi* the power of fertility. Wünyelfe, or the morning star, helps them communicate with spirits through dreams and obtain information about herbal remedies and ritual treatments. *Tralkan* (lightning) and *kura* (rocks) give *machi* strength (Bacigalupo 2001b:19).

Machi also draw on the power of the four elements: earth, water, air, and fire. They call on the power of waterfalls, lakes, and the earth, which are associated with reproduction, fertility, and social relationships. *Machi* spray water from their mouths or with branches during rituals, to call on the soothing power of water. Male sources of power are those that give a sudden burst of energy. Lightning, volcanoes, the sun, and rocks are considered male sources of power, which are needed during exorcisms and in dealing with catastrophic situations such as earthquakes, volcanic eruptions, and tidal waves. *Machi* light bamboo canes and smoke cigarettes during rituals to call on this fiery power.

Both female and male sources of power are thought to have young and old dimensions. In *machi* rituals, the power of the wind is represented in *machi*'s breath, and the power of the earth, in the *machi*'s heavy-step dance. Mapuche view these powers as either male or female.

Other Mapuche acknowledge that colonial and Catholic structures of authority, considered superior to natural phenomena, have affected Mapuche notions of divinity. The relationship between *machi* and divine beings is reminiscent of coercive colonial relationships in which Spanish authorities and Catholic priests laid claim to Mapuche bodies, souls, and land. Mapuche spirits similarly lay claim to *machi*'s bodies and souls. Contemporary Mapuche sociospiritual hierarchies also reflect the Mapuche's defeat by the Chilean state and their subsequent inferior position due to loss of land and autonomy under the reservation system and Christian missionization. The Mapuche deity Ngünechen, for example, first appeared in the nineteenth century as a response to the hierarchical political and religious structures imposed by Chilean society. The image of this deity combines various male colonial symbols of authority with Mapuche nature and ancestral spirits. The term *genche,* the root of the deity's name, first appeared in 1601 to refer to the Spanish *patrón* and landowner, who held social, economic, and political power over his Mapuche workers. This hierarchical relationship was projected onto the spiritual realm, and Ngünechen became the patron, dominator, and governor of the earth and people, combining the power of all the Mapuche nature spirits (*ngen*) and ancestral spirits that live in the sky (*wenu püllüam*) (Bacigalupo 1997). Ngünechen became the donor of benefits, blessings, harvests, animal and human fertility, and health.

Ngünechen also came to be perceived as a sacred family that incorporated Catholic, military, and Mapuche ancestral authorities. Old Man

(Fücha Wentru Ngünechen or Chaw *Dios*) is associated with the wisdom of God, Jesus, the apostles, the sun, and ancient chiefs; Old Woman (Kuse Domo Ngünechen or Ñuke *Dios*), with the power of fertility, the wisdom of the Virgin Mary, the moon, and ancient *machi;* Young Man (Weche Wentru Ngünechen), with the military powers of Chilean officers and with unbridled male sexuality and lightning; and Young Woman (Ulcha Domo Ngünechen), with unbridled female sexuality, childbirth, and the stars.[4]

The authority that Chilean religious and civil institutions hold over the Mapuche is replicated in the power that spirits and deities have over all Mapuche, and especially *machi*. Spirits and deities rank higher than humans and coerce them into certain behaviors. Spirits and deities punish humans with illness, drought, and bad luck if their demands are not met, and they reward humans with health, well-being, and abundance if they are. Mapuche incorporate and resignify these colonial hierarchical systems in order to reinforce Mapuche identities and norms. The spirit being that *machi* fear and revere the most is Ngünechen, who is often pictured as an old man with a white beard. Mapuche are like the Kuna in Panama in that the traditional features of social and cultural life transform the new into the old, incorporating and absorbing the outside, changing the world in order to stay the same (Taussig 1993). Mapuche, however, also incorporate colonial structures and systems of authority that transform traditional thought patterns, creating a new, hybrid sense of self.

Many Mapuche today view Ngünechen as a moral Mapuche deity equivalent to the Christian God. Machi José stated: "The God that appears in the Bible also means God in Mapuche. Ngünechen means God." Machi Ana argued that "being Chilean, being foreign, whatever, it does not matter. We are all children of the same God." Longko Daniel explained the relationship between Ngünechen and the Christian God in *machi* practice: "Of course, today that is mixed. This is so much so that in their prayers *machi* talk about Ngünechen, Chaw Ngünechen, and even Jesus Christ. They talk about God. Sometimes they talk about God instead of Ngünechen. They mix this religious thing, civilized ideas with what they understand by Ngünechen . . . They are different names, but it is the same person, which is the supreme being. They change their language to talk about Ngünechen in Spanish like God, but they know that it is no different. The difference is only in the image."

Some *machi,* however, stress the differences between Ngünechen and the Christian God. According to Mapuche intellectual Manuel Lincovil, "The elders say that Ngünechen is different from the God of the Bible.

In their view it is their god. In order for them to be the same they would have to believe that Ngünechen sent his son Jesus Christ to look for and save those who were lost in sin. Only this way would Ngünechen be the true God. And, in the *ngillatun* ceremony, the *machi* prays to several gods, gods of the mountain, of the water, gods of the east, believing that is where God who will give them help is."

Mapuche reinterpret the concept of the Trinity in terms of their traditional notion of a four-part spiritual being and incorporate colonial family and social hierarchies as well as the notion of punishment (*castigo*). The four social and divine personas of the deity Ngünechen—Old Woman, Old Man, Young Woman, and Young Man—not only constitute Mapuche wholeness but also are arranged hierarchically according to kin relations. Husbands and fathers (associated with hierarchy, authority, and warfare) rank higher than wives and mothers (associated with fertility, nurturance, and healing). Parents and grandparents (associated with wisdom) rank higher than children (associated with unbridled sexuality and life energy). Spirits and deities (associated with wisdom and parenthood) rank higher than humans (associated with ignorance and childhood). And generation in general ranks higher than gender (an elderly mother ranks higher than a young son but lower than her husband or father; a brother ranks higher than his sister).[5] *Machi* are inferior to spirits and deities but superior to other humans who are not *machi*. They are simultaneously daughters or sons of the *machi* who initiated them; daughters or sons of the deity Ngünechen, from whom they obtain knowledge; brothers or sisters of their *machi* cohorts; and wise old parents and grandparents of ordinary humans and their ritual community. These different social and spiritual positions and relationships are what have allowed *machi* to experience the world as different people and to gain varied forms of knowledge and power.

Machi's Gendered Tools for Healing

The principles of generation, gender, knowledge, and fertility present in the deity Ngünechen are also thought to be present in *machi* and in every aspect of nature and life (Bacigalupo 1998a). The tools and natural items that *machi* use in healing are not merely utilitarian but are linked symbolically, through gendered and generational metaphors, to many different domains of reality, such as Mapuche natural and sacred geography, plants, nature and sky spirits, ancestors, the human body, the world

Figure 3.1. *Machi* with her *kultrun*, covered by goatskin and filled with stones, darts, and herbal remedies (photo by Ana Mariella Bacigalupo).

of human relations, and domesticated crops and animals. *Machi,* their symbols, and their tools for healing have powers that participate in the construction of reality and represent the meaning of the human condition in relation to the spiritual and natural worlds. As representations of Ngünechen and of nature and ancestral spirits, *machi*'s symbols possess spirit, power, and vital force and effect this power in ritual. Some symbolic items, such as the *kultrun* and the *rewe,* effect the power of the four aspects of Ngünechen; others effect the power of either the younger couple or the masculine or feminine aspects of Ngünechen.

The *kultrun* is a shallow drum often consisting of a bowl of laurel (*triwe*) or oak covered by a goatskin (Fig. 3.1). The size, depth, and thickness of the *kultrun* bowl vary from *machi* to *machi*. Ramón, a man who makes Mapuche musical instruments, said: "The materials I work with are alive . . . The spirits of *machi* ask them to make their drums deeper and rounder than those I make to sell to *wingka*. The *machi* spirit chooses the sounds and tells the *machi* in a dream, and I make the *kultrun* . . . to fit those sounds."

Mapuche often conceive of the *kultrun* as a womb and as representing the Mapuche universe, which contains Mapuche knowledge, education, medicine (*lawen*), and thought (*rakiduam*). Like the *rewe*, the *kultrun* possesses the four generational and gender qualities of Ngünechen. A *machi* often shouts "Machi!" four times into the *kultrun* before it is covered with the skin, so that the drum holds her spirit and strength as well as those of the four people in Ngünechen. Inside the *kultrun, machi* place pairs and groups of four of objects considered to be male and female. Corn, maize, seeds, wool, animal hides, laurel leaves, *kopiwe* flowers (*Lapageria rosa*), *llancato* (precious stones), and old coins are viewed as female because of their association with life, growth, and fertility. Mapuche often equate the crashing sound of these items inside the *kultrun* with the sounds of sleigh bells, rain, or waterfalls, all female elements associated with health, well-being, and giving birth. Darts, bullets, chile, *foye* leaves, pieces of charcoal, and volcanic rocks are considered male because of their association with exorcism, war, or fire (Bacigalupo 1998b). *Machi* often paint their *kultrun* with a cross that divides the drum's face into quarters and represents the *meli witran mapu,* or fourfold division of the world. This symbolism includes the four corners of the Mapuche earth, or *mapu,* the four seasons, the four winds, the four celestial bodies (Grebe 1973), and the four principles of Ngünechen. The center of the cross represents the middle of the earth, the place where the Mapuche locate themselves and their *ngillatuwe,* or collective altar (Marileo 1995:93–102). The center is also the place where the *machi*'s *rewe* is located—the center of the earth and the place where different worlds meet and communicate. The space above the *kultrun* represents the *wenu mapu,* or upper skies; the skin is the *mapu,* or earth; and the base represents the *munche mapu,* or underworld.

The concept of *rewe,* or "the purest," refers to a tree of life or axis mundi that faces east and serves as a nexus between the human and spirit worlds and is also the symbol of *machi* practice. The *rewe,* with its fourfold gender and generational aspects, is whole like Ngünechen because it merges the different worlds of humans and spirits. Mapuche often refer to the *rewe* itself as *foye* or *canelo.* During colonial times the hermaphroditic *foye* tree legitimated male *machi*'s co-gendered status as sacred, powerful, and meaningful. It also reinforced and polarized ancestral Mapuche notions of female and male powers that allowed male *machi* to move between them. Once a symbol of peace, the *foye* tree today has become a symbol of office for both male and female *machi* and the place where the *machi*'s spirit resides. It represents the *machi*'s ability to move between worlds, generations, and genders and to embody the wholeness of Ngünechen.

Machi each have their own *rewe* at home, where they maintain their personal connection with their possessing spirit (*machi püllü* or *filew*) and travel to other worlds regularly during *küymi,* or altered state of consciousness (Fig. 3.2). The *machi's filew* is believed to live in the altar. The step-notched pole *rewe* is usually made from laurel or oak, which is considered feminine. Branches of *klon* (*maqui,* or *Aristotelia chilensis*), *triwe* (*Laurelia sempervirens*), *foye* (*Drymis winteri*), and *coligüe* (bamboo, or *koliu*) are tied to its side. *Machi* believe that all plants have sacred powers and use a variety of vines, ferns, and other plants in healing, but *foye, triwe,* and *klon* are especially important in ritual contexts, representing the gender, generational, spatial, and cognitive categories used by *machi.* The bark, roots, and bitter leaves of the *foye* are considered "hot" and are believed to have masculine, exorcising, and antibacterial qualities. *Machi* place knives, volcanic rocks, and *chueca* sticks—associated with masculinity and warfare—on the top and steps of the *rewe* to protect the *filew* against the attacks of evil spirits. They also place *kopiwe* flowers, food, drink, and herbal remedies—associated with femininity, seduction, and nurturance—on the steps or at the foot of the *rewe* in order to feed, heal, and seduce the *filew.*

The forms, colors, textures, effects, and fragrances of plants are gendered and linked metaphorically to other realms of reality. *Triwe,* or laurel, for example, is considered to have healing, soothing, integrating properties, which are feminine, and is rubbed over the patient's body. It is used against fever, boils, rashes, indigestion, headaches, bad temper, tachycardia, and antisocial behavior. At the same time, *triwe* can give protection against evil forces—a masculine quality—by means of its bitter sap. The *klon* plant represents the community, or *lof* (Gumucio 1999:143). While *foye* and *triwe* trees connect *machi* to other worlds and protect them against evil, *klon* grounds them to the world of the living and to their commitment to patients and community.

Mapuche believe that plants are powerful and participate directly in the world of humans and spirits. They identify some plants as possessing the fourfold qualities of Ngünechen. The *meli-ko-lawen* (marsh marigold, *Caltha sagittata*), for example, concentrates the healing power coming from four streams (*meli*) of water (*ko*). Running water, particularly *trayenko,* or waterfalls, is viewed as having the power of life and healing, and *machi* often visit waterfalls in order to ask for rain and good luck. *Meli-ko-lawen* is one of the most celebrated cure-all plants associated with the qualities of Ngünechen and must be treated with respect. When I went with Machi Abel to collect *meli-ko-lawen* at a nearby waterfall, we prayed at the site where it grew and left some coins there.

Figure 3.2. *Rewe* with branches of *foye* and *triwe* trees tied to it and offerings of flowers, stones, and knives on its steps (photo by Ana Mariella Bacigalupo).

Context and the actions, moods, and motivations of humans, in turn, affect the efficacy of plants. One day I promised Machi Pamela that I would arrive at her house early to witness a rogation for one of her female patients, who was looking for a husband. Because of car trouble, however, I arrived in the late morning. I was upset that I had missed the ritual.

Pamela and her patient were stripping the female *nulawen* plant, known for its sweet-smelling flowers and powers of love magic. I reached over to help them pull off the leaves and flowers, but Pamela stopped me. "You are upset," she said. "You can't touch the *nulawen*. You will spoil its love magic."

Plants that are not linked to the gender and generational qualities of Ngünechen are often viewed ambivalently, because they have no role in Mapuche cosmic ordering. Some *machi* ingest *palo de bruja* (*Latua pubiflora*) or the seeds of the *miyaya*, or *chamico*, plant (*Datura stramonium*) in order to produce hallucinations, divine the future, exorcise evil spirits, and treat pain, mental illness, asthma, and rheumatism. *Machi* who do not use hallucinogens are often critical of those who do, sometimes labeling them "*kalku*" (witch), because it is assumed that they will use these plants to poison others. Machi Hortensia said that she did not use *miyaya* or *palo de bruja* because only "bad *machi* who do not trance on their own use these herbs." Nevertheless, two of the *machi* I worked with asked me to get *palo de brujo* for them when I traveled to an area where the herb was abundant. *Machi*'s relationships with specific types of plants, particularly with those on their *rewe*, affect the way they are perceived and classified by others.

A *machi*'s *rewe* is closely tied to the *machi*'s persona. His or her *filew* often lives in the *rewe*, and *machi* fall ill when the *rewe* becomes too old or slanted with time. When *machi* change their *rewe* during *ngeykurewen* rituals, in which they renew their powers, they usually leave the old *rewe* to rot in a stream. Some *machi*, such as Rocío, believe that an old *rewe* always keeps some of the *machi* spirit and can be put in the stream to rot only after the *machi* dies.

Machi's *rewe* have different numbers of steps, but the number is not related to the knowledge, prestige, or powers of the *machi* or to the different worlds she visits, as Grebe, Pacheco, and Segura argue (1972). Rather, the more agile *machi*, who can climb up the *rewe* and jump from it, tend to have higher ones, and less agile *machi*, lower ones. Old Machi Nora had a four-step *rewe*, young Machi María Cecilia had a seven-step one, and aged Machi Pamela had no steps at all on hers. *Machi*'s ascent of the *rewe* during rituals is a performance to communicate to onlookers that the *machi* has entered into ecstatic flight, but it is not required to produce the ecstatic state itself.

Some *machi* also place a *llang-llang*—an arch made from *foki* (vines) in the form of a rainbow (*relmu*)—above their *rewe* to represent their intimate connection with the spirits of the forest, especially the *ngen* nature spirits that they meet in their visions. Rainbows are the visual manifestations of the power emanating from the *foki* of the forest. Juan Carlos Gumucio describes a *machi* who saw the *llang-llang* as "embracing her like the rainbow" (1999:151). When a *machi*'s helpers spit water over the *machi*'s head, they are emulating the rainbow and invoking its powers.

Foki act as intermediaries and communicators between the forest and the world of humans via the rainbow, in much the same way as *machi* are active intermediaries between humans and spirits from other worlds via the *rewe*.[6] This is evident in the drawings of Mapuche cosmology made by Machi Marta and Machi Jorge, in which they depict their *rewe* both on the earth and in the *wenu mapu,* or sky, while rainbows appear in the forests on the earth, the places where visions take place (Figs. 3.3 and 3.4). Both *machi* and *foki* have the ability to request powers through prayer. A Mapuche woman described by Gumucio (1999:151) saw *foki* "climbing on the trees and doing their *ngillatunes* [prayers]" in the same way that *machi* ascend the *rewe* (literally or metaphorically) to pray to the spirits.

The relationship between *machi* and *foki* is reciprocal. Machi Rocío claimed that "*foki* hug and discipline to tie the *machi* to the forest," but *machi* also depend on *foki* to gain the powers or forces of the forest. *Machi* can become intermediaries between humans and the spirits only once they have both the powers of the forest, granted by *foki,* and the powers of the sky, granted by *filew*. Intertwined *foki* represent the embracing young couple in Ngünechen as well as the powers of unbridled fertility and generation. One type of vine, the *kopiwe,* grows wild in the shade of native forests, and Mapuche associate it with the wild spirits of the forest, which resist social norms, forestry companies, modernity, and urbanization. *Machi* use *kopiwe* vines and flowers to seduce or appease spirits during initiation or renewal rituals and as offerings in order to stay connected with the spirits of the forest. According to María Cecilia, "the *kopiwe* is a young woman who cannot be domesticated but lives in the forest with ancient traditions."

Kopiwe flowers appear in April and May to remind neophytes that it is time for them to renew their commitment to their spirits. *Machi* use *kopiwe* to help with the symptoms of their initial calling and with sudden encounters with evil spirits. They also use the roots, stems, and leaves of the *kopiwe* to treat venereal diseases, gout, and rheumatism (Bacigalupo 1998a). As symbols of sexual health and fertility, *kopiwe* vines may produce these effects on others.

A necklace made from *llankalawen* (*Lycopodium paniculatum*) leaves is

Figure 3.3. Machi Marta's drawing of Mapuche cosmology and her initiatory dream where her *rewe* appears in the earth and in the Mapuche *wenu mapu*. Machi Marta also depicts evil spirits in the underworld.

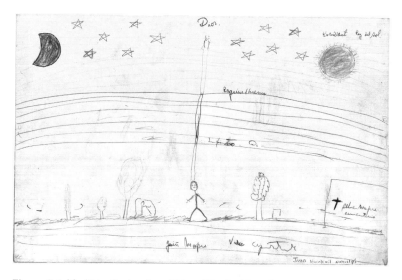

Figure 3.4. Machi José's drawing of himself in the Mapuche cosmos. José has a direct channel of communication with God, which overrides the different cosmological levels.

the male counterpart of the *kopiwe*. The name *llankalawen,* or "precious medicine" (Moesbach 1992:107), derives from *llanka,* the name of a precious green stone used in sacrificial offerings and for indemnity payments (Augusta 1966:127). *Machi* also use the plant for dressing wounds. Other vines important to *machi* practice include the *wenu-likan* (sacred stones from the sky); the *witral-lawen* (medicine of the loom), which weaves itself into people; and the *wichil-wichil* (very curved *foki*), the coils of which are charged with spiritual energy (Gumucio 1999:15–151).

Other tools that *machi* employ during rituals also symbolize the vitality and fertility of Young Woman and Young Man. Those associated with Young Woman include the *kaskawilla,* four bronze sleigh bells that are thought to contain the sound of sacred waterfalls and rain; the *guada,* or calabash, representing a womb with seeds in it; and the *metawe,* a clay vessel that *machi* fill with *muday,* a drink made from fermented maize or wheat that Mapuche perceive as the liquid of life and that is sometimes associated with semen or milk. The symbol most obviously associated with the powers of Young Man is the *trutruka,* a trumpet made from a horn and a hollow *coligüe* cane. The sound passes through the long cane of the *trutruka* and comes out through the tip of the horn, resembling ejaculation. The *pifilka,* or wooden flute, made from laurel wood, is also associated with Young Man. Ordinarily, only young men play the *trutruka* and the *pifilka*.

Machi use *koliu,* or *coligüe,* canes to fashion temporary *rewes* at their patients' houses. These canes are associated with the *machi* warring and exorcising complex and with the masculine powers of Old Man and Young Man. *Koliu* represent power in both the physical and the spiritual senses and are related to the concepts of freedom, strength, and sovereignty and the ability to battle enemies. Originally, Mapuche warriors used *koliu* to make their *waki,* or lances, and *machi* today often refer to the canes as *waki* (or *koliu* when they are used for ritual purposes; Juan Ñanculef, personal communication, 2003). Machi Javiera, for example, called the *koliu* "*marri epu milla waki*" (twelve spears of gold).

In addition to making temporary altars from *koliu* poles, *machi* plant them beside their step-notched *rewe* to exorcise evil spirits. A *machi's* male helpers strike *koliu* canes or *chueca* sticks (*wiños*) together above the *machi's* head to help her enter into trance during *datun* (complex healing rituals) or *nguillatuñma* (rogations). *Chueca* sticks, too, are associated with the warring complex. Traditionally, *chueca* games were played before going to war and to resolve conflicts between lineages. Today, *chueca* is often played in the context of *ngillatun* rituals.

Figure 3.5. The *ngillatuwe* represents the male and female aspects of the deity Ngünechen in nature and the cosmos (photo by Ana Mariella Bacigalupo).

The Mapuche cosmos and the balance between the gender and generational aspects of Ngünechen are expressed at the level of ritual community in the *ngillatuwe*, or collective *rewe*. The *ngillatuwe*, also referred to as *la cruz* (the cross), is a pole with the face and arms of Ngünechen or an ancestor of the ritual community carved on it. Often, blue and white crosses, representing the powers of the sky, are planted beside the pole, along with branches of *foye, triwe, boldo* (*Peumus boldus*), *klon,* and fruit trees.[7]

The *ngillatuwe*—the carved pole, crosses, and branches—serves as a collective axis mundi that connects the different worlds of the Mapuche cosmos to the ritual community, which consists of four *lof mapu* (communities and their land), each with its *longko*, or community head (Fig. 3.5). *Ngillatuwe* face east and are believed to protect the religious community from catastrophe, illness, infertility, and evil originating outside its boundaries. At the *ngillatuwe*, *machi* obtain knowledge about the religious community and its future and petition for the fertility and wellbeing of its people, animals, and crops. Catholic priests in the area often bless the *ngillatuwe*. An old woman from Pillamtumapu said: "When we planted the *ngillatun* cross, we brought branches of apple tree, *maqui*, and planted them at the cross as we prayed. First the [Catholic] priest came to pray at the cross and to bless it. He came to say a mass here, a Catholic priest from Padre de las Casas. In May we planted the cross, and the fifteenth of December they did a big prayer at the *ngillatun,* that's when *machi* came."

Ngillatun fields, where *ngillatuwe* are located, are sacred, uncultivated spaces often referred to as *milla lelfel* (golden flatlands), but they can be moved periodically. Because *ngillatun* fields and *ngillatuwe* are representations of the Mapuche cosmos, they can be conceptualized in different locations. Longko Daniel said: "One of the guys told me he would come to the *ngillatun* only if the cross was moved to another place, because it gave him a bad feeling there. The cross was moved to another place and the land around it became sacred." Destroying or desacralizing the *ngillatuwe* brings cosmic chaos, bad luck to the ritual community, and divine punishment to the evildoer. Longko Daniel explained the consequences of harming the *ngillatuwe* by recounting the story of a hunter who died instantly after shooting at a *ngillatuwe* pole in a field, and another about a family nearly all of whom died within a year after sending someone to cut down a *ngillatuwe* cross. Machi Leonor told a version of Daniel's first story in which two gringos, or foreigners, died in a car accident after laughing at the *ngillatuwe.*

Ritual symbols become instruments through which *machi* effect individual or collective healing because they represent the cognitive categories of the Mapuche and capture the powers of the cosmos. This cosmic power can be unleashed in rituals by individual symbols that possess the gender and generational aspects of Ngünechen or that, collectively, unite different meanings and realms of perception and practice.

Gendered Discourses of Divination:
The *Machi-Dungumachife* Couple

At seven o'clock one summer morning, Machi José sat at a small wooden table in the doorway of his kitchen, facing his *rewe.* He welcomed his first patient, a nineteen-year-old man, as his sister Amelia heated his drum on the open fire. The patient had lost his job and heard noises on the roof of his house at night. He had been wandering aimlessly, and his family feared the presence of evil spirits. José nodded as the man placed a worn T-shirt and three thousand-peso bills on the table. José laid three laurel branches on the T-shirt and crossed two knives directly below it. "We will find the evil and treat it," he said as he secured a green and black shawl around his shoulders with a woman's pin made of heavy silver. He tied a purple scarf around his head and pulled it over his eyes. José drummed his *kultrun* and began a divination song:

> I must be strong, my heart must be strong, eeeeeeeee.
> I have herbal remedies, I have remedies for you, eeeeeeeeee.
> His blood is too weak, weaker than others;
> My heart, my heart is here;
> Now the *machi* shall know . . . I am seeing his blood, his heart, his bones, eeeeeeeee.
> His bones, his heart, his heart . . .
> His heart, his heart, his blood, his blood . . .
> Chaw Dios, you who manage the earth above, Ñuke Dios,
> Give me strength to talk loudly,
> Give me good words, good knowledge, eeeeeeeeee.

José held the drumstick in his right hand, his body rocking to the left with every beat of the drum. His head rolled loosely from side to side. Amelia stood behind him and spat water over his head to help him concentrate. His body contracted and trembled as the ancient *machi* spirit of his grandmother possessed him. Mapuche view both the action of being possessed and the language of the trancing *machi* as feminine. In divination contexts, *machi* self-identify as children and servants of the spirits and beg them for healing knowledge.

Machi José used humoral medicine, in which bodily humors, organs, and body parts are believed to affect the behavior and character of the patient. Like most other *machi,* he analyzed the patient's blood, heart, sweat, and bones to diagnose the illness and her relationship to the social world (family, community, fellow workers), the spiritual world, and the cosmos. People perceived as having "weak bones, blood, and breath" are believed to be ill. Blood represents kinship, and bones are the most lasting repository of the person's power and identity.[8] José believed I had weak blood because I didn't eat enough and lived far from my blood relatives. Blood and bones are strengthened with food, specific herbal remedies, moral behavior, and rituals to appease or exorcise spirits. Food, emotions, and spirits also affect the balance between hot and cold elements in the body and may cause illness. An excess of heat is often viewed as the presence of an alien substance—a virus, a bacterium, or an evil spirit.

José drummed softly near his left ear and spoke the knowledge granted to him by the spirits: "His bones are not strong, he feels a lot of heat, sometimes he sweats too much, *alelalelalelalel.* You seem very calm, but this calmness will not last . . . I see illness, pain, fights, tears, and a lot of suffering."

Amelia, meanwhile, crouched close by and began conversing with José's *machi* spirit using the masculine language of the *dungumachife,* the ritual interpreter, who stimulates the *machi*'s discourse by repeating his or her words, agreeing with the *machi,* and interjecting specific questions about illness, evildoers, transgressions, relationships, remedies, sanctions, and actions:

AMELIA: What is the problem?

JOSÉ: There is envy in the family, conflict over a piece of land.

AMELIA: Who produced this?

JOSÉ: A distant family member works with evil spirits. The boy is sensitive, and the evil has taken root in his head and stomach.

AMELIA: Will he live?

JOSÉ: I have good remedies . . . I have medicine and he will get better. The illness is not so serious.

AMELIA: What are the remedies?

JOSÉ: He should take *alwe lawen* [*Satureja multiflora,* for digestive problems] and *allfeñ lawen* [medicine for skin ailments] for his skin. The boy needs to take my remedies with faith, and we need to perform a healing ritual soon, otherwise he can go crazy or die.

Scholars interested in healing teams have often focused on male shamans and their female spouses who have been trained and initiated together and who work interdependently to effect ritual healing, or on women who work as ritual interpreters for their shaman husbands (Rasmussen 1995:38–39; Tedlock 2003:). The *machi-dungumachife* couple offers a new dimension to such healing partnerships, based as it is on complementary gendered ritual discourses.

The intimate dialogue of *machi* and *dungumachife* during the *machi*'s altered state of consciousness (*küymi*) reflects a relationship between ecstatic feminine symbolic discourses and formal, masculine, ritual-language discourses, similar to that between the discourses of medieval female ecstatics and male Catholic priests. Hernán, the son and *dungumachife* of Machi Rocío, explained:

She speaks in Mapudungu but in a symbolic language. So, for example, instead of talking about the sweater she will say any other word, and I need to interpret and understand what she says and tell the other people so that they really know what she is saying . . . The *machi* calls her spirit and then when she enters into trance she greets everyone, and when the spirit is leaving she says her good-byes. So one knows when the words she is going to say are finished . . . *Machi* need to have a *dungumachife*. The other day a *machi* was doing a diagnostic ritual and went into trance when she was not supposed to, and there was no *dungumachife* to receive what she said while she was in trance. Because of this she was in trance all night and very ill afterward.

The *dungumachife* also elicits information from the *machi* about the patient's illness and treatment. The *dungumachife*'s masculine discourse differs from the discourses of other traditional male Mapuche authorities such as the *ngenpin* and *longko*. The *ngenpin* is an orator, chosen by the spirits, whose words carry power and make rituals effective in a way similar to that of liturgical Latin for a Catholic mass. The *ngenpin* invokes a community's ancestral spirits in a contemporary context. The *longko*, or community head, engages in political issues and addresses community needs and conflicts. The masculine language of *longko* and *ngenpin* is related to history, genealogy, forms of social organization, and hierarchy, whereas that of the *dungumachife* mediates between the sacred discourse of the *machi* and the needs of the patient or community. Machi Marta explained: "When the spirit comes to me, it comes on very strongly and for a long time. There has to be someone who knows how to receive the word properly, remember it, and then tell me what I said when I no longer have the spirit with me. It is as if God sends me writing through the *machi* [spirit], and the *dungumachife* tells it. My husband does not 'talk' [act as *dungumachife*] at all. He says he gets dizzy with so many words. He has to find someone around to receive words for me."

The *machi-dungumachife* couple performs the words of the divine knowledgeable couple and determines the future of a patient or community. The *machi* performs the role of Old Woman Ngünechen, and the *dungumachife* performs the role of Old Man. Because the purpose of this dialogue is knowledge, not fertility, *machi-dungumachife* couples are not necessarily spouses or even people of the opposite sex. The gendered performative act and the close personal relationship between *machi* and *dungumachife* take precedence over the sex of either. Machi Pamela, for example, often had her daughter Beatriz perform as her *dungumachife*, and Machi José often had his sister Amelia or Jaime, the son of another *machi*, perform as his.

Figure 3.6. *Machi* playing in the front row at a *ngillatun* ritual (photo by Ana Mariella Bacigalupo).

Collective Wholeness in *Ngillatun* Rituals: Body and Performance

At six in the morning on December 12, 1996, I stood beside Machi José, Machi Norma, two *longko,* and a small gathering of other men and women at their community's collective altar, the *ngillatuwe.* Flanked by branches of *foye, triwe,* and *klon,* the *ngillatuwe* stood in the center of the ritual field in Dafenco, Chile. The two-day collective *ngillatun* ritual had begun. The participants had donned traditional clothing: blue head scarves or festive, multicolored hair ribbons, skirts, and black shawls for the women; ponchos and hats for the men. We stood facing east, the cool air cutting into our faces, the dew soaking our shoes. One of the men painted our faces: a white cross on the left cheek and a blue cross on the right to remind us of the powers of the *wenu mapu.* As the sun rose, José and Norma sang praises to Ngünechen in increasingly louder voices. We dipped the tree branches in the water trough at the *ngillatuwe* and sprinkled the water toward the sun as we prayed to the different people in Ngünechen—Old Man, Old Woman, Young Man, and Young Woman (Fig. 3.6).

As the donor of all life, Ngünechen grants fertility to humans, animals, and crops and bestows salvation, wealth, and health on the ritual community (Bacigalupo 1997; Foerster 1993:78–80). If the Mapuche do not reciprocate with offerings, animal sacrifices, and propitiations, Ngünechen will punish them with drought, scarcity, and poverty. The *ngillatun* is the ritual at which they make such offerings and ensure Ngünechen's continued blessings. The term *ngillan* means "to ask for," and *tun* refers to an action. *Ngillatun* can be any type of prayer or petition to the spirits, whether individual or collective, but Mapuche most commonly apply the term to collective rituals involving several communities, or *lof*, that come together to form a ritual community. The purpose of *ngillatun*, like that of death rituals, is to integrate the ritual community through purification, sacrifice, and the community's relationship to ancestral and regional spirits or deities. People in rural Mapuche communities often perform *ngillatun* before and after the harvest to request abundance, fertility for the land and animals, and well-being for the entire ritual community (Bacigalupo 1995, 2001a). Most Mapuche believe Ngünechen will be angered if a *ngillatun* is filmed or recorded and will curse them instead of granting them blessings. I honored this belief by not recording the *ngillatun* prayers.

On this day, two Mapuche women laid offerings of maize, beans, and ceramic jugs filled with the drink *muday* at the foot of the *ngillatuwe*. A man cut the throat of a black sheep and poured the blood into a bowl beside the other offerings. He tied another black sheep to a stake on the east side of the *ngillatuwe* to request black clouds and rain. Machi José and Machi Norma drummed their *kultrun*.

Machi go into altered states of consciousness during *ngillatun* rituals only if the community is in danger and important messages need to be relayed. Both Norma and José tranced during this *ngillatun*. Norma spoke about the urgent need for the community to return to traditional ways of life and perform periodic *ngillatun*. José warned about the drought and scarcity that would ensue if the community did not resolve its conflicts and cooperate to produce collective well-being.

Norma, five other Mapuche women, and I played calabash rattles and sleigh bells while Raquel and Fabiana, the *machi*'s helpers, followed the *machi*'s rhythms on their *kultrun*. None of the women wore silver jewelry. During *ngillatun* rituals the *filew*, or generic ancestral *machi* spirit, is not seduced with jewelry and flowers, as it is during *machi* initiation and renewal rituals, but comes as a willing messenger of Ngünechen. Mapuche believe that displays of wealth, status, and hierarchy in *ngillatun* rituals detract from the humble mood and the sense of ritual community. When I asked a Mapuche woman why she was not wearing her silver breastplate (*trapelakucha*), she whispered: "If Ngünechen sees the silver, he thinks we are being arrogant. He will punish us with frost and misfortune."

The next day, people arrived from the three other communities that participated with Dafenco in *ngillatun* rituals. The four communities took turns hosting the annual *ngillatun,* so that each performed a ceremony once every four years. The visitors sat on benches under arbors arranged in a U around the edges of the ritual field, opening to the east, the place of beginnings. They exchanged visits, food, and drink with the other participants.

We danced back and forth and side to side in five rows facing the *ngillatuwe.* At the front, a row of *machi,* musicians, and *dungumachife* followed a row of Mapuche women from Dafenco dressed in traditional clothing. Behind them came a row of women guests and others wearing everyday skirts, and finally two rows of men. The side-to-side dancing in front of the *rewe* replicated the *machi*'s swaying between *foye* and *triwe* branches at the *rewe* while traveling to other worlds; it also represented the ritual community's oscillation between dualities such as male-female, health-illness, abundance-scarcity, self-other, and exorcising-integrating. Two men with sticks and wearing masks representing Spanish conquistadores (*koyon*) kept the dancers in straight lines.

The *machi* began playing a beat called the *tampultun,* and four young *choyke* dancers, mimicking the mating dance of the male *choyke,* or Patagonian ostrich, circled the *ngillatuwe* sixteen times, in four sets of four.[9] With *choyke* feathers in their headbands, they bowed their heads, lifted their knees, and flapped their wings, fashioned from white sheets. The *choyke* dancers teased and flirted with the unmarried young women to symbolize seduction, unbridled sexuality, and life energy. Twice during the ritual the dancing changed, and we moved around the *ngillatuwe* in two concentric circles defined by gender. These circles represented the workings of the ritual community and the ideal complementary roles of the masculine and feminine in Mapuche communal life. Men, in the outer circle, represent the community to the outside world, whereas women, in the inner circle, are constructed as guardians of traditional lore and the family. I danced with the women, moving counterclockwise as we played rattles and sleigh bells. The men danced clockwise in the outer circle, playing *pifilka, trutruka,* and horns (Figs. 3.7 and 3.8). An older woman dancing beside me explained: "We women have more traditional dress. We listen more to Ngünechen. We are close to the earth, so we have to be right beside the *rewe.*"

A group of Mapuche men on horseback, carrying blue and white flags, performed the *awün.* Beginning behind the *ngillatuwe* on the east side,

Figure 3.7. Young Mapuche men mimic the mating dance of the *choyke*. The dancers symbolize sexuality and fertility and tease and flirt with unmarried women (photo bought at the market in Temuco).

Figure 3.8. Two concentric circles of dancers at a *ngillatun* ritual. Women dance on the inside circle and men on the outside one (photo by Helmut Schindler, published in Helmut Schindler, 1990, *Bauern und Reiterkrieger: Die Mapuche-Indianer im Süden Amerikas.* Munich: Hirmer Verlag).

they circled counterclockwise around the dancers, imitating the movement of the sun and covering us in dust. After four sets of four rounds, they brought their horses to the *ngillatuwe* and made them breathe heavily on the *machi*'s heads and backs, to give them strength. The circle of ramadas, the circles made by the galloping horses, and those made by the *choyke* dancers were spatial representations of the ritual community and wholeness.

"Why do they repeat everything four times?" I asked the woman by my side.

"It has to be four," she replied, "as in Ngünechen—four parts to be complete." A Mapuche intellectual overheard me and added: "The *awün* is the totality of the cosmos. When the *choyke* dancers come from the east, it is as if they were coming directly from the sky. We are making totality."

The *ngillatun* creates cosmic wholeness and community through the ritual exchange of food and drink, the circling of the ritual field by horses during the *awün,* and the dancing of the ritual community around the *ngillatuwe.* The most significant manifestation of wholeness, however, is the people's collective enactment of the microcosm represented by the co-gendered deity Ngünechen. Machi Norma and Machi José each separately performed the role of Old Woman, and their *dungumachife* became Old Man. Two young men and two young women dancers (*llankan*) stood with lances behind the *machi* and the *dungumachife,* performing the roles of Young Man and Young Woman. The mating dance of the male *choyke* dancers was a manifestation of Young Man, deploying messages about crop yields, animal husbandry, and human sexuality.

Because the older couple in Ngünechen represents the performative aspect, divorced from the actual age or sex of the performer, *machi* and *dungumachife* of any age and sex can become these two. In this case, Machi José enacted Old Woman; in another example, Machi María Cecilia was only eighteen when she first performed Old Woman. Because the young couple represents the physical dimension of generation and gender, associated with specific bodies and sexes, young men must perform Young Man, and young women must perform Young Woman. When one of the *choyke* dancers fell sick during the afternoon dance and one of the girls asked Machi José if she could replace him, José replied: "The *choykes* must be all young men. We need another young man." He handed the girl a calabash rattle and told her to go and play at the *ngillatuwe.*

The divergence between the performative and bodily dimensions of generation and gender reflects the different relationships that the young and old couple have with the Mapuche universe. The young couple represents the unbridled forces of life energy and sexuality (sperm and eggs, menstrual and birth blood, sexual fluids), which play an important role in the maintenance and change of the cosmos. Female and male sexual fluids and sexual forces are crucial for human survival and healing and for the fertility of land and animals, but they can also be dangerous and interfere with spirituality. In order to be productive and sustain the Mapuche group, sexual fluids must remain balanced and controlled through social rules, gender roles, marriage, kinship, and divine mandates.

The old couple control knowledge about life and the universe. They divine the future, give advice, and dispense fertility, abundance, and well-being to the community. Elderly, abstinent *machi* have symbolic control over the powers of fertility and sexuality because they do not produce the menstrual blood, sperm, and sexual fluids that interfere with spirituality. Elderly *machi* are less bound by the surrounding network of interaction, gender roles, and taboos and have the knowledge and maturity to direct rituals. Elderly female *machi,* like postmenopausal women in northern India, are perceived as cooler and more self-contained, and their social identities are in some ways more like those of men (Lamb 2000:13). Young, sexually active *machi* of childbearing age are perceived as having limited powers. They are symbolically transformed into old people by being called Papay (Old Woman) and Chachai (Old Man) in order to officiate in rituals.

The complex relationship between the symbolic meaning and the bodily experience of gender and generation supports the complementary paradigmatic world order presented in the Mapuche creation myth, as well as asymmetrical social gender relations. Mapuche women and men are both responsible for ensuring fertility. Whereas men take precedence in political activities between social groups, women, as *machi,* predominate in the relationship between humans and the spirit world. Mapuche gender relations are therefore complementary, though as political intermediaries men hold higher prestige than women in mainstream Chilean society.[10]

Ngillatun rituals were not always led by *machi.* Until the beginning of the twentieth century, *ngillatun* in the south-central valleys of Chile were led by male *ngenpin* (orators) who propitiated specific ancestors of a patrilineage and recounted genealogy and history through formal prayers. *Ngenpin,* or men who "know how to pray" and "carry the words of others" (Augusta 1934), were elders and community chiefs—political, lineage, and spiritual leaders of their communities (Faron 1964:187).

They did not enter altered states of consciousness, though when a *ngen-pin* died, a male member of the patrilineage "inherited" the orator's spirit and speaking abilities. *Ngenpin* still officiate in *ngillatun* in the cordillera area (Pewenche) and the southern Mapuche area (Williche), where ritual congregations are smaller and tied to specific ancestral spirits and where land is more abundant (Bacigalupo 1995, 2001a:217, 254).

In areas between the south-central valleys and the Andean foothills, population has increased tremendously since the early twentieth century, and land has become scarce and eroded. There, *ngillatun* rituals began to be led by both *ngenpin* and *machi*, the latter of whom control the powers of fertility through their association with the moon.[11] Machi Sergio explained: "Before, *ngillatun* ceremonies were performed by *longkos* and all the members of the community. This [officiation by *machi*] is something that occurred recently." *Machi* officiators either belong to the ritual congregation that holds the *ngillatun* or are paid professionals from other communities.

Machi's performances in *ngillatun* in the south-central valleys also help compensate for the loss of ritual knowledge and oratorical ability by young men who might have become *ngenpin*. A man from the Williche area explained: "I think it is because youngsters are not interested in learning how to pray, sing, speak in ritual language [*ngillatucar*]. If the *machi* see that there is no one adequate to take on this role in the *ngillatun*, they can take it, because they have more power and knowledge . . . The fact that there are no *ngenpin* near Temuco demonstrates that young folk do not know how to *ngillatucar* anymore. The older generations are interested in maintaining tradition, so the *machi* has to replace the *ngenpin* in their functions."

Today, *machi* who officiate in *ngillatun* rituals in the south-central Mapuche valleys maintain cohesion among growing ritual congregations that no longer have ancestral spirits in common. They invoke the pan-Mapuche deity Ngünechen and regional deities as general ancestors of the whole congregation, not of a specific patrilineage (Faron 1963:153).[12] Mapuche from this area believe that *machi*'s spiritual powers and their ability to contact Ngünechen through altered states of consciousness are more effective than the formal prayers of the *ngenpin*. Longko Daniel explained:

> The *ngillatun* is something we all believe in. Ninety-nine percent of the community believes we are doing a prayer with good intentions. Young people sometimes do not believe in *machituqueo* [a *machi*'s curing]; they

think their friends are going to laugh at them. But most of them do believe in the *ngillatun*. The youngsters who went to the *ngillatun* the other
day maybe criticized some things, but none of them laughed at the cross,
at the *machi*. They know the *machi*'s prayers bring good things to the
community. They have more faith in *machi* than in the *ngenpin*. Anyone
with a good tongue and heart can be a *ngenpin*. But to be a *machi*, you
have to have God's support.

The collective enactment of cosmic unity and holistic personhood in
ngillatun rituals led by *machi* is an innovation crucial to the reaffirma-
tion of Mapuche identities within a new social order beyond that of local
patrilineages or community or ethnic identity. When Mapuche perform
Ngünechen, they embody Mapuche cosmology and *habitus,* the "system of durable dispositions" that regulates practices and representations
(Bourdieu 1977:72). At the same time, these performances are always
dialogical (Bakhtin 1986). They include a variety of Catholic and military
symbols, and the significance of *ngillatun* rituals is in constant transformation. Anthropologists have viewed *ngillatun* as ways to create ethnic
solidarity and integration in the ritual congregation (Dillehay 1985;
Faron 1964). Mapuche today view the collective enactment of the gender
and generational dimensions of Ngünechen in its broader religious, economic, and political dimension. Through Ngünechen, *machi* obtain the
good harvests, fertile animals, and well-being that allow the community
to survive, while at the same time they create the basis for a pan-Mapuche
identity.[13]

The Healing Rituals of *Machi:*
The Individual Performance of Wholeness

It was midnight in the community of Ralli on January 23, 1995. Machi
Pamela lay on the floor while Machi Ana played her drum loudly over her,
imploring Ngünechen to forgive Pamela and let her live. I had arrived at
Pamela's house early that morning to find two of her daughters sobbing
and Pamela lying on a mattress in the living room, dressed in her best
black woolen wrap and the heavy silver pin she used to protect herself
from evil spirits. Her eyes were closed, her face was white and clammy,
her hands were cold. I could feel no pulse. Her daughters said she had
been dead for over two hours and that they had washed her and changed
her clothes in preparation for the funeral.

Pamela's daughters had sent me and her brother-in-law, Tomás, to fetch Ana, who belonged to the same school of *machi* practice. Ana arrived at Pamela's house that night and discussed Pamela's illness with her daughter Beatriz:

> BEATRIZ: We have faith in you. Some hours ago my mother lost consciousness for many minutes; we didn't know what to do . . . We didn't think she would recover . . . When she began to react again, then we thought we should do something because she is not an ordinary person. Ordinary people have ordinary illnesses but with *machi* the situation is different . . . She isn't well; she was saying goodbye . . .
>
> ANA: She has her illness in her stomach. In the middle of her body . . . When the illness goes up, then her head becomes dizzy.
>
> PAMELA: I'm dizzy.
>
> BEATRIZ: The *wingkas* say it is problems with blood pressure . . . Yesterday I asked the doctor if it was the gall bladder. "No, it's not that," he said. "It is *nervios*," he said. Only *nervios*. When she gets mad it manifests itself. She shouldn't get mad anymore . . . "You have to be calm," he was telling her.
>
> ANA: But what is a person to do if they have a stubborn heart? . . .
>
> TOMÁS: Will you need *triwe, foye*?
>
> ANA: *Triwe, foye* for the *iaf-iaf* branches . . . For spiritual force we use *kuwi* and the *kürako* vine [*Pseudopanax valdiviensis*].

Nervios is an illness with physical, emotional, and often spiritual components that is common among Mapuche and many other people in Latin America. Like Pamela, many who experience *nervios* feel out of control and alien in their own bodies. They experience disorientation, dizziness, and fainting, fits of crying or anger, insomnia and headaches, sensations of hot and cold, and body aches. Some of the conditions giving rise to *nervios* include the breakdown of family networks, loss of loved ones, and concern for the well-being of friends and family members. As Setha Low (1994:141–142) describes it: "*Nervios* is constructed by local discourses and institutions, then expressed and acted upon as a metaphor of social, psychological, political or economic distress. The relationships between *nervios* and embodied distress, therefore is culturally mediated, both in terms of what forms of distress cause suffering and in terms of its metaphorical expression." Machi Pamela's experience of *nervios* had been aggravated by the recent death of her son and the soul loss she had subsequently suffered because she ritually sacrificed her spirit horse to feed the mourners at the funeral and to ensure that her son would travel to the *wenu mapu*.

Machi Ana performed an emergency *ulutun* to diagnose Pamela's illness, as well as a rogation for Pamela. Pamela's grandson Carlos slit the throat of a sheep, and Pamela and Ana drank the warm blood mixed with chile to gain strength. Because Ana was not going to be possessed by spirits and would not travel to other worlds during the *ulutun*, she did not need her ritual entourage of *dungumachife* and male and female helpers.

Ana's drumming, praying, and herbal remedies brought Machi Pamela back to consciousness, but she still needed a *datun*, a complex healing ritual, to treat her serious *wenukutran*. Ana would be back on Friday to perform the ceremony. In the meantime, she instructed Pamela to drink chamomile tea, to avoid getting angry, to start saving money to buy another spirit horse, and not to watch television.

Pamela asked me come to her *datun* to shake *foye* and *triwe* branches to scare off evil spirits and to play sleigh bells. I had often helped Pamela in the healing rituals she performed for other people and sometimes recorded them. Pamela decided I should record the first half of her *datun*— before midnight—when her illness would be diagnosed, but not the second part, when her future would be decided, lest it offend Ngünechen.

On Friday evening I went with Tomás to pick up Machi Ana, her brother, who was also her *dungumachife*, and her niece, who served as her ritual helper (*yegülfe*, in the case of a female helper). Ana prayed to her *rewe*, asking her spirit for permission to go and heal Pamela, and spat water on the *rewe* as an offering. She arrived at Pamela's house and inquired about her health. The two of them bragged competitively about their shamanic powers and the patients they had healed. Meanwhile, Tomás, Carlos, and I prepared the remedies for the ritual. Tomás planted two *coligüe* with *triwe* and *foye* branches tied to them outside the kitchen door, on the east.[14] I placed the soothing herbal remedies (*triwe, nulawen, limpia plata*) in one wooden bowl and the remedies meant to exorcise evil (*llanten, fulcon, foye*) in another. Pamela's daughter Alba heated the skin of Machi Ana's *kultrun* to deepen its sound.

Pamela lay face up on a sheepskin on the floor, bare-breasted and in a petticoat, with her head toward the kitchen door. Carlos placed pots with *foye, triwe,* and *klon* branches at her feet and head. Ana sat on a low stool beside Pamela, smoking a cigarette in order to concentrate on her divination. She donned her silver breastplate and her headdress for pro-

Figure 3.9. A *machi* is healed with prayers, massage, and herbal remedies (photo by Ana Mariella Bacigalupo).

tection against evil spirits and placed two crossed kitchen knives behind Pamela's head. She played the sleigh bells and *kultrun* softly in a drumbeat called *metrumtun* as she called the spirits and narrated the history of her calling, powers, and initiation in four phases; her *kultrun* was heated after each phase. Then Ana named a variety of nature spirits and ancestors and spoke of the places where they lived. She called the names of Ngünechen as well as those of a variety of nature spirits, Jesus, the Virgin Mary, and God in order to gain power to heal, and she announced the arrival of her spirit (Fig. 3.9). By naming the spirits, *machi* bring them into being and into the ritual space. The spirits are pleased when *machi* demonstrate that they know who they are, and they show willingness to give healing knowledge to the *machi*.

Ana wiped the sweat from her brow, and her niece pulled her head scarf over her face as she proceeded with a faster beat used to enter into *küymi*. Pamela referred to this beat, the *tayilün*, as *trekan kawellu kultruntun*, or the drumbeat of the traveling horse on which *machi* gallop to other worlds and gain knowledge. Six young men from the community who were also present clashed *koliu* canes above her head and screamed: "¡Ya ya ya ya!" Ana's head shook and she entered *küymi*.

Ana played a forceful beat often referred to as *trompümkultrun* (Ñanculef and Gumucio 1991:5) as she began the *pewuntun* (divination), communicating with nature spirits, twelve warring spirits, and Ngünechen.[15] She described her divination as "seeing like an x-ray" and "unraveling like a thread." Mapuche view evil as attaching itself to people, trapping and weakening them, tying them up, agitating them, contaminating them, knotting their life paths, and confusing them. Healing takes place as the *machi* exorcise the evil spirits lodged in the bodies, souls, hearts, and households of their patients by shooting or stabbing them and by vomiting, purging, and cleansing. Ana rubbed Pamela's arms and legs with the blunt side of a knife to unravel the knots caused by witchcraft, purify and strengthen Pamela's spirit, and lift it so that she would be influenced by the calming realm of the upper world and the healing powers of Ngünechen.[16] The healing process is one of transformation from knotted to unraveled, contamination to purification, weakness to strength, and agitation to calmness.

Then Ana exorcised the evil spirits from Pamela's body. She sucked what she saw as snakes and stones from Pamela's stomach, spat them out, and rubbed Pamela's body with a mixture of bitter *foye* leaves and firewater. In doing so, she embodied Young Man and knowledgeable Old Man. She played the drum loudly over her head and screamed war cries, to which the other participants responded. "Four powerful sergeants, old kings, old and new generals," she prayed, "don't let it stay here. Make it leave to its territory . . . Push it to a side, unravel it. Don't let them beat us. We came to win. Kill those enemy *wekufe* spirits, revive her heart, revive her blood . . . The rifle, the machine gun—let it destroy their hearts with bullets . . . Disintegrate its heart with bullets . . . May they leave defeated." Pamela later described the pounding sound made by Ana's drum as male, warring, and exorcising.

Ana walked through every room of the house and then circled the house, beating the walls with a stick. Carlos, Tomás, and the other men followed her, thumping pitchforks, hatchets, and knives on the ground to kill evil in the same way knives and guns kill living beings. Pamela's daughter Alba carried a pan with a smoke exorcism of burning *foye* leaves, sulfur, and chiles, while her daughter Beatriz sprinkled ammonia and chlorine in our footsteps with a *foye* branch.

Ana returned to Pamela's side. As she sang, she massaged Pamela with herbal remedies while her niece-helper played the *kultrun*. Then the helper and I rubbed Pamela's body with "soft" herbal remedies while Ana embodied Old Woman and Young Woman. Ana played her *kultrun* again, this time face down over Pamela for maximum therapeutic effect.

She asked Ngünechen to forgive Pamela for her transgressions and to integrate her back into her *machi* practice, family, and community. She prayed: "Old Woman visionary, Virgin Mother, daughter stars of the morning, help your daughter *machi*. She was chosen in the womb of her mother to be an orator, a sacred singer. Awaken her spirit of service. Bring her back to life, unravel her like a thread . . . You chose her to be a *machi;* allow her to finish her assignment, father God . . . Give her heart, blood, and tongue for service; . . . untie her tongue; . . . give her bones for service so that she can have her prayer, her discourse, her song."

Then Pamela tranced unexpectedly. She swayed, holding onto her breasts and playing sleigh bells as she faced east. Her body trembled uncontrollably, and she screamed that she saw visions of huge black dogs—a form of evil—at her feet. She ordered Carlos to shoot at the visions with her revolver. Carlos complied.[17] He brought in Pamela's chosen sheep and made it dance to the music. Pamela spat into her hand and the sheep licked the saliva, a sign that it had accepted her spirit.

Anthropologists have distinguished between patients' trances, which do not make them conduits for the spirits but rather put them in touch with their inner being, and the trances of shamans, who control the alteration of their own consciousness; the patient's consciousness is controlled by the shaman (Laderman 1994:192). Machi Pamela was exceptional in being both patient and shaman. As patient, she was put in touch with her inner being, but her consciousness was not controlled by Machi Ana. Pamela, too, became a conduit for the spirits, who demanded that she renew her kinship ties to spirit animals and the *filew,* the ancestral *machi* spirit.

During the course of this *datun,* Machi Ana simultaneously embodied all four parts of the deity Ngünechen; she became a co-gendered and co-generational being. She expressed this embodiment in her prayer: "Old Man, creator of *machi;* Old Woman, creator of *machi;* Young man, creator of *machi;* Young Woman, creator of *machi:* You have given me herbal remedies. You chose me. I am your *piuke* [heart]. I am your *rakiduam* [thought]. I am you. Now, with my heart of service with four big and powerful people in it, I will revive her [Pamela's] heart."

Then Ana entered into a state of *konpapüllü.* This is the final part of the trance, in which the *filew* reveals the cause of the illness. Ana asked me not to record this section, because it was the most delicate part of the ritual. Her helper played the *kultrun* while Ana held branches of *triwe* and *foye* in her hand and shook the temporary *rewe* made from *coligüe* planted outside the kitchen door. She buried her head in the branches tied to the canes, swaying between them. Beatriz spat water over Ana's head. Carlos, dressed as a *choyke,* then danced with Ana, bringing her back to her ordinary social gender roles and an ordinary state of consciousness (*chetu*). The *dungumachife* placed two knives on Machi Ana's chest and slid them along her arms to help the spirit leave. As Ana and Pamela regained normal consciousness, Pamela's daughters and I set the table for the midnight feast, during which the *dungumachife* summarized the spirit's explanation of Pamela's illness:

> This daughter was sent evil . . . Evil spirits came to see her. The evil *witranalwe* became a man and was transformed into a dog. He came to see her; that is why she became ill. They were competing with *filew* . . . Also she hasn't performed the activities typical of her being. Before, she had a chosen sheep and saddled horse. Now she doesn't pray to the celestial mother, the celestial father that chose her . . . there is where she is failing. They almost took her language away. But there were people who interceded on her behalf, saying: "She will have her saddled horse again. We already have it for her."

During Pamela's *datun,* as in all *datun* rituals, the officiating *machi* became the Mapuche microcosm. Because the spirits and Ngünechen duplicate the physical world of humans—family relationships as well as social and spiritual hierarchies—to call them forth by song and to embody them is to mimetically gain control of the world they represent. By assuming different positionalities during the healing ritual—servant and daughter of Ngünechen, mother and superior to Pamela, father warrior who scares away evil spirits, and Ngünechen itself—Machi Ana linked worldly and spiritual realities. Like Kuna shamans (Taussig 1993:106), *machi* are not just subjects but also the mimicked other about whom they chant.[18] *Machi* chant themselves into the healing scene and exist there not only as chanters but as the spirits and deities chanted about. Embodying the different parts of Ngünechen, *machi* see the world through different "modalities of personhood" (Bem 1993) and points of view.[19]

The genders of spirits remain permanent, whereas *machi* move between gender identities or combine them. Machi Ana assumed masculine, feminine, and co-gendered identities for the purposes of healing and divining. She became masculine in order to exorcise illness, bad thoughts, and suffering from Pamela's body through spiritual warfare, with the help of ancestral warriors and Jesus. She became feminine to forgive and integrate Pamela back into her ordinary self, life, and profession by embodying Old

Woman, the morning star, and the Virgin Mary. She became old to gain knowledge about the causes and cures for illness and affliction. She became young to gain the stamina to defeat evil forces. It is this ability to cross genders and generations that allows *machi* to embody Ngünechen—male, female, young, and old—and in doing so to transcend gender and the boundaries of the ordinary world, embody wholeness, and become divine.[20]

Conclusion

The gender and generational aspects of the Mapuche mind-body complex are a paradigm for understanding the Mapuche's hierarchical family and social relationships as well as their ordering of the cosmos. While the gender and generational characteristics of symbols, spirits, and deities map the world (social, environmental, and spiritual) by remaining constant, those of *machi* shift and change in different ritual contexts, expressing different Mapuche social and spiritual positionalities in order to gain power. In Mapuche rituals, these gender and age dimensions are tied to specific young male and female bodies when sexuality and fertility are to be emphasized, and to older, desexualized bodies when knowledge and wisdom are to be expressed.

Mapuche ritual practices, however, also show that gender and age are not just characteristics of the sexed physical body but indicators of certain qualities of personhood, types of social and political relationships, and modes of cosmological ordering. Cosmic wholeness is expressed through the co-gendered and dual generational qualities of Ngünechen; it is performed by *machi* at the individual, relational, and collective levels. Divination rituals stress wholeness through the complementary relationship between feminine ecstatic discourse and the masculine discourse of translation and interpretation. Collective *ngillatun* rituals, in which different participants enact the various gender and generational aspects of the deity Ngünechen, achieve wholeness collectively as fertility and well-being. Healing rituals subsume difference, and *machi* become whole persons by moving between gender and generational notions or combining them. By becoming whole and replicating the power of Ngünechen—individually, relationally, or collectively—*machi* are transformed and transform Ngünechen itself, creating a power that can be used to create a new world, to transform the essence of beings, for healing or for evil. *Machi* share in and take character and power from Ngünechen and are responsible for the changes they bring about in social and cosmic ordering.

Machi's diverse manifestations of ritual wholeness—and their gender and generational dimensions—have implications for Mapuche identity politics. *Ngenpin* no longer propitiate ancestral spirits of the patrilineage to benefit the ritual congregation; rather, *machi* and ritual participants collectively perform the hybrid Mapuche deity Ngünechen, it combines colonial hierarchies with Mapuche cosmic ordering to effect well-being for all Mapuche. *Machi*'s collective performances of wholeness thus help to create a pan-Mapuche identity. This new hybrid identity, in turn, has economic, religious, and political implications, shaping the way in which Mapuche engage with the non-Mapuche world.

Ritual expressions of wholeness and self move beyond the *machi*'s individual mind-body complex into other domains of knowledge and experience. By being both human and spirit or deity, chanter, and the subject of chanting, *machi* embody the different dimensions of Mapuche identity and their various possibilities in the world. The Mapuche mind-body complex is central to the maintenance and change of this cosmos and at the same time dependent on human agency and choice, cultural practice, and social process. The mind-body is a paradigm not only for individuality but also for sociality, politics, and cosmology. Cultural concepts affect the way in which Mapuche view the qualities of Old Man, Old Woman, Young Man, and Young Woman as well as the meanings of physical and spiritual characteristics and experiences. In turn, *machi*'s experiences of embodiment and ensoulment affect cultural concepts and social and political practices. *Machi*'s ritual expressions of wholeness are comments on Mapuche personal, ethnic, political, and moral identity.

These diverse expressions of ritual wholeness also have implications for theories of gender and embodiment in the context of shamanic practice. *Machi*'s relationships to the spirit world indicate no simple correspondence between a *machi*'s sex and sexuality, on one hand, and masculine or feminine perspectives, on the other. In ritual contexts, *machi*—regardless of their sex or sexuality—transcend the everyday gender and generational categories ascribed to sexed bodies by moving among the masculine, feminine, young, old, co-gendered, and co-generational characteristics attributed to spirits. *Machi*'s ritual performances of fluid gender identities illustrate Judith Butler's notion (1990) that gender is not a fixed condition but a state of mind and body that is maintained through reiterative performance. It also highlights the artificial relation of gender to bodies and sexualities.

But the performance of fluid concepts of gender during ritual does not preclude the construction of stable, gendered social roles for *machi* as women and men in daily life.[21] Indeed, *machi*'s performances of gen-

der fluidity and co-genderism in ritual contexts are possible precisely because the Mapuche maintain highly polarized notions of masculinity and
femininity, which are expressed in *machi* symbols, the gendering of discourses, and the permanent gender identities of spirits.[22] *Machi*'s individual creativity lies precisely in the ways they privilege particular aspects
of the feminine and masculine qualities of spirits over others to varying
degrees, according to context. Messages about gender in *machi* rituals
thus range from enforcement of gender difference to encouragement of
gender fluidity.[23]

   Machi's complex identities involve both holistic ritual identities that
are independent of the sex of the actor and national majority notions of
personhood and gender as determined by sex. *Machi* are both unique
persons who switch gender identities in ritual in order to become whole
and women or men in their everyday lives.

   I now turn to the diverse gendered relationships *machi* develop in
ritual as they engage with deities, spirits, and spirit animals. Their spiritual relationships, forged through kinship, marriage, and mastery, reflect
complex historical, social, and ethnic relationships as well as Mapuche's
diverse notions of personhood.

CHAPTER 4

Ritual Gendered Relationships: Kinship, Marriage, Mastery, and *Machi* Modes of Personhood

At this moment I beg you to remain by my side, Father of the Sky, Mother of the Sky, Old People from Above, Old Grandmother, Old Grandfather. You who are the owner of all remedies that live in the blue sky, don't allow me to remain truncated . . . I humble myself before you. Mount me on your horse and don't allow me to weaken . . . You have remedies at the tip of your rewe. I ask you to give them to me for my work, to help people. I also ask you not to punish me, as my only job is to use the remedies that you reveal to me. Isn't it you that made me be in this job to serve others? That is what I am saying, Father God, Mother God.

—EXCERPT FROM A DIVINATION BY MACHI JOSÉ,
   DECEMBER 21, 2001 (TRANSLATED FROM MAPUDUNGU
   TO SPANISH BY ARMANDO MARILEO)

Kinship, marriage, and mastery—the closest and most durable gendered social relationships among Mapuche—are used by *machi* in ritual to create bonds with the spirit and animal world. *Machi* are individual women and men in their everyday lives, but in ritual contexts their sex and age become secondary as they engage in various relational personhoods that link them with animals and spirits.

In this chapter I explore the ways in which spiritual kinship ties, spiritual marriages, and relationships of mastery between *machi*, animals, and spirits—manifested during initiation, healing, and death rituals—reflect historical ethnic and national relationships, social and gender dynamics, and complex understandings of personhood. The spiritual relationships of *machi* reflect the gendered power dynamics of marriage and seduction, possession and ecstasy, hierarchical kinship systems, and colonial mastery and domination. These gendered spiritual relational personhoods and their associated altered states of consciousness are shaped by the legacy of colonization: political and religious authorities; the loss of autonomy by Mapuche communities; the incorporation of horses and sheep into the subsistence economy; the imposition of agriculture and the reservation system; and missionization. *Machi* are kin to their spirit animals and to other *machi* who initiate them; they are spirit brides who seduce their *machi* husbands into possessing them; and they are masculine mounted warriors, masters of spirit animals, who travel in ecstatic flight to other worlds. These spiritual relationships reflect a complex understanding of personal consciousness in which *machi* are agents of their actions but at the same time share self with the spirits and are dominated by them. The gendered spiritual positionalities of *machi* in ritual contexts are both embodied and ensouled. Experiencing the world as different people, they gain varied forms of knowledge and power through the exchange of bodily substances as well as through spiritual means. In doing so, they offer a new perspective on current discussions among anthropologists about embodiment, ensoulment, and personhood.

The relational personhoods of *machi* vary according to region, *machi* school of practice, and individual. For this chapter I have selected the *machi* initiation, healing, and death rituals and narratives that best illustrate the gendered relationships between *machi* and other spirit, human, and animal beings.

María Cecilia's Initiation: The Forging of Spiritual Kinship with *Machi* and Animals

Eighteen-year-old María Cecilia bowed her head as she sat beside her newly planted *rewe,* the step-notched tree trunk altar that connects the human world with spiritual ones. She wore a blue head scarf and an elegant black shawl with a pink stripe. Her necklaces of blood-red *kopiwe* flowers and *llankalawen* leaves and her heavy silver breastplate swayed as she turned from side to side, beating her new drum, or *kultrun,* with four red suns painted on its face. María Cecilia's *machi* spirit—her *machi püllü,* or *filew* (literally, "the knowledgeable one")—lived simultaneously in the *wenu mapu;* in María Cecilia's head, *kultrun,* and *rewe;* and in the spirit horse and sheep with whom she exchanged breath and blood. Possession, spirit travel, dreams, and visions would give María Cecilia the knowledge to divine, heal, and grant blessings.

During her initiation ritual, María Cecilia forged ties of spiritual kinship with other *machi* and with animals by exchanging bodily substances with Machi Juana and Machi Elena—her initiating *machi*—as well as with a cock, a sheep, and a horse, which became her spirit animals.[1] *Machi* and animals share essences and qualities of being, as do family members. They gain various types of power from each other and protect each other from illness and witchcraft.

By virtue of her initiation, María Cecilia became part of the *machi* school headed by Juana. *Machi* of the same school share similar symbols, spiritual concepts, and practices and heal each other. In addition, María Cecilia's initiation recognized her inheritance of the *machi* spirit, something that is ordinarily passed down through the mother's side of the family, unlike social kinship, inheritance, and succession, which are patrilineal. María Cecilia had inherited her *machi* spirit from her great-grandmother. She had experienced visions of drums and *foye* trees and felt chronic pain in her bones and stomach. She finished secondary school despite her illness and then went to live for a year with Machi Juana, from whom she learned to control her altered states of consciousness, read dreams, perform rituals, and prepare herbal remedies.[2]

I became close to María Cecilia and her family during the eight months preceding her initiation ritual. I visited her natal home, where her father, Edmundo, lived with his elder wife, Marcela, his younger wife, Carolina, and his and Carolina's two daughters and ten-year-old son. Eduardo and María Cecilia asked me to photograph the initiation so that they would have mementos of the event, despite Mapuche taboos on photographing rituals. Mapuche often believe that photographs steal their soul and can be used for witchcraft or, as is often the case with tourists, to objectify them.[3] On April 16, 1992, the day of María Cecilia's initiation, or *machiluwün*, Machi Juana and Machi Elena visited her in the community of Trarilongko. For two days, from dawn to dusk, they healed María Cecilia of the spiritual illness (*machikutran*), caused by a *machi* spirit, that pressures the neophyte to become a *machi*. María Cecilia legitimated her status as a *machi* by publicly demonstrating her ability to drum, sing, and enter and exit altered states of consciousness in order to speak to humans and spirits.

Edmundo, her father, tied the animals to stakes on the left-hand side of her *rewe*. He circled their eyes, noses, and mouths with blue paint, the color of the sky, so that their senses and skills would be put at the service of María Cecilia's spiritual gifts. He then slit the ears of the sheep and the cock's crest and collected the blood in a shallow wooden bowl. Some of the blood he rubbed on the underside of the horse's stomach; the rest,

Figure 4.1. Female *machi* with her spirit horse and sheep during an initiation ritual. Blue markings on the animals and the necklaces around their necks indicate their spiritual partnership with the *machi* (photo by Ana Mariella Bacigalupo).

María Cecilia drank. María Cecilia tried to strengthen the spiritual kinship among her animals by making the horse drink sheep blood with her. The horse resisted and bucked, so María Cecilia sprinkled blood over her *rewe* instead, to reinforce the connection between her spirit horse and her own *machi* powers. A young man rode María Cecilia's horse around the field, after which she inhaled the horse's breath (*neyen*)—a source of *newen* (strength, power)—and forced her own breath through its nostrils (Fig. 4.1). The ritual exchange of blood and breath unites *machi*, animals, and spirits in kin relationships. Blood, breath, and saliva are spiritual foods that can be magically acted upon to give a *machi* or an animal particular powers, but they are also profound indications of kinship and life force shared among *machi* and between *machi* and spirit animals.

Juana and Elena moved slowly up the path toward María Cecilia's house, turning from side to side with each beat of the drum, each followed by an entourage of helpers: four *ñankan*, men who play flutes and dance with the *machi* while she is in *küymi*, or an altered state of consciousness; a *dungumachife*, or "master of words," who speaks to the *machi* while she is in an altered state of consciousness and interprets the metaphoric language spoken by spirits into a language understood by all; two *yegülfe*, or women helpers, to heat and play the *machi*'s drum and hand her herbal remedies; and four *afafanfe,* male helpers to crash *coligüe (koliu)* canes over the head of the patient, help the *machi* enter or exit an altered state of consciousness, and help her exorcise evil spirits.

María Cecilia mirrored the movements of her two *machi* teachers. The three of them danced around the *rewe* in slow, purposeful movements, playing sleigh bells and holding knives and *foye* branches to their ears in order to protect themselves from evil spirits. The three *machi* circled the *rewe* counterclockwise as they danced forward, side by side. Each *machi* faced a male partner who danced backward (Fig. 4.2). Two young men led María Cecilia's sheep and cock around the *rewe* and made them "dance" to the *kultrun* rhythms played by the *machi*'s helpers, in order to endow these spirit animals with *machi* powers.

María Cecilia lay on a bed of herbs while Juana and Elena smoked and then rubbed her with the sacred leaves of the *foye, triwe,* and *klon* trees, spraying her periodically with mouthfuls of water. They sang and drummed over María Cecilia to heal her of her *machikutran*. They begged her *filew* to grant her power and healing knowledge and divined her future as a *machi*. Then each *machi* prayed and played her *kultrun*. A cacophony

Figure 4.2. Three *machi* dancing forward and counterclockwise around the *rewe* with their ritual partners, who dance backward (photo by Ana Mariella Bacigalupo).

of prayers, drumbeats, and flutes filled the air. The eight male helpers periodically clashed *coligüe* canes above María Cecilia's head to help her enter into an altered state of consciousness. Each *dungumachife* in turn conversed with his assigned *machi,* blocking out the words and sounds of the others. The *dungumachife* listened intently, memorizing the *machi*'s words in order to repeat them to the participants after the ritual. Any omission could cost him his health or that of the *machi.*

While possessed by *filew,* each of the *machi* in turn climbed María Cecilia's *rewe,* her tree of life, which would allow her to communicate effectively with other worlds. They swayed between the *foye* and *triwe* branches planted on either side. I danced counterclockwise around the *rewe,* too, holding hands with a group of Mapuche women. All of us wore blue head scarves and black shawls and carried *triwe iaf-iaf* (bunches of laurel leaves). A group of men danced clockwise around the circle of women. Juana and Elena exhaled over María Cecilia's head in order to grant her their powers and initiate her into their *machi* school as spiritual kin. Two men slashed the neck of a sheep and bled it into a bowl. The three *machi* drank the blood to consolidate their personal and spiritual kinship ties and to feed their respective *filew.*[4]

The participants celebrated the consolidation of María Cecilia's spiritual kinship ties over a dinner of roasted sheep and potatoes. The *dungumachife* summarized and interpreted what each *machi* had said while in an altered state of consciousness. They discussed similarities and differences in interpretation and concluded that María Cecilia's ritual had been successful and that she now belonged to Juana's school of *machi* practice. The *filew* was satisfied with her performance and offerings but warned her that she must live a life of sacrifice, or the *filew* would leave her.

Kinship created by ritual sharing of breath and the blood of sacrifice supersedes the blood ties of biological kinship. Just as Mapuche sons and daughters are incorporated into the social patrilineage through blood ties with the father, so María Cecilia was incorporated into the spiritual matrilineage of *machi* by acknowledging the spirit of her *machi* great-grandmother and by sharing breath and sacrificial animal blood with other *machi* and spirit animals. She often referred to Machi Juana as "mother" and to her cohorts within the school as "sisters." María Cecilia's spiritual kinship ties express a larger notion of an ordered social body composed of various bodies and souls (human and animal) and their social relationships. Once spiritual kinship is established with spirit animals, the bodies of *machi* and those of their spirit animals become interchangeable. *Machi*'s animals can experience illness on the *machi*'s behalf, and *machi* become ill if their spirit animals or *machi* cohorts are hurt or killed. As do the Kulina (Pollock 1996:320), a group of Amazonian Indians living in Brazil, Mapuche believe bodies and souls share the qualities of social relationships. Mapuche spiritual kinship is an expression of the relational dimensions of personhood, which are acquired, shared, and transformed rather than constrained within a single human body.

Seducing a Spirit, Becoming a Bride

"*Machi* make necklaces out of *kopiwe* flowers and *llankalawen*, like jewels," said Machi Rocío. "The *filew*, the *machi* of the sky, looks down, he sees these ancient jewel plants, and he likes it. He sees the silver shining in the sun. 'Eeeeh, how pretty,' he says. It attracts him. He sees the *machi*'s head, all blue in the head scarf like an offering calling him, and down he comes into the *machi*'s head."

Machi's passages between the human and spirit worlds are negotiated individually through intimate relationships with spirits involving seduction and marriage. Spirits and *machi*, like other women and men, have different qualities of being and various (culturally defined) interests and roles and are united as couples through marriage and seduction. The *machi* bride is a human body dressed in women's clothing, open to the spirit world. Both male and female *machi* become spiritual brides who seduce and call their *filew*—at once husband and master—to possess their heads to grant them knowledge. They perform this seduction by wearing symbols of femininity and wifeliness: blue or purple head scarves; necklaces of red *kopiwe* flowers and *llankalawen* leaves (female and male symbols; respectively);[5] women's black shawls; and silver jewelry. The *filew*-husband is interested in the performance of wifeliness, not in the sex of the person under the *machi* clothes. The ritual transvestism of male *machi* does not transcend the categories of woman and man but, rather, draws attention to the relational gender categories of spirit husband and *machi* wife as a couple (*kurewen*). María Cecilia, like most other *machi*, periodically renewed her marriage ties with her spirit in a ritual called *ngeykurewen*. The action of *ngeykun* refers to the *machi*'s swaying between the *foye* and *triwe* branches tied to the *rewe*, and the term *kurewen* refers to the coupling of *machi* bride and spirit husband (Bacigalupo 1996a:83; Métraux 1942:302; Titiev 1951:120).

Perceptions of erotic relationships between *machi* and *filew* and the symbolism of the head both mirror and transgress Mapuche gender relationships. Just as the community chief, or *longko,* represents the community, so *machi*'s heads are the loci of spiritual brideliness. Rural Mapuche women typically place great value on modesty, so they hide their hair by braiding or tying it and covering it with a head scarf, a straw hat, or a cloth baseball cap. They perceive young urban Mapuche women who cut their hair or wear it loose as seductive and promiscuous. *Machi* use traditional Mapuche women's head scarves, shawls, and silver jewelry in novel ways to attract and seduce the spirits. Contrary to Mapuche women's seduction of men, however, *machi*'s seduction of *filew* is positively valued as a skill available only to those who have power, and it enhances *machi*'s reputations.

Machi's spiritual seduction offers a unique perspective on erotic spirituality that privileges gender identity and performance over anatomical sex or sexual penetration. Studies of gender identities in Latin America have focused on the ways in which specific sexual acts—that is, acts of penetrating or being penetrated by others—create gender.[6] They associate gender variance with sexual variance, whereas *machi* do not. *Machi* of either sex may, in their everyday lives, perform penetrating acts, receptive acts, or both with either men or women, or they may remain celibate, yet they still become spiritual brides in order to seduce the spirits. Male *machi,* who do not construct themselves explicitly as brides of spirits or God in the same way female *machi* do, still view their commitment to *machi* practice as a marriage. Machi Sergio stated: "I cannot get married because I am a *machi.* All my time and dedication go to healing others. I am committed to my profession, and God does not allow me to have a family."

The power of spiritual seduction is so great that a *machi* can use it to delay initiation and alleviate spiritual punishment. On May 27, 1995, Machi Pedro invited me to a healing ritual (*datun*) for a young girl who had a *machi* calling but who was being punished by her *filew* because she had not yet been initiated. The girl's feet bled with open sores, and she went into an altered state of consciousness frequently and uncontrollably for hours on end. Pedro drank a concoction made from the juice of *foye* leaves and metal particles scraped off a knife. He covered the girl's body and the four stakes of *foye* and *triwe* branches placed at each corner of her sheepskin bed on the dirt floor with silver jewelry and necklaces made from *kopiwe* flowers. This was to seduce the spirit in order to decrease the severity of the girl's spiritual illness.

After the four introductory prayers (*llelipun*), in which Pedro narrated his calling to be a *machi* and described his powers, and the *metrumtun,* or calling of the spirits, Pedro rubbed the girl's body with *trive* leaves. He then threw a knife toward the door four times to expel the evil spirits that had made the girl ill and to divine the outcome of the ritual. If the knife pointed toward the doorway, the spirit had accepted the offering; if it faced inward, the spirit was unhappy. The spirit's response was ambiguous. Twice the knife fell pointing toward the doorway, and twice facing inside. Pedro asked us all to donate silver jewelry for the girl to wear in order "look prettier for the spirit," and he repeated the ritual again at five o'clock the next morning. He asked the spirit to be patient, arguing that the girl would be initiated as a *machi* as soon as she learned to speak Mapudungu and her family saved enough money to pay for the initiation. This time the knife pointed toward the doorway three of the four times. Five years later, the girl had learned to speak Mapudungu and became initiated as a *machi*.

There is a certain homology between *machi*'s spiritual marriages and human marriages. By marrying a *machi püllü*, a *machi* commits to an exclusive, lifelong relationship with a spirit, which conflicts with the *machi*'s sexual and romantic relationships with humans, regardless of the sex and sexual orientation of the *machi*. Jealous spirits punish *machi* who have romantic and sexual encounters by making them ill, and the spirits must be appeased with offerings, gifts, and prayers (Bacigalupo 1996b). As a result, people who become *machi* are often widowed, single, or have exceptional partners who are willing to break away from conventional gender roles and accept that *machi* must attend to their patients and ritual obligations over and above their families and partners. Scholars have often viewed the practices of female shamans as an extension of the reproductive processes of menarche, fertility, and motherhood (Glass-Coffin 1998; Sered 1994; Tedlock 2005). Mapuche shamans, on the contrary, believe that parenthood, fertility, sex, and family life conflict with *machi*'s spiritual roles and weaken their powers. As spiritual brides, *machi* participate in the cosmic process of fertility and reproduction, which holds priority over and conflicts with their personal sexual and reproductive lives.

The relationship between a *machi* bride and the *filew* husband who possesses her also reflects colonial hierarchical relationships in which male colonial authorities—saints, apostles, mounted generals, and Spanish kings—held power and authority over indigenous people and women. *Machi* brides express the limited participation of women in the patrilineal social and political realm. At the same time, they demonstrate that, through ritual practice, wives actively negotiate relationships between male lineages and between male-dominated structures of social and political power. Spirits do not spontaneously possess *machi* brides; *machi* seek to seduce them. Furthermore, *machi* control their altered states of consciousness and willfully embody the spirit and gendered hierarchies that order their world.

Machi's spiritual marriages are both similar to and different from the sexualized hierarchical power relationships that obtain between voodoo and Oyo-Yoruba Shango priests and the spirits that possess them. These priests are viewed as horses who are ridden by the spirits. The mounting action of the spirit rider suggests a form of control whereby horseman-ship, spirit possession, and sexual penetration are homologous and the bride-horse is inferior to the master-husband and has limited self-control (Bourguignon 1976; Matory 1994:7, 69). *Machi* brides are inferior to their spirit husbands, but their possession experiences are neither invol-untary nor uncontrolled.[7] *Machi* are not horses penetrated and subsumed by the will of their riders but humans who control their interactions with their spirit husbands through seduction. *Machi*'s seduction of spirits and deities who are superior to them is a way for them to gain control over the sociospiritual hierarchies that run their lives. Furthermore, Mapuche spirit horses are not slaves or messengers for spirits but represent the power of the sky.

Master of Animal Souls: The *Machi* Mounted Warrior

> Father creator of the sky . . . take me over the earth, show me the earth above. "May he ride on his horses," you are saying, Mother Creator, Father Creator. May they protect me. The horse of the earth above has me with my head hanging. They lift my heart. They lift my head. I come from ancient grandparent *machi*. They gave me power. I want to ride on the horses from the upper worlds. Here I am, the child of the ancient people waiting for your horse to lift me . . . I am a being who rides on horses, who knows herbal remedies . . . My other self, my other power is riding on a horse.
>
> —EXCERPT FROM MACHI JOSÉ'S DIVINATION PRAYER

Machi gain knowledge, power, and control over the spirit world through horsemanship and mastery over spirit animals in the same way Spanish horsemen and colonial institutions gained control over Mapuche people. While *machi* brideliness reflects subtle forms of agency whereby *machi* gain knowledge through feminine seduction, horsemanship is a spiritual relationship that involves an explicit hierarchy and *machi*'s domination over spirits and is associated with masculinity and warfare. Mapuche metaphors of lifting, elevating, and raising, and especially those of mounted horsemen who travel to the sky, are metaphors of communication with the divine. Horsemanship, mounting, and mastery over animals are symbols of masculinity, fortitude, agility, and prestige for *machi,* as they were for colonial Spanish and Mapuche warriors who battled each other between the sixteenth and the late nineteenth centuries. Mounted Spanish conquistadores believed they were defeating infidels and evil while gaining land and riches for Spain, and later Chilean mounted warriors defended the independence of the new Chilean nation. Some *machi* mimic powerful conquistadores on horseback to bring out their spiritual power. As masculine mounted warriors and masters of animals, *machi* defeat evil spirits and foreignness and gallop to other worlds to gain knowledge of the universe. History is replayed and transformed in ritual. *Machi* gain sacred power from performing the attributes of the Spanish colonial and Chilean national armies and can use that power for healing or destruction.

In some contexts, Mapuche view horsemanship, dogs, pigs, horses, and bulls as foreign and associate them with colonization and witchcraft. Usually, however, *machi* view horses, sheep, chickens, and cattle as indigenous, associate them with well-being and abundance, and value horsemanship and mastery over animals. Mapuche warriors quickly incorporated Spanish horses, sheep, and cattle into their livelihood. They created a cavalry to defend their land and liberty. Cattle raising became a main source of sustenance for the Mapuche until the imposition of reservations in 1884, when they turned to sedentary agriculture. Having many animals was a symbol of power, prestige, and wealth (Alvarado, de Ramón, and Peñaloza 1991:84, 87, 89). Horses and, to a lesser extent, sheep and cattle became important parts of Mapuche sociopolitical, ritual, mythical, and military ideologies. In one version of the Mapuche deluge myth, only humans who rode on horses were saved. Collective *ngillatun* rituals always include the *awün*—an event in which mounted Mapuche warriors, carrying flags and lances and shouting war cries, gallop counterclockwise around the altar (Fig. 4.3). They do battle with the winds in order to control the weather (Alvarado, de Ramón, and Peñaloza 1991:145) and celebrate the power of horsemanship, the horse, and Mapuche identity. José explained: "The horse is spiritual power, it gives me strength. It is also a means of transport . . . The horse is my cavalry. Bad people have dogs as their cavalry."

Figure 4.3. Mapuche circle the ritual field on their horses during the *awün* to do battle against the winds and celebrate the power of horsemanship, the horse, and Mapuche identity (photo by Helen Hughes).

Machi strengthen their bodily defenses and ability to heal by personi-fying male mounted warriors (*machi weichafe pura kawellu*), often re-ferred to as "guardians," "nobles," and "kings," who shelter *machi* during an altered state of consciousness.[8] A *machi* must mount a spirit horse in order to become initiated: "I saw the saddled horse in my dream," said Machi Rocío. "I knew that if I rode I would be a *machi*." Fabián explained that, after initiation, *machi* ride spirit horses during rituals in which they experience themselves as spirits that have knowledge and power. Machi Ana claimed that *machi* rode spiritual horses to other worlds in order to gain power and knowledge—to "know the situation of the universe." When I told José that I had dreamed about his healing songs, he replied: "I sometimes ride my horse to visit people in their dreams and cure them spiritually."

Machi are also described as warriors who ride their *rewe* like horses as they ascend the steps in their travel to other worlds in magical flight. Weapons and war imagery give the *machi* knowledge and strength. *Machi* view themselves as masculine mounted warriors who defeat evil, illness, and suffering. They use guns, knives, and war cries to kill illness or drive it from the bodies of their patients or from their land, household, or community. Machi José viewed his spiritual horse itself as a weapon: "I'll knock down evil with my horse and finish with it." To help them defeat evil, *machi* often call on the power of *chueca* sticks—sticks used in playing the ritual game of *chueca* during *ngillatun* rituals and on other festive occasions (Fig. 4.4). The word *chueca* is semantically equivalent to warfare, and in the past the game helped strengthen Mapuche warriors before battle. *Machi* perform spiritual warfare as a way of aggressively advocating the opposition between, on one hand, self, Mapuche tradition, and life and, on the other, non-Mapuche culture, death, and otherness (Bacigalupo 1998b). Machi Javiera prayed:

> With all your teachings I will ride my horse for this ill son of mine. I will incense the horse with smoke; I will sweat knowledge. I will sweat petitions . . . Come, become my tongue and come into my head. Come and live in my heart . . . Take me, you twelve *chueca* sticks of war, my twelve arrows of war, my twelve knives of war that will allow me to travel through the universe and give me my knowledge. My twelve horse breaths, my twelve walking horses, my twelve spirit horses . . . My superiors have given me my strength. They feed me with knowledge and advice. They take me to the sky. I shall go to the sky. I shall be doing war . . . knowledge of war, teachings of struggle . . . This is the end of my greeting, my petitions, Old Woman of discourse, Old Man of discourse, warrior chiefs, wise people.[9]

Machi are also masters over other animals besides horses: they gain power, strength, and life force from special sheep, horses, chickens, and sometimes cows or bulls. *Machi* drink the saliva of their spirit animals and blood from the ears. They receive the animals' breath on their faces, heads, and backs to strengthen them; the ritual participants eat horse and sheep meat. During initiation and *ngillatun* rituals, Mapuche tie a sheep, a horse, and sometimes a bull or cow to a stake near the *ngillatuwe* or *rewe,* and horsemen take their horses to the *machi* so that she can feel the horses' breath on the face, head, and back. Sometimes, the horse's breath is the "breath of life" (Alvarado, de Ramón, and Peñaloza 1991:91) that restores the *machi*'s strength after he or she enters into an altered state of consciousness, embodies a spirit, and travels to the *wenu mapu.* Machi also receive breath from their spirit animals daily. Machi José sang of the life-giving qualities of his spirit horse's breath: "My heart has strength again. My head has strength again. Your breath has lifted my being."

Most *machi* choose a sheep, horse, chicken, cow, or any combination

Figure 4.4. The ritual all-male game of *chueca* is semantically equivalent to warfare, and in the past it helped strengthen Mapuche warriors before battle (photo bought at the market in Temuco).

thereof as spirit animals, to be initiated along with the *machi,* just as María Cecilia's were. *Machi* do not ride these spirit animals, make them work, or slaughter them. Instead, the animals are expected to protect and help the *machi.* The human *machi*'s well-being receives higher priority than that of her spirit animal. If a *machi* is ill or is cursed, ideally, the spirit animal will get sick or die on her behalf. If a spirit animal dies, the *machi* must replace it with another or she will become weak and ill. The term *machi filew* or *püllü* refers to the *machi* spirit as such, but also to the physical embodiment of the spirit, usually human but sometimes animal.[10]

Not all *machi* can afford a spirit horse at home, so they keep other animals with different power attributes to protect them. Machi Rocío, for example, kept a sheep and a cow. Instead of exchanging saliva with them or drinking their blood, she bathed them in herbal remedies. Machi Pamela had a *machi* sheep with whom she exchanged breath. She prayed: "My heart is happy that my sheep has arrived again. By having my sheep I can scream louder . . . Before, my tongue was stuck. My tongue was small . . . Now this did not happen, I am revitalized. I have recovered my strength."

Bulls are strong and grant power to *machi,* but horses are considered more powerful in the spiritual world because of their gracefulness and agility. Gloria, a Mapuche potter, said: "When bulls are castrated they lose their strength, but horses have much more power than any cattle . . . The spirit asks the *machi* to have a horse . . . Bulls are not as useful to *machi*." Other *machi* believe that the agility and spirituality of the horse can be combined with the strength of the bull. Machi María Cristina prayed: "I am looking for teachings. I implore for a horse-bull and for an ox-bull."[11]

Machi share spirit and life force with their spirit animals, and their lives are intertwined. If a *machi*'s spirit animal is killed, part of the *machi* dies, too, and she suffers drastic physical and spiritual consequences. When seventy-eight-year-old Machi Pamela's son died from heart failure in 1994, she ritually sacrificed her spirit horse to feed the mourners at the funeral and to ensure that her son would travel to the *wenu mapu* on the horse instead of lurking nearby and tormenting the living. As we saw in Chapter 3, Pamela became sad and weak after her son's death and felt pain in her chest, stomach, and head. She experienced fever, fainting, confusion, and amnesia, which she interpreted as soul loss. When Pamela fell into a cataleptic state, Machi Ana came to heal her. After forty minutes of massage, drumming, and prayers, Pamela regained consciousness. Ana said that Pamela's spirit horse was angry because she had killed it, and that in doing so had killed herself in the same way—stabbed with a knife in the heart and lung. Pamela had been hospitalized a few weeks before and diagnosed with cardiac weakness; blood and fluid were accumulating in her lungs. She interpreted the diagnosis as a reflection of the spiritual suicide and soul loss she had experienced when her spirit horse was killed.

Ana obtained the power to heal Pamela from the deity Ngünechen in the guise of four mounted warriors. She asked them to revitalize Machi Pamela: "Old Man mounted on your horse, Old Woman mounted on your horse, Young Man mounted on your horse, Young Woman mounted on your horse . . . come together with your four saddled horses to see this sister and strengthen her spirit of service, strengthen her heart . . . This sick *machi* with a clean heart will mount her horse . . . She must mount her horse with good faith to regain her vitality and the activities of her being." Machi Pamela agreed: "I need a horse to make me feel happier, stronger. I will not get sick, because Chaw Dios will be watching over me. I will be invincible."

Machi share self with horses, master them, and become spiritual mounted warriors who appropriate the power of Spanish conquistadores and Chilean generals to literally or symbolically ascend the *rewe*, travel in ecstatic flight to other worlds, and kill evil spirits. At the same time, *machi* are neither horses nor riders but humans who propitiate the powers of the *wenu mapu* in the form of horses. They draw on the power of Ngünechen in the deity's guise of four mounted warriors. These multiple *machi* powers and positions, along with those of seduction and brideliness, are paired with different altered states of consciousness that grant *machi* a broad experience of the universe.

Machi's varied gendered relationships with spirit beings in ritual are both embodied and ensouled. The paradigm of embodiment alone—the lived experience of being in the body—is insufficient as a model from which to understand *machi*'s ritual relationships. Rather, *machi*, like some other non-Western people, experience a continuum of states of being that include body, mind, personality, consciousness, and self or soul (Halliburton 2002), states in which people possess not only bodies but also multiple spirits (Laderman 1992; Pollock 1996).[12]

Machi ritual practice extends Bourdieu's notion of *habitus* (1977:85)—the process by which social structures and history are transformed into durable dispositions of the body—to express a history that is embodied, ensouled, and transformed in ritual performance. Different states of individual and collective bodies (*trawa*), consciousness (*zuam*), and soul (*püllü*) continuously interact with one another in the ritual relationships of *machi*. Spiritual kinship and spiritual mastery are marked by exchanges of bodily substances such as voice, breath, blood, and saliva, while spiritual marriage involves shamanic illness and the symbolism of the mounting of the head. At the same time, *machi* have many intangible modes of experience separate from the body during altered states of consciousness in which their own soul, or *püllü,* either remains distinct from or merges with the souls of spirit beings such as the *filew,* the *machi püllü,* and Ngünechen.

Personhood, Possession, and Ecstatic Travel

Machi's varied, gendered, ritual relationships with spirit beings offer new perspectives on shamanic altered states of consciousness. In this section, after discussing previous approaches to gender and shamanism, I explore the ways in which three perceptions of self and ritual gendered relationships with spirits on the part of *machi* contribute to current discussions of shamanic altered states of consciousness and personhood. *Machi* view themselves as independent persons who have symbiotic relationships with spirits in their everyday lives; they share personhood with spirits during ecstatic flight; and they each have a persona separate from that of the spirit during possession, although the persona of the spirit temporarily predominates.

Many ethnographers continue to accept older Euro-American assumptions about personhood, gender, and sexuality as natural, precultural universals and to project these concepts onto shamanic altered states of consciousness. Many ethnographers throughout the world still subscribe to the classic, male-dominant paradigms proposed by Mircea Eliade (1974: 328–329, 346–347, 411, 453, 507) and I. M. Lewis (1966:321–322; 1969:89), in which men are shamans because they travel to other worlds and experience ecstatic, transcendent spiritual knowledge, which they control and remember. Conversely, women and "passive" homosexual men, who are like women in affect and dress (Matory 1994:228–229), are defined not as shamans but as mediums because they are physically and spiritually "mountable" by the spirits who possess them. These embodied possession experiences are characterized as unwilled, involving impersonation and a change of identity (Rouget 1985:3, 325), and therefore as amnesic and uncontrolled (Bourguignon 1976:12).[13]

Researchers of Mapuche shamanism replicate these older gendered notions of possession and ecstasy. Some have reported that spirits possessed female and feminized male *machi* and that the *machi*'s soul was displaced (Alonqueo 1979; Kuramochi 1990; Métraux 1973). René San Martín (1976:92) writes that male *machi* do not experience possession but travel with their spirits in ecstatic flight to other worlds; he gives no information about female *machi*. This perspective does not account for the fact that *machi*—male and female—experience both possession and ecstasy, engage with spirits of different genders, and incorporate both female and male symbols and roles in their practices. Anthropologists have viewed the distinction between ecstasy and possession as one of control or lack of control over an altered state of consciousness, but if the altered state is sought, "then the question of 'control' or 'possession' is a matter of ideology, techniques, theatrics, or audience perception" (Tedlock 2003). *Machi*'s entrance into and exit from both possession and ecstasy is willed and controlled. When unwilled possession occurs among Mapuche, it is not considered shamanic. Mapuche who experience unwilled possession are characterized either as neophytes who have a spiritual calling but need training or as people who are possessed by evil spirits.[14]

Machi ecstasy is not superior to possession but involves greater risk and skill. The ecstatic *machi* must be able to control her spirit horse in order not to be captured by an evil spirit as it travels through different worlds. *Machi* do not cease to experience possession because they are shamans but engage in possession, ecstasy, or both, according to the specific ritual situation. They call their spirits and become possessed at the beginning of healing and initiation rituals, and they engage in ecstatic flight to gain additional healing knowledge and to rescue lost souls in other worlds. These experiences are echoed in the findings of scholars who argue that shamans engage in alternate states of consciousness (e.g., Frigerio 1988). And although the ability to undergo ecstatic magical flight may require greater skill than does mastery of possession (Peters 1981:109), most shamans can experience ecstasy, possession, and visionary altered states of consciousness (Basilov 1976:149; Hultkrantz 1973:29; Tedlock 2003).

Many authors have linked the alleged predominance of female me-diums and the scarcity of female shamanism to women's social or sexual deprivation. In societies where possession cults are "peripheral to the morality system" (Lewis 1969:189; see also idem 1966:321–322), par-ticipants—women and effeminate men—are said to be drawn from the periphery (Eliade 1974:507). According to Lewis (1969), women be-come shamans only in areas where state bureaucracies and doctrinal reli-gions have discredited the practice of shamanism. Other scholars have fol-lowed Lewis's lead to argue that the power female shamans gain within their families and communities from their spiritual calling to heal others compensates for women's peripheral social status (Basilov 1990; Harvey 1979; Lewis 1969; Wolf 1974). Female mediums have been constructed, too, as women who seek to heal themselves by compensating for sexual deprivation (Obeyesekere 1981; Spiro 1967) and resisting the power of men (Boddy 1989; Lambek 1981). Yet, if women are in fact universally deprived, as Lewis argues, why is it that more women do not become shamans (Kendall 1999:893)?

Other contemporary authors have challenged these perceptions, assert-ing that the deprivation hypothesis does not explain the predominance of female shamans around the globe in spite of the suppression and discred-iting of shamanic practice by state authorities (Balzer 1996; Basilov 1990; Humphrey and Onon 1996; Kendall 1985; Tedlock 2005). Women are shown to become shamans because of specific historic conditions (Bal-zer 1996; Kendall 1999:894), to create "new forms of speech and new local and global histories" (Tsing 1993:254), and to work alongside male shamans (Tedlock 2003). The last is particularly noticeable among the Mapuche, where women and men shamans coexist, with one or the other predominating according to specific economic, social, and political cir-cumstances and the gendering of social and spiritual space.

Many scholars, however, continue to focus on the everyday gender identities of shamans as women or men, neglecting the different gender identities they assume during an altered state of consciousness. I believe possession and ecstasy are expressions of different gendered relationships between spirits and hosts, and not direct comments on the everyday gender, sex, or sexuality of the *machi* practitioner. Rather, by rendering these everyday identities secondary, ritual personhoods use gender to express the hierarchical relationships between Chilean authorities and Mapuche authorities, masters and servants, parents and children, husbands and wives. *Machi*'s descriptions of their altered states—ecstatic flight as a masculine action and possession as a feminine action—are contingent on the *machi*'s personal consciousness in relation to that of spirits and deities.[15]

In everyday life and in ordinary states of consciousness, *machi* are generally viewed as persons who possess *zuam* (consciousness) and who are authors and agents of their own thoughts, actions, and emotions. In order to be a person, a Mapuche must have a *piuke* (heart), the locus of *nünkün* (emotion), as well as *rakiduam*—thoughts, knowledge, and wisdom. Seeing, knowing, and empathy are central to *machi* practice. *Machi* decide whether and whom to marry, make friends, vote, are involved in politics. *Machi* autonomously decide which patients to see and which rituals to perform, how much to charge, and how to bolster their popularity and compete with other *machi*.

But although *machi* are held accountable for their actions in everyday life, they are never true agents of their destiny.[16] After initiation, a *machi*'s personhood is shaped by her relationship with spirits and by their demands. *Machi* usually inherit a *machi püllü,* the individual spirit of an ancestral *machi,* and also gain divinatory and healing knowledge from a *filew,* a powerful, generic ancestral *machi* who guides them through their ecstatic travels to other worlds. Ngünechen, the deity that fuses Mapuche ancestral spirits and colonial authorities with the Christian God, Jesus, and the Virgin, also provides advice and punishes *machi* who stray from traditional norms.

These spirit beings expect *machi* to live up to impossible ideals. They ask *machi* to dedicate their lives exclusively to the spirits, not to marry, to avoid modern technology, and to speak exclusively in Mapudungu and not in Spanish, the official language of Chile. Spirits place taboos on drinking, dancing, socializing, sex, and nontraditional clothing. They are angered if *machi* have lovers or spouses, travel in cars, or use cellular phones, and they punish them with illness and suffering.

Machi negotiate their needs and desires with their spirits, appeasing them continually with prayers and offerings. Machi Rocío described one of her struggles with her *machi püllü* in a dream narrative: "In my dream there was a *machi* who didn't show her face. 'Extinguish the fire,' she said. 'No,' I said. And the spirit was mad. 'You are not your own owner,' the spirit said. 'I command you. Extinguish the fire . . . Play your *kultrun* and pray for that poor ill man.' And that is what I did, because if one does not do what the spirit says in the dream, one becomes ill."

Some *machi* find the burden of spiritual marriage unbearable. As we will see in Chapter 8, Machi Fresia was unable to fulfill the demands of the spirit she inherited from her great-grandmother or to resolve the conflicts she had with her spirit. She finally decided to uproot her altar and abandon her *machi* practice.

During ordinary states of consciousness, *machi* and their spirits are perceived as separate persons in symbiotic relationship. The *filew* is the power, or *newen*, that makes the *machi*, and the *machi* is the human who makes the power tangible and effective through ritual practice. Thus, even human *machi* may be spoken of as *filew*, just as *filew* may be referred to as *machi*. Although *machi* are subject to the *filew*'s demands and desires, and the *filew* influences the *machi*'s personality, they remain separate persons. Ramiro, a Mapuche intellectual, elaborates on the relationship between the personhoods of *machi* and of spirits:

> RAMIRO: There are two elements to the *machi* person: the physical, which is individual, and the *püllü*, which is inherited . . . Machi Jacinto is physically Jacinto. But his *püllü* is that of his great-grandmother. So when the *püllü* comes into him, which is the character who acts? The character of the *machi*—a great-grandmother.
>
> MARIELLA: When Machi Jacinto dies, which is the spirit that is inherited by another *machi*? That of Machi Jacinto? That of the great-grandmother *machi*? Or that of the great-grandmother *machi* transformed by Machi Jacinto?
>
> RAMIRO: That of the great-grandmother *machi*, because it is the *machi* identity that is inherited. But there is also the individual *püllü* of Machi Jacinto, so the spirit says: "I have also served this other *filew* called So-and-So."

During ecstatic states, *machi* share self with the *filew*. The *filew* is the intermediary or messenger between humans and Ngünechen that speaks the god's demands, knowledge of remedies, and advice through the *machi*. Mapuche consider ecstatic flight—as a mounted Mapuche or a Spanish warrior—a masculine action in which male and female *machi* travel to

Figure 4.5. *Machi* experiencing *konpapüllü* is held by her *dungumachife* (photo by Helmut Schindler, published in Helmut Schindler, 1990, *Bauern und Reiterkrieger: Die Mapuche-Indianer im Süden Amerikas*. Munich: Hirmer Verlag).

other worlds to obtain power objects, acquire knowledge about healing, and recover lost souls from the hands of evil spirits. *Machi* describe themselves as the *filew* "flying to the sky," "riding the spirit horse," and "sitting beside Ngünechen to listen to his words." At the end of *datun* healing rituals, *machi* experience an ecstatic state labeled "*konpapüllü*." The term has multiple meanings: "the spirit who enters and does here," derived from *konün* (to enter), *pa* (to do here), and *püllü* (living spirit); "the spirit who divines here," derived from *koneu* (divination), *pa*, and *püllü*; or simply "with the spirit." At the time of *konpapüllü*, Ngünechen or the *filew* merges with the *machi* to reveal the cause of the illness and gives advice and knowledge about healing remedies. *Machi* remember their experiences as spirit beings in detail and recount them often (Fig. 4.5).

The way in which *machi* share personhood with spirit beings during ecstatic flight is complex. They draw on the discourse of possession to describe ecstatic flight as multiple, multilayered possessions in which the *machi* and the *filew* go into *küymi* (an altered state of consciousness) and the *filew* "speaks the words of Ngünechen through the *machi*'s mouth." Mapuche sometimes refer to *machi* in trance as *filew* or as Ngünechen. Ramiro, whom I quote earlier, commented that "the *machi püllü*, the *filew*, and Ngünechen can be the same or different according to context."

In an interview on December 28, 2001, Machi Rocío explained this process:

> MARIELLA: When you are possessed, which spirit comes?
> ROCÍO: The spirit that one has, the *machi püllü*. A *machi* without power is no good. One has to have power.
> MARIELLA: When your head becomes drunk and you go into *küymi* [an altered state of consciousness], who arrives?
> ROCÍO: *Filew*, Ngünechen, *machi püllü*. They are all the same.
> MARIELLA: But if you inherit a *machi* spirit from your grandmother, that spirit is not Ngünechen.
> ROCÍO: One has to inherit a spirit first to be a *machi*. That is the *machi püllü*. That is the spirit that comes to one. The words of Ngünechen, the *filew*, come through the *machi püllü*. When the *machi* is in *küymi*, the *machi püllü, filew*, and Ngünechen are the same.

These multiple, multilayered possessions between the *machi*, the *machi püllü* or *filew*, and Ngünechen are comparable to the two sets of mimesis observed by Michael Taussig (1993:120): one between the person and the copy represented by her soul; and the second, the mimetic conjunction between the soul and the spiritual cosmos. *Machi*, like Panama's Kuna chanters, have a decisively mimetic component built into their speech, whereby the speaker is always retelling, reviewing, or reinterpreting something said before (Taussig 1993:109). They hear the message of Ngünechen through the words of the *filew* and the *machi püllü*, who interpret them. The *machi* repeats and interprets the words of the *filew* and the *machi püllü* in her ecstatic discourse. The *machi*'s words, in turn, are repeated and interpreted by the *dungumachife* on behalf of the ritual participants.

During possession states, the *machi* becomes a feminine bride, and his or her head is mounted by a spirit, a process called *longkoluupan*. The *machi*'s personhood remains distinct from that of the spirit, and the spirit speaks directly through the *machi*'s mouth and body while he or she remains absent.[17] While possession strengthens the interpersonal ties between spirits and their human spouses (Boddy 1994:421), it also keeps their personhood separate. *Machi* claim they do not remember the possession experience because they separate themselves from the spirit, who speaks. In practice, however, *machi*'s possession states are always under control, and *machi* are both aware and unaware in what Carol Laderman (1991:88) calls "a balance between remembering and forgetting."

Machi distinguish between light and deep possession and consider the latter more prestigious and powerful. During light possession, the spirit inhabits the *machi*'s body but does not replace his or her soul, a phenomenon that Rolf Foerster (1993:106) refers to as "revelation." *Machi* are aware of the spirit's presence and understand its advice and demands, but it is the spirit, not the *machi,* who speaks. The possessed *machi* serves as a spokesperson for spirits. *Machi* forget their own persona but remember the ritual, the performance, and sometimes the actions and words of the possessing spirit. Machi Pamela described her personal soul, or *püllü,* as "sitting beside" her body while she was being possessed by the *filew.* Machi Marta described the experience this way: "The *filew* is up in the sky but also in the *rewe* guarding the *püllü.* When the *filew* comes to me I feel a heat rising in my body and I am gone. I stay at the *rewe,* I am Marta. The *filew* takes over. While God talks to the *filew,* the *machi* talks to the people. The word of God is repeated."

During deep possession, the *machi*'s person is completely separated from that of the spirit, who takes over and replaces the *machi*'s soul. *Machi* rarely remember anything of what transpired except for the drumming rhythms. Machi Fresia explained: "When the spirit is here, I disappear. So there is a change. When the spirit is not with me, then I am here. When the spirit arrives, then I am not here where the spirit is talking. *Machi* are double persons because sometimes she is here and sometimes she is not the person with whom people are talking" (interview, November 24, 1991). Like the Haitian voodoo practitioners whom Erika Bourguignon observed, *machi* perceive a continuity between the possessing spirit and the culturally defined identity of a generic spirit such as *filew* or Ngünechen, but a discontinuity between the possessing spirit and the human vehicle, who has no memory of or responsibility for the actions carried out by her or his body when it becomes the residence of a more powerful spirit. At the same time, some cases of possession show an obvious continuity with the conscious motivation of the possessed (Bourguignon 1965:47, 53, 57). In such cases, the temporary replacement of the *machi*'s self by that of a spirit does not challenge the integrity of the *machi*'s self but, rather, provides increased scope for fulfillment by providing the self with an alternative set of roles. Possession becomes an idiom of communication whereby spirits have a place not only during public ceremonies but also in everyday domestic life (Crapanzano and Garrison 1977:10–12; Lambek 1980:319).

During Mapuche rituals, *machi* or candidates for *machi*-hood (*machil*) are the only people who are possessed or who engage in ecstatic travel.

Knowledgeable elder Mapuche, *ngenpin* (orators), *dungumachife,* and some dancers and musicians understand the power and meaning of Mapuche ritual prayers, songs, and dances, but the *machi* alone is responsible for establishing the connection between the *wenu mapu* and the earth. *Machi* criticize, for example, the collective possessions that take place in Senegalese possession rituals. When Machi Abel participated in an international folk music festival in Germany, he was struck by the Senegalese music and dance troupe: "Not everyone can be a communicator, a spiritual messenger. How it is that one spirit possesses all those people at once? They must be possessed by the devil."

Machi stress the relational nature of humans, animals, and spirits, but in practice they operate in both relational and individual modes of personhood. They stress their relational selves in order to legitimate themselves as *machi* with strong spiritual powers who gain power from colonial authorities, ancestral spirits, and spirit animals. They emphasize their individual personhood when asserting their agency and volition in everyday life and in distancing themselves from possessing spirits who take over their bodies and speak through them.

Death: Severing Relationships and the Rebirth of the *Filew*

In the Temuco area, *machi*'s spiritual kinship, their marriage to the *filew,* and their ability to be animal masters and mounted warriors are broken at death. Mapuche perform a special funerary ritual called *amulpüllün* ("making the soul leave") in order to help the *machi*'s personal spirit, or *püllü,* find its way to the *wenu mapu* and to sever all the *machi*'s social and spiritual ties with animals, spirits, other *machi,* and other humans. *Machi* often know when they are going to die. In December 2001, Machi José told me that he would probably die in January because his spirit horse was weak. "I am in spiritual competition with other spirits who are not positive like me, and I think I am going to lose because they have really screwed me up. If I survive January, then it means I won the battle and I will live." José survived January but died on March 21, 2002.

Machi's spirits eventually become the *filew*—the generic spirit of *machi*—and are invoked by living *machi* and other Mapuche in rituals. The relationship between a deceased *machi* and his or her family is particularly important because the *machi* spirit, or *filew,* will eventually be "reborn" in a descendant, usually in someone from the mother's side of the family. Funerary rituals for *machi* closely resemble *machi*'s *ngeykurewen* (renewal) rituals, and *machi* who know they are soon to die sometimes organize a *ngeykurewen,* buy food and drink, pay the helping *machi* and musicians, and then die shortly beforehand. In late August 1996, Machi Pamela said to me:

> I had a dream that told me I had to do a *machi purrun* here in the house. I dreamed that people were dancing *purrun* and *choyke.* "I have to do a *baile de machi,*" I said. God said: "You have to go out and find people, get all the things you are going to need. You have to bring a good *tru-truka* player. You have to have *choykes* for the *purrun.* There has to be meat. There has to be a powerful *machi,* a good *machi.*" I dreamed that it was Machi Ana who would come and help me make my spirit strong again . . . I thought: "I will do my *baile* the fourth of October, the day of Saint Francis. Maybe I will renew my powers, or maybe it will be my last *baile de machi.*

I was in Cambridge, Massachusetts, when Pamela died, and I was unable to attend her funeral in southern Chile. I have reconstructed the events as they were described to me by Pamela's daughter Beatriz and by Machi Ana when I visited them in December 1996.

On September 10, 1996, Pamela walked from house to house inviting friends to her renewal ritual and paying for the musicians and the *machi* who would perform. She drank large quantities of cheap red wine and arrived home drunk and tired. On the morning of September 11, Tomás, her brother-in-law, went to wake her and could not. Beatriz came and recognized that Pamela's heart was not beating. Beatriz and her sister Alba took off Pamela's silver jewelry and placed it in a box, together with her ritual headdress and her sleigh bells. Each of her daughters kept some of the jewelry. Beatriz decided that I should keep Pamela's headdress of multicolored ribbons and her ring.

Early on the morning of September 15, after a four-day wake, Machi Ana came to perform the *amulpüllün* to bid Pamela's spirit farewell. Ana prayed so that Pamela's *püllü* would leave hastily and not remain on earth to haunt her family. Ana told Pamela's family to destroy her belongings and not to mention her name. She prayed for Pamela's personal soul, or *püllü,* and told the family not to think of Pamela anymore—otherwise, they would call her spirit back. Pamela would eventually return as a *filew* who would guide another *machi* in the family. The *filew* would have some of Pamela's personal characteristics; Beatriz claimed it would have a fiery temper.

The *amulpüllün* reversed Machi Pamela's initiation ritual. Her brother-in-law broke off the heels of her shoes so that her spirit would not clomp around the house tormenting her family. Instead of consecrating a new *rewe* for Pamela, Machi Ana pulled her old *rewe* out of the ground and left it in a nearby stream to rot. "Pamela's body will rot in the cemetery; her *rewe* has to rot, too. Pamela has to become earth again," she said. Instead of blessing Pamela's spirit sheep, the mourners killed and ate it. Pamela's *püllü* would ride the spirit of her sheep to the *wenu mapu*. The mourners danced *purrun*, circling counterclockwise around Pamela's coffin with flowers and laurel leaves in their hands. Young male *choykes* danced to remind the mourners of the beauty of life and the living.

The local priest prayed over the coffin and blessed it with holy water. After eating Pamela's spirit sheep, the mourners followed the funeral car. Ana and three of her helpers played *kultrun* while the men played trumpets and flutes to honor Pamela as they would have a military chief. Ana explained: "We buried her with honors just like a military person—with trumpets, with flags—because she battled against evil just like a military man." Pamela's brother-in-law slashed the skin of her drum and placed it on the casket, together with the intestines of her spirit sheep and the blue and white flags that were ordinarily planted beside her *rewe*. The mourners buried the coffin. Pamela's grandson planted a cross at the head of the grave. The mourners painted her tombstone blue and placed an image of the Virgin Mary on it. Pamela had often called on the powers of the Virgin Mary to help her heal, and Beatriz thought she would need the Virgin to accompany her on her voyage to the *wenu mapu*. Pamela was buried with her feet facing east, so that the next morning her *püllü* could walk up into the sky and become a *filew* in the *wenu mapu*. Pamela's *filew* would sit beside Ngünechen, waiting for the moment to embody a new *machi*.[18]

In December 1996, Beatriz chided me for grieving for Pamela: "Don't cry. It is not good to remember her because you will call her spirit back."

"I want her back," I sobbed.

"No," Beatriz sighed, "you wouldn't know the spirit. She would do witchcraft on all of us."

Living *machi* in the Puren-Lumaco area of the Araucanian region, in contrast, perform rituals on the *cuel*, mounds under which *machi* and *longko* are publicly buried. Through these rituals *machi* maintain social, spatial, and religious relationships with the dead of the local elite who speak through the *cuel* (Dillehay 1995). At death, *machi* sever relations with ordinary living persons but maintain connections with living *machi*. In the Mapuche areas where I worked, closer to the city of Temuco, there are a few mounds, but nothing like those of the Puren-Lumaco area, and *machi* do not engage in the same kind of public memorializing of the dead. Rather, I observed and was told of private memorializations of specific ancient *machi* by neophytes who had inherited their shamanic powers. For example, Tom Dillehay (personal communication 2003) reported that one *machi* using a mound near Temuco stated that it was her personal *filew* and her way to rejuvenate her powers and medicine. In the Temuco area, a tension exists between the severing of *machi*'s ritual relationships with spirits at death so that they can be transformed into *filew* and the remembering of ancient *machi* spirits who are later embodied and ensouled by new *machi* or who give powers to family members. Longko Jaime's gift of ritual speech, granted by Machi Nora, his deceased mother, exemplifies the latter: "I dreamed that my mother came walking down the path toward the *ngillatuwe,* and I was walking up the path. We met in front of the *ngillatuwe.* 'You must loosen your tongue,' she said. My lips trembled for several days . . . She gave me a gift. I dreamed that I spoke well, so many words came out so well . . . Then, when I was praying in the *ngillatun* ritual, many words came out just like in the dream, and people admired me. They were in agreement that I should be *longko*" (interview, December 28, 2001).

Conclusion

The complex workings of *machi* personhood offer a new way to think about the relationship between body, mind, and spirit and the ways in which shamanic spiritual experiences and altered states of consciousness are gendered. Male and female *machi* experience both relational and individual modes of personhood, and their ritual experiences are embodied and ensouled. Feminist theologians and scholars of feminist spirituality have created a dichotomy between men's symbols and experiences, which transcend and invert everyday experiences, and women's symbols and experiences, which build from social and biological processes. Men's experiences are characterized as focusing on opposition and elaborating on discrete stages between self and other through contradiction, inversion, and conversion (Bynum 1986:13). Women's experiences are viewed as embodied (rather than as nonphysical), lived (rather than otherworldly), relational (rather than solitary, competitive, or adversarial), processual (rather than goal oriented), and immanent (rather than transcendent) (Alcoff 1994:96–97; Glass-Coffin 1998:187–188; Ochs 1983:21;

Ruether 1987:67). Anthropologists of shamanism acknowledge that shamanic power and the spiritual power on which it draws flow between worlds (Houston and Stuart 1989) rather than existing within this world (immanence) or outside the boundaries of this world (transcendence). Some continue to see relationality among humans and between humans and spirits as particular to women shamans (Glass-Coffin 1998:188, 191) and project the correlation between gender differences in the use of symbols in American and European Judeo-Christian traditions onto gender differences in local shamanic philosophies and therapeutic strategies.

In Chile, to the contrary, relationality is crucial for both male and female *machi,* and perceptions of bodily experiences, as well as those of the soul, must be read within their cultural context rather than universalized. The spiritual experiences of *machi* are gendered not according to their biological sex or everyday gender identities but according to the power dynamics involved in ritual relationships involving spiritual kinship, spiritual marriage, and spiritual mastery.

Mapuche consider out-of-body ecstatic flight a masculine action associated with the image of mounted conquistadores and Mapuche warriors, and embodied possession as a feminine action associated with brideliness toward possessing spirits. Yet, *machi* experience both of these drum-induced altered states of consciousness regardless of their sex, using one or another according to purpose and specific ritual context. Contrary to classic theories of shamanism, Mapuche do not view ecstasy as superior, more controlled, or more transcendent than possession, nor does possession involve a loss of self. In fact, *machi*'s experiences of possession and ecstatic flight have much in common. Both altered states of consciousness are voluntarily induced and controlled. Possessed *machi* are double persons who have a certain awareness of the ritual performance, whereas *machi* conceive of ecstatic flight as multiple, multilayered possessions in which the shaman's self merges with that of her spirit while that spirit, in turn, is possessed by other deities and spirits. The classic dichotomy between embodied possession as characteristic of women and ecstatic flight as characteristic of men may say more about the gender biases and politics of researchers than about the people they study.

Shamanism, however, is not just a question of varying altered states of consciousness or of expressions of power and resistance (Boddy 1989; Comaroff 1985; Stoller 1995). Shamanism is not a "desiccated and insipid category" (Geertz 1966:80) but a widespread "historically situated and culturally mediated social practice" (J. Atkinson 1992:309) connected both to local circumstances and histories and to national and transnational contexts (J. Atkinson 1992; Balzer 1996; Joralemon 1990; Kendall 1998; Taussig 1987; Tsing 1993). The different relational personhoods and positionalities of shamans, animals, and spirits are expressions of cultural meaning and of ethnic and national relationships in various social and political contexts. *Machi*'s ritual relationships through kinship, marriage, and mastery, and their associated altered states of consciousness, reflect the complex and contradictory relationships between Mapuche and Spaniards, women and men, and humans, animals, and spirits. These relationships can be hierarchical or complementary; they can highlight the agency of the *machi* or merge her personhood with that of other spirit beings.

Machi's spiritual marriages represent the contradictions inherent in feminine control and power in a patriarchal social system. When *machi* brides are possessed by husband spirits, they illustrate the superiority of spirits and deities over humans and of Chilean authorities over Mapuche ones, as well as the limited participation of ordinary women in the patrilineal social and political realm. At the same time, spiritual brideliness illustrates how women are able to negotiate pragmatically with local male authorities in the same manner in which Mapuche negotiate with Chilean ones. *Machi*'s positive valuation of spiritual seduction as the tool for entering the spirit world and the prioritization of spiritual marriage over social marriage set *machi* apart from other women and offer a new reading of feminine sexuality in a spiritual context.

As masters of animals and mounted warriors who travel in ecstatic flight, *machi* gain control over the hierarchical institutions that regulate Mapuche people and use their power for their own purposes. Multiple, multilayered possessions provide the context for the merging of a *machi*'s personhood with those of masculine, mounted, Mapuche and Spanish warriors as well as the Chilean religious and civil authorities who control their lives and futures. In this context, shamans are not the children or brides of hierarchical spirits and deities but are deities and authorities themselves. It is from this position of power that shamans know about the universe and are able to change situations. By becoming male authorities in order to change the world, *machi*, in an attempt to define their own destinies, reverse the inferior position that Mapuche hold in relation to the Chilean state. At the same time, *machi*'s powers, destinies, and lives are intertwined with those of the animals they dominate. *Machi* are part of a larger social body in which Mapuche and non-Mapuche, masters and animals, share personhood and in which foreign authorities and beings become part of and transform the Mapuche self.

Outside of ritual contexts, however, *machi* are viewed as women and men who must abide by the gender norms of mainstream Chilean and Mapuche society in order to be legitimate and successful. In the following two chapters I look at these imposed gender norms, first by showing how Spanish colonialists misread *machi*'s ritual co-gendered identities and transvestism by drawing on Spanish tropes of sodomy, the criollo penetration paradigm, and contradictory Spanish Catholic notions of women as pious virgins or perverse witches. Then I show how these notions have been appropriated and transformed in contemporary Chilean national discourses about homosexuality and in Chilean and Mapuche notions of men's and women's roles.

CHAPTER 5

The Struggle for *Machi* Masculinity: Colonial Politics of Gender, Sexuality, and Power

One long winter evening in August 1629, in a hamlet headed by Longko Maulican south of the Bio-Bío River in Chile, a *machi weye,* or male shaman, healed a bewitched native boy with the help of ancestral spirits and a *foye* tree. Longko Maulican's slave, Francisco Núñez de Pineda y Bascuñán, a twenty-two-year-old of Spanish descent, born in Chile, watched wide-eyed and terrified in a dark corner. To him, the *machi weye*'s appearance and spiritual practices were those of a *puto,* or male gender invert, a perverse sodomite engaged in devil worship:[1]

> An Indian with such a horrible figure entered. His outfit, his perverse face and shape expressed what he was . . . His features, dress, and body made him look like Lucifer because he was not wearing pants but was a *weye.* Instead of pants he was wearing a *puno*—a cloth that is wrapped around the waist and is used by women with a long shirt on top. His hair was long and loose while others wear their hair braided, and his nails were so deformed that they looked like spoons. His face was very ugly, and he had a cloud in his eye that understood everything. His body was very small, his back was broad, and he limped. Just looking at him caused horror and gave me to understand his vile exercises . . . Those that take on the role of women are called *weye,* which in our language means nefarious ones and, more precisely, male inverts [*putos*] . . . They become *machi* because they have a pact with the devil. (Núñez de Pineda y Bascuñán 1863:107, 157–159 [hereafter, Núñez 1863])

The sick boy lay on a sheepskin on the dirt floor of his father's thatch hut. A sacred *foye* tree had been planted at the boy's head to serve as a conduit for spirits who descended into the *machi weye*'s body. They gave him knowledge about the circumstances under which the boy had been be-witched, about the required treatment, and about the final outcome of his illness. Several laurel (*triwe*) branches were placed beside the *foye* to lower the boy's fever. The *machi weye*'s drum hung from the *foye,* and a lamb was tied to its base. While several women sang and played drums, the *machi weye* slit open the lamb's chest, placed its still-beating heart in the *foye* tree, and began periodically to suck blood from it. Next, he blew tobacco smoke over the boy's chest and stomach and then slit them and sucked some of the venom out of his body. Miraculously, the boy's wounds healed immediately, leaving no scars. The *machi weye* then became pos-sessed by a helping spirit. His eyes rolled back and his body bounced like a ball on the floor while his drum imitated its owner, jumping beside him. He told the participants that an enemy had poisoned and bewitched the boy during a drinking party, that the venom had spread throughout the boy's body, and that soon it would reach his heart and kill him (Núñez 1863:159–160). Young Francisco was deeply affected by this experience: "I commended myself to God . . . and after I saw this horrible spectacle, my soul became anguished, my hair stood on end, and I was sure that his [the *machi weye*'s] body was possessed by the devil" (Núñez 1863:160).

Francisco Núñez de Pineda y Bascuñán wrote the only eyewitness ac-count of an encounter between a colonial agent and a *machi weye* and the only known seventeenth-century narrative by a Chilean criollo, a locally born person of Spanish descent. Colonial agents were either Spanish or criollo, but it was the former who wrote most of the seventeenth-century chronicles. Born in Chillán, Francisco lacked the power and prestige of Spanish-born authorities, yet he drew on Spanish understandings of gen-der, religion, and power, which linked shamans' bodies with devil wor-ship, gender inversion, and perverse sexuality. He saw the native *weye*'s body as deformed and repulsive. He interpreted the *machi weye*'s long hair and nails and his waist wrap as effeminate and linked them to sodomy and perversion. Finally, he read the *weye*'s possession and divinatory abilities, his miraculous surgery, his jumping drum, and his sucking of blood as expressions of native devil worship.

Francisco's criollo status was also important in the way he shaped his own identity and that of the people by whom he was enslaved—who were known as Mapuche from the mid-eighteenth century onward. Trained as a Jesuit priest, Francisco fashioned himself as Spanish, Christian, and masculine to erase his criollo origins. When he committed a few "juvenile blunders," his father, Alonso—a famous Spanish conquistador—enlisted him in the Spanish army so that he could prove his worth. Francisco was captured by Mapuche warriors at the battle of Cangrejeras on May 15, 1629. When he was enslaved by a Mapuche chief, his ethnicity, gender, and beliefs were interpreted ambivalently by the Mapuche and by some Spaniards, too. Francisco wrote a 560-page chronicle of his seven months of captivity in an attempt to legitimate his Spanishness by condemning *machi weye*.

Spanish and Hybrid Lenses

Like most other colonial agents and Jesuits, Francisco Núñez de Pineda y Bascuñán perceived the colonial encounter in gender and racial terms and interpreted it through the prism of the devilish versus the divine. He embraced Thomas Aquinas's notion that there existed a "natural, God-given law," expressed in Christian religious orthodoxy, which constrained pleasure, nonreproductive sex, and European bodies. He deemed people and practices that fell outside of orthodox categories "unnatural," "abominable," and "against the divine order" (Núñez 1863:107, 157–159). He associated honor with images of powerful, masculine, Spanish soldiers and Christian souls, and shame and stigma with the bodies of *machi weye*. In typical Spanish fashion, he constructed Mapuche's sensual practices— healing, feasting, dancing, and sex—as devilish and effeminate. Following Christian ideals of masculinity, he resisted bodily enjoyment and the sexual advances of Mapuche women (Núñez 1863:134, 136–137, 148, 205).

Spanish perceptions of sexuality, gender, and religion permeated most aspects of the Spaniards' experience, but they did not prepare Francisco or his Jesuit contemporaries for understanding *machi weye* or the roles they played among the Mapuche. *Machi*'s bodily healing practices, dress, and demeanor were especially challenging to Francisco's Spanish Christian masculinity. Like most Jesuits, he stigmatized *machi weye* as *putos* because he believed they had "womanly desires for men," "dressed in skirts," and "were like women." He repudiated *machi weye,* who were thought to enjoy being penetrated by men, as "sodomites." He considered Mapuche in general to be "sodomites," "gender inverts," "effeminates," and "devil worshipers," and female *machi* to be witches (Núñez 1863; Ovalle 1888; Valdivia 1887). Differentiating between Spanish and indigenous, Christianity and witchcraft, reproductive sexuality and sodomy, and masculinity and effeminacy became a way of policing the boundaries between a privileged Spanish self and an abject, indigenous *machi*.

When Spaniards arrived in Chile, they projected their classificatory schemes onto Mapuche realities and used them as a rationale for domination. Colonial agents used contrasting Spanish perceptions of Mapuche men to advance different political agendas. Their depictions of Mapuche warriors as brave, masculine, barbaric, and dangerous helped to explain Spanish military defeats and justify the enslavement of Mapuche. The Spaniards' sexualizing and demonizing logic was a rhetorical strategy and a weapon against *machi* and polygamous Mapuche chiefs. If male Mapuche spiritual and political authorities led lives of sexual excess, sodomy, and perversion, and if female *machi* were witches, then Spanish colonization and evangelization were "justified." The discourse of sexuality and evil became a Spanish tool for molding Mapuche subjects to colonial power. Judgments about sexuality are deeply embedded in the history of scholarly explanations of who acquires power, who deserves it, and who gets to keep it (Weston 1998:20). Lust and leisure are attributed to those "unfit to rule"; domesticated sexuality and managed sensibilities are attributed to those who stand above—and who label—those troubled categories (Stoler 1995:194). In Chile, *machi weye* and female *machi* were forced to conform to Spanish notions of sexual propriety, modesty, and decorum and to become Christian to avoid persecution.

How did Francisco's use of Spanish categories differ from those of other Spanish colonial agents? How were he and the Spanish categories he learned affected by his enslavement to a Mapuche chief? What happened to his status as a Jesuit and a soldier in the Spanish army during his captivity? Francisco's narrative is exceptional for two reasons. First, as a criollo, he knew himself to be different from Spanish soldiers, who believed they were powerful and superior to the Mapuche simply because they were Spanish. Francisco had to consciously appropriate Spanish identities and power ideologies, first to model himself and then to manipulate Mapuche gender identities and religious practices through these lenses.

Second, his enslavement to Longko Maulican reversed the way colonial power dynamics were ordinarily played out in terms of race and gender. Mapuche and Spaniards questioned Francisco's Christianity, his masculinity, and his Spanishness in the context of his enslavement. He had to be pleasant and accommodating to Mapuche chiefs. The Mapuche infantilized him as "little Álvaro," and Maulican became his native father, protecting him against Mapuche men who wanted to kill him. Maulican wore Francisco's conquistador clothes while Francisco wore the "vile clothes" of Indian men (Núñez 1863:84, 59, 103–105), which made him

neither Spaniard nor Indian. The Mapuche viewed him as an asexual outsider who, like a woman, served a male *longko* and acted as an intermediary between different groups. Because Francisco held ambivalent status
and evangelized boys, the Mapuche believed he had shamanic powers and
requested herbal remedies and prayers from him (Núñez 1863:182–183,
220–221).[2]

He, in turn, challenged Spanish notions of superiority by describing
his Mapuche friends in Spanish manly terms—as noble, generous, brave,
and smart (Núñez 1863:123–124)—and by portraying his seven months
of captivity as "happy ones." His narrative illustrates the ways in which
Mapuche and Spanish perspectives were negotiated and gradually became intertwined, transformed, and integrated.

I first read Francisco Núñez de Pineda y Bascuñán's account of his encounter with a *machi weye* in 1987 while studying history at the Catholic
University in Santiago, Chile. The Spanish intellectual tradition, which
refused indigenous people a place in history, and the agendas of Spanish soldiers, authorities, and Jesuits, which led them to construct *machi*
as witches and devil worshipers, were obvious to me. Yet, I thought of
gender and sexuality as empirical facts, not as theories, interpretations of
the world, or parts of a particular intellectual history. My Chilean Catholic education, infused with colonial perceptions, had not prepared me to
question the "natural" relationship between sex, gender, and sexuality.
I thought that Spanish assumptions about effeminacy and masculinity
were universal, and I assumed that Mapuche and Spanish notions of gender inversion were synonymous. I could not read beyond the Spanish
sodomy tropes to see the gender identities of *machi weye* as having been
performed; I could not see gender as a central category for organizing
sexual acts and bodies or for defining identity and sexuality. Influenced
by Chilean machismo, I assumed that gender inversion was automatically
associated with effeminacy and passive sexual intercourse and that sodomites were equivalent to effeminate homosexuals. I saw men who were
penetrated by other men as more homosexual than their partners. Like
most other Chilean academics, I was blind to the ethnic, political, and
power implications of the sodomy labels that colonial agents had hurled
at indigenous people.

I began to recognize Chilean assumptions about gender and sexuality
and my own cultural and academic baggage when, as a graduate student
in anthropology at the University of California, Los Angeles, I encountered American notions in which homosexuality was defined mainly by
choice of same-sex object. My views broadened further when I began

to explore *machi*'s flexible gender and sexual epistemologies during my ethnographic research in southern Chile in 1991. The contrast between American and Chilean popular homosexual identities and Mapuche gendered systems prompted me to take a closer look at Chilean majority readings of both colonial and contemporary gender identities and sexualities of male *machi*. I saw discrepancies between those contemporary identities and sexualities and Chilean national stereotypes, many of them based on Spanish sodomy tropes. Colonial assumptions and modern Chilean misreadings of colonial texts had distorted Mapuche gender epistemologies and *machi weye* subjectivities.

In the rest of this chapter, I reread the gender identities of *machi* in the colonial period by taking colonial power dynamics into consideration. I contrast Mapuche perceptions of *machi* with those of Spanish and criollo soldiers and Jesuit priests and explore the process by which the two groups' categories gradually merged. In later chapters, we will see how the resulting gender norms help shape the identities of *machi* in contemporary Chile.

The Battleground of Masculinity

Once the Spaniards crossed the Bío-Bío River into Mapuche land, they met resistance from accomplished guerilla warriors who had long defended their territory against Inca expansion. Unable to conquer the Mapuche, in 1643 the Spaniards signed a royal treaty recognizing the sovereignty of the Mapuche nation south of the Bío-Bío River. In 1673 Father Diego de Rosales (1989:114) asked why Spain, which had been able to conquer the Aztec and Inca empires, had been defeated by naked Mapuche warriors who battled with simple wooden weapons.

The Mapuche were difficult to conquer because they were hunters and horticulturalists organized in small, seminomadic, endogamous, patrilineal kin groups. The power of Mapuche lineage heads, or *longkos*, was local; victory over one *longko* in no way guaranteed dominance over others. Mapuche groups skilled in guerilla warfare consistently destroyed precarious Spanish settlements (Alvarado, de Ramón, and Peñaloza 1991; Olivares 1864–1901). The Spaniards' introduction of the horse and metal weapons in the seventeenth century increased Mapuche warring and spiritual power. In skirmishes, mounted Mapuche warriors were more agile than armor-clad Spanish soldiers, and *machi weye* used horse spirits as spiritual mounts to travel to other worlds and kill enemy souls.[3]

Mapuche resistance to Spanish colonization and later to Chilean pacification became legendary. Finally, in 1883, the Chilean republic defeated
the Mapuche rebels with a large, well-equipped army and the support of
longkos loyal to the republic. The Mapuche became secondary citizens of
the Chilean nation-state.

Spaniards and Mapuche associated spiritual and political power with
gender in ways both similar and different, and both parties used their gendered lenses to represent the practices of the other in their own terms. In
Spain, men held the reins in institutions of power. Spaniards viewed practices of politics and warfare as masculine, performed by masculine kings
and knights. They often associated piety and spirituality with femininity
and women, yet celibate male priests held institutional religious power.
The Jesuits considered themselves "soldiers of Christ" who battled against
the devil and against the vices and sins of the Mapuche (Olivares 1864–
1901).[4] The Spaniards believed that Christian forces had participated in
the spiritual conquest of Chile. They described the Apostle Saint James
leading the Spaniards into battle with his cross, and the Virgin Mary
blinding Mapuche warriors with light and dust (Acosta 1894:246; Ercilla
y Zúñiga 1933; Rosales 1989:387–388; Sosa 1966:180).

In Mapuche society, co-gendered males, who moved between masculinity and femininity and combined, in varying degrees and according to
context, the identities, performances, occupations, modes of dress, and
sexualities associated with Mapuche women and men, held precedence.
Nevertheless, Mapuche political power was considered masculine and was
traced through the male line. It was associated with waging war, hunting,
cattle herding, and men's dress. Mapuche spiritual power was considered
feminine, and though it, too, was traced through the male line, it was
associated with healing, horticulture, and women's dress. Co-gendered
machi weye combined feminine spiritual power and masculine political
power, contrary to Spanish assumptions about how men controlled both
social and spiritual orders.

Machi weye were the sons of prominent *longkos* (Rosales 1989:159) who
were initiated into shamanhood through dreams and trance states. They
learned to use herbal remedies along with their mental faculties in specialties including surgery and bone setting (*gutaru*), healing with herbs
and invocations to the spirits (*ampivoe*), locating those who caused illness
through witchcraft (*ramtuvoe*), autopsies (*cupuvoe*), divination (*pelonten*),
and midwifery. There were also those who performed witchcraft through
the use of magical darts and poisoning (*kalku*) (Molina 1901:156, 181).
I believe *machi weye* were not male gender inverts, as the Spaniards be-

lieved, but one of three types of Mapuche co-gendered male practitioners called *weye,* who oscillated between embodying femininity and masculinity in varying degrees. (The other two were the *boquibuye* and the
foquiweye or *foyeweye,* who were the priests of the *foye* tree, and the young
weye, who performed fertility dances in collective rituals.)

Female *machi* also existed in the seventeenth century, but the chroniclers had limited access to them and little interest in documenting their
practices. Most colonial references to *machi* concern *machi weye,* because
of the chroniclers' interest in documenting male warfare, "sodomy," and
putos. This does not mean that *machi weye* outnumbered female *machi* or
that female *machi* were less important in Mapuche society.

The special co-gendered identities of *machi weye* allowed them to combine the male roles that the Spaniards valued most: roles in warfare and
spirituality. For one thing, *machi weye* performed spiritual warfare against
the Spaniards. They propitiated the spirits of Mapuche warriors and
machi spirits (spiritual warriors) who continued warring against Spanish
souls in the sky, using as weapons lightning, thunderbolts, and volcanic
eruptions (Rosales 1989:155–161). With curses, *machi weye* blew tobacco
smoke toward enemy land. They divined the locations of Spaniards and
determined the outcomes of confrontations by performing magic in bowls
of water (Rosales 1989:135). They invoked the moon, the sun, and the
planets during military divinations to gain power to cure the wounded
and take vengeance on their enemies (Ercilla y Zúñiga 1933:45, 147; Oña
1975:15, 21). *Machi weye* consistently advised Mapuche chiefs to eliminate
the Spaniards (Rosales 1989:384). It is unclear whether *machi weye,* like
the co-gendered Native Americans that French and English colonizers
called "berdaches" (Callender and Kochems 1983; Katz 1976), actually
fought alongside warriors, but they accompanied Mapuche warriors to
the battlefield and performed spiritual warfare from the sidelines (Fig.
5.1). They pierced their tongues and penises with wooden spindles and
offered their blood to the spirits (Vivar 1966:134), requesting spiritual
protection for Mapuche warriors in exchange.[5]

Machi weye employed words as weapons, too. Many of them were re-
nowned public orators (Rosales 1989:159–160) who used discourse to
call on the powers of their ancestors and belittle Spanish warriors. They
invoked a co-gendered warring spirit called Epunamun—"two feet" (Valdivia 1887)—that had huge limbs and what the Spaniards described as a
divine "dual sexual nature."[6] This spirit granted the Mapuche knowledge
of warring skills and the gifts of strength, valor, and integrity. Excep-

Figure 5.1. The Mapuche believe that the souls of Spanish and Mapuche warriors and *machi* continue battling in the skies. *Machi weye* performed spiritual warfare against the Spanish by propitiating the spirits of Mapuche warriors and *machi* to kill Spanish souls, using as weapons lightning and thunderbolts (figure from Ovalle 1888: between 322 and 323).

tional Mapuche warriors, as well as Spanish warriors, who were thought to control the power of lightning through their muskets, were labeled Epunamun (Ercilla y Zúñiga 1933:34; Rosales 1989:478).[7]

Today, Mapuche spiritual warfare against enemy spirits is no longer a political tool but has become an essential component in the ritual healing of bodies and communities. *Machi* kill evil *wekufe* spirits using spiritual warfare during exorcisms performed at all healing, initiation, and collective fertility rituals (Bacigalupo 1998b). *Machi*'s warfare ideologies have also remained part of *chueca,* a ritual war game played with sticks and a hard rubber ball to resolve conflicts between competing teams. *Machi* give the players spiritual power gained from ancestral spirits and herbal remedies to grant them the strength, valor, and the power needed to win (Alvarado, de Ramón, and Peñaloza 1991:146–147; Matus 1912:185; Medina 1882).

Mapuche ideals of co-gendered sexual warriors and sexual-spiritual *machi weye* clashed with the Spaniards' polarized notions of religiosity. These were embodied, on one hand, in the ideal of a hypermasculine Spanish soldier who should resist sensual pleasure and, on the other, in the purportedly celibate Catholic priest. Yet, there were also instances of identification with the other. Both Spaniards and Mapuche established parallels between the gender identities of celibate Catholic priests and celibate "*weye* of the *foye* tree," or *boquibuye* (*foyeweye*). *Boquibuye,* chosen from among the most prestigious *longko,* carried sacred *foye* branches as symbols of peace during war parleys and lived isolated in caves, which the Spaniards labeled "monasteries." They wore long cloths wrapped around their waists in place of breeches, but the Spaniards saw these as "priestly robes," not as the garments of *putos.* They wore their hair long, as did *machi weye,* or wigs made from seaweed (Núñez 1863:361–362; Rosales 1989:168, 209, 1154). The Spaniards considered this hairstyle priestly, not effeminate.

The Jesuits associated *boquibuye* with their own spiritual militias, in which obedience, poverty, and chastity on the part of men of the same rank encouraged homosocial cohesion and homoeroticism while preventing same-sex practices (Geirola 2000:160–161). The Jesuits saw their friendships and those between *boquibuye* as traditionally masculine, because they rejected everything feminine and womanly. Mapuche, in turn, projected the co-gendered identity of the *boquibuye* onto Jesuit priests. Chief Guaquimilla portrayed a Jesuit priest bearing a *foye* branch as a *boquibuye* whose co-gendered qualities were thought to grant well-being to animals, people, and nature in general: "They called him *father and mother* and filled him with compliments and gifts . . . His happy coming was not limited to the people to whom he brought this enormous good. The animals, herbs, flowers, streams, and brooks, too, were leaping with pleasure" (Ovalle 1888:292; emphasis added).

Mapuche constructed Jesuits as powerful *machi*, and priests often played with this image to gain Christian followers. Father Alonso del Pozo, for example, claimed that his holy water healed the sick, and he told *chueca* players they would win if they went to Mass. When Fray Alonso revived a dying boy, the Mapuche believed his powers were superior to those of the *machi* (Rosales in Pinto 1991:55, 58), undermining their prestige. *Machi* countered that the Jesuits were witches who used baptism and confession to hex and kill Mapuche (Olivares 1864–1901:289).

The Spaniards struggled to represent Mapuche chiefs and *machi weye* in ways that legitimated their own image as masculine soldiers and authorities and as pious missionary priests who controlled the faith, will, and bodies of their colonial subjects. This was no easy task. The Mapuche ideology that associated spirituality, co-genderism, and warfare posed serious problems for Spanish gendered categories of representation, in which masculinity was usually associated with warfare and effeminacy, most often with witchcraft. How could Mapuche value both masculine warriors and devil-worshiping, effeminate, sodomitical gender inverts? How could these male gender inverts—who influenced the outcome of battle through spiritual warfare—have social power and prestige? Why did Mapuche men have sex with sodomites, invoke a hermaphroditic warring spirit, and label their outstanding warriors with its name?

The Spaniards imagined Mapuche men to possess simultaneously the most admirable and the most despicable qualities of humankind. To them, Chile was an exotic land of mythic giants, pious Indians, and noble warriors, isolated from the civilized world. They revered Mapuche warriors for being masculine, ferocious, brave, and honorable (Rosales 1989:113, 114, 116) and admired their muscular bodies. Spanish epics speak of Mapuche titans with superhuman strength, agility, and beauty, and especially of the Mapuche heroes Caupolicán and Lautaro (Ercilla y Zúñiga 1933; Oña 1975).

Romanticized images of Mapuche warriors have persisted in the Chilean imagination. The Chilean army named its regiments after Mapuche heroes and place names, and the Nicaraguan poet Rubén Darío (1941) lauded Caupolicán's mythical qualities.

Nevertheless, colonial Spaniards also imagined *Machi weye* and Mapuche chiefs as embodying the darkest side of human existence, the one

Spaniards feared and abhorred the most. As "devil worshipers" (González de Nájera 1889; Leiva 1982; Vivar 1966), "*putos,*" and "sodomites," *machi weye* were especially noxious to both Spanish Christian and military masculinity. They challenged Spanish notions of God and morality and military notions of manhood. Mapuche chiefs were depicted as savages who tortured their prisoners of war and ate their beating hearts during rituals. They were said to have used prisoners' heads to drink and divine from, leaving the bodies to scavengers (Rosales 1989:128). Similar perceptions continued throughout the nineteenth and twentieth centuries. Máximo Lira (1870) depicts a *machi weye* trying to burn alive a young Spanish woman and a priest.

Such images defied Spanish ethics, morality, codes of honor, and notions of social and religious order. If this was what Mapuche spiritual and political authorities were like, wrote the chroniclers, then conquest, evangelization, forced labor, and enslavement were necessary and justified.

Dressed Bodies, Sexed Bodies, and Gendered Clothes

Transvestism, gender inversion, and *hermaphroditism* are umbrella terms used by anthropologists that often obscure more than they reveal about indigenous sex and gender performances.[8] Mischa Titiev (1951:115), for example, writes that the office of *machi* in colonial times "was generally held by men, and it is practically certain they were abnormal, at least with respect to sexual conduct. Some of them may have been hermaphrodites, the rest were berdaches or transvestites, and widespread indulgence in sodomy was common." His observations about colonial *machi* were based on traditional Euro-American assumptions that gender is the cultural reading of biological sex — the idea that there are only two sexes, and they are "naturally" associated with a particular gender performance, dress, and manner. People whose bodily sexes combine male and female anatomy in varying degrees are considered hermaphrodites, whereas those who have the body of one anatomical sex but whose gender performance, dress, and manner are those associated with the other "natural" sex are labeled "inverts" and "transvestites." Cultural feminists have critiqued these assumptions, arguing that sexuality and gender are shifting, fluid categories (Flax 1990; Garber 1992; Haraway 1991). Biological sex is itself a gendered notion that depends on culturally generated perceptions of difference for its meanings and its ability to appear "natural" (Butler 1990, 1993; Hausman 1995).

In the eyes of colonial Spaniards, however, vaginas were ideally linked to womanhood, skirts, and "passive" sexual intercourse, whereas penises were ideally linked to manhood, breeches, and sexual penetration. Because Spanish soldiers and Jesuit priests saw gender, dress, and manner as ideally linked to bodies and sexual acts, they sometimes labeled transvestites and gender inverts "hermaphrodites," and they associated both categories with "deviant" sexuality. The Irish Jesuit priest Thomas Falkner (1774:117) notes: "The male wizards are obliged (as it were) to leave their sex, and to dress themselves in female apparel, and are not permitted to marry, though the female ones or witches may. They choose for this office those who at an early time of life discover an effeminate disposition. They are clothed in female attire." The body and its dynamics are sites for the most deeply entrenched beliefs held by a culture. The Spaniards perceived Spanish male bodies, dressed in men's clothing, as natural and correct. Native bodies had to be made to conform, to learn their Spanish gender, in order to be considered part of society.

Although effeminacy, gender inversion, cross-dressing, and passive sexual intercourse all meant different things for Mapuche in colonial times, many chroniclers fused them. To them, cross-dressing meant gender inversion, and gender inversion implied a passive sexual role. Colonial agents confused sodomy and cross-dressing and heaped sodomy epithets on natives throughout Latin America without ever observing any sexual practices.[9] They assumed that *machi weye,* who wore skirts, loincloths, necklaces, rings, and braids, along with those who had "feminine mannerisms and gait" by Spanish standards, and those who cooked and gathered herbs necessarily engaged in "receptive" sexual intercourse with men (see Febres 1882; Havestadt 1882; Núñez 1863:107, 159; Ovalle 1888; Pietas in Gay 1846:488; Rosales 1989; E. Smith 1855).

Spaniards and Mapuche held different ideas about what constituted men's and women's dress, behavior, and roles and how these related to gender identity and sexuality. Because the chroniclers viewed Mapuche men through the lens of gender deviance and sodomy, they failed to notice that *machi weye* also assumed male identities, roles, and dress—particularly in the context of warfare—and that they sometimes had sex with women (Pietas in Gay 1846:488). Indeed, the loincloth (*puno*) worn by *machi weye* was not, as Núñez de Pineda y Bascuñán claimed, a woman's dress but a garment male warriors wore during battle and in games of *chueca* (Núñez 1863:61; Rosales 1989:161). Mapuche women's dress consisted of a long piece of black wool cloth held together at the waist with a sash (Ovalle 1888:114). Men wore woolen breeches called *chiripa,* sleeveless shirts, and a square poncho (Góngora Marmolejo 1862:2; Quiroga 1979:83). *Machi weye* sometimes donned women's necklaces and rings (Gusinde 1917:97; Pietas in Gay 1846:488), but their long hair—which the chroniclers considered feminine—was stylish for both Mapuche men and women (Vivar 1966:50–51).[10]

Spaniards and Mapuche had very different understandings of the relationship between gender and genitals. In Spanish eyes, all gender identities except those of "woman" and "man" were unnatural and were often determined by hermaphroditic bodies. The Spaniards labeled *machi weye* and the co-gendered warring spirit Epunamun "hermaphrodites" because they believed them to be products of a monstrous fusing of male and female bodies and genders.[11] Hermaphrodites represented the confusion of sexes, desires, and dispositions that represented social, moral, and sexual chaos.

Few *machi weye* were in fact hermaphrodites; most were Mapuche with ordinary male genitals who were culturally defined as possessing co-gendered status. Mapuche did not ordinarily associate co-gendered status with a hermaphroditic body, and they referred to hermaphrodites not as *weye* but by a separate term, *alkadomo,* meaning "male-female" (Febres 1882:23).[12] Yet symbolically, hermaphroditism became for Mapuche a signifier of co-gendered status and was positively valued. It represented the ability to combine spiritual and warring powers and served as a synthetic representation of the complementary female and male powers of spirit beings.

Twentieth-century Chilean national gender ideologies and their representations of male *machi* developed from the Spanish colonial association between gender performance and sexuality. If a man displays dress or behavior considered inappropriate for men, it raises doubts about his heterosexuality because it stands outside the stereotype of masculinity and the heterosexual binary model. Scholars throughout the twentieth century depicted male *machi* as "inverts," "transvestites," "effeminate," and "homosexuals" (Hilger 1957:68, 128, 249; Latcham 1915:281). Martín Gusinde (1917:97) writes that *machi* "follow the custom of sexual inversion, which can be proved by their preference for jewels and womanly adornments." As we will see in later chapters, *machi* juggle these majority representations with ritual gender bending.

Machos, Sodomites, and *Maricones*

Time and again, contemporary Mapuche told me that *maricones* (effeminate, sexually receptive men, or "faggots") and *homosexuales* (homosexuals) did not exist traditionally among the Mapuche—that these practices were brought by the Spaniards. Colonial agents, of course, did not hold twentieth-century notions of homosexuality as a permanent social identity combining a "pathological psychological orientation," same-sex object choice, and "deviant sexual practice" (Halperin 2000:110). They did bring with them the discourse of sodomy. Some Mapuche males engaged in same-sex acts, but it was Spaniards who labeled males who engaged in anal intercourse "sodomites." Contemporary Mapuche and Chilean popular notions of homosexuality as based on sexual position find their roots in New World colonial sodomy tropes.

The chroniclers' readings of *machi* practice as sexual, marginal, and deviant relied on the Spanish assumption that Christian morality was natural and that sexual practices not leading to reproduction were sinful vices. Colonial agents and Jesuit priests—like the Spaniards who encountered North American Indians with co-gendered identities—equated *machi weye*'s gender variance with sodomy and prostitution. In 1606 Father Luis de Valdivia, for example, translated the Mapuche term *hueyun* (*weyun*) as "nefarious sin" and *hueyuntun* (*weyuntun*) as "the act of committing the nefarious sin" (Valdivia 1887:H6). Of course, Mapuche's own references to the gender identities and sexualities of *machi weye* scarcely appear in the colonial written records.

The sketchy accounts of *machi*'s gendered identities written by Spanish Catholic priests, missionaries, and soldiers were heavily colored by the antisodomitic spirit of the Counter-Reformation. Technically, sodomy included any nonprocreative sexual act in which semen was spilled outside the "natural receptacle" of the vagina (Jordan 1997:56). Spaniards, like Mapuche, believed that the distinction between same-sex acts and opposite-sex acts was less important than the distinction between sex that was potentially reproductive and sex that was nonreproductive. In practice, however, the Spaniards mostly punished anal intercourse between males; sodomy between men and women was less likely to be witnessed or denounced (see Greenberg 1988:277).

In sixteenth-century Spain, Inquisitorial and popular discourses used accusations of sodomy against two contrasting groups: wealthy, aristocratic men; and ethnic and religious outsiders. The Inquisition tagged older, wealthy, aristocratic Christian men who lusted after and were thought to penetrate lower-class Spanish boys as sodomites because they engaged in "unreproductive erotic disorders" and challenged Christian norms (R. Carrasco 1986:44, 83–84, 95, 156). The boys who were thought to have performed the receptive role received lighter punishment because they did not spill semen outside the natural receptacle of the vagina.

Spanish popular discourse also labeled lower-class adult men, those belonging to other ethnicities and belief systems, and those who were marginal in Spanish society, such as Jews and Moors, as sodomites (R. Carrasco 1986:27, 166–174). In these cases, the heavier stigma rested not on the penetrating partner but on the receiver. The satirical literature often depicts sodomy as associated with race, effeminacy, heresy, and loss of humanity. Effeminacy, in turn, was associated with inferiority, lust, sin, and disorder (Horswell 1997; Saint-Saëns 1996). Femininity belonged not just to women but to anyone who enjoyed penetration. Lower-class Spanish men and women held the strongest antisodomitic sentiments and denounced such practices to the Inquisition (R. Carrasco 1986:22).

In the New World, colonial agents often used receptive sodomy labels against Indians as a way of policing ethnic, social, religious, and status relations. Most Spanish authorities in the Americas came from the poorer, lower social classes. They sought to gain wealth and titles of nobility through their conquests. Natives were identified with "sodomitical" Moors, whom the Spaniards sought to exterminate (Monter 1990:276–299; Perry 1990:118–136). The conquistadores Hernán Cortés and Vasco Núñez de Balboa characterized cross-dressed Indians in Mexico and Panama, respectively, as sodomites, thereby eliminating any possibility of reading native bodies in local terms. Balboa set a precedent in 1513 when he had forty Quareque Panamanian noblemen who had been accused of sodomitical practices fed to his dogs (Goldberg 1992:180–185).

The male-dominant Spanish culture—still reflected in Chilean hierarchies—spoke directly about male sexual practices because they threatened the sexuality and selfhood of lonely Spanish soldiers, administrators, merchants, and priests. The chroniclers spoke only indirectly or inversely about female sexual practices. They labeled female *machi* "witches" but did not target them in sexual terms the way they did *machi weye,* whose "deviant" sexualities were more dangerously antagonistic to the Spanish patriarchal order. Deviant male sexuality, witchcraft, and Indianness were linked as negative examples against which the Spaniards constructed their masculinity. The colonies were construed as sites in which European virility could be demonstrated precisely because the conditions of intense male camaraderie and isolation there meant that masculinity could easily be unmade (Stoler 1995:175). Colonial agents (e.g., Gómara 1554:43) considered both active and passive partners in anal sex to be sodomites, but they used the active-passive ideology to portray their superiority to native male political and spiritual authorities. Colonial agents in Chile created an opposition between an ideal masculine, penetrating, Spanish Christian man and an abject, sodomitical chief or *machi* who played a receptive role in sexual intercourse with men.

Francisco Núñez de Pineda y Bascuñán, as a criollo, embraced the stigmatizing notion that indigenous people were passive, effeminate sodomites, in order to legitimate himself as Spanish and masculine. He projected New World sodomy labels, associated with native ethnic difference and receptive anal intercourse, onto Mapuche realities and put his own words in native mouths: "They believe that the nefarious sin is vile, with the difference that the man who takes on the role of the man is not offensive like the one who takes on the role of a woman" (Núñez 1863:107).[13]

Mapuche may have had a joking acceptance of receptive same-sex acts between men, as did some Native American tribes, but I doubt that they considered these acts vile, and they certainly did not share Núñez's notion of "nefarious sin." It is possible that he interpreted Mapuche joking about male same-sex acts as criticism or that one of his Mapuche Christian converts noticed his aversion to male same-sex passive sexual roles and criticized such practices to appease him. Through experience, Mapuche—like many other indigenous peoples influenced by European or American missionaries (Greenberg 1988:78–79)—learned to suppress, deny, and criticize the sexual practices that colonial agents and priests abhorred. It is also conceivable that the Jesuit conquistador himself depicted his Mapuche male friends as condemning sodomy in order to ingratiate them to the Spaniards. One can only speculate about what concepts Mapuche men used in talking with Núñez about male same-sex acts and what actually took place in the oral exchange that prompted him to write this statement about their condemnation of sodomy.

The importance of Núñez's statement lies in his observation of the different meanings colonialists ascribed to the penetrating and receptive sexual positions in male same-sex intercourse. Spaniards and criollos disapproved of attraction between men, and Jesuits labeled both penetrating and receptive male partners in anal intercourse "sodomites." A man who was penetrated by another man, however, was considered more noxious than the one who penetrated him. Spaniards stigmatized receptive sexual positions as "passive" and effeminate—as emulating "feminine subjugation"—but considered penetrating sexual positions "active" and associated them more often with the masculinity and status held by men who penetrated women. The penetrating partner maintained some inkling of "masculine privilege." Roger Lancaster (1992, 1997a), Don Kulick (1998), Richard Parker (1999), and many others have documented the ways in which some popular sexual traditions in contemporary Latin America have been configured along this active-passive dimension and interact with the competing sexual paradigm of the upper classes, which is based on choice of sexual object. Núñez's statement demonstrates that male passive and active sexual roles were also very much a part of colonial power dynamics in Hispanic Chile. These categories became two of the many criteria that define modern popular Chilean homosexuality.

Popular Chilean male homosexual identities are associated with passivity and effeminacy because colonial agents thought of *machi weye* as sodomites—effeminate men who engaged in passive sexual relations with other men. In contemporary Chile, lower-class men who are perceived as masculine, active partners in same-sex intercourse are sometimes considered to be less homosexual than are passive partners, because colonial agents in Chile less frequently targeted men who penetrated other men as sodomites.[14] Spanish soldiers asserted their virility and "superior" ethnicity and religious beliefs by symbolically being "on top," dominating male *machi,* who were constructed as feminine, indigenous, pagan, and "on the bottom." In Chilean majority discourses throughout the nineteenth century, gender deviance was read as homosexuality. The Mapuche terms *weye* and *weyetufe* were defined as "*hombre homosexual*" (homosexual man), "*homosexual pasivo*" (passive homosexual), and "*maricón*" (Febres 1882:106; Montecino 1999:52)—the last a heavily stigmatized word that also serves as a synonym for coward, liar, and betrayer.

Pious Women, Witches, and Masculine Transgressors

Female *machi* more easily fell into Spanish categories of the feminine than *machi weye* fit Spanish notions of masculinity. The colonizers believed that Mapuche women were naturally more pious than men, but women who resisted evangelization or healed others with herbs were labeled as evil witches and devil worshipers. Both Spanish categories for women—pious souls and witches—were projected onto female *machi* and became quickly incorporated into popular belief.

The few existing colonial records on female *machi* mention that they were often daughters of powerful *longkos* and became healers after being initiated into a *machi* school of practice (Ovalle 1888:21; Rosales 1989:159). The chroniclers assumed that female *machi* were women because they dressed in women's clothing and performed women's work, such as collecting plants, cooking, seeding, and making textiles and ceramics (González de Nájera 1889:287; Núñez 1863:278, 329; Ovalle 1888:21, 158, 388, 406–407; Rosales 1989:159). According to the chroniclers, Mapuche men viewed women as economic assets and property. A Mapuche man's wealth was measured by the number of wives he could "buy" through bride-price, and Mapuche women who were unproductive or did not have children could be returned to their fathers (González de Nájera 1889:44, 89; Quiroga 1979:83). There is no information about female *machi*'s sexualities during the colonial period, and aside from Diego de Rosales's brief note about women and men "exchanging clothes" during rituals (1989:141), no allusion to Mapuche women wearing men's clothes appears in the literature. A few references to female *machi*'s "sexual irregularities" (Guevara 1913:262) appeared sporadically in the nineteenth and twentieth centuries, but these practices were less stigmatized than those of male *machi* because they did not threaten Spanish male sexualities and personhood.

The Jesuits believed that female *machi* could be more readily converted to Christianity on account of their "natural virtuosity." Father Alonso de Ovalle's seventeenth-century narrative of the conversion of female *machi* intimates his Jesuit readings of female piety and the exclusivity of Christian faith. In it, female *machi* "witches" become "virtuous Christian women" in the hands of priests. Jesuits expel the "art of the devil," for example, from the bodies of four female *machi* using Christian symbols as divine healing objects. One *machi*'s "horrific nocturnal visions" cease "miraculously" when a priest places a rosary around her neck. Another *machi* is "exorcised" when a priest presses a relic of Saint Ignatius onto her body while invoking Jesus' name (Ovalle 1888:388, 407). The Jesuits' exorcising techniques were similar to those of *machi*, but in Jesuit eyes, relics and rosaries were saintly and miraculous; *machi* drums and *foye* trees were instruments of native witchcraft. Jesuits used baptism as the sole marker of Christian faith and assumed that baptized *machi* would lose their powers and abandon their spiritual healing practices.[15]

The Spaniards also constructed female *machi* as witches. Sometimes they portrayed all Mapuche as demonic, but they thought women and effeminate men were especially prone to seduction by the devil.[16] Chroniclers depicted Mapuche women as ambitious, jealous, and untrustworthy and believed that Mapuche men controlled them by treating them roughly, by having them eat separately, and by making the women stand behind them during public meetings (Núñez 1863:61, 193, 453–454; Rosales 1989:152). Spanish soldiers and priests condemned all bodily experiences and associated femininity with lasciviousness and lack of will and control.

The Mapuche believed that illness and death were produced through witchcraft, poisoning, and invisible darts, and they feared those who performed such acts, but they distinguished between healing and witchcraft. The Spaniards grouped all *machi* practices under the term *witchcraft,* translating the Mapuche term *kalku* as "effeminate witch" or "agent of the devil who works against Christian law" (Valdivia 1887). *Machi*'s divinations using animal livers, exorcisms of patients through sucking and blowing, use of herbal remedies and stones, and ritual drinking, dancing, and games were all interpreted through the rubric of witchcraft (see Dougnac 1981:104–105; Leiva 1982:212; Ovalle 1888:407; Rosales 1989:135, 142, 155, 159, 184). In 1626 the first diocesan synod in Chile condemned the practices of *machi* as well as those who visited them (Casanova 1994:124).

Throughout the colonial Americas, social and political biases and fears of the power of women healers led to their being accused of witchcraft (Glass-Coffin 1998; Karlsen 1987; Klaits 1985; Silverblatt 1987). Most of the women accused by Spaniards were unmarried or older widowed women—those who were independent of men or who were perceived as threatening or competing with the power of men in some way. In the seventeenth and eighteenth centuries, Spaniards held numerous proceedings against Mapuche women, and some men, who were physically punished until they confessed to standard, European-style witchcraft (Casanova 1994:139–150). By the mid-eighteenth century the association between women and witches had become part of popular belief, and Mapuche themselves stabbed and burned Mapuche women they thought were witches (Anonymous 1890:16–17; Gómez de Vidaurre 1889:325–326; Robles Rodríguez 1942:12).

The chroniclers also presented an alternative image of Mapuche women as "strong, brave, and masculine" (Ovalle 1888:22–23; Rosales 1989:495, 38, 252), because they performed well-respected roles and participated in community activities in a way Spanish women did not. "Chilean women are so masculine that, on important occasions and when men are scarce, they take up weapons as if they were men and play in *chueca*" (Ovalle 1888:115). Mapuche women also played important roles as peace negotiators and in recovering prisoners of war (Bacigalupo 1996a:64). Because women were inferior to men in Spanish gender ideologies, colonial agents believed men should take on all important social positions. Female *machi* who performed important roles and were valued in Mapuche society were considered masculine by Spanish standards.

Colonial prejudices about the inferior or superior qualities of the female sex and assumptions about female sexuality, femininity, and womanhood influenced the ways in which female *machi* are perceived today. Contradictory representations of female *machi* as pious women, feminine witches, and masculine women have permeated the contemporary Mapuche imagination. References to female *machi* as *monjas* (nuns), *ángeles* (angels), and *brujas* (witches) are common, and the term *marimacha* (butch, or masculine, woman) is occasionally applied to female *machi* who systematically transgress norms of behavior for Mapuche women.

Co-Gendered Identities and Alternative Sexualities

In colonial times, Mapuche recognized and valued at least one gender identity aside from that of women and men—that of the co-gendered *machi weye*—and accepted many different types of sexual acts. In their view, gender and sexuality were *performed;* they did not follow naturally from anatomy. If—taking Spanish perspectives into account—we examine the Jesuit priest Luis de Valdivia's Mapuche-Spanish dictionary of 1606, we find that several seventeenth-century Mapuche terms suggest the existence of co-gendered identities. As translated by Valdivia, the terms *chegelcen* (to be made a man), *chegelun* (to make oneself a man), *cacudueltun* (to disguise oneself by wearing a dress), and *kureyen* (to use as a woman) all imply that gender was made, performed, and enacted rather than determined by sex or sexual identity.

The value Mapuche placed on co-gendered identities and gender transformation, and the Spaniards' abhorrence of gender inversion, were founded on the two groups' different valuations of masculinity and femininity. A Mapuche man who abandoned his male gender to become a *machi weye,* a nonman, did not undergo a profound loss of status, privilege, or power, because womanhood and femininity were socially valued. A Spanish man who became effeminate and lost his manhood, however, lost the privilege men held over women and effeminates in Spanish society.

The concept of third-gender persons was created by Euro-American scholars to describe people around the globe with gender identities distinct from those of women and men. Such persons are labeled "crossgendered" or "transgendered" because their gender and sex do not match up according to the Euro-American woman-man binary system. Some writers argue that the terms *third gender, alternate gender,* and *two-spirit* allow us to go beyond the woman-man binary and explicate multigendered societies (Garber 1992; Herdt 1984; Nanda 1985; Roscoe 1991; Wikan 1991). Yet, in its attempt to universalize what is really culturally variable and context specific, the third-gender concept itself draws on Western woman-man gender binarism. In this context, the third-gender notion reinforces the Euro-American idea that sex is naturally associated with gender and fixes the gender subjectivities of women, men, and third gender as static and permanent (Epple 1998; Kulick 1998; Prieur 1998).

I use the term *co-gendered* to refer to *weye* to reinforce the idea that the identity of *machi weye* continually fluctuated between the masculine and the feminine.[17] Mapuche associated the masculine with political and warring abilities and the feminine with spirituality. *Machi weye* moved from being men (masculine) to being nonmen (feminine) when conducting spiritual warfare and rituals. In everyday contexts, the masculine was ideally associated with men and the feminine with women—an ideal also held by colonial agents.

Women and non-*weye* men ordinarily defined themselves in relation to this second, everyday binary. *Weye* were held to it in daily life, too, and the distinction between *weye* and women then became relevant. Males' sexual relations with *weye* were not the same as their sexual relations with women, and even as nonmen, *weye* retained their position in the patrilineage and did not have husbands. In this context, *weye* were perceived as men.

It is unclear whether the Mapuche in colonial times viewed female *machi* as having their own distinct co-gendered identity or whether they considered them to be women. The chroniclers make no reference to a Mapuche term for female *machi* who resembled Native American female berdaches.[18] Nor do they mention female *machi*'s combining political and spiritual power to perform spiritual warfare. Nevertheless, contemporary female *machi* do have co-gendered identities in ritual contexts. They move from being women (feminine) when healing to being nonwomen (masculine) when conducting exorcisms and killing evil *wekufe* spirits.

Co-gendered identity was the basis for *machi weye*'s sexualities. Mapuche did not consider sexual partners of the same physical sex but not of the same gender to be sodomites or deviants. Sexual acts between *machi weye* were taboo, however, because they belonged to the same co-gendered category. *Machi* were what Brackette Williams (1996:96) calls "heterogendered," in the sense that they engaged in sexual acts with people belonging to genders other than their own, who could be anatomically either male or female. However, these sexual acts did not denote a permanent identity or a social category. *Machi weye*'s sexual acts cannot be subsumed under the modern notions of homosexual, heterosexual, or bisexual personae.

The Spaniards' stress on *machi weye*'s passive same-sex acts over other aspects of their gender roles severely distorted their image. I believe that sex with males was a secondary, derivative, feature, not a precondition of *weye* status. *Weye* engaged in penetrating sexual intercourse with women as well as receptive sexual intercourse with men (Pietas in Gay 1846:488), and they remained celibate while preparing for rituals or battle.

Machi weye's co-gendered identities also became the basis for alternative sexualities. Certain nineteenth-century Mapuche terms refer to genital acts that had spiritual and nonreproductive connotations. The term *püllitun,* translated by the Jesuit missionary Andrés Febres as the "sin of sodomy between two men" (1846:60), actually means "to take, receive, or create spiritual power and strength" (Valdivia 1887). It refers to spiritual, nonreproductive sexual intercourse between males (Augusta 1934:202; Febres 1846:19). The term *antükuram,* meaning "an egg without an embryo," refers to nonreproductive intercourse between people of any gender (Catrileo 1995:152).

The Mapuche were not alone in connecting nonreproductive sexualities and spirituality. Like many Native American peoples, they recognized a spiritual dimension associated with institutionalized gender variance.[19] These Mapuche nonreproductive spiritual sexualities were positively valued and contrasted with Spanish notions of nonreproductive sexuality as sodomitical practice.

Machi today are often labeled according to popular Chilean national sexualities and gender ideologies in which masculinity and penetration are valued over femininity and receptive intercourse. The categories of masculinity, femininity, and homosexuality themselves have shifted over time and continue to change in different contexts. *Machi*'s co-gendered identities persist in ritual contexts, and sexualities based on gender or sexual position continue to play important roles in *machi*'s lives. Even today, some Mapuche label male *machi* "*domo-wentru,*" or woman-man. These co-gendered identities provide *machi* with legitimacy in ritual but do not undercut national hierarchical constructions of sexual identity and gender in everyday contexts, a point I return to in Chapter 7.

Feminizing Spirituality

The relationship between gender and political and spiritual power among the Mapuche shifted dramatically in the mid-eighteenth century as missionary zeal and sociopolitical and economic change transformed native communities. As other Mapuche institutions gained political power, *machi* were stripped of their influence and regendered as solely feminine and spiritual. Various circumstances led to the repudiation of the roles of male *machi* and the raising of females to these positions of spiritual authority. Local Mapuche clans disappeared, and political power became unified and concentrated in the hands of a few permanent, macroregional sociopolitical organizations with a pan-Mapuche identity (Boccara 1998). The line of male ancestral spirits whom the *machi weye* invoked for the benefit of a small, lineage-based community became less relevant. Sociopolitical interests replaced the ideal of the co-gendered warrior as the Mapuche became sedentary agriculturalists, suffered military defeat by the Chilean army in 1883, and were placed on reservations in 1884. The number of male *machi* decreased substantially after the final "pacification" of the Mapuche in the late nineteenth century; spiritual warfare and male military divination were no longer needed (Faron 1964:154). Missionization by homophobic Catholic orders (Foerster 1996; Pinto 1991) that rejected "unmasculine" male *machi* also contributed to the decline in their numbers and the rise of female *machi* (Bacigalupo 1996a:97–100). Missionization was facilitated by the division of Mapuche patrilineages among different reservations, so that they no longer had ancestral spirits in common.

Female *machi* predominated throughout the nineteenth and twentieth centuries as land fertility became a major concern for Mapuche.[20] With pacification, the Mapuche were relegated to small plots of eroded territory, and agricultural production became crucial for survival. Collective *ngillatun* rituals were now performed primarily to ask deities for bountiful crops and fertile animals. Both female and male *machi* were considered *ngenküyen*—owners of the moon—who controlled the powers of generation and fertility (Latcham 1922:433).

Gradually, however, Mapuche incorporated Spanish Catholic sex-based notions of gender into their beliefs and began to reject effeminate male *machi*. The idea that female *machi* were more effective at ensuring land fertility became generalized throughout the twentieth century, and those who officiated in collective *ngillatun* rituals came to be called "*machi* moon priestesses" (*machi kuyen domo*).

The shift to predominantly female *machi* was gradual, but it produced a permanent change in the way Mapuche conceived of the relationship between gender and spirituality. Chilean perceptions of spiritual power and political power as contrasting phenomena had a profound effect. By the beginning of the twentieth century, Mapuche were associating the spiritual power of *machi*—as well as witchcraft—with femininity and per-ceiving it as conflicting with the political and social power of male chiefs. The legitimacy of male *machi* as spiritual intermediaries was threatened by the imposition of the Chilean ideal of the male role as political and public. Today, the spiritual power of *machi,* associated with femininity, is independent of political power and is passed down through the female line, often through a maternal grandmother. When *machi* lost their politi-cal power, the spiritual power and female bodies of female *machi* accorded them status and prestige in other realms of Mapuche society—something that was much more difficult for male *machi* to achieve.

Colonial Legacies

Almost four centuries have passed since Francisco Núñez de Pineda y Bascuñán encountered a *machi weye* and labeled him a *puto,* a sodomite, and a devil worshiper, and since Alonso de Ovalle found female *machi* to be either pious women or witches. The sociopolitical, religious, and economic circumstances in which *machi* live today are very different, but the colonial penetration paradigm continues to shape Chile's power sym-bolism. Colonial ethnic, sexual, and power relationships still mold Chile's majority discourses, and the *machi* body, with its desires and gendered powers, is still a site of identity and difference between colonizer and colonized. National perceptions read femininity as inferior, penetrated, and on the bottom, and masculinity as superior, penetrating, and on top. Feminine identities, receptive sexual positions, and marginal ethnicities remain devalued in the national imagination. Chileans view *machi* as feminine and marginal to the modern patriarchal state. They use the dis-course of effeminacy and homosexuality as a tool for domination to mold *machi* to state-defined masculinities.

The gendered perspectives of colonizer and colonized are no longer easily distinguishable, for the Mapuche have created hybrid gender ideologies. Ideologies created in the colonial record a polarization between a powerful, masculine conquistador who speaks about *machi* genders in Spanish terms and a subaltern, indigenous, effeminate *machi* who is silent. In contemporary Chile, conflicting indigenous voices and diverse notions of gendered and sexual selves and others coexist within a single social fabric. Heavily stigmatizing labels of homosexuality and witchcraft are used not only by the Chilean majority but also by Mapuche themselves, who police internal boundaries of deviance, tradition, and personhood. Labels of homosexuality are like accusations of witchcraft in that people use them to ostracize those with whom they have personal conflicts, those who do not fit their notions of social order, and those they perceive as threatening to themselves or the community.

Three gendered binaries shape the way contemporary *machi* see themselves and the way others view them. Structured by different principles, these three binaries give rise to different sexual ideologies and are linked to systems of power.

The first gendered binary is that defined by biological sex and associated with men and women in Mapuche, Spanish, and Chilean national discourses in the context of everyday life. Female *machi* who behave in ways considered unwomanly are labeled "masculine," and male *machi* who behave in ways considered unmasculine are labeled "effeminate." This binary gives rise to an aspect of Chile's national sexual culture that is based on the principle of homology. That is, a homosexual man is defined by his choice of sexual object, and the bond of sexual partners is based not on power and domination but on their identity of desire, orientation, and sexuality (Lancaster 2001). Mapuche often label male *machi* who engage in sexual acts with other men as homosexual regardless of their gender identities. Mapuche and *machi* themselves, however, do not self-identify as homosexual and view all types of homosexuality as antithetical to masculinity.

The second binary is defined by the criollo penetration paradigm, in which penetrating men are opposed to receptive nonmen and women, and masculine men are opposed to effeminate nonmen and women. Spanish sodomy tropes and notions of effeminacy colonized Mapuche ideologies and gave rise to another aspect of Chile's national sexual culture. This one is based on the principle of "heterology," in which male homosexuality is associated with gender transitivity and sexual position. According to this perspective, it matters not only with whom but also how and in what context one has sex (Halperin 2000:112; Lancaster 2001; McKee Irwin

2000). Mapuche label male *machi* who are effeminate and transvestite as a certain type of homosexual, a *maricón* —a passive, anal-receptive, feminized man. In practice, who is active and who is passive remains uncertain. Macho men throughout Latin America are sometimes penetrated by their effeminate male partners (Kulick 1998; Prieur 1998; Schifter 1998).

Nevertheless "active" and "passive" remain signifiers of power and masculinity. Male *machi* who do not meet Chilean and Mapuche standards of manhood and male dress or who are suspected of deriving pleasure from being penetrated are called "*maricones*," whereas those who master the rules of conventional masculinity and penetrate others are considered machos. The Chilean sexual ideology of domination affects even homosexual men themselves, who favor masculine gay identities over effeminate ones. In 1995 the Homosexual Liberation Movement (Movimiento de Integración y Liberación Homosexual, MOVILH) refused to admit effeminate homosexuals in order to maintain its members' images as masculine homosexuals.[21] The Chilean majority continues to view female *machi* and effeminate male *machi* as witches. Male gender inversion, passivity, and witchcraft remain linked in Chilean popular notions of homosexuality, to which many Mapuche ascribe.

The third binary, that of the genders "man" and "woman," is defined by the ritual co-gendered identities of *machi,* which oscillate between the two or meld them. Historical Mapuche notions of co-gendered identities and alternative sexualities have remained pervasive in the prescribed contexts of ritual. Contemporary male and female *machi* engage in ritual performances of feminine, masculine, and co-gendered roles. Their ritual co-gendered identities influence *their* everyday identities, and Mapuche construct *machi* sexualities in relation to all three gender binaries. The language of co-genderism also legitimates *machi* practice and "traditional" culture and has served as an important symbol for Mapuche identity politics and fundamentalist ideologies.

Contemporary Mapuche have also incorporated Catholic discourses about gender and sexuality that combine the principles of homology and heterology with concepts of normality and deviance. Catholic discourses in Chile assume that the "natural" function of the penis is that of the inserter, the natural function of the vagina, the receptor. Thus, heterosexual couples are "natural" and "normal." Same-sex acts, male effeminacy, transvestism, and men who are penetrated by others are "inverted" and "deviant"; both the practices and the actors are labeled "homosexual." Catholic discourses have shaped Chilean national discourses, media representations, and public opinion. Michelle Bachelet (2006–2010) is the only Chilean president who has met with organizations of homosexuals, and until December 23, 1998, the Chilean Penal Code criminalized anal intercourse between consenting adult men with up to five years of imprisonment.[22]

Although political correctness does not allow the Chilean press to directly attack homosexuals, it foments homophobia by associating homosexuals with violence, immorality, promiscuity, prostitution, and AIDS (Torres 1997). Polls conducted in Santiago in 1996 and 1997 showed that 74 percent of the population abhorred homosexuals and 44 percent believed homosexuality should be prohibited because it was "unnatural" (Guajardo 2000:127). The numbers are even higher in rural Mapuche areas, where people tend to be more conservative.

In describing contemporary male *machi*'s sexualities and gender identities, anthropologists have either used historical Mapuche notions of co-genderism anachronistically or have drawn solely on Chilean Catholic homophobic notions. These representations seriously misrepresent Mapuche's contextual negotiations of *machi* gender identities and sexualities. Some anthropologists have portrayed contemporary male *machi* as equivalent to historical *machi weye* and Native American berdaches (Métraux 1967; Murray 1995:284; Titiev 1951). The permanent co-gendered identities of *machi weye* and berdaches, however, were different from the ritual co-gendered identities of contemporary male *machi,* who self-identify as men in their everyday lives. Anthropologists have replicated Chilean homophobic notions of gender and sexuality when describing male *machi* in everyday and ritual contexts. They have drawn on both the principles of homology and heterology and equated male *machi*'s partial transvestism during ritual with effeminacy, homosexuality, and abnormality (Hilger 1957:68, 128, 249; Latcham 1915:281; Titiev 1951:115–117). Some scholars have characterized female *machi* as masculine and occasionally homosexual, and male *machi* as effeminate and usually homosexual (Bengoa 1992:142–143; Degarrod 1998; Faron 1964:152; Hilger 1957:68, 128, 249; Métraux 1967; Montecino 1995). Anthropologists understand the distinction between sexual practices (behaviors in which one engages) and sexual identities (something one is) (Weston 1991:64), but when writing about same-sex acts cross-culturally they often reduce homosexuality to sexual practice, labeling the practices and sometimes the participants as homosexual regardless of local understandings of these acts (Davis and Whitten 1987; Elliston 1995).

Anthropologists have not analyzed the different ways in which contemporary Mapuche combine the national notions of Chilean Catholics and traditional Mapuche ones to describe the gender identities and sexualities of male *machi* in everyday, ritual, and public or political contexts. As we will see in Chapters 7 and 8, *machi* have devised diverse ways to maintain some aspects of their co-gendered colonial-era identities while using the majority's gendered ideologies of political and spiritual power for their own ends. First, however, I look at the ways in which gendered national discourses—heirs to colonial beliefs and power relations—and the discourses of Mapuche resistance movements coerce and construct *machi* and at how *machi* appropriate, transform, and contest these gendered images in their hybrid healing practices while constructing themselves as traditional.

CHAPTER 6

Machi as Gendered Symbols of Tradition: National Discourses and Mapuche Resistance Movements

Machi María Ángela smiled straight at the camera and beat on her shamanic drum as she posed for photographers beside Chilean president Eduardo Frei at the presidential palace on August 5, 1999. She wore the festive garb of Mapuche *machi:* heavy silver jewelry, a black wool shawl, a blue apron with lace, and multicolored hair ribbons tied in a rosette on her forehead (Fig. 6.1). Frei performed Mapuche ritual by holding a branch of the sacred *foye* tree and drinking *muday.* He recognized the ethnic dimension of Mapuche problems and promised to "construct a democratic coexistence based on respect and equal opportunities for original ethnicities" (*Las Últimas Noticias,* August 6, 1999). A few journalists asked the male *longko* who were present how they viewed the encounter. But the *machi*—women and a few partially transvestite men—were never interviewed. When the *longko* spoke, the *machi* legitimated them by beating their drums in the background.

Outside the presidential palace, other *machi* drummed to express support for Mapuche resistance movements that were attempting to retake Mapuche land from forestry companies, private energy companies, and the state's highway authorities. They also backed a request for the suspension of martial law imposed by Frei in Mapuche communities and the release of Mapuche political prisoners.[1]

Most Mapuche, including *machi,* were aware of the contradiction between Frei's public pro-indigenous performances and his government's neoliberal policies. Mapuche protest groups created a pamphlet featuring a much-publicized photograph of Frei drinking *muday* with *machi,* over the ironic caption "¿Cuánto Vale el Show?" (How much is the show worth?). Chile's democratic presidents since 1990 have used *machi* in their political campaigns to present themselves as pluralistic. Yet, they perpetu-

Figure 6.1. President Frei, and his minister of the interior, holding *foye* leaves, stand for the national anthem at the presidential palace while female *machi* and other Mapuche women sit in the background with their drums (photo by the Consorcio Periodístico de Chile).

ate national gender ideologies and the neoliberal policies instituted under the military dictatorship of Gen. Augusto Pinochet (1973–1990), even while instituting new forms of power and reaping the legitimacy gained from democracy.

The Mapuche suffered further assimilation and expropriation of their land under Pinochet's dictatorship. Chile's return to democracy saw the passage of the Indigenous Law in 1993. That law recognizes the Mapuche culture and their language, Mapudungu; protects some land and water rights; and created CONADI (Corporación Nacional de Desarrollo Indígena—National Corporation for Indigenous Development), which implements state policies regarding indigenous people. The law, however, did not grant Mapuche any significant political or participatory rights within the state.[2] They have the right to vote, but they are marginalized from national politics, and their own political systems go unrecognized. The Indigenous Law does not recognize the Mapuche as a people or grant them the right to self-determination and autonomy.

The protection of Mapuche land was violated by presidents Eduardo Frei (1994–2000) and Ricardo Lagos (2000–2006) in the name of national development. They built a series of hydroelectric plants along the

Bio-Bío River in the Mapuche-Pewenche communities and a highway that ran through other Mapuche communities. Frei and Lagos subsidized forestry companies that logged Mapuche ancestral territories, destroying ancient forests and depleting water resources in the area (Instituto de Estudios Indígenas 2003; Muga 2004). Frei argued that national development projects were necessary to "modernize" Chile and make it competitive in the global market, but those projects effectively threatened the livelihood and identity of Mapuche. Even though most Mapuche are now urban dwellers, the southern ancestral territories remain central to their cosmology, shamanic practices, and identity politics.

After the "celebration" of the Columbian quincentenary in 1992, indigenous groups throughout Latin America organized both pan-indigenous and local resistance movements.[3] Mapuche resistance movements gained momentum at the end of the 1990s in response to an increasing number of national development projects in Mapuche territories. The two most important such movements, Consejo de Todas las Tierras (Council of All Territories), led by Aucan Huilcaman, and Coordinadora Malleko-Arauco (Malleko-Arauko Coordinator), struggle for the cultural rights, autonomous self-government, and equal political participation of the Mapuche nation within the Chilean nation-state. Chile's constitution, however, recognizes only one people, one nation, and one state, thereby denying the multicultural and pluriethnic character of the country (Instituto de Estudios Indígenas 2003). Chile's presidents have viewed Mapuche demands for self-determination and autonomy as threats to the state (Bengoa 1999:199–200.[4] Socialist president Michelle Bachelet promised the constitutional recognition of indigenous peoples, but the right-wing Renovación Nacional and Unión Democrática Independiente parties in Congress rejected the motion in 2006. As of this writing, Bachelet has not addressed Mapuche demands for self-determination and autonomy.

The administrations of Presidents Frei and Lagos viewed Mapuche demands in terms of development and equality instead of recognizing their cultural rights (Richards 2004:148). They used two strategies against Mapuche resistance movements. First, they increased the number of development projects handled through CONADI. The Orígenes Program in particular claims to have established a new relationship between the government and indigenous people by promoting development using local cultural and ethnic models. CONADI's policy of indemnifying Mapuche for their land, however, contradicts the state policy of prioritizing national and transnational economic interests in Mapuche land over Mapuche interests and seeking to incorporate the Mapuche into the global economy.[5] Second, these governments treated Mapuche political demands as terrorist acts, to be punished juridically. Lagos applied Pinochet's antiterrorist law against Mapuche protesters.

Machi and *longko,* as icons of Mapuche society, have become key symbols in confrontations between Mapuche and the state. *Machi*—nowadays predominantly female, although male *machi,* who preponderated in earlier times, are again growing in numbers—play the traditional role of contacting ancestral and nature spirits and deities through altered states of consciousness in order to transform illness into health and conflict and unhappiness into well-being. *Longko,* the male, secular heads of communities, who inherit their posts, address community needs and conflicts and carry the knowledge of Mapuche history, genealogy, social organization, and hierarchy. Members of Mapuche resistance movements have used *machi* and *longko* as representatives of Mapuche spiritual and political traditions, respectively, and as symbols of an autonomous Mapuche nation. As I show later, the images ascribed to *machi* and adopted by them in relation to resistance movements—images that rely heavily on notions of gender roles in Mapuche and Chilean society—are varied and often contradictory.

Participants in Chile's national discourses since the early nineteenth century have used gender analogically to express a relationship of power and subjugation between the modern state and the traditional Mapuche, with *machi* and *longko* as their main cultural symbols. National gendered constructions of the Mapuche, sometimes internally inconsistent, stem from what Gerald Sider (1987:7) has called a "contradiction between the impossibility and the necessity of defining the other as the other—the different, the alien—and incorporating the other within a single social and cultural system of domination." Participants in Chile's national discourses use gender to "folklorize," marginalize, and assimilate female *machi* and male *longko* in the interests of diverse nationalist agendas.

The Chilean ruling class is, to use Pierre Bourdieu's words, a "beneficiary of economic, social and symbolic power expressed in economic and cultural capital and society's institutions and practices" (quoted in Tarifa 2001:26–27). Power, however, is not just the ability to use state images and discourses to coerce others but also the ability to produce pleasure, new systems of knowledge, goods, and discourses (Foucault 1980:119). Resistance of any kind is what Lila Abu-Lughod labels a "diagnostic of power." Resistance to one system of power often means conformity to a different set of demands (Abu-Lughod 1990:42, 53), and conformity to and transformation of systems of power create new forms of resistance and power relations. Mapuche have developed responses to national images of themselves that range from embracing folkloric, gendered images of *machi* and *longko* to transforming those images and challenging nationalist discourses through resistance movements. *Machi*, in turn, draw on national images of male and female, tradition and modernity in order to devise their own gendered strategies for negotiating with national and Mapuche political authorities.

In analyzing the many and often contradictory views of *machi* and their participation in Mapuche and national politics, I underscore the way Mapuche activists and national politicians use images of female *machi* in the pursuit of their own agendas. I argue that female *machi* and male *longko* play complementary leadership roles in their dealings with Chilean political authorities and that Mapuche resistance movements have manipulated public images of female *machi* in ways that emphasize their roles as icons of tradition. These images reinforce national gender restrictions while promoting pan-Mapuche agendas. I begin by describing the stereotypical images of Mapuche in general and *machi* specifically that have been created by the larger Chilean society, stereotypes that *machi* sometimes resist and sometimes transform and use for their own ends.

Gendered Constructs of Mapuche and *Machi* in Chile

Since colonial times, Chileans have dealt with Mapuche in any of three primary ways: by folklorizing them, by marginalizing them, and by attempting to assimilate them. These three approaches are mutually contradictory in that marginalizing is an attempt to exclude Mapuche from national society, assimilation is an effort to include them—if only on terms set by the nation-state—and folklorizing encompasses elements of both. Each approach involves its own set of stereotypes of Mapuche, and particularly of *machi*. The negative images that gave rise to and were created by the marginalization of the Mapuche—that they were barbaric, ignorant, dirty, and so forth—are the same images that assimilationists aspire to overturn by educating the Mapuche, de-Indianizing them, and converting them to Catholicism. Therefore, I neglect assimilation in favor of establishing the key images of folklorization and marginalization before turning to Mapuche and *machi* adaptations of and challenges to these stereotypes.

All such images are directly related to dominant Chilean notions about female "domestic" and "spiritual" spheres and male "public" and "political" spheres (M. Rosaldo 1974), notions that Mapuche themselves have adopted in some contexts. When Chile became a nation-state in 1818, national discourses that divorced spiritual and political power became increasingly important to *machi* practice. As we saw in Chapter 5, *machi* were then stripped of their formal political power and regendered as feminine and spiritual. Both Chileans and Mapuche characterize public presentations of self, formal political and religious leadership roles, political ideology, law, rationality, urbanity, and formal negotiations with state powers as masculine. Mapuche of both sexes see women as marginal to the world of formal politics, which they consider the realm of men.

In contrast, emotion, intuition, pragmatism, rural life, the intimate domestic realm of the family, the informal roles of healer and shaman, and the world of altered states of consciousness and spirits are characterized as feminine (Bacigalupo 1994b, 1996a; Degarrod 1998). Mapuche believe that, when social norms and spiritual orders are transgressed and relationships become strained, Mapuche women are better than men at negotiating between people and appeasing offended spirits.[6] *Machi,* whether male or female, are especially viewed as effeminate because of their connection with the spirit world. As we have seen, regardless of a *machi*'s sex, he or she dresses in female clothing and jewelry during certain rituals in order to "seduce" the spirits. These gendered notions, although important signifiers in both national and Mapuche discourses, are not entirely borne out in Mapuche's everyday lives. As we will see in Chapters 7 and 8, women's, men's, and *machi*'s roles do not always fit neatly into the domestic-public dichotomy.

Despite the complexity of gender roles in Mapuche's daily lives, Mapuche women often reinforce the ideological polarization between the male, urban, public, political realm and the female, rural, private, family realm. On March 8, 2002, for example, a group of Mapuche women interrupted Pres. Ricardo Lagos's celebration of International Women's Day to criticize him for honoring women in public positions of power while ignoring rural Mapuche women (*La Tercera,* March 9, 2002). They claimed that Lagos constructed discrimination against Mapuche women in terms of national gender inequalities (see Richards 2004), erasing racial, cultural, and class differences among women. The protesters, in turn, ignored the existence of the many urban Mapuche women, those who are professionals, and those who work in Mapuche nongovernmental organizations. During the presidential elections in January 2006, the Mapuche Araucanian region voted for Sebastián Piñera—a right-wing authoritarian man—rather than for socialist single mother Michelle Bachelet. One Mapuche woman argued: "Women govern their houses, but the country should be governed by a man with authority."

Female *machi* and male *longko* are cultural symbols that publicly connote tradition, history, and the various relationships of power, subjugation, and integration between the state and the Mapuche. Under the folklorizing approach, participants in national discourses have constructed the Mapuche as the folkloric soul of the nation—as symbols of the Chilean past to be celebrated in exhibitions and performances at special times, places, and events. This folkloric discourse is strongly gendered. The Chilean state, which constructs itself as modern, masculine, urban, and civilized, views Mapuche warriors of the past—and, when convenient, *longko*—as appropriate symbols of virility and military zeal.[7] It idealizes such warriors, who fought for their freedom, as emblems of independence and the basis for a patrilineal, patriarchal Chilean nation. The army, for example, named its regiments after Mapuche heroes and places, and a popular football team is named after the Mapuche warrior Colo-colo. Chilean poet Pablo Neruda (1951), nineteenth- and twentieth-century indigenist novelists (Blest Gana 1968; Lira 1867, 1870), and jurist and politician Andrés Bello all lauded the heroism and mythical qualities of colonial Mapuche warriors while ignoring Mapuche political demands of their time. A statue of the Mapuche warrior Caupolicán was placed on Santa Lucía Hill to commemorate the founding of Santiago—though it depicts a near-naked North American Plains Indian with feathered headdress rather than a Mapuche man in the traditional *makuñ* (poncho) and *chiripa* (breeches).

At the same time, national discourses reject contemporary Mapuche leaders who sympathize with resistance movements, wear traditional *makuñ,* and carry *waki* (spears) as subversives who threaten national sovereignty. Mapuche leaders may in some instances present themselves as "colonized males who question their masculinity and virility" (Degarrod 1998:348), but in others they promote images of virile Mapuche warriors both as icons of ethnic resistance against the state and as symbols of Chilean patriarchal nationalism. On May 30, 2003, the Consejo de Todas las Tierras requested that the statue of the conquistador Pedro de Valdivia—a symbol of colonization and domination in Santiago's central plaza—be replaced by one of the Mapuche hero Lautaro as a symbol of the Chilean nation (*El País,* May 30, 2003).

In folklorizing Mapuche women, participants in national discourses have stereotyped them as passive retainers of the nation's soul, either as rural, folkloric mothers of the nation or as wives of the nation. Female *machi* in particular symbolize the way in which Chileans conceptualized Mapuche throughout the nineteenth and twentieth centuries—that is, as exotic remnants of past folkways who had to remain unchanged in order to be authentic. *Machi* are often depicted on postcards and tourist brochures as symbols of the "authentic" Chile, and Chilean politicians use such images to gain the votes of indigenous sympathizers. With what Renato Rosaldo (1989:68–87) calls "imperialist nostalgia," the dominant class mourns the loss of indigenous traditions that have been destroyed by "progress." *Machi,* whether female or male, are feminized in these nostalgic representations and cherished because of their symbolic value as bearers of pristine tradition. Meanwhile, living *machi* and their healing practices remain stigmatized.

While glorifying Mapuche warriors, the state has historically infantilized and feminized Mapuche in order to justify its military occupation of the Araucanian region and establishment of the reservation system (1830–1884), the colonization and redistribution of Mapuche land (1884–1929), and the suppression of Mapuche rights under Pinochet (1973–1990). The neoliberal state projects itself as the epitome of modernity, a European nation in South America. It assumes the role of a father struggling to bring development and economic progress and characterizes Mapuche as "feminine and puerile" because they are "incapable of self-organizing and easily manipulated by the Left, terrorist groups, ecological groups, and foreign nongovernmental organizations" (*El Mercurio,* March 7, 2002). The state believes it must subjugate Mapuche through military action and violence as well as protect them, civilize them, and legislate and solve their problems (Bengoa 1999; Villalobos 2000). The impact that Michelle Bachelet will have on these gendered national symbolic constructions remains to be seen.

National discourses reject and feminize Mapuche when the state needs to justify its paternalism and the exploitation of Mapuche lands and people in the name of national development and progress. In this context, state discourses may argue that the Mapuche have been feminized, integrated into the state, and transformed into "Christian Chilean farmers" (Degarrod 1998:342). But few Mapuche view themselves in this way, and the state does not ignore Mapuche demands to be recognized as a sovereign, autonomous nation—demands that have increased in strength and scope. The state constructs Mapuche men who oppose state discourses of progress and development and who demand autonomy and sovereignty not as feminized but as masculine, barbaric terrorists who challenge civilization and law and order.

Female *machi* and male *longko,* conversely, have become symbols of tradition, in accordance with the Mapuche worldview that women and men, spirituality and politics, work together, in balance, to maintain the Mapuche nation and promote Mapuche mobilization. *Machi* and *longko* have become symbols of Mapuche tradition not because they are "disapproved by the ideology of dominant society" (Degarrod 1998:348) but for the opposite reason. Chile's presidents have tried to appropriate *machi* and *longko* as symbols of the nation in an effort to ameliorate the political clout that Mapuche resistance movements have gained with *machi* and *longko* as their symbolic representatives. Chile's presidents, constructing themselves as representatives of the masculine state, have related to women and indigenous people in general by using gendered kinship metaphors. Salvador Allende (1970–1973) perpetuated the existing national notions of women as the wives and mothers of the state (Boyle 1993:158; Miller 1991), but, unlike other political leaders, he also addressed them as workers and citizens and created SERNAM (Servicio Nacional de la Mujer, National Women's Secretariat) to incorporate women into national society (Valdés, Weinstein, Toledo, and Letelier 1989). Augusto Pinochet (1973–1990) cast himself as father and husband of the nation and addressed women as mothers of the nation who were morally superior and keepers of the faith (Boyle 1993:160–161). Chilean presidents in the post-Pinochet era have continued to view women as mothers, wives, and victims who need to be protected, although President Lagos took a somewhat more progressive stance on women's rights (Richards 2004:53–54). These democratic presidents have claimed to support indigenous people on their own terms but remain paternalistic, imposing what they believe to be economic progress while negating the Mapuche right to self-determination and limiting their participation in local politics as mayors or regional authorities.

National images of *machi* and *longko* as representatives of folklore who are ineffective as politicians or negotiators with the modern state have allowed Chile's presidents to construct themselves as inclusive and pluralistic. Ricardo Lagos, for example, manipulated folkloric images of *machi* and *longko* by having some of them stand onstage with him during his election campaign while in the background a choir sang in Mapudungu. When Lagos took office in March 2000, he sent minister of development and planning Alejandra Krauss to the southern city of Temuco, where she danced with *machi* in a collective ritual. In January 2006, presidential candidates Sebastián Piñera and Michelle Bachelet, in a last-minute effort to gain votes, organized competing political events during which they danced with *machi* and *longko* and promised to recognize indigenous people.

The state encourages the use of distinctive indigenous symbols as markers of cultural difference. Yet, real communities of indigenous people are hidden beneath such symbolic markers in the discourse of cultural diversity and pluralism (Hill and Staats 2002). The report by Lagos's Commission for Historical Truth and New Treatment of Indigenous People (Comisión de Verdad Histórica y Nuevo Trato), which appeared in 2003, promises to recognize the Mapuche as a people and grant them greater political participation in parliament and communal government. It also promises to recognize Mapuche territorial rights. But the report says nothing about easing the state's repressive policies toward the Mapuche or about self-determination, autonomy, or the legitimacy of local Mapuche authorities. Dozens of Mapuche leaders were arrested as political prisoners under Lagos's "antiterrorist" laws, which deprived detainees of the right to a speedy trial and allowed prosecutors to withhold evidence from defense lawyers (Guerra 2003). Some Mapuche have been tortured or killed by police, who act with impunity.[8] Ironically, Mapuche anthropologist Rosamel Millamán—one of the members of Lagos's commission—was beaten and detained by police during a raid on the community of Rofue.

By fossilizing the actions of *machi* and *longko* in a folkloric past, nationalist discourses erase contemporary realties of exploitation and domination (Alonso 1994:398) and obscure the roles *machi* and *longko* play in contemporary national politics. These discourses devalue the contemporary role of *machi* as spiritual leaders and of *longko* as political leaders of a people with its own history, demands, and agency, and they ignore the dynamism of Mapuche cultural practices. Chilean national discourses envision the nation of the future as a modern one composed of assimilated citizens who have forgotten their indigenous past but colored by occasional performances of indigenous culture as a folkloric construct. Perhaps the global economy will transform the "people without history" into "cultures without people" (Hill and Staats 2002).

Just as national discourses folklorize Mapuche in gender-specific ways, so do they marginalize them. Nineteenth-century novelists depicted the Spanish conquerors as masculine and the conquered indigenous people as feminine (Del Solar 1888; Larraín 1870).[9] Nineteenth-century historians constructed the Mapuche as barbaric and excluded them from Chilean history (Pinto 2002:343–346). In order to justify their invasion and expropriation of Mapuche land and the relocation of Mapuche on reservations in the 1800s, Chileans portrayed them as lazy drunkards and savages who obstructed progress (see, e.g., *El Araucano,* February 1, 1929). As recently as the end of the twentieth century, Sergio Villalobos (2000) claimed that the Mapuche were barbaric and effeminate because they engaged in homosexuality, witchcraft, revenge, and polygamy. Even today, national discourses stand Mapuche in opposition to Chileans of European descent, who are associated with the upper classes, education, masculinity, and power.[10]

Above all, it is *machi*—including male *machi*, because they are partially transvestite during rituals—who have become the ultimate symbols of the stigmatized margin of Chilean society: the feminine; the sexually deviant; the traditional; the indigenous; the rural; the poor; the spiritual; and the backward. The Chilean press and church perpetuate associations between passivity, domesticity, reproduction, womanhood, and lack of political power, depicting female *machi* as fertile Catholic earth mothers who perform private healing rituals. *Machi*'s drumming and singing, their trance states, and their use of herbal remedies and massage are considered backward feminine superstitions, inferior to the knowledge of the Chilean intellectual elites. As symbols of the past who heal with the help of herbs and spirits, *machi* are often seen as irrational sorcerers, threats to the church and Western medicine, and impediments to the Mapuche's becoming modern Chilean citizens (Bacigalupo 1994b, 1996a; Degarrod 1998). Alternatively, the media sometimes portray female *machi* as archaic women who are disappearing with modernity and who pose no threat to the state or to Catholic morality (*El Mercurio,* June 2, 1999).[11]

Male *machi* are marginalized in national discourses because they are viewed as effeminate and therefore challenge male-dominant national models. As we will see in Chapter 7, male *machi* often perform chores considered "womanly" by Mapuche and Chileans alike, and they wear women's scarves and shawls during rituals to call on the spirits. National homophobic discourses often depict male *machi* as deviant, effeminate homosexuals who threaten national masculinities and Catholic morality and therefore are inappropriate as national symbols.

Some Mapuche themselves subscribe to national images of *machi* as marginal, apolitical, irrational country folk who are easily manipulated by both Mapuche and Chilean politicians. Some organizations created by urban Mapuche leaders in the early twentieth century, such as Unión

Araucana and Sociedad Caupolicán, became complicit in national discourses to produce demonized versions of female *machi*. They viewed
female *machi* as ignorant, deceitful women who disobeyed their husbands
and knew how to manipulate poisons to weaken or kill innocent men (*El
Araucano,* September 1, 1927; Degarrod 1998:348; Foerster and Montecino 1988:59–60). These organizations petitioned the government to
prohibit *machi* practice because it was "fraudulent" and to prohibit collective, communitywide rituals (*ngillatun*) because they were "immoral"
and "irrational." In a classic case of Gramscian ideological hegemony, the
dominant group's meanings and values permeated the whole of Chilean
society without appearing to be imposed, and Mapuche organizations
themselves legitimated the interests of the dominant classes. Unión Araucana negated ancestral culture and argued for assimilation and modernization. Sociedad Caupolicán argued for the gradual incorporation of
national values into Mapuche culture (Degarrod 1998; Foerster and
Montecino 1988). As recently as December 2001, a thirty-five-year-old
Mapuche woman who worked at the National Center for Indigenous
Issues (Coordinadora Nacional Indianista, CONACIN) told me: "*Machi*
are wise in their communities, in their culture, but ignorant about politics
. . . . The state and the Mapuche politicians manipulate *machi* . . . A politician or anyone can convince them, and they will go and march."

Whereas assimilation eliminates indigenous identity, folklorization
and marginalization undermine it more subtly. What is at stake in all
three processes is who has the power to define indigenous identities. As
we will see, *machi* themselves both conform to and defy national stereotypes and systems of power, sometimes employing them for their own
ends and sometimes ignoring them as they go about their business. Next,
however, I want to show how Mapuche resistance movements themselves
have adopted and elaborated on such images of *machi*—especially female
machi—for purposes never intended by the state.

Machi in Mapuche Resistance Movements

Mapuche, challenging Chileans' assumptions about the boundedness and
homogeneity of Mapuche culture and politics, have developed diverse responses to Chilean national images. The contradictions, conflicts of interest, doubts, arguments, and changing motivations and circumstances of
indigenous politics are best approached through what Lila Abu-Lughod
(1990:42) calls "ethnographies of the particular." Some Mapuche par-

ticipate in resistance movements that seek political recognition of the Mapuche as a people and promote their autonomy as a nation. Others believe empowerment comes only through integration of the Mapuche into the modern Chilean state and participation in existing national structures of power. Some support right-wing ideologies and Pinochet's legacy; others embrace the ideologies of the democratic governments. Mapuche sociologist Marcos Valdés (2000) shows that Mapuche's political demands for autonomy or integration and their requests for economic benefits from the state are not mutually exclusive. Mapuche, regardless of their political ideology, seek from the government health, education, and social security benefits, for example, and the return of ancestral land. Some Mapuche question national images of *machi* and *longko;* others appropriate these images but use them for their own ends.

Female *machi* and male *longko* play different but complementary leadership roles in local Mapuche society and in their relationships with national political authorities. Mapuche view *longko* as active, gregarious, and pan-Mapuche and as both urban and rural, traditional and modern in their secular leadership roles. They associate *longko* with political activities and warfare, traditionally the masculine domain. They view female *machi* as passive, local, rural performers of spiritual roles and of roles associated with Mapuche women, such as healing, making herbal remedies, and tending gardens. Female *machi* must negotiate their broader political roles with other Mapuche leaders—*longko* and *presidentes* (elected, non-traditional political representatives of the community)—who are most often men. *Longko* who lead Mapuche resistance movements appropriate and elaborate on national images of female *machi* and resignify them as symbols of ethnic history, cultural integrity, and ancestral rights in order to legitimate claims to land and to a Mapuche nation.

Mapuche resistance movements such as the Consejo de Todas las Tierras and Coordinadora Malleko-Arauco, in which *machi* and *longko* play important roles, have both reinforced and challenged national images of *machi*. Mapuche activists' contradictory uses of gendered images of *machi* enable us to trace the ways in which conflicting notions of power work together and the ways power relations between Mapuche and the state are transformed. The resistance movements reinforce national gendered restrictions and stereotypes but also resist national interpretations of *machi,* promoting, instead, pan-Mapuche ones that advance their own agendas.

Mapuche resistance movements are increasingly supported by the civilian population, NGOs, and the United Nations. In 1999, 80 percent of Chileans believed the Mapuche had been victims of illegal assaults against their property and of the repressive state apparatus (Vergara, Aravena, Correa, and Molina 1999:129). Foreign governments have criticized Chile's violation of Mapuche human rights, and international NGOs and environmental movements have supported Mapuche resistance to the forestry industry.[12] Rodolfo Stavenhagen, the human rights commissioner for the United Nations who visited Chile in July 2003, criticized the government for violations of human rights and for the corrupt judiciary system used against Mapuche. He recommended that the Indigenous Law prevail over other national laws for exploiting resources, that CONADI be granted more money to buy indigenous land, and that Mapuche be consulted about development projects in Mapuche territory. He also urged that the legitimate protests and social demands of Mapuche not be criminalized and that the government grant amnesty to Mapuche political prisoners (J. Marimán 2004).

In a strategic move, Mapuche activists appropriate national folkloric images of female *machi* as symbols of the traditional, the feminine, the ecological, and the marginal and politicize them as representing ethnic history, pan-Mapuche cultural integrity, and ancestral rights.[13] They capitalize on the rhetoric of marginality and oppression for political aims, constructing female *machi* as links to the past and to nature rather than offering any empirical evidence for such connections. The Consejo de Todas las Tierras uses *machi* images in legitimating its requests for ethnic sovereignty and territorial autonomy, in negotiating periodically with the government and forestry companies for land, and in gaining international support for the Mapuche cause (Fig. 6.2). The Coordinadora Malleko-Arauco does not engage in dialogue with the government and uses *machi* solely as symbols of Mapuche tradition and resistance. Both movements argue that the ideals of modernization and progress proposed by the Chilean government do not benefit the Mapuche and trample their individual and cultural rights. In 2005 politically unaffiliated Mapuche founded the Consejo de Autoridades Tradicionales (Council of Traditional Authorities) to counteract the images of *machi* and *longko* used by Mapuche resistance movements.

Mapuche intellectuals Pedro Cayuqueo and Wladimir Painemal (2003) argue that the Chilean government's indigenist policies have been designed to disarticulate Mapuche resistance by institutionalizing Mapuche life in organizations such as CONADI and replacing traditional leadership with administrative leadership. The government has also fostered conflict and fragmentation among Mapuche organizations by legitimating the specific territorial identities of some groups that have concrete,

Figure 6.2. Mapuche protest graffiti in Metrenco featuring the *machi's kultrun* as a symbol of Mapuche identity and resistance. The expression "Fuera Usurpadores de Tierra" (Get out, land usurpers) is a protest against Chilean farmers, forestry companies, and the state highway system, which have taken land from Mapuche communities. The expression "Newen Peñis" (Power or strength, Mapuche brothers) incites Mapuche to unite against the usurpers (photo by Ana Mariella Bacigalupo).

nonpolitical goals rather than engaging with the political demands of the Mapuche movement as a whole. Mapuche intellectual José Marimán criticizes both territorial fragmentation and Mapuche fundamentalist notions that Mapuche who are intellectuals, urbanites, or professionals are "colonized Mapuche."[14] Such perceptions, he argues, have effectively blocked the creation of a Mapuche nation with a common political project for autonomy and self-determination (Cayuqueo and Painemal 2003; J. Marimán 2003, 2004). Marimán, Cayuqueo, and Painemal all agree that Mapuche's common experiences of colonization and domination must be used to strengthen Mapuche identity and create awareness of the Mapuche as a nation that spans Chile and Argentina. This is one of the purposes of *Azkintuwe* (www.nodo50.org/azkintuwe/), the first Mapuche Internet newspaper, created in 2003.

Mapuche activists use folkloric national discourses in ways never intended by the state. They selectively manipulate symbols and discourses for purposes of resistance, political mobilization against forestry companies, and attempts to create a new Mapuche nation with a territorial base. Although most Mapuche are urban dwellers, land has remained central to Mapuche identity, autonomy, and self-determination.[15] At a time when the actual location of an increasingly urban Mapuche culture is uncertain, the idea of a culturally and ethnically distinct homeland becomes even more salient. It is at such times that displaced people cluster around remembered or imagined communities attached to imagined homelands (Gupta and Ferguson 1997:39).[16] Being "from the homeland" is a more important form of engagement with Mapuche identity than is the reality of being fixed to a rural community.

Because the United Nations views indigenousness as bound to cultural and territorialized practice, this is also the point from which indigenous people have been able to argue most convincingly for rights to land, natural resources, and self-determination (Muehlebach 2003:251, 253). As Rudi Colloredo-Mansfeld (2002) shows for Ecuador's Otavalo, indigenous self-determination is not bounded by indigenous territories; instead, the Otavalo engage in "relational" and "situational autonomy" linked to the geographical mobility of peasant careers. Similarly, urban Mapuche are not bound by their ancestral lands. But they do not have the political clout to negotiate the terms of their "relational self-determination" disconnected from cultural and territorial demands. As Andrea Muehlebach writes (2003:258), "the rights to self-determination and territory are a starting point from which indigenous peoples could properly negotiate more equitable futures for themselves."

Mapuche notions of tradition are less about preservation than about transformative practice and the selective symbolization of continuity. Like most other indigenous peoples, Mapuche use their historical consciousness to create themselves in history rather than simply inheriting static traditions from the past. Because the practical limits on invention are primarily political, not empirical, a tradition can accommodate a great deal of interaction and hybridity without losing its integrity (Clifford 2000; Conklin 1997; Hill and Staats 2002). Unlike participants in the national agenda, who appropriate indigenous traditions as agentless symbols of indigenousness, members of resistance movements actively create relations between past and present, spirits and land claims, *machi*, and the struggle for Mapuche autonomy.

The logging of Mapuche ancestral land has become the key area for physical and symbolic confrontations between Mapuche and the Chilean state. Heavy logging has produced severe soil erosion, crippling the self-sufficiency of Mapuche communities (Millamán 2001:10–11). Majority discourses often depict Mapuche who pursue environmental causes as subversives who oppose national development and have become pawns of foreign environmental groups. Mapuche activists view the bodies and souls of *machi* as inextricably bound up with ancestral land and with the environmental and sacred knowledge critical for the survival and reproduction of the traditional Mapuche lifestyle. They portray *machi* as guardians of knowledge of the forest who obtain their life force and power to heal from nature spirits, or *ngen,* and who need herbs that grow only in their ancestral forests. *Machi* experience visions of *ngen* spirits, who grant them knowledge to heal. Some *machi* powers are believed to reside in the forest. Mapuche believe that female *machi* will suffer physical illness, spiritual harm, and loss of power if ancestral land is appropriated by others or affected by ecological disaster.

Forestry companies and the government are aware of the symbolic relationship between *machi* and ancestral land and know of the central role *machi* play in Mapuche resistance movements. After a confrontation between Mapuche protestors and police in the community of Catrio Ñancul, agents for the company Forestal Mininco cut down the community's *rewe* with chain saws (Barrera 1999:186). By symbolically destroying the *machi*'s powers and legitimacy, Mininco attempted to prevent them from performing rituals in which spiritual powers and the appeal of tradition could be used to mobilize the Mapuche against the logging industry.

Mapuche resistance movements' image of female *machi* as earth mothers and guardians of the land, which corresponds to national folkloric images of *machi,* are strategically chosen and situationally deployed to engage Mapuche from different communities and to legitimate an autonomous Mapuche nation with a fixed, rural territorial base. These movements have used what Gayatri Spivak calls "strategic essentialism," an appropriation of essentialism—the idea that people have essential qualities, properties, or aspects—by oppressed groups. Such groups are aware that their "essential attributes" are cultural constructs but invoke them in particular circumstances as powerful political tools (Landry and MacLean 1996:124). The value of female *machi* as instruments for strategic essentialism became obvious to me when I saw women who were not *machi* presented as *machi* during Mapuche protests and marches. A Mapuche man explained: "It is easier to bring ordinary Mapuche women to play the drum. There is less protocol to follow, and then if the protesters are drenched or beaten, it is less embarrassing when the women are not *machi* . . . As long as the journalists think they are *machi,* that's fine."

Mapuche resistance movements draw on essentialist notions of a utopian homeland defended by traditional *machi* for purposes of ideological and political mobilization. Yet, just like Chilean national assumptions, these notions disregard the changing dynamics of Mapuche culture, as reflected, for example, in Mapuche proposals for industrial development and by Mapuche who sell their forested land to the lumber industry in order to survive.[17] The image of a utopian Mapuche homeland has also created identity problems for the predominantly urban Mapuche. Although many such people maintain ties to relatives in rural communities, their identity is not predicated on a rural land base.[18]

Some Mapuche intellectuals, like anthropologists, have rejected strategic essentialism by exploring the constructed aspects of Mapuche culture and the dynamic and context-specific aspects of particular communities. Mapuche historian and sociologist José Ancan (1997), for example, criticizes the perspective of strategic essentialists because they hail the rural community as a timeless, uncontaminated refuge of the "real Mapuche" and gloss over the complexities of urban Mapuche ethnicity. Yet, as the rural land base, associated with motherhood and the bodies of female *machi,* has come to stand for Mapuche society, Mapuche increasingly see recovering their land as the only way to regain their identity and self-determination and create alternative forms of power in resistance to those of the Chilean state.[19] While *machi* and Mapuche activists adopt national images for their own ends, they also challenge national gendered discourses by offering new readings of the relationship between *machi* and politics. Although traditional Mapuche gender ideologies associate femininity with spirituality and masculinity with politics, *machi* do perform some local political functions in their communities.

The plaza of Temuco features a statue of a female *machi* with her drum that illustrates the diverse readings made of such women (Fig. 6.3). The statue stands in the capital of the Mapuche homeland as a symbol of the Mapuche as traditional and rural. It represents a region and an ethnicity that have been politically and historically marginalized from the state, which is symbolized by statues of the founding fathers in Santiago. The positioning of a female *machi* at the center of the public political-administrative space of the Araucanian region, however, recognizes *machi* as symbols of national folklore. Mapuche resistance movements, in turn, have appropriated this statue as a symbol of the traditional Mapuche nation. It marks the place where such movements began and the capital of what the Mapuche define as their autonomous nation. At the same time, the statue continually engages with actors and symbols of modern life, as *machi* do in their pragmatic relationships with national symbols. The Falabella de-

Figure 6.3. The statue of a female *machi* with her drum in the plaza of Temuco illustrates the diverse readings of female *machi* through gendered discourses of tradition and modernity (photo by Ana Mariella Bacigalupo).

partment store and the Catholic church loom behind it, businesspeople and doctors pass by it on their way to work, and Mapuche protests take place at its feet.

Tradition and Hybridity in *Machi* Practice

Machi argue that their practices are traditional, but in reality they stretch and reinvent the notion of tradition for their own ends, show the traditional-modern dichotomy to be artificial, and transgress it by engaging in dynamic, hybrid healing practices (Bacigalupo 2001b; J. Marimán 2004). *Machi*'s traditional forms of expressive behavior have expanded rather than disappeared under the pressures of modernity. They incorporate and resignify Catholic, national, and biomedical symbols and modern technology in local terms and use them as sources of spiritual power. Spanish horses transport spirits between worlds; the sacred heart of Jesus is associated with the beat of the drum; antibiotics become exorcising remedies. *Machi*'s brightly colored, lacy aprons, which have become a symbol of traditional Mapuche womanhood, are closely patterned on the clothing of Chile's former colonial elites. Machi Hortensia's "traditional" *ngeykurewen* included guitar and accordion music, and she invoked Jesus, not the ancestral *filew* spirit, as her teacher. Some *machi* use the Chilean flag as an emblem of power in individual healing rituals as well as in collective *ngillatun,* and even General Pinochet can be a symbol of authority propitiated for good or evil (Fig. 6.4).

Machi juggle these various religious, medical, and political symbols and represent themselves diversely according to who else is present and what the others' intentions and context may be. Such processes have been described as the "invention of tradition" (Hobsbawm and Ranger 1983). *Machi* practice is a system in which meaning, identity, and relations are continually created with every performance (Guss 2000:12). This flexible notion of tradition is crucial to the maintenance of Mapuche culture. As the Mapuche writer Elicura Chihuailaf puts it (1999:48–49), "traditional culture is what allows the Mapuche to transform their communities in their social, political, and economic aspects without relinquishing being indigenous."

The indigenized Virgin, Jesus, and God acquire magical powers far greater than those of their Christian manifestations and are shaped by durable, traditional Mapuche notions. Most Mapuche reject Catholic notions that God is male, that Mary was a virgin, and that Jesus had

Figure 6.4. A *machi*, his patient, and helpers pose with the Chilean flag after an all-night healing ritual. The *machi* used the flag to draw powers from the Chilean nation-state in his rituals (photo by Ana Mariella Bacigalupo).

to die on the cross in order to save humanity. In Mapuche Catholicism, God is male and female like Ngünechen; Mary is a divine mother and the moon, which grants fertility; and the cross symbolizes death or the connection between the human and spiritual worlds but has little to do with Jesus. Most Mapuche are baptized for protection from evil spirits, and they ask priests to bless funerals and *ngillatun* rituals with holy water in order to enhance agricultural fertility. When *machi* incorporate images of the Virgin, Jesus, or the Bible into their healing, they rub them on the patient as if they were herbal remedies or use them to exorcise evil spirits. Some *machi* believe that becoming initiated or renewing their powers on days that coincide with key Catholic celebrations, such as the Immaculate Conception or Christmas, will increase their powers and grant them protection from evil spirits. In turn, the Catholic churches in Mapuche areas ask *machi* to officiate at the celebration of the Mapuche New Year (*wetripantu*) at the local church. Besides embracing the ritualistic aspects of Catholic Mass, Mapuche espouse Catholic discourses about morality and evil, but shamanic practices show this opposition to be contextual, contradictory, and ambiguous.

Machi also have complex interactions with several other mainstream religions. The Baha'i have gained followers among the Mapuche by recording and playing *machi* music and prayers. Evangelical pastors depict *machi* practice as the art of the devil, and Mapuche often view evangelical religion as conflicting with *machi* practice. Yet, the two often overlap. Pentecostalism has become popular in some Mapuche communities because it reproduces the central elements of Mapuche ritual and the role of *machi,* such as possession, ancestor propitiation, healing with the help of spirits, and speaking in tongues (Foerster 1993:156–157). Ana María Oyarce (1988:44) observed an evangelical *machi* who diagnosed illness while she was in trance; she prayed and sang in Mapudungu and rubbed a Bible instead of a *kultrun* on patients during her healing rituals. Fabián, a Mapuche intellectual, and Ramón, Machi Javiera's husband, discussed the case of a *machi* neophyte who became an evangelical pastor:

FABIÁN: Pepe was preparing to be a *machi,* and his parents did not support him. He became an evangelical. He prays in Mapudungu and gives herbal remedies, and people say that it works, too. But he really has a *machi püllü* [spirit].

RAMÓN: He has a good basis to be a *machi,* a good *küymi* [trance]. He throws and collects the knowledge that he has. Very good. His singing, too. Now he is an evangelical pastor.

MARIELLA: I thought that *machi* did not mix with the evangelicals.

FABIÁN: Yes, that's why there must be something very complicated in his memory. In his head.

In recent years, *machi* have increased in number, and they defy folkloric stereotypes as they independently develop strategies for expanding their services in modern Chile. Fabián told me: "Fifteen years ago I said that *machi* practice would end in fifty years, and now fifteen years have gone by and there are new *machi* all over the place. So I was completely wrong . . . There are many more *machi* than I ever imagined" (December 27, 2001). *Machi,* both male and female, are not just rural practitioners but also flourish near urban centers. Despite their being stigmatized in Chilean national discourses, they increasingly attract clients from among non-Mapuche as well as urban Mapuche. They make appointments with their patients by cellular phone and travel to Chilean and even Argentine cities to exorcise houses and bring patients luck in love, money, and work (Bacigalupo 2001b). They treat Mapuche for spiritual illness produced by maladjustment, discrimination, and poverty, and non-Mapuche for stress, depression, and insomnia. They bless indigenous monuments, universities, and schools and see patients at intercultural health hospitals and consulting rooms.[20] Indeed, as Michael Taussig writes (1987:237), shamans are the "shock absorbers of history."

An increasing number of *machi* maintain offices akin to those of medical doctors in major cities, where they see their urban patients. Machi María Cecilia and Machi Juana, for example, traveled to Santiago five days every month between 2002 and 2006 to treat patients in a room they rented in a dilapidated building. Their cell phone numbers and schedules were posted outside, and a steady stream of patients arrived from nine in the morning until nine at night. Most of the patients came for depression or soul loss, bad luck or evil spirits, or physical ailments such as liver, kidney, and stomach problems, swelling, fever, and arthritis. The *machi* curtained off part of the building's central courtyard, where they had a gas stove on which they prepared herbal remedies, and they kept a drum in their room to perform prayers and divinations. Machi Myriam saw patients twice a week in a doctor's office at an intercultural health hospital and was lobbying to be hired at another. Machi Sergio saw patients in consulting rooms in different towns every day except Sunday.

Like other Mapuche, *machi* present one image of themselves to fellow Mapuche and another to non-Mapuche. *Machi* sometimes enact national perceptions of shamanic practices, playing on their customers' sense of the traditional in order to retain their clientele. This became apparent to me one winter evening in July 1995, as Machi María Cecilia, her family, and I watched a soap opera on an old black-and-white TV plugged into a car battery. When a truck driven by *wingka* came up the driveway, everyone jumped up. María Cecilia's brother hid the television set and the car battery.[21] Her sister helped her put on her *machi* scarf while her mother went outside to greet the visitors. María Cecilia explained later that because *wingka* have a "mental picture" of what it means to be a *machi,* if they saw her watching TV or speaking in Spanish instead of Mapudungu they would question her authenticity and her power to heal.

Machi's engagements with discourses of tradition are complex. They are guardians of tradition, punished by spirits if they engage with the media and rewarded if they satisfy consumer images of the exotic. At the same time, *machi*'s pragmatic hybrid practices engage productively with biomedicine and Catholicism in urban contexts, as long as they construe these practices as traditional. So-called traditional *machi* gender identities, too, are products of hybridization.

As we will see in the following two chapters, male and female *machi* have found diverse, paradoxical ways to negotiate their shifting ritual gender identities and powers with everyday expectations for women and men in contemporary Mapuche society. They conform to and challenge the gendered expectations of their *machi* spirits, as well as Chilean national and Mapuche notions about gender and sexuality, as they struggle for legitimacy in their everyday lives and their healing and political practices.

CHAPTER 7

The Responses of Male *Machi* to Homophobia: Reinvention as Priests, Doctors, and Spiritual Warriors

Eugenio and Daniel—both *longko* of their respective communities—drank a carton of Gato Negro wine as they mused about my research on male *machi* one summer evening in December 2001. The two drew on Chilean homophobic discourses to joke about the manliness, gender performances, and sexuality of male *machi*. They applied to male *machi* the derogatory Chilean terms "*coliwilla*," "*maricón*," "*marica*," and "*homosexual*" and viewed *machi* as effeminate, transvestite, deceitful, cowardly, and passive. Yet, paradoxically, Daniel and Eugenio also respected male *machi* and recognized the importance of their traditional co-gendered performances and transvestism during rituals that ensured health, wholeness, and well-being.

The *longko*'s ambivalent response to male *machi* as people whom they at once respected and deplored reflected their competing Chilean Catholic and traditional Mapuche ideologies of gender and sexuality. Like most other Mapuche, Eugenio and Daniel tried to reconcile these conflicting perceptions by legitimating male *machi*'s co-gendered identities and spiritual practices as being akin to those of celibate Catholic priests and by masculinizing their healing practices as being like those of medical doctors:

> EUGENIO: Why is it that male *machi* are *coliwilla* [effeminate homosexuals]?
>
> DANIEL: Male *machi* are powerful, but they like pigs' legs [men's bodies]. Both men laugh.
>
> MARIELLA: Just because they use head scarves and shawls in ritual doesn't mean they are *coliwilla*. Besides, what's wrong with that?
>
> EUGENIO: How is it going to be normal for two men to be together?

You've been around too many gringos. How many male *machi* have kissed you?

MARIELLA: None.

[Daniel and Eugenio laugh.]

EUGENIO: You see—a man who is macho would at least have tried.

EUGENIO'S wife, AURELIA, chides him: How can you say that? Not all male *machi* are like that. Machi José and Sergio are special, like priests, like doctors. They have power, we have to respect them.

DANIEL jokes: You never know what the priest hides under his robes. You never know what the doctor hides under his coat. You never know what the *machi* hides under the shawl.

[We all laugh.]

AURELIA: They say that because they are drunk, but when the community did not want Machi José to perform at the *ngillatun,* Eugenio defended him. They laugh now. But when they are sick, when they need a *ngillatun,* they go begging the male *machi.*

DANIEL: That's true. There are few male *machi,* but they are stronger [than female *machi*] . . .

EUGENIO: They may be stronger, but they wear women's clothes. Machi Jacinto wears women's clothes to work. He must like pig's legs.

MARIELLA: Jacinto is married and has children. You say he is *coliwilla* just because he wears a *killa* [woman's shawl] during rituals?

EUGENIO: If I wore a skirt and a shawl, what would you think?

DANIEL: *Mi'jita rica* [Gorgeous babe]!

In calling male *machi* "*coliwilla,*" Eugenio and Daniel subscribed to Catholic discourses in which any form of sexual or gender variance is viewed as unnatural and threatening to family values, society, and morality. They saw homosexuality partly as a matter of choice of sexual object, and they labeled male *machi,* whom they believed engaged in sexual acts with other men, "abnormal." Partly, they viewed it as associated with gender transitivity and sexual positions, and they called male *machi* whom they viewed as transvestite "effeminate," or those engaging in passive sexual acts "*coliwilla.*" The discursive act of labeling a male *machi* "*coliwilla*" and as "liking pig's legs" was a form of rejection because it placed the *machi* in an inferior position vis-à-vis national power dynamics, state-defined masculinity, and Catholic morality.

Machismo, the ideology of male dominance and superiority that feeds aversion toward and stigmatization of effeminate men, who are thought to be penetrated by others, remains strong among Mapuche. Machismo structures the relationship between men and women but also that between men. It is "a system of produced identities, desires and practices: it defines what a man is, and what he isn't, what he should want, and what he shouldn't; what he may do, and what he may not do" (Lancaster 1992:277). By rejecting male *machi* as *coliwillas,* Eugenio and Daniel attempted to assert their masculinity in terms of its national signifiers.[1] Mapuche men like Eugenio and Daniel, who are doubly marginalized from the structures of power of the Chilean state because of their ethnic identity and low socioeconomic status, are particularly vested in participating in the ideal national image of heterosexual masculinity, in order to try to reverse their own marginality.

Nevertheless, Eugenio and Daniel sought male *machi* to perform at collective *ngillatun* rituals in their respective communities and visited male *machi* periodically for healing and advice. Machi José healed Eugenio from *kastikutran,* a spiritual punishment illness, which he experienced when a community member sold part of the communal ritual field to a stone quarry. Another male *machi* treated Eugenio for the stomach pains and nightmares he experienced while waiting for some new communal land promised by CONADI (National Corporation for Indigenous Development), which he needed to host a collective *ngillatun* ritual.

Eugenio and Daniel negotiated contrasting national and traditional Mapuche gender ideologies. They grudgingly accepted male *machi's* ritual co-gendered identities, partial transvestism, and performance of womanly roles for the sake of ritual efficacy. But they also expected male *machi* to legitimate themselves in terms of any of three prestigious, public male roles—the celibate priest, the medical doctor, and the politically active spiritual warrior.

Priests are like male *machi* in that they mediate between the natural and the supernatural worlds on behalf of humans and hold moral authority but also wear skirts and have a sexuality distinct from that of ordinary family men. By reconstructing themselves as celibate Mapuche priests, male *machi* remind city folk that they are Catholic while claiming that priesthood has always been a traditional Mapuche co-gendered role. Although many Mapuche now subscribe to the penetration paradigm, the notion of homosexuality as same-sex acts, and the belief that there is a relationship between male gender inversion, transvestism, and homosexuality, they do not ordinarily view Catholic priests in those terms.

In Chile, medical doctors are predominantly men. Male *machi* are like doctors in that they possess knowledge of medicine, diagnose illness, prescribe remedies, and treat. Male *machi* who identify themselves as doctors gain authority and prestige. Male *machi* also assert their masculinity by politicizing their spiritual practices in activist arenas. Sometimes they revive and masculinize their colonial roles as spiritual warriors by associating themselves with contemporary military authorities. Like Chilean generals, male *machi* protect individuals, families, and the nation by warring against enemy beings.

In the rest of this chapter, I explore the ways in which three male *machi* have, in their everyday lives and practices, either fulfilled or challenged the gender expectations of their *machi* spirits, the public roles assigned to males in Chilean society, and Mapuche notions about gender and sexuality. After introducing the three, I examine the different ways in which they have reconciled their ritual co-gendered identities, partial transvestism, and special sexualities with the need to masculinize themselves in their daily lives. Finally, I look at the ways in which these three *machi* have reinvented themselves as celibate priests, spiritual doctors, and politically active spiritual warriors in order to deflect accusations of homosexuality or witchcraft. These newfound roles also allow male *machi* to legitimate their spiritual and healing practices and regain their political role.

A Call to Healing

Machi Sergio: Prestige and Legitimacy

I met Machi Sergio while in the company of Fresia, his initiate, in March 1991. Sergio lived with his mother in a large, yellow wooden house on a hill. His five-step *rewe*, which held his *machi* spirit and healing power, faced east outside the kitchen and was flanked by flags in white and blue, the colors of the sky. Sergio, a robust, single, forty-year-old, emerged wearing a track suit and a blue head scarf. He was happy to see Fresia, who had lived with him for a year while she learned *machi* lore, and he readily agreed to participate in my project. I continued to work with him and observe his rituals until December 2002.

Sergio had been born into a prestigious Mapuche family, wealthy by local standards, and had lived in his house since birth, according to Mapuche traditional patrilineal and patrilocal norms. He inherited his *machi* spirit from his paternal uncle, and his mother knew he would be a *machi* even before he was born: "When I was pregnant with him I saw a vision that took me up to heaven and showed me potatoes, herbs, wheat . . . Abundance and wealth is what I saw. This never happened with my other sons. Then I told my husband that surely this baby was going to be a man and a *machi*."

Sergio was possessed for the first time when he was eight, and he became ill. "At night my mother said I was twisting like a lizard . . . I suffered a lot, and this suffering made me compassionate toward the suffering of others." Sergio was too young to be initiated, but he dreamed about playing a *kultrun* and began healing people with herbal remedies. He also went to the local school: "My teachers would always wonder why I was alone. I did not like school—the teachers telling me what to do, punishing me." Sergio began his *machi* training with Machi Jorge but left him because their *machi* spirits "were incompatible." He then underwent training with a prestigious female *machi* and finally became initiated when he was nineteen: "Every day of my life I say thank you for letting me help so many different people, see different places, how other people live, be with rich people, poor people."

Sergio's family supported his *machi* practice, and he maintained a good relationship with his community. His younger brother served as his assistant in healing rituals, and his uncle sometimes performed as his *dungumachife*. Sergio had many patients within and outside his community: "There is no rejection of me in the community, and whenever my people ask me for a remedy, I give it to them, whether they pay for it or not."

Sergio enhanced his popularity as a *machi* outside his community by attending to poor patients for free and becoming a public representative of Mapuche culture. He explained Mapuche traditions on the radio, taught at the local school, worked with an intercultural health hospital, and appeared regularly in the newspapers for blessing new schools and offices in the area. Sergio gave his herbal recipes for forty-seven ailments to the Mapuche pharmacy created in 2003 by a Mapuche intercultural hospital. The Mapuche pharmacy successfully markets and sells these recipes as herbal extracts taken as supralingual drops.

Sergio also wanted to use the media to publicize himself and increase his clientele. He asked me to make a video of his rituals and give his real name, his cell phone number, and the location of his house and consulting rooms, to be broadcast on Chilean national television. Some Mapuche criticized Sergio's engagement with the media and anthropologists, and his sharing of medicinal knowledge with the Mapuche pharmacy, but this has had little effect on his practice because of his legitimacy in the community.

Machi Jorge: Marginality, Wealth, and Witchcraft

Machi Jorge, whom we met in Chapter 2, drove a large pickup truck, a commodity that set him apart from his neighbors. Adjacent to his cooking hut, or *ruka,* stood a wooden house, painted blue, where Jorge, his sister, her husband, their children, and Jorge's two male helpers all slept. He had an additional wooden house with a room containing a long wooden table and chairs, where patients waited and slept if necessary. Facing the kitchen door was his thick, four-step *rewe.*

Unlike Sergio, Jorge was suspected of witchcraft from the start. His family was poor and of low status. People believed he had inherited his powers from his maternal grandmother, whom they considered to have been a *kalku.* He began curing when he was still a boy and became a *machi* suddenly at the age of eleven, during an earthquake. He did so without the help of another *machi* and without undergoing the shamanic training that would have granted him legitimacy in the eyes of the community. Nora, a prestigious eighty-four-year-old *machi* from a nearby community, expressed the view that Jorge was born a witch: "I've known Jorge from the time he was a little boy. I saw him collecting *kolliwai* [*Colliguaja odorifera,* a plant with a toxic sap] at night. He would play his *kultrun* at night. This is what *kalku* do . . . He has an evil voice, he does evil to people. His family is no good. He did *brujería* from the time he was young."

As a *machi,* Jorge found his clientele outside his ritual congregation. Mapuche tend to place their faith in *machi* whom they know only by reputation and who therefore can have no interest in performing witchcraft against them. A man from Jorge's community said: "We do not go to Jorge because he may have reason to practice witchcraft against us. With someone from far away, he has no reason to, especially if they are paying him good money like the gringos do." A patient from a distant community waiting to be treated by Jorge for the first time said: "I don't know him more than by hearsay. People have told me he is a powerful *machi* and can tell who has sent the evil. Other *machi* don't know that." These patients went to Jorge for treatment of a variety of emotional, spiritual, and physical ailments and were usually satisfied with his healing. People also paid Jorge to officiate in *ngillatun* outside of his ritual congregation. Both of these practices built his reputation outside his community.

The wealth Jorge had acquired as an adult, seemingly quite suddenly, and his popularity among outsiders increased his neighbors' suspicions that he was a witch. Mapuche associate both excessive poverty and excessive wealth, because they challenge the ideals of reciprocity and egalitarianism, with social marginality and witchcraft. According to Mapuche logic, people become poor and marginal when they transgress social or moral norms and are punished by the deity Ngünechen and their community. Poor Mapuche are unable to contribute their share of material goods for community rituals and events. People become wealthy when they forge Faustian pacts with evil spirits, challenge the local sociopolitical hierarchy, or sell Mapuche knowledge to foreigners. As in some parts of Africa (Comaroff and Comaroff 1999; Geschiere 1997), witchcraft is tied to the new distribution of power and goods brought about by capitalism and state bureaucracy. One man from the community explained Jorge's family's initial poverty as "God's punishment because they behaved badly." When Jorge suddenly became wealthy in local terms through his successful healing practice, his community claimed that he had sold the blood and souls of his family to evil *wekufe* spirits in exchange for prestige, money, and material belongings.

Most *machi,* in order to maintain their legitimacy in the ritual congregation, learn to balance their individual gains with demonstrations of selflessness, commitment to the community, and dedication to their spirits. By redistributing their wealth, *machi* protect themselves from accusations of witchcraft. Jorge stood apart in that he acted in his own self-interest, ignoring community well-being and selling shamanic knowledge for his own benefit. His community ostracized him for doing so, and Jorge became a scapegoat for all the misfortunes that befell his ritual congregation.

Jorge's media appearances and his work with foreign anthropologists exacerbated the idea that he was commodifying Mapuche imagery and knowledge to gain fame and fortune. His picture appeared on postcards sold in the marketplace in Temuco, he participated in an annual folkloric music festival, he advertised his skills on the radio, and he appeared periodically on Chilean national television. Other male *machi* balanced these sorts of engagements with outsiders by also performing local communal duties, maintaining social etiquette, and abiding by some *machi* or Catholic traditions. Machi Abel, for example, sold Mapuche crafts to tourists and participated in folk festivals in Europe and Chile, but he also made flags and aprons for *machi* rituals. Jorge claimed that he was more traditional than other male *machi* because he worked from home rather than at intercultural hospitals, but he was less successful than others in working for the community's well-being.

As indigenous identity is redefined throughout Latin America in terms of knowledge rather than practices, outsiders increasingly recognize shamans as bearers of valuable knowledge and representatives of their people (Conklin 2002:1050–1051). Anthropologists sought out Jorge precisely because he was knowledgeable about Mapuche traditions and *machi* lore. He consulted at museums in Chile and the United States, and he agreed to have his initiation ritual filmed by anthropologists for a fee. Ironically, by paying Jorge as a consultant and identifying him as a representative of traditional Mapuche culture, anthropologists and foreigners inadvertently perpetuated local notions that he was a wealthy, individualistic witch. His community believed he was selling Mapuche identity along with people's bodies and souls. It was outraged when, in 2002, Jorge sold his old altar to a museum in the United States instead of leaving it in the river to rot, as is traditional.

As in all cultures, a structural and symbolic articulation exists between Mapuche individuals and the collectivity. Mapuche allow for individual identity, variation, and innovation among *machi,* as long as they are enacted within culturally determined possibilities for social action (Bacigalupo 1996b). Although the community had ostracized Jorge's family, once Jorge became "wealthy" it expected him to advocate for their well-being and to share his wealth through traditional norms of reciprocity and solidarity. Jorge wanted to be accepted as a prestigious *machi,* but the community held his questionable background against him and demanded more than he would give. Jorge realized he could gain more power and wealth by violating community norms and engaging with outsiders. His wealth and prestige outside the community gave him access to alleged *wingka* numinous powers and witchcraft that surpassed those of local Mapuche. Jorge believed that the authority he gained through his *wingka* connections would grant him the prestige that local Mapuche sociopolitical hierarchies did not.

Machi José: Conflicted Encounters with Spiritual Power

I first met José together with his friend Carlos, my host brother, in February 1992. Carlos and I approached two wooden huts. One of them was a kitchen with two adjacent bedrooms where José's parents and his two single sisters slept. José, his nephew, and his patients slept in the other hut. Outside, facing the kitchen door, was Jose's *rewe,* its four steps painted with blue and white stripes. José, a stout thirty-six-year-old with dark hair and inquisitive black eyes, came to meet us wearing jeans and a blue sweater. "I would like to come and talk to you about your life, your *machi* practices," I told him. He nodded and said: "And about God. You have to learn about God before the final judgment day . . . *Machi* cannot adore the *pillan* [ancestral or volcanic spirits], which are evil. *Machi* have to adore God exclusively; they cannot even go through the saints."

José had a personal interest in appearing in my book, because he believed God would judge him favorably for helping me. "They told me in a dream that you would write this in a passage among the pages of your book . . . and they told me that I would appear in a photo . . . If you do your work well, the same work that you do will be written in the sky . . . It will be like a bible about me." Like Michael Taussig's Colombian healers (1987:264), Jorge believed that the Bible and official books of Chilean law leaked magic into the hands of the people they dominated. He used the Bible to construct himself as Christian and civilized and to distance himself from the books on popular magic sold in the marketplace, which he viewed as satanic.

Like Machi Jorge, José was born into a poor family with no prestige in the community. When he became sick at the age of six, his parents, worried that he might die like his three younger brothers, had welcomed the help of a *naturista* (natural healing practitioner) who happened to drop by. José said: "He offered my father a *contra* so that we would not continue being ill, but he didn't know he would do me evil. He put a drop here on my nose, and since then every time I'm ill I relive that moment. Every time I want to pray to God, the smell comes back to haunt me."

Over the next twenty years José experienced what he described as "unknown spiritual illnesses located in the brain," the symptoms of which included fatigue, fever, headaches, dizziness, joint pain, insomnia, high blood pressure, and amnesia. Sometimes he attributed his long illness to the "evil" brought by the *naturista* and to "telepathic attacks" sent by other *machi* whom he felt he was fighting "psychologically." At other times he believed he had a *machi* calling and was granted powers directly from God: "The *machi* spirit came into my body at birth, but I didn't know it. When I was a child my eyesight would get foggy and I would begin to see red, green, and blue. This was my spiritual illness . . . the illness went to my blood, my head. I felt destroyed, oppressed . . . I had a strong desire to pray to God but didn't know how."

José went to the Catholic primary school and church in Quilmawe and by age twelve was using herbal remedies to heal others. He studied electricity and mechanics at the technical secondary school in Temuco but refused to do the practical training in order to complete his degree. He worked the land with his father until he came across *infitun* witchcraft—

rotten eggs and lamb guts buried in his fallow fields to render them infertile and a dead bird in the corral to make his animals sick. After this incident, his harvest was poor, many of his animals became sick and died, and José grew ill. In addition, his whole plantation of sugar beets "disappeared" one night in 1973, and José claimed his well was poisoned. He attributed these events to witchcraft practiced by neighbors who wanted to exterminate him and his family: "They bewitched us. First they wanted to destroy us economically and then morally."

José visited different health practitioners in the hope of exorcising the witchcraft and healing his shamanic illness. He was treated by Machi Claudia, by a *naturista,* by an evangelical priest, by a parapsychologist, by a psychiatrist, and by a gypsy. Each of these practitioners influenced his worldview but was unable to heal him (Bacigalupo 1994b:423–442). José began to have premonitory dreams about storms, catastrophes, and harvests, and he predicted the breakup of the Soviet Union. He also had a *machi* vision:

> The sky opened up and I saw a person riding a horse come down, and that person came to explain everything to me. About the different levels in the sky, about hell, everything. They came down with their secretaries and gave me two blue flags from the sky. There was a cassette that was functioning in the sky which reflected the earth on a screen . . . I spoke to the Holy Ghost. Then after that an angel came to inform me . . . I was lifted up to the sky. My spirit ascended and my body was left thrown there [on the floor] . . . I was protected by two guards who helped me from above.

José, again like Jorge, went through no *machi* training, but unlike Jorge, his *machi* powers were seen as legitimate. Machi Claudia considered his illnesses, dreams, visions, and herbal knowledge proof enough that he was a *machi* and initiated him in July 1991. José was in *küymi* for three days and learned all he needed to know from the Holy Spirit: "I felt so relieved. I was so uncomfortable before. I was almost crazy. I was psychiatrically uncontrolled, disturbed."

José's excessive use of the image of the Holy Ghost, his psychologizing of shamanism, and his obsession with evil cannot be understood in terms of traditional *machi* norms. His initial symptoms and imagery were close enough to those of other neophytes to have been considered a *machi* calling, but when he accused other *machi* of bewitching him, the community believed he was *wesa longko* (crazy) (Bacigalupo 1994b:423–442). By distinguishing between *machi* and psychotics and arguing, at first, that José's behavior was not shamanic but abnormal, Mapuche demonstrated that shamans are not ordinarily considered mentally ill from the local point of view.[2]

José's case also demonstrates the flexibility of Mapuche culture and shows how the classification of a person as normal or abnormal can change. Not only was he eventually accepted as a legitimate shaman, but, despite the similarities between his and Machi Jorge's backgrounds, José was never considered a witch because his Christian discourses resonated with Mapuche Catholic views.

After his second initiation as a biblical *machi* in May 1992, José changed his behavior and *machi* imagery to conform more closely to those of other *machi*. He planted a new *rewe* so that others would respect his *machi* practices and gained control over his *küymi* states. He also adopted the public persona of a *machi*. He no longer drank and danced in public. He began to invoke Ngünechen and nature spirits instead of the Holy Ghost in his rituals. This format was acceptable to his growing number of patients. His Catholic morality and his donations to Mapuche families in need increased his prestige. By 1995 José was one of the most popular *machi* in the area and was training three other men and three women to be *machi*.

The Gender Identities and Sexualities of Male *Machi*

FABIÁN [a *machi* initiate]: Male *machi* are not like other Mapuche men. They can't have positions in the community. They can't drink and get into fights. They can't have women, because it takes away their powers.

MARIELLA: Are male *machi* men?

FABIÁN: Of course they are men. They are special men, like priests who don't have a family because they dedicate themselves to God. Priests can't fight. They can't have women. But they are still men.

MARIELLA: Some Mapuche say male *machi* are more effeminate.

FABIÁN: The men who are chosen to be *machi* by the spirits of God have certain special faculties. They are sensitive, intuitive, like women. That is why they have to be more effeminate. More exquisite. Some male *machi* are homosexuals, but not all of them. Just like some priests are homosexuals, but not all of them . . .

RAMÓN [Machi Javiera's husband]: In ancient times there were *machi malleo* [co-gendered *machi*].

FABIÁN: What's *malleo?* Is it effeminate? Homosexual?

RAMÓN: Possibly. Most male *machi* are single, they don't get married, and they like men. It is an embarrassment to have a male *machi* in the family, because people talk. But sometimes God punishes one and so there is a male *machi* in the family or in the community.

MARIELLA: Why is it a punishment?

RAMÓN: Because they say they [male *machi*] like men . . . that's bad. How is a man going to like another man?

MARIELLA: Some Mapuche say they don't marry because they are like priests. Is this idea of their liking men true or gossip?

RAMÓN: They say that in part it is true. Because I once saw—and I won't say who—a male *machi* kissing another man, a taxi driver. Do you think that is normal? I don't think that is right. Kissing between men and women is fine, but not kissing between men.

FABIÁN: I have the spirit of a *machi,* but I'm not weird. I'm not homosexual. (Interview, December 27, 2001)

Contemporary Mapuche interpret male *machi*'s co-gendered identity through the lens of national perceptions of homosexuality in diverse ways. Machi Rocío, for example, in an interview in late 2001, explained that male *machi* inherit *machi* spirits from women on the mother's side of the family and that their gender performances become feminized in the process: "Male *machi* inherit the spirit of a grandmother *machi* and then they have to become like women . . . because they say that male *machi,* one month they are like men but another month they are like women. If they have a woman they have to sleep with the woman. They have to sleep with their patients. But female *machi* don't do that. They respect them." Longko Melinao agreed: "When men become *machi* they become more like women, and men don't like that . . . It is looked down upon, and that's why men avoid that profession." Rocío, too, claimed that male *machi*'s co-gendered ritual identity led them to desire both women and men. Ramón compared contemporary male *machi* who were "single and like men" with historically known co-gendered *machi,* whom he referred to as "*machi malleo.*"

But Rocío, Ramón, and Fabián also stressed that *machi* were men in their everyday lives. Fabián referred to male *machi* as "special men" chosen by the spirits, and Ramón constructed male *machi* as homosexual men. Rocío believed that male *machi* retained the "sexual appetite of men" and were sexually more active than female *machi.*

Mapuche sometimes distinguish between *machi*'s co-gendered ritual identities, effeminacy, transvestism, and homosexuality, and at other times they lump them together. Fabián characterized male *machi* as sensitive and effeminate. He believed that they should not have women because they would lose their powers, but that not all male *machi* were homosexuals. Ramón, in contrast, argued that being a *machi* was a punishment, because most of them were homosexuals. He used the term *homosexual* to refer to all same-sex practices by male *machi*. Mapuche also describe male *machi* as homosexuals to outsiders unfamiliar with co-gendered identities. Ramiro, a Mapuche intellectual, wrote me an e-mail message stating: "Just now a gringa came to see about the gender theme. She wanted to confirm with me if male *machi* were homosexuals. Imagine the bitterness I felt when I had to tell her that that was what it was" (July 16, 2002).

Mapuche often see male *machi*'s same-sex relationships as less homosexual than same-sex relationships between ordinary Mapuche men, because of *machi*'s co-gendered ritual identity. But sexual acts between a female *machi* and another woman are considered more acceptable than those between male *machi* and other men, because male *machi* are believed to perform the "passive" or "receptor" role.[3] Mapuche subscribe to the penetration paradigm and consider "receptor" males to be more homosexual than "inserter" males, who often retain their identity as machos. Like Fabián and Ramón, other Mapuche view all forms of homosexuality as abnormal and sexually deviant.

Male *machi*'s actual sexual practices are as varied as those of other Mapuche and non-Mapuche men. Some have male lovers, some female, some both; some remain celibate; and a few are married. Sexual acts between *machi* of either sex are taboo because they share a ritual co-gendered identity. Male *machi* are aware of the power dynamics involved in the labeling of sexual acts and gender performances. They do not assume a permanent homosexual identity, and they readily contest Mapuche or national readings of them as *maricones* or *homosexuales*. Male *machi* self-identify as masculine, heterosexual, or celibate men in their everyday lives, regardless of their gender performances and the sexual acts they perform with others.[4] By legitimating themselves according to national discourses of gender and sexuality, male *machi* attempt to avoid being labeled "marginal" and "deviant."

Sergio and José: The Celibacy Argument

Male *machi* protect themselves from accusations of effeminacy and homosexuality by identifying as married and heterosexual (two *machi* named

Pedro and Jacinto are examples) or as single and celibate like Catholic priests, as in the cases of Machi Sergio and Machi José. Because Sergio and José had had girlfriends in the past, most Mapuche viewed their decision to become celibate as the result of demands from their respective *machi* spirits rather than as cover-ups for same-sex desires. One Mapuche man, nevertheless, told me that Sergio was an effeminate homosexual who had secret relationships with men, like many Catholic priests.

Machi Sergio became vulnerable to spirit attack when one of his former girlfriends spurned him. He subscribed to the dominant Catholic male notion of woman as temptress and believed that his *machi* spirit had enabled him to renounce women. He thought his *machi* practice was incompatible with marriage:

> Before I became a *machi* I had a dream where I was walking up a path and naked women were beckoning to me, trying to tempt me. I looked at them and then continued on my path. This was a test that God had put to me . . . *Machi* must go around taking care of other people and love them like their own family . . . I can't have a family of my own. Can you imagine having kids and a wife and coming back late, or not at all? How could they grow up properly or be happy?

Machi José, similarly, had concluded that God did not want him to have a girlfriend, because he became ill when his high-school sweetheart cheated on him. Since then, he had viewed all women as deceitful, evil creatures, "like Eve," and had become celibate. He claimed that male *machi* should never marry:

> A priest does not marry, a monk does not marry. A good *machi,* who has more power than a priest, more power than a mother, more power than the pope, more power than a bishop, does not marry . . . The Bible says that a person who adores God should not marry. It is totally prohibited . . . Our ancestors in the time when the Bible was written were unmarried. Jesus did not marry. My inheritance comes from Noah and Jesus . . . I would like to have children but there are certain impositions that tell me "no." I have to work for God and for my fellow humans.

At the same time, in order to assert his heterosexual masculinity in his community and to dispel another rumor that he had a relationship with a young man, José did not try to disprove a rumor that I was his girlfriend.

Jorge: Sexual Ambivalence

The Mapuche imaginary often conflates the categories of *kalku* and *maricón* into one powerful but marginal being that travels at night to feed on the blood of others, seduce and pervert their bodies, and kill them. Mapuche *kalku* and *maricones* are created through the accusations of others, much in the way successful *machi* are created through praise. Mapuche often perceive *kalku* as perverse *machi* who, under the pretense of healing, use their powers and knowledge to bring illness and death to the community. Similarly, *maricones* are considered abject beings who pretend to be women but whose uncertain gender performances and sexuality lead them to seduce and destroy the identity of men. Because human identity is associated with standard forms of gender and sexuality, those who do not appear "properly" gendered have their sociality and humanity questioned (Butler 1993; Halberstam 1998). Chilean and Mapuche dominant notions read effeminacy, passive homosexuality, and transvestism as sexual deviance and link them with sorcery and perversion.

Mapuche, however, view persons who are sexually and morally ambivalent as even more threatening than sorcery-associated *maricones*. Although male *machi* who are labeled "*maricones*" may be considered "deviant" sorcerers, their actions and motives are predictable. *Machi* with changing sexuality and desires, who are believed to use both positive and negative powers, are the most feared by Mapuche, because it is unknown when they will strike. Machi Jorge was suspected of being this type of *kalku*.

Machi are supposed to have only one guiding spirit, but Machi Pamela claimed that Jorge worked with several and that his sex and sexuality changed with the moon. Like the Chilean majority, she saw anatomical sex as a guiding metaphor for sexuality. She associated Jorge's changing character with his shifting between good and evil spirits, between active and passive sexual roles, and between male and female sex organs: "When the moon is growing, then Jorge has a penis. When the moon is getting smaller, then he has a vagina. He changes. One month he has the spirit of a woman and another he has a spirit of a man. This is why he can [both] cure someone and do harm, and you never know when he is working with the *witranalwe* and when he is not . . . Chaw Dios does not like this kind of thing, *machi* with changing spirits, *maricones*."

In this context, Pamela used the term *maricón* to refer to Jorge's alleged deceitfulness and transgression of acceptable social identities. Jorge was male and female, man and woman, *kalku* and *machi*, passive and active, and he desired both men and women. Shifting sexuality was a sign of co-gendered divinity during colonial times but has come to be associated with witchcraft by seduction. Like Punkure and Punfüta, the nocturnal *wekufe* spouses, Jorge was thought to seduce men and women in their dreams, dominate their thoughts, and take their will. At those times, it was said, he called on the evil powers of the *witranalwe* and his blood-sucking child wife, the *añchümalleñ*. Jorge was also said to assume a passive sexual role with his male lovers but an active sexual role with female lovers in his everyday life. Jorge was once married and had a son, but in 1991 he claimed he was single and did not like to talk about his married life. A man from Jorge's community said: "His girlfriends never last him more than one month, then the next month he has a young guy living with him."

Because Jorge's relationships with men challenged conventional notions of masculinity, they were often read as witchcraft. Members of his community argued that he and his assistant, Dago, were lovers, although I was unable to assess whether this was really so. Jorge's family accepted his close relationship with Dago, but people within and outside of his community were critical of his alleged relationships with young men. Local Mapuche men assert their masculinity by boasting about being household heads, having many children, and drinking, and they joked about Jorge's alleged effeminate homosexuality. Jorge's transgression of acceptable male-male relationships infringed on their own sense of masculinity. Longko Daniel said, "We don't have anything against male *machi*. Sáez [a Mapuche man from a neighboring community] was also a *machi* at one time. He was sensitive, but not a *zas* [effeminate homosexual] . . . Jorge disparages us men. He changes from one sex to another. No one knows what to expect."

Outsiders, too, relied on Chilean national homophobic discourses to construe Jorge as deviant. A student working with Sandro, an anthropologist and old friend of Jorge's, drew on the notion that *maricones* were aggressive deviants in order to invalidate Jorge's healing knowledge: "I'm tired of his screaming at us. He makes us eat food we don't like and gets angry if we don't. On top of this, he's a *maricón*. What we are supposed to learn from him, I don't know." Sandro was one of the few people aside from Jorge's family who tried to understand his allegedly changing sexuality and view it in a positive light. Sandro drew on male *machi*'s sexual practices during colonial times to construct Jorge's sexuality as typically shamanic and therefore different from that of ordinary people: "People see *homosexualidad* as bad when it is practiced among 'normal' people, but the *machi* is essentially asexual, so there is no problem with this." Mapuche in general, however, criticize male *machi* for alleged effeminacy, passive homosexuality, or sexual ambivalence and sometimes associate them with sorcery.

The Ritual Transvestism and Gender Roles of *Machi*

One complex code through which male *machi*'s gender ambiguity is communicated is transvestism. Shamanic ritual transvestism does not necessarily translate into gender or sexual variance in a shaman's daily life. Numerous male shamans from Siberia, for example, including some Sakha, many Yukagir and Evenk, and some Ob-Ugrians, wear cloaks fashioned after women's dresses during their séances, even when they are far from being "soft men" in everyday contexts (Balzer 1996:169).

In Chile, male *machi*'s clothing and gender performances have been interpreted through multiple lenses. Some Mapuche view male *machi*'s ritual transvestism and womanly role as demands from the spirits, not as manifestations of effeminacy or homosexuality. Ramiro told me during an interview in December 2001: "Machi Jacinto is married and has children. He is like any man. People become scandalized when a *machi* wears women's dresses to work. That's the issue. Mapuche men make cruel jokes [about homosexuality] without thinking of the consequences." Other Mapuche view male *machi*'s transvestism as an indication of effeminate homosexuality. In order to protect themselves from this label, male *machi* remain only partially transvestite in ritual contexts and dress in men's clothes in everyday contexts. A *machi*'s marital status influences the way his clothing and gender performances are read. Married male *machi* are assumed to be heterosexual and can wear more women's clothes and perform more womanly tasks than single male *machi* without being viewed as effeminate or homosexual.

Dominant Chilean notions of manly gender performances have also influenced the way *machi*'s clothes are read by others. Ramiro told me that non-Mapuche coded all Mapuche traditional clothing as womanly: "In olden times Mapuche men didn't wear pants, they wore *chiripa*. Now, when men *machi* wear chiripa, people say they are wearing women's clothes. Chileans think that traditional Mapuche clothes are feminine. In order to be treated like a man one has to dress like a Chilean."

Male *machi* have tried to respond to these multiple expectations. Their practices involve a complex layering of Mapuche and Chilean signifiers of

Figure 7.I. Male *machi* dressed in everyday clothing with a head scarf and shirt (photo by Ana Mariella Bacigalupo).

masculinity, femininity, and ethnicity, orchestrated through the clothing of their bodies. In their daily lives male *machi* wear Western-style pants and hats and Mapuche men's *makuñ,* which mark them as masculine. Yet, their bright scarves and silver bracelets for warding off evil show them to be different from ordinary Mapuche men (Figs. 7.1, 7.2, and 7.3).

Male *machi*'s gender performances are indeed different from those of other Mapuche men. As boys, male *machi* rarely participate in national signifiers of masculinity such as fighting and playing soccer. Typically, *machi* spirits do not allow male *machi* to perform rural Mapuche men's tasks such as working the land, cutting wood, and doing wage labor. Nor do the spirits allow them to drink in public. Some Mapuche understand male *machi*'s special gender roles, whereas others criticize them for being effeminate because they do not perform "masculine" roles. Some Mapuche use the term *maricón* to refer to male *machi*'s effeminate gender performances, even though they do not see them as homosexuals. Paulina referred to Machi Abel as *mariquita* (little *maricón*) because he did not cut wood or work the land, although she believed that he liked women and would eventually marry. Male *machi* respond to such perceptions by performing some rural Mapuche women's roles, such as collecting and preparing herbal remedies and cooking, but avoiding others, such as

Figure 7.2. Male *machi* dressed in ritual clothing, which includes a chief's poncho, or *makuñ*, scarf, and feathers (photo bought at the market in Temuco).

Región de la Araucanía
Temuco - Chile

Figure 7.3. The author with male *machi* dressed in a chief's poncho, a scarf, and a *guaso*, or peasant hat (photo by unidentified Mapuche).

spinning, weaving, sewing, and making pottery, that would clearly mark them as effeminate.

Sergio: Priestly Robes

Sergio and I waited at the bus stop after two afternoon healing rituals. He wore men's pants, a Mapuche man's *makuñ* over a shirt or sweater, and a hat. His silver bracelet and the colored scarf around his neck signaled that he was no ordinary man. While he was healing that afternoon Sergio had worn multiple colored scarves around his neck and head, two *choyke* feathers in his hat, and a purple silk cape that he described as "priest robes." I asked him why he did not wear a *killa* during his rituals, as Machi Jacinto did. He responded: "I am like a priest. I wear traditional *machi* clothes that are like priests' robes. I don't wear women's clothes. I am not like *machi* Marta . . . She is really a male *machi* who wears a *chamal*. That is only for women." Male *machi* do not approve of exceptional male *machi* like Marta, who dressed in women's clothing every day and assumed the identity of a woman. By constructing his ritual clothes as traditional *machi* clothing or priestly robes, and not as women's clothes, and by criticizing Marta's transvestism and gender-crossing, Sergio distanced himself from possible rumors about his own effeminacy or homosexuality (for an in-depth discussion of Machi Marta, see Bacigalupo 2004a).

Sergio had not played soccer or fought while in high school: "I would see the boys my age run after the ball and I thought how dumb they were . . . I just didn't want anyone to yell or scream at me; I didn't want any fighting. I wanted peace and quiet." Now Sergio drank at home: "Being out of one's house makes it easier to have evil thrown at one, especially if one gets drunk. That's why I eat at home, and if I drink, I drink at home." He focused on the restrictions his *machi* spirit placed on him rather than reflecting on how tasks were gendered: "I can't do any physical work. I feel dizzy and faint. I have to keep my strength for curing. The other male members of my family plow the land." Sergio cooked occasionally and prepared herbal remedies, but he performed none of the other chores considered womanly.

Jorge: Transvestism as Sexual Ambivalence

Jorge was like a typical urban Chilean man in that he ran his household and was its main provider. His other family members performed domestic tasks, tended the animals, and worked the land. Jorge dedicated himself exclusively to his *machi* practice and performed neither men's nor women's chores. His drinking in public with other men did not enhance his masculinity. Other Mapuche viewed it as a transgression of his spiritual role, which reinforced the notion that he was a witch.

Jorge's masculine everyday clothes and his partial transvestism during rituals were read as signs of his changing sexuality, his moral ambivalence, and his engagement with both positive and negative spirits. Jorge wore men's pants, a sweater, a woolen *makuñ*, and a man's hat as everyday garb. During rituals he replaced the hat with colored kerchiefs and feathers, changed his *makuñ* for a women's shawl, and added a silver cross and bracelets to ward off evil. His ritual clothing was similar to Machi Sergio's and more masculine than Machi Jacinto's; the latter wore an altered version of a woman's *chamal* and a *killa* during rituals. Other Mapuche, however, interpreted Jorge's ritual clothing as effeminate, but not Jacinto's and Sergio's. Sergio avoided being labeled a homosexual by successfully constructing himself as a celibate priest and by drawing on his family's prestige. Jacinto avoided it because he was married, had children, and received the support of his community. Jorge's family, on the contrary, was marginal, and his community viewed him as sexually and morally ambivalent because of his alleged relationships with young men and his inability to construct himself according to socially acceptable men's roles.

José: Masculinizing Priestly Robes

At five o'clock on the morning of April 21, 1995, Machi José and I drove to the previously evangelical community of Chanco to perform the first collective *ngillatun* ritual held there since 1960. José borrowed my man's *makuñ* and tied a blue scarf around his neck. "You are not going to wear a *killa?*" I asked as I pinned my *killa* on over my black dress and flowered apron. "No," José replied, "they need to know that I am a Mapuche man with special powers. If I wear a *killa* like you or too many scarves, then people talk bad. They say male *machi* are like women. They need to learn to respect us. They need to understand that we [male *machi*] heal and give blessings like priests, like Jesus, with our *kultrun* and our prayers." In this context, José looked like a traditional Mapuche man.

Machi José masculinized and urbanized his everyday dress and manners to such a degree that it affected some Mapuche's belief in his ability to engage spirits. He wore a parka or leather jacket when he was in Temuco or Santiago: "I don't want them to look at me and know that I am a *machi* and that I am different." Julio, who later became José's *dungumachife,* remarked that "most people don't believe in male *machi* like José because they are not feminine enough."

José was like Sergio in that he had not played soccer in high school. But Mapuche viewed him as masculine because he worked the land and had undergone training to be an electrician and a mechanic—men's jobs in Chile—prior to his initiation. José justified leaving these masculine jobs by associating himself with Jesus: "Jesus Christ did not plow; he planted a spiritual seed. I must do the same." José was not accused of being homosexual although he remained single and often wore a *killa* and a purple head scarf during divinations. José believed that "alcohol is the devil" but, like other Mapuche men, drank at home with his family and friends.

Mapuche view male *machi*'s gender identity and sexuality ambivalently because of the tension between their spiritual and everyday roles and identities. Mapuche revere male *machi* as people chosen by the spirits yet criticize them if they abide fully by their spirits' demands that they wear women's clothing or engage in womanly roles. Mapuche may construct male *machi* as homosexuals and witches yet expect them to have some degree of sexual or gender variance, like priests, in order to be legitimate *machi*. If a male *machi*'s gender performance and sexuality are too masculine—as in José's case—then Mapuche may think he has lost his spiritual powers. Male *machi*'s clothing, gender performances, and sexual identity are balancing acts designed to satisfy the contradictory demands of Mapuche spirits and humans. The masculinity of male *machi*, however, depends not on their gender performances and sexualities alone but on their ability to construct themselves in prestigious, national, public male roles.

The Reinvention of Celibate Priests, Doctors, and Political Men

Chilean national discourses emphasize the division between effeminacy, domesticity, and *machi* practice, on one hand, and masculinity and prestigious public roles, on the other. Male *machi* challenge these notions by associating themselves with national male positions of prestige while retaining their status as traditional Mapuche practitioners. Male *machi* legitimate their co-gendered roles by identifying as celibate Catholic priests, and they masculinize themselves as prestigious doctors and political men.

Some male *machi* have productively inserted themselves into modern life by exercising a "moralistic Catholicized shamanism" (Chaumeil 1992:108), by experimenting with new shamanic forms inspired directly by modern medicine, and by engaging with Chilean presidents and their political ideologies. The predominantly male professions of priest, doctor, and politician carry great political weight in Chile, where religion, health, and politics go hand in hand. Former president Gen. Augusto Pinochet, for example, changed the Constitution in order to present himself as a legitimate president who promoted Christian values, and not as a military dictator. The Catholic Church has also exerted great influence over Chilean politics. Because of Catholic influence, abortion remains illegal, and divorce was legalized only in 2004.

Machi offer benefits to the population by challenging majority discourses and reinventing themselves in these prestigious public roles. With the privatization of the health-care system in 1981 and the impossible rise in prices of pharmaceutical remedies, many people who can no longer afford doctors have turned to *machi*. *Machi*'s holistic health-care system offers herbal remedies and rituals at reasonable prices. *Machi* compete with psychologists and priests in delivering advice about self-improvement, relationships, and spiritual and moral matters. Although male *machi* do not assume political positions of authority, they influence community decisions, identify with specific national political ideologies, and politicize their spiritual practices.

Mapuche Priests

The celibate Catholic priest is an acclaimed male authority figure in Chile who is neither heavily masculinized nor sexualized but holds social prestige. Male *machi* who reconstruct themselves as celibate Catholic priests hold moral authority and justify dedicating their lives to their spiritual calling.

Male *machi* perform *ngillatun* rituals on behalf of a ritual congregation in the same way priests conduct Mass. Machi Nora's son Jaime said: "The *ngillatun* is the same as the [Catholic] priests who have their church, only the Mapuche do their religion once every four years." Longko Daniel added: "Doing a *ngillatun* without a *machi* is like a mass without a priest, like an evangelical meeting without a pastor. There always has to be a *machi* to direct it." Sergio, José, and many other male *machi* officiated as *machi*-priests in the collective *ngillatun* ceremonies in their respective communities.

Machi Sergio adhered to a Catholic morality and performed his role as Mapuche priest accordingly: "I must dedicate myself to God and to prayer. God gives a little light and tells us to follow that path and you will find God, but all of this is guided by God." He believed that altruism, humility, penance, and forgiveness were crucial for *machi* practice. Sergio initiated three *machi* into his *machi* school of practice, which he viewed as a monastic order involving discipline and sacrifice. He expelled evil from patients' bodies and souls but did not denounce evildoers or practice ritual vengeance, because he believed that "those who wish evil on others only bring evil back unto themselves."

Sergio thought Catholicism was a complement to *machi* practice. He found great similarities between *machi* rituals and the Catholic Mass. He was never ordained, but he began conducting Mass in Mapudungu, together with the bishop, to pray for peace when Chile was on the verge of war with Argentina in 1978. In December 2001 he said: "The bishop still comes and invites me to go to Mass with him. He wants the Mass to be played with Mapuche musical instruments. I give people the host, I play my *kultrun* in the church." At the same time, Sergio used predominantly Mapuche symbols, not Catholic ones, when healing. He wore an archiepiscopal cross around his neck as a *contra,* to protect himself against evil spirits, but kept no images of saints, the Virgin, or Jesus in his house, nor did he invoke them for healing.

Machi José had wanted to be ordained as a Catholic priest. He received his First Communion in 1964 at the age of nine and visited the Catholic church in Quilmawe frequently. He read the Bible throughout high school and applied to enter the seminary at twenty-one but was rejected. The church caretaker threw him out, claiming he made the church dirty. José did not return to the church but instead began to draw on Mapuche notions of spirituality: "Our race has its own church. They are always trying to impose on us, saying that only the Catholic Church or the evangelical church is the real one, but no. God has the face of a Mapuche." José burned his crucifix because he opposed the use of Christian images, but he drew on the concepts of sin, heaven, hell, and divine punishment. He linked his own illness and suffering to that of Jesus Christ and drew on the Catholic doctrine of Christ as God and man. In this way he synthesized the paradox of divine spirit and human body.

By 1995 José was identifying himself as a "Mapuche priest" and "biblical *machi*," because he read the Bible and was possessed by the Holy Spirit. He rejected the church and its authorities but believed God had made him a Mapuche priest: "I have a lot of authority. I can baptize and marry people . . . nobody knows what God left me. Only I know." José believed he was superior to other *machi* because he read the Bible, and superior to priests because of his spiritual powers:

> A good *machi* like me has more powers than a Catholic priest, because they are chosen here on earth, they decide to take on that role . . . *Machi* come from the spirit world and are ordained directly by the creator of all of us. Our prayers are stronger. When have you ever seen that a Catholic priest can make it rain or stop raining? But a *machi* who prays in the *ngillatun* can, because God is in nature and listens to the *machi* . . . I am a true Mapuche priest. Not the kind that killed Jesus. (Interview, December 17, 1995)

Machi Jorge, too, claimed a priestly identity for himself, but not altogether successfully. He told journalists that he was "like a priest, an authority" (*Diario Austral,* September 27, 1987). But he was not celibate nor did he act like a priest. Jorge was not invited to perform as *machi*-priest in his community's collective *ngillatun* ceremonies, although he was often a paid performer at other ones.

Whereas José drew on Jesus as a model, Jorge viewed himself as the Mapuche Jesus Christ, which won him the reputation of being *agrandado*—superior, contemptuous, or arrogant. "I want to renew my powers the day Jesus was born. I am the Mapuche Jesus Christ," Jorge told me. He renewed his *machi* powers on Christmas Day and changed his four-step *rewe* for a larger, seven-step one to demonstrate that he was the most powerful and prestigious of *machi*. Jorge believed that his identification with the healing powers of Jesus would gain him respect and legitimacy in his Catholic community, but his neighbors could not reconcile his aggressive, authoritarian, and changeable character with that of a Jesus-like figure. One woman said: "It is a sin that he says he is Jesus. He is not God. Jesus was giving and sacrificed himself for his people. Jorge does none of this." Mapuche engage in direct, reciprocal relationships with spirits; they reject the idea of one powerful Mapuche messiah who represents the entire ethnic group and becomes the sole negotiator between Mapuche and the divine (Foerster 1993:145–147).

In sum, Sergio and José sought different types of legitimacy in their roles as "Mapuche priests." Sergio wanted the support of the church and the bishop, and he adapted his ritual practices to fit the format of the Mass. José despised the church and its authorities but believed he had spiritual and priestly power granted directly by God. Whereas Sergio embraced priests and priestly roles, José used the discourse of priesthood to gain recognition but believed that Mapuche spirituality was superior. Jorge—standing in contrast as usual—was not recognized in his priestly role because instead of seeking legitimacy from the church or the Bible he drew solely on his self-perceived experience as the Mapuche Jesus.

Medical Doctors and Priestly Healing

Male *machi* who identify themselves as doctors gain authority and prestige, masculinize their healing practices, and distance themselves from accusations of witchcraft associated with effeminacy. Some *machi* work with doctors in diagnosing the ailments of patients at intercultural hospitals (*El Sur,* March 14, 2002; *El Mercurio,* September 20, 2001). Manuel Lincovil, a *machi* working at the intercultural health center in La Pintana, a suburb of Santiago, said he could no longer handle the enormous flow of patients who came to see him, 80 percent of whom were nonindigenous (*Apples for Health* 2001). Machi Abel had so many patients that Chile's Internal Revenue Service (Servicio de Impuestos Internos, SII) wanted to tax his earnings.

But *machi* who become too much like doctors and impart healing knowledge in an authoritarian manner are also viewed as witches. *Machi* usually try to avoid such accusations by combining their medical practice with processual, empathetic, and involved healing techniques, which they associate with priestly behavior. Some of the healing practices of Sergio, Jorge, and José illustrate the way male *machi* draw on the ideologies and methodologies of medical doctor and priestly models.

SERGIO: RELATIONAL HEALING
AND CONSULTING ROOMS

Sergio attended to a steady stream of patients in rooms he rented at the archbishop's see in El Dorado on Fridays. He diagnosed patients' illnesses by looking at urine samples, a method called "*willentun.*" I talked to his patients about their ailments and observed some of their diagnoses. Sergio treated local Mapuche and non-Mapuche farmers, mestizo housewives, and landowners of German descent who came seeking respite from a variety of physical, social, and spiritual illnesses. He switched back and forth between Spanish and Mapudungu and between traditional

Figure 7.4. Patients waiting in a *machi*'s consulting room modeled on that of a doctor's office (photo by Ana Mariella Bacigalupo).

Mapuche, Catholic, and biomedical models to accommodate the linguistic preferences and cognitive frames of his patients.

Sergio admired medical doctors' power and modeled his "consulting rooms" in different towns on those of a doctor's office (Fig. 7.4). Patients awaited their turn in a waiting room. Sergio gave them bottles of herbal extracts from the Mapuche pharmacy or dried herbs, and he advised others to buy Western pharmaceutical drugs such as antibiotics, anti-inflammatories, and painkillers to complement his herbal medicines. He learned about medicinal herbs through dreams and also read medical journals.

But Sergio's healing strategies differed from those of doctors in some important ways. Doctors send urine samples to be analyzed at a laboratory, whereas Sergio used them for holistic divination. Sergio had no biomedical training and brought herbal remedies (as extracts or dried herbs) for common ailments to his consulting room for patients to prepare at home. His fee for diagnosis was 4,000 pesos (US$6.00), but his patients paid according to their means. Sergio criticized medical doctors for being unable to divine the cause of illness and for the depersonalized treatment and lack of spirituality in the practice of biomedicine:

Hospitals often make people worse . . . Doctors don't allow [people] to heal gradually, surrounded by friends and family . . . and don't measure the side effects of the remedies they give to patients . . . Doctors learn their knowledge through books, not through spirits, as *machi* do. *Machi* know things mentally because of God's gift . . . When I treat a patient I follow everything—his life curriculum, we could say—what she is like, why he is ill. All of those things *machi* know . . . *Machi* don't ask you: "How are you? What hurts?" But if you go to the doctor, you have to say: "It hurts me here," and then the doctor draws a conclusion . . . I wonder if doctors are mentally praying for that body they are operating on?

Most of Sergio's patients were women. He had a good reputation for healing what he called "women's illnesses," including menstruation problems, symptoms of menopause, and ovarian cysts. I brought Sergio my urine sample to diagnose; I had been experiencing dizziness, headaches, cramps, and inflammation of the bladder and ovaries. He shook the bottle and held it up to the light seeping through the window: "You have to look at everything: color, consistency, clarity [of the urine], the patient's personality, the illness, the situation—it all comes through." He linked my physical symptoms to three locally recognized illnesses—chills, nerves, and women's illnesses. He related these illnesses, in turn, to my emotional state, which he diagnosed as undecided, scared, and fragile.

"You have nothing serious," he said. "You do not have evil. You have to drink 'tea for women' and *alwe lawen* for nerves. For your cramps take eucalyptus leaf baths. This herb, *chilka (Baccharis glut)*, is for menstruation, and this one, chamomile, is for chills." Then he advised: "You have to be surer of yourself. With time you are going to have luck in everything . . . There is a power that helps you a lot, and prayer will help it stay this way, but you have to pray."

Sergio believed in the power of the mind, heart, and spirit and in the need to empathize and suffer with his patients: "As a *machi* you cannot abstract yourself from your patients . . . You have to suffer spiritually. You have to put your mind there and work, fight . . . it is more mental than medicinal." At the same time, he expected his patients to be involved in their own healing and destiny: "Patients also have to put their *piuke* and *rakiduam* into the healing process for it to work . . . You, Mariella, have to say: 'I will finish this work no matter how difficult.' And you can do it if your mind and your heart are on it . . . It will all fall into place."

Sergio also focused on the relationships between patients and their families in his healing. He made patients recognize their own faults, forgive others, and find ways to resolve social conflicts. His treatment of Emilia, who was experiencing witchcraft, domestic violence, and boils on her arms, illustrates this:

SERGIO: You feel dizzy. You have headaches. You think you are pregnant but you are not. Are you having problems with your husband?

EMILIA: He screams at me. The other day he gave me a black eye.

SERGIO: Someone in the family is sending you evil. There is a *kalkutun*. I have remedies against witchcraft. You can take *ruda, foye* . . .

EMILIA: He has a woman. She did love magic on him. They are both trying to poison me [*illeluwün*, or poisoning with food].

SERGIO [ignoring Emilia's love magic hypothesis]: Do you want to work things out with your husband or not?

EMILIA: I don't know.

SERGIO: When did you grow apart? Why?

EMILIA: About six months ago. We had money problems.

SERGIO: What was your fault in this?

EMILIA: I was angry because we never had money. He came home late.

SERGIO: He was wrong to hit you but you also have some fault in this fight. You constantly throw in his face that he doesn't make money. You suspect him . . . The herbal remedies will make you better for now, but if you want this to turn out, you have to put in your own effort. You have to be more gentle, lady. I put the remedies, but you must put your heart into this.

Sergio and I visited the small, dark house in Rucalikan where Emilia lived with her husband, Patricio, and her parents. Sergio began with a *sahumerio.* He sprinkled firewater and ammonia around the house, and Emilia followed him with a pan containing burning leaves of eucalyptus, *foye,* and absinthe. Sergio told Emilia and Patricio that they needed to talk and perform a *sahumerio* every Saturday. Emilia believed that Patricio had been won by his lover through love magic—a type of witchcraft involving the manipulation of human sentiment. By blaming the witchcraft on a family member and not on Patricio's lover, Sergio took some of the pressure off the couple's relationship. Sergio also made them combat the witchcraft together and participate actively in their own healing.

Sergio also focused on how Emilia and her family could change their attitudes in order to better themselves. "You can't be like this," he chided Emilia. "You have to give without expecting anything in return. Find ways to help your family. If you give with the heart and the mind, God will return to you ten times over." Sergio did not believe in love magic, which is practiced mainly by female *machi,* and made Patricio accountable for his actions: "You have a good wife. Treat her well. You have to support her. Find a good job and leave that other woman. God will reward you."

Sergio acknowledged the double standard for women and men in Chilean society but counseled Emilia and Patricio to act within their gendered social roles. Emilia should acknowledge her fault in the conflict and forgive her husband in order to save her marriage. Patricio should act according to Sergio's expectations of married men by providing for his family, supporting his wife, and leaving his lover. Sergio was like a Peruvian *curandero* in that he reinforced patriarchal ideologies but also helped women gain moral leverage within the system (Joralemon and Sharon 1993:268) and made patriarchal authority conditional (Glass-Coffin 1998:183). He believed that social norms and order were linked to the moral order established by God. Emilia and Patricio suffered from conflict and witchcraft because they had transgressed their gender roles, and they needed to embrace them again in order to regain their health.

Sergio masculinized his practice by drawing on the models of the priest and the doctor. Like a priest, he stressed the patient's self-improvement and forgiveness as required for healing to work, and he opposed witchcraft, ritual revenge, and love magic. He linked the doctor and the priest models by renting a "doctor's" consulting room while highlighting the advantages of holistic healing over medical treatments and hospital care. Sergio demonstrated that male *machi* were unlike ordinary men in that they had special insights into women's illnesses and problems and could heal them by using an empathetic, relational model and abiding by the gendered constraints of the social system. At the same time, he demonstrated that male *machi* were different from female *machi* by rejecting love magic.

JORGE: AUTHORITARIAN HEALING AND RITUAL REVENGE

A long line of patients stood holding urine samples and waiting to be diagnosed by Jorge on a Tuesday morning. Using authoritarian, goal-oriented strategies, he treated a large number of Mapuche from outside his community, as well as *wingka* patients. Jorge was quick, efficient, and assertive in diagnosing illness in an attempt to gain the authority attributed to medical doctors and to legitimate and masculinize his healing. He put as many as three urine samples on the steps of his *rewe* at once and diagnosed one patient's ailments while the others waited. Then he took each patient separately into his *ruka* to talk with him or her privately.

Jorge made little effort to soften his medical-doctor style. Sometimes he behaved quite aggressively with patients. I watched him diagnose the illness of a middle-aged Mapuche woman. He stared at her urine sample. "Have you gone to the doctor about this?" he asked.

"No," answered the women timidly.

"That is a lie," Jorge screamed. "I can see it in the urine."

The woman stuttered nervously: "I did go to the doctor a long time ago, but I'm not going anymore."

This incident convinced her of Jorge's foresight and powers. Jorge viewed his patients as victims of illness and witchcraft whose healing depended on his powers and knowledge. This contrasted with Sergio's approach, in which patients were active agents who took responsibility for their actions and participated in their own healing. Jorge's neighbors, however, did not view his assertive healing strategies as masculine or typically shamanic. They considered Sergio's Catholicized morality and his empathetic, relational approach to his patients as typical of male *machi* and Jorge's aggressive healing strategies as typical of witches.

Jorge called himself a *machi,* a "spiritual doctor," and treated Mapuche and *wingka* patients in either Mapudungu or Spanish. He received only patients he felt he could cure and sent those who had serious physiological problems to the hospital. Jorge had undergone formal training as a nurse and believed his experience in the two medical systems masculinized him and gave him an advantage over other *machi.* Many of Jorge's patients were uncertain about whether they were suffering a spiritual illness, a physiological illness, or both, and Jorge drew on both medical systems in diagnosing them. He gave his patients herbal remedies, injections, and antibiotics and performed *datun* rituals for both Mapuche and *wingka.*

Being a nurse and seeing *wingka* patients caused Jorge problems among Mapuche fundamentalists. An old man from his community said: "He is ridiculing our traditional religious system and way of curing. He is either a doctor or a *machi,* but not both. This cannot be. He also attends to so many *wingka*. This is not right. A *machi* should attend to Mapuche first." Jorge's intercultural healing at home contrasted with the practices of Machi José, who worked at an intercultural hospital but gave priority to Mapuche epistemologies and methodologies over those of biomedicine.

Jorge became unpopular in some surrounding communities, too, for bringing his own helpers when he performed *datun* rituals there instead of asking people from the patient's family to participate. The participation of people from the patient's household and community, who offer care and support, is crucial for healing in these holistic rituals. By breaching traditional, collective, holistic models of healing, Jorge created an impersonal model similar to that of medical doctors, which increased people's suspicions that he practiced witchcraft. Machi Pamela said: "He came to this community to cure a person and he brought all his own helpers. Nobody from here could go in. Why is that? When I cure people I allow anyone to come and help send the [evil spirits] away. If he didn't have something to hide, he would allow other people to participate."

Jorge's herbal remedies were thought to be powerful but dangerous. To test their effectiveness, Sandro, his anthropologist friend, once asked him for an infusion that would make him urinate. At first the remedy had no effect. But when he left the jar sitting for a few days and drank the gel at the bottom, his whole body accelerated. "I almost had a heart attack," he said.

Jorge was believed to manipulate the herbal remedies he gave his patients in order to convince them of his powers. Sandro observed Jorge giving a patient remedies that made the patient feel worse and, a few days later, the real remedy, meant to cure the illness. As the patient felt the contrast between these two states, he was convinced of Jorge's curing powers. Machi Fresia commented: "A *machi* like Jorge who does not work with just one spirit can manipulate patients. He can give them remedies to make them better for a while, charge them lots of money, and then they will feel bad again, but in the long run people will realize and leave him."

Jorge was one of the few *machi* who acknowledged that they performed ritual revenge, an older Mapuche practice in which *machi* reveal the name of an evildoer and offer to retaliate against him or her. Because this practice is highly antisocial, it contributed to Jorge's being accused of witchcraft. Like most other *machi,* Jorge considered a patient's family background, social relationships, and incidents preceding the illness crucial for understanding the cause of an illness and finding a cure. In treating an illness, he passed judgment on the patient and other members of the community and gave advice. Unlike Sergio and José, Jorge came up with a culprit and a reason for the evildoing and offered his services to "return the evil to the person who sent it." When Jorge said someone was the evildoer, his word usually confirmed community gossip and family interests. Jorge's patients sought his services to avenge themselves on alleged evildoers.

Jorge's community associated his practice of ritual revenge with witchcraft and sexual deviance. One of his healing rituals—for a twenty-four-year-old Mapuche man whose eighteen-year-old wife had died of pneumonia just a year after their wedding—was construed in this way. The widower was upset and became ill. He went to Jorge to be healed and to find out why his wife had died so suddenly. Jorge went to stay at the patient's house. According to community gossip, Jorge told the patient that he had to have sex with him in order for the cure to work, which the patient did. Jorge found out that the widower had a long-standing land conflict with a neighboring aunt. He told the patient that his aunt had hexed him and his wife, hoping they would both die so that she could keep their land. He offered to take ritual revenge. He asked Sandro to take a photograph of the aunt and give it to him, but Sandro refused, fearing he might use it to hex the aunt. Jorge believed that, by practicing ritual revenge, he allowed his patients to gain some control over *wekufe* spirits and evildoers.

Other *machi* in the area constructed Jorge's ritual revenge as witchcraft. Machi Nora held a Catholic, moralistic perspective and condemned Jorge for drawing on an older, dualistic Mapuche worldview, in which both good and evil had a place, in order to practice ritual revenge. Machi Marta, who practiced ritual revenge herself, labeled Jorge's particular form of practice "witchcraft": "Jorge himself sends evil to people because he wants them to be ill. He came here to play his *kultrun* at night. That is bad. Several people died shortly after because of the evil he sent them."

Jorge effectively masculinized himself as a doctor outside of his community, but within it his authoritarian healing strategies and practice of ritual revenge were viewed as witchcraft associated with homosexuality. These accusations never became a threat to Jorge's well-being, however, because he was feared in his community and had the support of Mapuche and *wingka* from outside who had faith in his healing strategies and benefited from his knowledge of traditional lore.

JOSÉ: SPIRITUAL HEALING AND A DOCTOR'S PRESTIGE

Machi José believed that Mapuche and Western medicine complemented each other, and he borrowed metaphors from one system to describe the other. He had no training in biomedicine but labeled himself a "spiritual doctor" who "operates spiritually." He believed that "doctors are ordained in the sky," as he was. José considered himself like medical doctors and unlike other *machi* in that he had a specific medicine for every physical illness, according to its location in the body: "I have different remedies for thirty-five illnesses—the gallbladder, the kidney, the liver, the lung, the heart, the blood, the head, stomach pains." He did not imitate the doctor's consulting room, as did Sergio and several other male *machi*, but in 1994 he began working with doctors at the intercultural hospital at Antümalal. José believed he was superior to medical doctors in diagnosing and treating spiritual illnesses: "Doctors don't know how to diagnose spiritual illness. And for this kind of illness, pills and injections can kill you." José did not use pharmaceutical remedies and claimed to have "special spiritual recipes" for cancer and AIDS.

José also drew on the priestly model and emphasized the roles of God and spirits in healing and illness, which protected him from accusations of witchcraft: "I can see the power that God gave me in the urine, in the clothes, in the blood, and in the heart. The heart suffers to adore God. Sometimes one does not realize, and we take remedies to lower blood pressure when, in fact, the error is that we have not adored our Father." José believed that all evangelists were possessed by the devil and needed to be exorcised.

Patients lined up outside José's house every morning, waiting for him to diagnose their illnesses by taking their pulse, looking at their urine samples, or drumming on top of clothing they had worn (*pewuntun*). Like Sergio, José instituted a standard fee of 4,000 pesos (US$6.00) for divinations but charged his patients only what they could pay for healing rituals.

One of José's specialties was exorcising evil spirits. He gave herbal *contra* medicine to patients poisoned with *fuñapue* and evil-spirit possession to make them vomit. José could see who had visited evil on a patient or family, but he did not reveal the identity of the evildoer, take ritual revenge, or perform love magic; he considered these practices to be witchcraft. He treated Deborah from Santiago, who had been diagnosed with lupus and also had evil spirits in her house: "She's bloated like a frog. She has been hexed and she is very angry," José told me.

Deborah complained: "I have such pain. The pain moves from one side of my body to another like a ball and bloats me . . . my head rings like a bell."

"That's the evil," José interjected.

Deborah continued: "There is an evil spirit that makes noises on my roof. It doesn't let me sleep. The other day the kitchen cabinet fell down. No explanation. Then a big bunch of worms fell from the roof. My house is possessed by the devil." She started to cry.

"Calm down. Now you are here in the south you will feel better. But you must have faith. And you should continue to go to the doctor. I need his help. First, you need to take the medicine I give you. Then I will go to Santiago and heal you and your house."

José's *datun* rituals focused on exorcising evil spirits and reestablishing good relationships among patients, their families, and their communities. José described eighteen-year-old Rodrigo's body as "hot" with witchcraft, which had spread to the whole family. One of Rodrigo's brothers had died, and they had heard the call of the evil *chon-chon* bird at night.

One evening at Rodrigo's home, José sharpened his knife to fight evil spirits and asked God for permission to heal the family. Rodrigo lay face up on a sheepskin on the kitchen floor, wearing only his shorts. His mother placed *foye* trees in pots at his head and feet. José rubbed the blunt side of his knife down Rodrigo's arms, legs, and face to cut the spiritual knots that tied the family to evil spirits. He rubbed Rodrigo with steaming herbs and then beat his *kultrun* loudly and circled the inside and outside of the house to exorcise evil spirits. We followed him, hitting the roof and the walls of the house with bamboo canes and screaming "¡¡Ya ya ya!!"

Jorge entered into *küymi* and revealed that a distant family member had hexed the family because he was envious of the things they could buy. This person had thrown a hexed piece of meat over the fence, which had made Rodrigo ill. José told the family to wear red yarn as *contras* and to help the community by acting to stop a housing project and prevent Mapuche from selling their land. Rodrigo's mother later dreamed that she had wrested the knife from a man who attacked her. When he was transformed into a chicken, she wrung his neck. She interpreted this as proof that the witchcraft had been exorcised.

José legitimated his practice by constructing himself as a masculine spiritual healer who merged the roles of doctor and priest. Like priests, he exorcised evil spirits, viewed evangelical practices as devilish, and believed in forgiveness. Like doctors, he had remedies for illnesses that affected specific body parts. Unlike Jorge, José worked with doctors in intercultural healing, offering spiritual recipes for physical illness. José's healing model was less authoritarian than Jorge's but more hierarchical than Sergio's. He focused on the power of God to heal others rather than on patients' self-betterment. But he did not view himself as the source of power and knowledge, as Jorge did, and was not tagged as an authoritarian witch.

HEALING STRATEGIES AND GENDER

Bonnie Glass-Coffin (1998:163, 185) characterizes the healing strategies of male shamans on the north coast of Peru as combative, depersonalized, and goal oriented. She argues that sympathetic healing techniques that are processual, relational, and involved are typical of female shamans. She views qualities such as acceptance, penance, illumination, and determination as characteristic of a "mothering model for healing," in which female shamans empower their patients by awakening their possibility for agency instead of victimhood (194). Similarly, Barbara Tedlock (2005:167, 169) describes male shamans embracing conflict and confrontation and female shamans using compassion, conciliation, and compromise to develop the healer-patient-plant relationship.

The cases of Sergio, Jorge, and José show that relational and authoritarian healing strategies among *machi* in Chile are linked not to gender but to a *machi*'s personal characteristics and practices. Sergio was the most empathetic and relational of the three, Jorge the most authoritarian, and José somewhere in between. Furthermore, male *machi* view the qualities that Glass-Coffin associates with mothering models as typical of priestly models. Mothering and priestly models draw on specific types of gendered roles to legitimate shamans' practices, but they do not reflect the qualities or healing strategies of women and men as a whole. The only healing strategy exclusive to female *machi* is love magic. Male *machi* either view love magic as witchcraft (José) or do not believe that human sentiment can be manipulated (Sergio and Jorge).

Male *machi* who are able to balance masculine doctor roles and co-gendered priestly ones effectively legitimate themselves without threatening their healing practices. Male *machi* gain prestige as spiritual doctors who know about pharmaceutical remedies and have consulting rooms. But they distance themselves from medical doctors' inability to divine, heal spiritual illness, and practice holistic healing. Male *machi* priests engage in relational healing strategies, exorcise evil spirits, and focus on spirituality and the healing power of God. Jorge's practice of ritual revenge was associated with witchcraft because it was the opposite of the priestly practice of forgiveness. Mapuche view male *machi* such as Jorge, who overdo the masculinity and authoritarianism of the doctor's role, as witches, and they see those who do not construct themselves as doctors at all as effeminate.

Spiritual Warriors and Political Ideologies

In Chapter 5 I show that colonial *machi weye* invoked Mapuche warriors to conduct spiritual warfare against the souls of Spaniards and that *machi*'s spiritual warfare was reduced to rituals and games once the Chilean state defeated the Mapuche and placed them on reservations in 1884. I argue that, during the nineteenth and twentieth centuries, Mapuche viewed *machi*'s spiritual roles as effeminate and antithetical to the male political position of *longko*. Contemporary male *machi* rarely take on positions of political authority, but they challenge the notion that male *machi* are apolitical and unmasculine by performing some local political functions in their communities and by participating in national political movements. *Machi* of both sexes hold spiritual, moral, and judicial authority, and to the extent that they represent the forces of good and control the forces of evil on behalf of the ritual community, they play a political role. *Machi* legitimate local community events, conflicts, and political processes as well as the authority of *longko* (Dillehay 1985).

Most Mapuche expect male *machi* to define themselves in terms of national political ideologies and to engage with political authorities primarily through such ideologies, as other Mapuche men do. Since the advent of democracy in 1990 under a civilian government, Mapuche men have increasingly aligned themselves along national political party lines and subscribed to party ideologies. Ideology is closely tied to the concept of power and refers to "shared ideas or beliefs which serve to justify the interests of dominant groups" (Giddens 1997:583). Most male *machi* define themselves along political party lines and participate in political events only with authorities with whom they share a political ideology. Mapuche view male *machi* who do not voice their political ideologies as effeminate.

Male *machi* link spiritual warfare to priestly roles as well as to the roles of masculine doctors, political movements, and military authorities. *Machi* spiritual warriors exorcise evil spirits as priests do, defeat bacteria and viruses as doctors do, and support political regimes and Mapuche resistance movements. Most male *machi* endorse the idea of a Mapuche nation with its own territory and self-government and celebrate the restoration of Mapuche communal land.[5] But they have different notions of the type of government that would be compatible with Mapuche nationalism. Sergio, Jorge, and José read their own enactments of the spiritual warrior through diverse political ideologies.

SERGIO: SYNTHESIS OF MILITARY AND SPIRITUAL AUTHORITY

Sergio was exceptional among *machi* in that he linked spiritual power with social inheritance and local political influence. Whereas most *machi* obtain their spiritual powers from their mother's side of the family, Sergio obtained his from his paternal uncle. He inherited his oratorical ability from his paternal grandfather, who was both a *longko* and a *ngenpin*. His *machi* spirit expressed intergenerational continuity. As Sergio put it, his ancestors had transformed his body (the locus of experience), his heart (the locus of emotion), and his head (the locus of thoughts and knowledge) in order to make him a powerful *machi* who understood the essence of life. His ancestors made "what is said" (words, oratorical ability) and "wisdom" (*machi* lore, tradition) "go forward," or become effective, in Sergio's rituals. At the same time, Sergio viewed his spiritual practice as incompatible with positions of political authority. He was not a *longko*, although he was influential in local decision-making.

Sergio found the military manly, appealing, and powerful. After he finished high school, he joined the army as a cook, but his *machi* spirit seized his body, making him ill so that he would abandon the military to become a *machi*. He recounted: "I told them: 'I have a *machikutran*. I have to go and get my remedies, and when I become a *machi*, then I will come and see you.' Then, when I became a *machi*, I went back to San Fernando [to the army base]. 'Now I'm a *machi*,' I told them. 'You were so agitated when you left,' they said. 'And now you come as a *machi*.' They admired me very much."

Sergio had a paradoxical relationship with spiritual and military authority. On one hand, he and his *machi* spirit viewed military service as incompatible with spiritual practice. Acceding to his *machi* spirit's will, he had challenged the military authority he found so appealing in order to accept the moral responsibility of being the next *machi* of his lineage and community. At the same time, he used physical discipline and images of military rank in his *machi* practice. He flogged his initiate Fabián because he did not listen to Sergio's instructions. Sergio also liked the military aesthetic. "Those in the military parade are so good-looking," he commented once as we looked at photographs of him and his mates parading in uniform.

Sergio resolved his paradox by synthesizing spiritual and military practice in his role as spiritual warrior. He believed the military was the representative of God—like priests—and that he was a warrior of God, akin to Jesuit soldiers of Christ, who killed evil beings. One of Sergio's friends who shared his perception told him: "You are doing well, my brother. God is taking care of you, because I saw you surrounded by military in my dream. You were standing in the middle. They were watching you, taking care of you. Nothing will happen to you." Sergio's synthesis of spiritual and military roles enabled him to volunteer for military action despite being a *machi*: "When Chile almost went to war with Argentina and there were trenches and tunnels here down south, I was ready to volunteer to fight for my general, Pinochet, and our country, Chile."

Sergio actively supported Pinochet during his public appearances between 1973 and 1989. Sergio was periodically invited to the presidential palace and was an honored guest when Pinochet visited the Araucanian region. He believed that Pinochet upheld Mapuche traditions, and he viewed himself as a representative of the nation-state run by Pinochet. He associated the blue stars and red suns painted on his *kultrun* with those of the Chilean flag: "There is not a prettier flag than the Chilean one . . . We all struggle for this country that is Chile."

Sergio associated Pinochet's military prowess with that of masculine, colonial Mapuche warriors, whom he invoked to exorcise evil spirits. He believed that spiritual warfare was typical of male *machi* and that his performances were more effective than those of others because he had Pinochet's support. Mapuche consider spiritual warfare to be a masculine strategy, but it is practiced by both male and female *machi*. Ana and Pamela killed evil spirits with gunshots, and Machi Edmunda saw a vision of a horse with a golden saddle standing in a pond as part of her *machi* calling.

Machi who use military images to exorcise evil spirits do not always support military regimes. Fifty-year-old Machi Pedro, who opposed Pinochet, viewed his *machi* spirit as a powerful warrior mounted on a horse with silver reins, stirrups, and breastplate. Sergio linked Mapuche ancestral spirits with Pinochet to justify his support for Pinochet's authoritarian ideology.

Sergio believed that the Mapuche's situation worsened after the return to democracy under presidents Aylwin (1990–1994), Frei (1994–2000), Lagos (2000–2006), and Bachelet (2006–2010). He refused to attend events involving democratic presidential candidates, even when Mapuche friends asked him to go: "Of the Chilean presidents, Pinochet was the best . . . I do not get involved with the politics of the new government [of President Lagos]. I no longer go to La Moneda [the presidential palace]. They no longer invite me, either. I don't want the government to manipulate me. Before, my General Pinochet helped Mapuche and listened to them. Now there are only fights. The people from CONADI come and say: 'This land belonged to your ancestors and we are going to give it to you,' but nothing happens" (interview, December 30, 2001).

Sergio believed that Mapuche should resist the modernist neoliberal projects of the nation-state under the contemporary democratic regime, but he did not conduct spiritual warfare against it. He argued that the

Mapuche should become an independent nation with political and territorial autonomy. Ignoring the existence of 800,000 Mapuche city dwellers, he invoked a romanticized idea of the return to an original rural Mapuche homeland. In an interview in December 2001, he said: "The Mapuche protests against building the dams in Quinquen and Alto Bio-Bío are good. When the Mapuche want to put a little pressure on, they can. It would be good for the Mapuche nation to have its own territory here in the south and not in the city. There should be a Mapuche mayor governing this territory, because this is our land of origin."

Sergio did not support the leaders of Mapuche resistance movements. He believed they promoted a socialist agenda instead of attending to Mapuche interests, which he believed were more compatible with those of authoritarian regimes: "Some Mapuche are not so bright and allow themselves to be manipulated. This Wilkaman guy [the head of the Mapuche resistance movement Consejo de Todas las Tierras], he does not represent the Mapuche, and he allowed himself to be manipulated by the socialists" (interview, December 30, 2001).

JORGE: THE MISUSE OF POLITICAL POWER

Jorge had no experience in the military, but he, too, supported Pinochet's authoritarian regime and the imposition of power. Authority and power are associated with manliness in national discourses, but Mapuche view individual misuse of authority as violating norms of sociality and egalitarianism and therefore as associated with witchcraft. Jorge violated the notion that male *machi* should not take on political positions. When the king of Spain visited Chile in 1990, Jorge misconstrued himself as "official representative of the Mapuche people," although Mapuche have no system of centralized authority. At that time Jorge also gave a Senate candidate the title of *longko*.

Many Mapuche were outraged at Jorge's actions. Ramiro, a Mapuche intellectual, remarked: "He had no right to do that. No one can call himself the official representative of the Mapuche. He has no right to give anyone the title of *longko*. Those are traditional community positions." Longko Daniel, from a neighboring community, added: "Many different communities are angry at what Jorge has done. But for money and fame, Jorge does anything. He really ruined his reputation among the Mapuche because of that" (interview, November 4, 1991).

The only other male *machi* I met who assumed a political position of authority was Machi Víctor, who stood as a candidate for mayor of Carahue. Víctor and Jorge were heavily criticized by their communities for assuming political positions that were viewed as conflicting with their spiritual roles. Female *machi*, however, would not have been allowed to present themselves in these positions in the first place.

Jorge worsened his reputation among Mapuche when he threatened some police officers with retaliation from General Pinochet. Jorge viewed Pinochet as a powerful military man and witch and linked his *machi* powers to Pinochet's powers to intimidate others.[6] Whereas Sergio admired Pinochet as head of the military and associated him with the spirits of colonial military authorities, Jorge viewed Pinochet as a military patron who would use his power to override police authority and conduct spiritual warfare against his personal enemies. When Jorge was arrested for public drunkenness in 1991, he told the police that, if he was not released immediately, Pinochet would avenge him. Jorge's community construed his threat as another example of the arrogance and misuse of power that characterizes witches loyal to outsiders and authoritarian governments.

JOSÉ: DEMOCRACY AND MAPUCHE RESISTANCE

Machi José opposed Pinochet's military regime and did not find secular military authority to be manly or appealing. Unlike Sergio, José believed that Pinochet was a witch who censured Mapuche traditions and abused *machi*. "Pinochet didn't respect *machi*," he said. "He had several *machi* shot on the bridge, and they were thrown into the river. During the dictatorship the person didn't count. It is not like in a democracy, where one has the right to speak. During the dictatorship they said one thing and that was the way it had to be. Totalitarian."

José showed his support for the post-Pinochet ruling alliance, Concertación de Partidos por la Democracia, by drumming at several of its political rallies. He believed in the democratic ideologies of the post-Pinochet era but did not take on a position of political leadership. He did not use his political connections to gain popularity in the media and increase his clientele: "As long as they don't film me, I go to the campaigns for the democratic presidents. I went to Carahue to meet Frei. I don't like to talk to the big men, though. I like to read what they say and think . . . Lagos is the best because he works for the Mapuche. He has expanded subsidized housing and benefits for the Mapuche."[7]

Although José supported the democratic regimes, he also criticized the repressive policies and antiterrorist laws Presidents Frei and Lagos applied against Mapuche who demanded the rights of self-determination

and autonomy. José believed that the Mapuche should retake their ancestral lands and use the media to gain international support. Like Sergio, he
proposed a return to a romanticized, rural Mapuche homeland:

> JOSÉ: The only way that people are going to realize the problem is for
> Mapuche to take over farms. Only then do the radio, the police arrive.
> That is when the information goes to other countries. Before then it
> does not go out.
>
> MARIELLA: Do you prefer to negotiate with the state or should the
> Mapuche be independent?
>
> JOSÉ: They should be independent. Because before, the Constitution
> recognized that the lands from the Bío-Bío River south belonged to
> the Mapuche. There could not be any *wingka* farmers. No gringos.
> But that was not respected, and they continued making more and
> more farms . . .
>
> MARIELLA: And what would happen to the Mapuche in Santiago?
>
> JOSÉ: They would have to come back south. (Interview, December 17,
> 2001)

José saw himself as a mounted spiritual warrior. He believed that
Mapuche resistance movements could use spiritual warfare as a military
strategy against Chilean secular, neoliberal policies, which he associated
with powerful non-Mapuche witchcraft. As a *machi* who combined the
authoritarianism of the medical doctor with the spirituality of the priest,
he associated spiritual warfare not with the secular military prowess of
General Pinochet, as Sergio did, but with fundamentalist religious militias such as that of Osama bin Laden. I spoke to Machi José three months
after the terrorist attacks in New York City and Washington, DC, on September 11, 2001:

> MARIELLA: How is your spirit horse?
>
> JOSÉ: I have the *püllü*. Like in the holy war. Osama bin Laden.
>
> MARIELLA: What do you think of bin Laden?
>
> JOSÉ: We have to support him.
>
> MARIELLA: Why?
>
> JOSÉ: Because we are religious, we adore the same God.
>
> MARIELLA: He killed a lot of people.
>
> JOSÉ: Yes, and so did the United States. The United States is the biggest
> terrorist of all. (Interview, December 17, 2001)

Machi of both sexes support the revival of tradition and the notion of a rural homeland promoted by Mapuche resistance movements, even if they do not participate actively in those movements. Male *machi*, however, tend to situate Mapuche movements in national and international contexts and link their mistrust of politics and power to non-Mapuche witchcraft. José viewed the terrorist attacks on the United States as a retaliation for Augusto Pinochet's military coup on September 11, 1973, which ousted socialist president Salvador Allende. Jorge viewed Pinochet and the United States, which promoted the coup, as powerful witches. The neoliberal economic model imposed by Pinochet applied U.S.-prescribed measures of privatization, eliminated restrictions on the circulation of capital, lowered environmental and labor standards, and created tax exemptions for foreign investors. But the neoliberal model was enacted only through the brutal control of political dissent.

Although from the same party as Allende, President Lagos staunchly promoted the free-trade agreement with the United States.[8] He continued to allow logging by transnational companies and the building of hydroelectric dams and highways on Mapuche land. The targets of José's proposed spiritual warfare were the secular neoliberal policies promoted by the United States and applied first by Pinochet and later by Lagos.

José was stressed and drinking heavily when I last saw him in December 2001. His community had criticized him for getting drunk while performing at a *ngillatun* ritual, and he was losing popularity. Drinking among men reinforces *compadrazgo* (co-paternity) and masculinity, but increasing alcoholism in Mapuche communities is linked to other factors such as poverty, low self-esteem, stress, and discrimination. José had lost thirty-five kilograms and undergone surgery for a peptic ulcer and gastrointestinal problems: "I had complications from the ulcer, from the liver, several problems. But it was not cancerous, it was treatable with pharmaceutical remedies and herbal medicine. It was a natural illness." José also interpreted his illness as having been caused by spiritual conflict: "I have spiritual competition with other spirits. I don't think I will win because they have me really messed up. If I can live through December I will have won the competition."

José lived through December but died of digestive extravasations in March 2002. Fabián, a friend of José's, believed there were physical, spiritual, and emotional components to José's illness: "He showed me a tumor and said that he had it because of this spiritual competition. I think he was also nervous because the Ministry of Justice summoned him to talk about the burning of the forestry company trucks by Mapuche individuals. José had nothing to do with this, but he was very nervous anyway. So this could also be the reason why he became ill and died. He was too nervous about the summons when I talked to him last, and now he is dead." José was neither the intellectual nor the material author of the protests against the forestry companies, but he believed he was their spiritual author. His nervousness stemmed from the belief that his spiritual competition against secular neoliberal policies was having unforeseen, violent effects.

Male *machi*, in short, carefully orchestrate their acceptable political practices to enhance their masculinity without threatening their spiritual roles, which Mapuche view as antithetical to political authority roles. Yet, in order to be considered masculine, male *machi* must subscribe to a political ideology and engage with political authorities through it. They have masculinized themselves by drawing on the image of the spiritual warrior to synthesize spirituality with military practice and diverse political ideologies on behalf of the Mapuche. Jorge linked Pinochet's military prowess with his own ability to conduct spiritual warfare against evil spirits and enemies. He believed that this spiritual-military power granted him the political authority to negotiate between the Mapuche and the Chilean and Spanish states. Sergio linked Mapuche ancestral warriors, Jesuit soldiers of Christ, and Pinochet's military dictatorship to conduct spiritual warfare against secular socialism. José linked Mapuche ancestral warriors with Mapuche resistance movements and fundamentalist militias to conduct spiritual warfare against the secular neoliberal policies of the Chilean state, instituted by Pinochet and promoted by the United States through witchcraft. He believed that Mapuche should negotiate with a democratic state because it listened to Mapuche demands and would eventually change the policies that were detrimental to them.

Conclusion

Male *machi* use paradoxical discourses about gender, as well as notions of spirituality, health, politics, and power, to legitimate themselves as both prestigious traditional shamans and modern masculine men. The ambivalent position of male *machi*, who respond to contradictory demands, offers insights into how gendered readings of power coexist with, conflict with, and affect *machi* practice. Male *machi* reconcile these different discourses in their daily lives by referring to one or another of them according to context. Local Mapuche ideologies legitimate male *machi* as bearers of spiritual power who need to engage in ritual transvestism and co-genderism in order to heal. But Mapuche also draw on national ideologies that read these gender performances as those of *maricones* and witches who threaten Mapuche masculinity as well as that of the modern Chilean state. In order to defend themselves against such labeling, male *machi* draw on the national ideology of male prestige and reconstruct themselves as priests, doctors, and politically active men who participate in national discourses of power.

As celibate priests, male *machi* can justify their ritual co-genderism, their transvestism, and their tendency not to marry. But, ironically, they simultaneously reiterate the church's condemnation of all same-sex practices and its belief in the naturalness of sex and gender, the very system that stigmatizes their co-gendered identities. By incorporating the Catholic morality of forgiveness, male *machi* legitimate their own empathetic, relational healing practices, and they use the model of the exorcist priest to justify their exorcism of evil spirits.

But Catholic morality has harmed the traditional practice of ritual revenge. Although ritual revenge makes evildoers accountable and gives victims some control over evil spirits, many Mapuche now view it as witchcraft. Male *machi* may gain legitimacy by associating themselves with the church, the Bible, and prayers to God. If a male *machi* claims to be God or Jesus, however, Mapuche believe he is a witch (Jorge) or crazy (José). The model of the Catholic priest legitimates male *machi*'s gender performances to some extent, but male *machi* who do not also reinvent themselves as medical doctors or spiritual warriors or who participate in national political ideologies are still viewed as effeminate.

Male *machi*'s performances of Chilean masculinity must be carefully balanced with their traditional spiritual roles. Male *machi* who masculinize themselves too much are believed to have lost their spiritual powers or even to be witches. In order to maintain his status as a shaman, a male *machi* must boast of his unique ability to divine and heal spiritual illness and to heal holistically, as no Western doctor or priest can. One of the ways in which male *machi* masculinize themselves without losing their spiritual role is by reinventing themselves as spiritual warriors who lack the stigma associated with co-gendered roles yet effectively synthesize femininity and masculinity, spirituality and politics. It remains to be seen whether the new images of the spiritual warrior will eventually lead to a positive reevaluation of *machi*'s co-gendered identities.

Male *machi* explain their engagement in contemporary politics by extending the traditional role of the Mapuche spiritual warrior rather than by drawing on the model of Chilean politicians. The image of male *machi* as spiritual warrior is successful because it conforms to Mapuche notions of the relationship between spirituality, militarism, and politics, as well as to Chilean perceptions of men's participation in politics. By not taking on political positions, male *machi* are able to maintain their authority as spiritual intermediaries. By allowing political ideologies to shape their spiritual understandings of power, male *machi* limit the number of political authorities with whom they engage and exchange favors. And despite male *machi*'s differing politics, the model of the spiritual warrior enables all male *machi* to strengthen the notion of Mapuche nationhood based on land, the revival of tradition, and resistance to the state's neoliberal policies.

Witchcraft is a productive lens through which to analyze male *machi*'s engagement with different gendered discourses of power and authority and the way notions of tradition and modernity shape the Mapuche ethos. Mapuche view witchcraft as antisocial because it threatens the integrity of the bodies of Mapuche men and women and of the body politic as a whole. Yet antisocial behavior, sexual desire, and solitariness exist in human behavior as the opposites of sociability, human love, and collectivity (Langdon 2004:309). Witchcraft, the counterpart of shamanism, is necessary in Mapuche society to maintain the tension between health and illness, life and death, individual gain and reciprocity, insiders and outsiders, normality and deviance that is believed to be part of the cultural whole.

Machi Jorge met different needs in Mapuche society from those filled by, for example, Machi Sergio. Whereas Sergio and José appealed to Catholic morality and models of empathetic healing, Jorge combined biomedical and traditional healing epistemologies and took ritual revenge for the ailments his patients experienced. Sergio, legitimated by his prestigious family background, maintained the traditional values of reciprocity and solidarity and the idea that shamans do not assume positions of political authority. Jorge, socially marginal in his community, sought alternative modes of legitimacy in prestige among outsiders, capitalist gain, self-proclaimed political and religious roles, and aggressive behavior. Jorge's case shows that witchcraft can be a personal, noninstitutional form of action that opposes collective identity and interests (Teixeira Pinto 2004), yet can still serve collective needs as a legitimate expression of political power (Whitehead and Wright 2004:14).

Contrasting notions of "tradition" held by outsiders and by Mapuche shape the way in which male *machi* are viewed. Anthropologists, museum personnel, and tourists viewed Jorge as a hypertraditional symbol of the Mapuche past and as a representative of the Mapuche because he embraced older shamanic practices such as shifting sexuality, ambiguous uses of power, and ritual revenge. Jorge found legitimacy in these constructions and claimed that he was "the official representative of the Mapuche people." His community, in contrast, saw him as marginal to contemporary Mapuche "tradition." Sergio, José, and Nora, who rejected Jorge, embraced moralistic, homophobic, Chilean, and Catholicized beliefs, which they reinvented, in their own syncretic practices, as traditional.

Mapuche expect "traditional" male *machi* to be celibate or heterosexual, to identify as Catholic priests and medical doctors, to be involved in politics, and to use empathetic, relational approaches to patients. Members of Jorge's community believed that, by incorporating and resignifying these foreign elements as traditional, male *machi* would participate in the prestige and privilege of dominant Chilean society and its neoliberal economy. Although Jorge made several attempts to adjust his practice to community demands, he was always unsuccessful. His shifting sexuality was apparent to the community, despite his earlier marriage. His attempt to engage Catholic sensibilities by presenting himself as the "Mapuche Jesus Christ" came across as arrogant and pretentious. Although Jorge gained some legitimacy by presenting himself as a doctor, his healing model was excessively authoritarian. Accusations of witchcraft against him strengthened his community's ideals of contemporary "cultural tradition."

Jorge's community also used his associations with anthropologists, the media, and museums to construct him as modern, individualistic, and uninterested in traditional Mapuche values of reciprocity and communal sharing. His lack of formal *machi* training, his marginal family, his sexual ambivalence, and his relative wealth all marked him as a witch who gained his powers from modernity. In the eyes of Jorge's community, he had become like an outsider who privileged his own interests above those of the community. He was a modern witch who sold shamanic knowledge, the soul and identity of the Mapuche people, for capitalistic gain.

Sergio and José, too, wanted to gain personal benefit from outsiders by appearing in the media (Sergio) or in my book (José), but they sought to legitimate their shamanic powers and enhance their good relationship with the community. They redistributed some of their wealth, supported community events, and integrated their outside contacts with traditional *machi* practices. Sergio taught Mapuche traditions on the radio, and José upheld Mapuche spiritual practices at the intercultural hospital.

Mapuche communities are transformed by male *machi* who perform some traditional practices and gender roles yet embrace capitalism and re-invent themselves in new roles as priests, doctors, and spiritual warriors. Capitalist consumption and male *machi*'s individual successes in these newfound masculine roles are both desired and criticized as antithetical to spirituality, morality, and community values. Accusations of witchcraft reflect both the shortage of equitable ways of integrating members of a community into a market economy and state system (Auslander 1993) and the rejection of norms and values associated with modern capitalism and national masculinities that marginalize Mapuche or benefit some over others. Accusations of witchcraft among Mapuche appear as cultural idioms tied to systems of gender inequality, modern processes of power, and cultural gatekeeping.

How will the new models of celibate priests, doctors, and spiritual warriors further transform the gendered images of male *machi* and their ritual identities and practices? What will the new paradigms of Mapuche witchcraft be as capitalist gain, individual success, and male *machi*'s new gendered models begin to play a larger role in Mapuche life and politics?

CHAPTER 8

Female *Machi:* Embodying Tradition or Contesting Gender Norms?

Because I am a machi, the owner of her son [mother-in-law] was angry.
"The bride has to sweep the house in the morning, and you will be gone, who
knows where you will be, that's why you are worth nothing to me. You will be
dragging around with your kultrun tied to you," that bad woman said to me.
What can I do if the spirit who sustains the person wanted it that way?
—EXCERPT FROM A PRAYER BY MACHI HORTENSIA,
   RECORDED BY JUAN ÑANCULEF

Most *machi* in Chile today are women, and Mapuche use the Spanish feminine article *la* in conjunction with the word *machi*. Some Mapuche argue that *machi* are predominantly women because "women stay at home and follow Mapuche ways more than men." Others stress that women are more accepting of their calling. According to Machi Ana's son: "Men decide not to become *machi* because they are embarrassed. But women are braver and prefer to become *machi* than always to be ill." According to Jaime, Machi Nora's son: "Women recognize the signs of *machi* calling and go to *machi* to be cured, while men go to the hospitals and allow themselves to die." Machi Ana believed that "spirits get along better with women" and that "women are more patient with the sick and know more about herbs." *Machi* spiritual power is usually passed down through the female line, often through a maternal grandmother—unlike social descent and inheritance, which are traced through the father's side of the family. Occasionally, as in Ana's case, a *machi* inherits spirits from both her mother's and father's sides.

Mapuche see female *machi* as symbols of tradition, domesticity, and womanhood, yet also, paradoxically, as masculine transgressors who, in their everyday lives and practices, stray from the gender roles and behavior expected of ordinary Mapuche women. Female *machi* are rural women marginalized from the Chilean state's structures of power because of their ethnic identity, their poverty and lack of education, their gender, and their healing practices. Mapuche's incorporation of Chilean gender notions reinforces the dichotomy between the public, urban, modern, masculine world of politics and the private, rural, traditional, feminine world of shamanism and witchcraft (Bacigalupo 1996a:109–114). Machismo, the ideology of male dominance and superiority over women, and Marianism, the cultural ideal of the Virgin Mary, constrain Mapuche women's behavior. "Good" Mapuche women are expected to stay home, accept male authority, and remain virgins or become mothers who are loyal to their husbands and families.

The dichotomy between the private-spiritual and the public-political is an important signifier in both Mapuche and Chilean national gendered discourses, but it does not reflect the complex practices of female *machi*. These women transgress gender norms, take on public ritual roles as *machi* moon priestesses, and travel away from home to heal patients. Female *machi* who officiate as moon priestesses in collective *ngillatun* rituals obtain fertility powers from the moon in order to petition for agricultural and animal fertility and well-being in behalf of the entire ritual congregation. They also draw on national gendered discourses for their own purposes. They capitalize on the notion that Mapuche women are apolitical in order to develop nonpartisan political relationships with a variety of politicians for pragmatic ends.

Mapuche accept female *machi*'s transgressions as long as they remain representatives of tradition and respectable daughters, mothers, and wives. Instead of justifying their co-gendered identities and attempting to disprove suspicions of same-sex acts, as male *machi* do, female *machi* generally abide by Mapuche patrilineal norms and try to prove their virtue under the terms of male-dominant Catholic discourses. Female *machi* gain prestige as representatives of custom who wear traditional Mapuche women's clothes, obtain their powers from the moon, forests, and spirits, and use those powers to ensure agricultural fertility and well-being.

Mapuche associate female *machi*'s shamanic practices with domesticity and view their position as distinct from the public positions of political authority held by male *longko* and *presidentes*. When female *machi* transgress gender norms and wield power independently from chiefs, the patrilineage, and their husbands, Mapuche label them "*mariconas*" (butches, betrayers, liars), "*brujas*" (witches), and "*mujeres de la calle*" (street women). Female *machi* may try to protect their reputation by reinventing themselves as virtuous Catholic women, nuns, or angels and by advising their patients to abide by traditional gender norms. Some female *machi* draw on the "mothering" model—empathetic relational healing practices equivalent to those of male *machi*'s "priestly" model—to justify their ritual work. Others construct themselves as medical doctors or priestesses to gain additional prestige.

In their everyday lives and practices, female *machi* sometimes fulfill and sometimes challenge gender roles, Catholic norms, and perceptions of Mapuche tradition. Continually faced with balancing their ritual practices against their roles as daughters, mothers, and wives, they must cope with the tension ever present between the social legitimacy they gain through marriage and motherhood and the opposing demands of spirit husbands and spiritual power. They use diverse strategies to reinforce their image as representatives of tradition, yet they may equally engage with the modern political world. To illustrate these points, many women appear in what follows, among them Machi Nora, Ana, Tegualda, Hortensia, Javiera, and, particularly, Rocío, Pamela, and Fresia. First, though, let me introduce Machi María Cecilia and her co-mothers, Marcela and Carolina.

The Paradoxical Gendered Roles of Female *Machi*

Twenty-one-year-old *machi* María Cecilia, her two mothers, and I talked about the roles of Mapuche women and female *machi* in January 1995. Fifty-year-old Marcela and thirty-five-year-old Carolina were co-wives in a polygynous marriage to Edmundo, a wealthy, fifty-five-year-old *longko* (Fig. 8.1).[1] Marcela, Carolina, and their daughters illustrate the variety of roles performed by Mapuche women. These roles are shaped by both Mapuche discourses of gender egalitarianism and Chilean notions of gender hierarchy. Marcela and Carolina played traditional Mapuche gender roles at home; María Cecilia healed and stood for tradition and womanhood in some aspects but not in others; Lola, Marcela's youngest daughter, worked as a housemaid; and Melinda, Carolina's eldest daughter, was employed as a seamstress.

Most Mapuche women uphold the ideal of gender complementarity. Carolina explained: "Mapuche women are important for the family. Mapuche men are more political and in touch with the community." Mapuche view the different gender roles as part of the Mapuche system of balanced, complementary opposites expressed in the Mapuche cosmos, society, and family (Bacigalupo 1994b, 1996a, 2000:281). Marcela

Figure 8.1. Mapuche co-wives in a polygynous marriage work together at home but maintain separate sleeping quarters. The eldest wife usually ranks higher than the younger one and has better clothing and jewelry as well as other privileges (photo by Ana Mariella Bacigalupo).

believed that gender complementarity generated gender egalitarianism, in which women and men had different roles but equal value: "Mapuche women and men work together on the land. Men do some chores, women do others. Everything has to be decided together" (interview, January 23, 1995).

Mapuche women highlight the differences between their gender roles, perspectives, and priorities and those of Chilean women. Mapuche women work together with their men, they say, to eliminate oppression and violence and to strengthen their communities (Bacigalupo 2003:49). Even when they focus on women's needs and interests, their central struggle is that of the Mapuche people as a whole, and they assert their differences from nonindigenous women (Richards 2004:152, 172). Urban Mapuche women such as Isabel criticize feminist assumptions about the universality of women's experiences and priorities: "Mapuche women have their own knowledge, medicine, and experience. But Chilean and foreign feminists think that we [Mapuche women] know nothing and impose their own ideas and goals. The world and priorities of Mapuche women need to be respected. We have women's organizations, but men and women work together for the family, for the community" (interview, December 20, 1999).

Mapuche ideals of gender egalitarianism and complementarity remain central to the way Mapuche view and represent themselves to others, although instances of both gender egalitarianism and gender hierarchy appear in their everyday lives (Bacigalupo 2000). Mapuche women discussed these issues during the first indigenous women's conference in 1995. Ana Llao-Llao drew on the gender-egalitarian Mapuche creation myth to argue that Mapuche had gender-egalitarian practices (Encuentro Nacional de Mujeres Indígenas 1995:80–84). Carolina Manke focused on the differences between Mapuche gender egalitarianism and the gender hierarchy imposed by the dominant Chilean society. Most of the women explained Mapuche men's machismo as being due to Chilean influence in the postreservation era (Encuentro Nacional de Mujeres Indígenas 1995:15–18). A few argued that the Mapuche practices of abducting women by force, polygyny, and patrilineal descent and inheritance were evidence that they had always been a male-dominant society.[2]

Mapuche activist Isolde Reuque held that gender complementarity furthered gender subordination because it limited women's activities to the home and justified a shortage of leadership opportunities for women (Encuentro Nacional de Mujeres Indígenas 1995:95; Richards 2004:164). In contrast, a group of urban Mapuche women used the discourse of complementarity to promote Mapuche women's political participation: "We are a people and this means equality between men and women. It is necessary for men to open up more opportunities for women's participation" (Richards 2004:171).

In traditional rural settings, gender roles often fit the Chilean stereotype of women's domestic and men's public domains:[3] men usually till and harvest the fields, sell agricultural products, mend tools, and do business in town, whereas women tend the gardens, spin wool, weave textiles, gather herbs, prepare herbal remedies, fetch water, and cook.[4] Women such as Marcela and Carolina, who remain in their rural communities, see themselves primarily as daughters, mothers, and wives. Because they are less likely to receive advanced education, they become symbols of traditional lore (Bacigalupo 1996a:74–95), gaining de facto power in their communities.[5]

Mapuche see female *machi*, too, as traditional models for Mapuche women; Isabel believes that female *machi* should reproduce traditional knowledge by teaching other women about herbal remedies. Mapuche men have more independence to travel to the city by themselves and to drink alcohol, whereas women must constantly guard their reputations. Marcela, for example, chided María Cecilia when she saw her boyfriend on the sly or spent too much time in town.

In other ways, Mapuche gender roles conform less strictly to the female-domestic, male-public stereotype and often overlap. Mapuche expect women to cater to their men in public, but family decisions are negotiated collectively at home. A forty-year-old Mapuche woman said: "I tell my husband how he should act. Although men decide, what women advise them often goes." Rural men and women both socialize children, tend animals, and cut firewood, and I observed women tilling the fields, harvesting, selling their vegetables and textiles, and making decisions as community presidents. I also saw men cooking, tending gardens, and fetching water (Bacigalupo 1994b). Wage labor has changed traditional Mapuche gender roles. Men now work on farms or as bakers in cities, and single women market their domestic skills as urban housemaids, cooks, or seamstresses, as Lola and Melinda did. The independence and mobility Mapuche women gain in these new jobs challenge rural Mapuche notions that women should remain at home, stay financially dependent, and travel only accompanied by men. Mapuche women who work as professionals or as leaders in Mapuche NGOs also challenge rural gender roles. Female *machi*'s challenges to traditional women's roles are especially noticeable, because female *machi* otherwise represent tradition and womanhood by working from home, wearing traditional dress, understanding herbal remedies, and speaking Mapudungu (Titiev 1951:115–117).

In many instances, female *machi* are not subject to the same restrictions and obligations as other Mapuche women. They may participate in community decision-making, which grants them higher status than ordinary Mapuche women (Bacigalupo 1994b, 1996a, 2000). One woman explained: "[*Machi*] are treated better in public than other women. They have more authority. And they have help in the house. They are the owners of their own money and are fat because they have money" (interview, January 24, 1992). Female *machi* travel on their own to patients' homes and various cities and are independent, forthright individuals. Machi Pamela and Machi Ana, for example, drank at bars and chided *longko* for their lack of knowledge of traditional lore. Ana, Nora, and Rocío were influential in community decision-making. Most female *machi* have women relatives who care for their children and perform domestic tasks for them.

Female *machi* usually give their *machi* role higher priority than their marriage, family, and domestic chores. Longko Daniel said: "Even when a female *machi* is making her best soup, or receiving a visitor, if someone comes to get her, she has to leave everything and go. First she is a *machi* and then she is a housewife." María Cecilia had no time to sew or weave and rarely performed any chores unrelated to her healing. Machi Ana felt ill if she stayed home too long: "I arrive at ten or eleven in the morning [from all-night healing rituals], and in the evening I leave again to heal somewhere else. I don't get to sleep at my house. When I remain at home for a week I feel ill, as if I am going to die. I no longer feel like eating, but when I go out and heal somewhere else I don't even get a cold."

Gender roles are the media through which female *machi* express their differences from other women. By looking closer at three *machi* in particular—Rocío, Pamela, and Fresia, all of whom I met in November 1991—we can explore the diverse ways in which such women grapple with Mapuche gender roles in their daily lives.

Rocío: Flexibility, Independence, and an Aversion to Cooking

When I met Machi Rocío, she was a sixty-eight-year-old widow who lived with an adult son and daughter in two wooden huts that served as kitchen and sleeping quarters. She owned a large plot of land and a vegetable garden, which made her wealthy by local standards. Her paternal grandfather had been a non-Mapuche who owned no land, but her maternal grandfather was a prestigious *longko,* and her maternal grandmother, a *machi* from whom Rocío inherited her powers. As a child she experienced *machi* dreams but did not tell her parents because she did not want to become a *machi*—it involved "too much work and suffering," she said. Although she suffered one *machi* illness as a child, her parents propitiated the spirits by purchasing spirit animals for her, and she was not ill again until 1976, after she had been married and borne thirteen children. It was then that she planted her *rewe* and was formally initiated as a *machi.*

Rocío held flexible gender roles. Her brother had died when she was young, and Rocío and her four sisters had performed tasks ascribed to both women and men: "We plowed the land, took care of the animals, and harvested [like men], we wove and cooked [like women]. We worked hard." Later, Rocío worked with her husband sowing, planting, and working the vegetable garden. She found it difficult to combine domestic chores and healing. She continued to work in the vegetable garden and make textiles for sale, but her daughter Pía did the cooking, cleaning, and washing. Rocío felt ill if she got near the fire. Leo, her son, told me: "She would say, 'Why don't you make the food?' She became bad tempered. When she leaves the house to heal others she rests a bit. She is okay for a few days. She feels bad when she gets near the stove or the fire, when she doesn't go out to heal."

As a new *machi,* Rocío spent a great deal of time healing away from home. Leo remembered: "They picked her up one day and brought her back the next day, and there were already two people waiting to take her. Sometimes she spent more than fifteen days away. Finally, we pressured her so that she wouldn't leave the house alone so much."

Rocío thinks female *machi* have higher status than ordinary women: "*Machi* have to be treated with more respect because they are sent here by God. They treat me better, they give me everything—wine, meat. They serve me before other people."

Male *machi* make their own decisions about when to leave the house, but Mapuche typically ask a female *machi*'s husband or children for permission to take her to heal a patient. Rocío, however, asked her spirit— not her husband or children—for permission to leave the house. She did not believe that making decisions on her own or traveling to other communities masculinized her: "The ones who say female *machi* can't go out, those are *machistas.*" Rocío liked working in the garden and making textiles, but she viewed all other domestic tasks as incompatible with the mobility and high status accorded to female *machi*. She argued that female *machi* did not have to abide by gender norms, though she acquiesced to her family's demands that she spend more time at home.

Pamela: Conserving and Defying Gender Norms

Pamela, when we met in 1991, was a robust, seventy-seven-year-old widow, *machi,* and midwife. She lived with her brother-in-law, one of her daughters, and a grandson. Like Rocío, Pamela was wealthy in local terms, and she shared her plot of land with her son Mario and his family. Like Rocío, Pamela had grown up with her mother and maternal grandparents, because her father was a landless non-Mapuche. Her family, however, had been very poor. She met her husband, Horacio, while she was herding animals, married him at seventeen, and lived with her in-laws in the same community.

Pamela had special dreams—about a horse, about playing the *kultrun,* about herbal remedies. Then, in 1960, she received her *machi* powers suddenly during a devastating earthquake, in a vision that included huge lightning bolts. "Now Chaw Dios bosses me," she said. "I cannot decide things on my own." As a lightning shaman, Pamela effectively conducted spiritual warfare against evil spirits and was masculinized in the process.

Pamela had no brothers, and her father was absent during her childhood, so she performed tasks associated with both boys and girls. She made textiles like the girls and cut wood, tended to animals, and plowed like the boys. After she married Horacio, Pamela healed, worked in the vegetable garden, and wove textiles, which she sold to help support her six children. Unlike Rocío, Pamela also cooked and cleaned. Horacio worked the land with the help of his *compadres* and occasionally engaged in wage labor. When he died in 1976, Pamela became the head of the household.

Once she was widowed, Pamela began to challenge Mapuche gender norms by assuming what Mapuche describe as "manly behavior." She drank and swore in public. She became independent and opinionated: "I make my own decisions. When I want to go out, I do. When I don't want to, I don't. I don't ask permission from anyone. I am my own boss." Tomás, Pamela's brother-in-law, took over some of Horacio's tasks, but Pamela no longer had the help of Horacio's *compadres*. Instead of asking Tomás to create new work alliances for her, Pamela made her own *compadres* and performed some men's tasks herself: "I work alone in my house for my money. I grab my hammer, my ox, my ax to cut wood. Women also have strength." In 1991 Pamela was still plowing, mending fences, and digging ditches, despite her age. "All I have I have earned by the sweat of my brow. I don't owe anyone anything," Pamela told me. Her friends called her "Pamela loca" (crazy Pamela) because her behavior was extreme even for a female *machi*.

Pamela's community punished her gender transgressions by claiming that her *compadres* were her lovers and by labeling her *"mujer de la calle"* and *"maricona,"* thereby attempting to pressure her into changing her behavior. Pamela complained: "They are frightened of me because I work like a man. They say I am a *maricona* because I am the boss in the house. They say I'm a *mujer de la calle* because I have men friends who help me plow and harvest." Moreover, some Mapuche believed that Pamela had inherited her *machi* spirit from her maternal grandmother, Ester, who was considered a witch. They thought Pamela had a contract with the evil *añchümalleñ* and *witranalwe* spirits, who made her wealthy in exchange for her kin's blood. The community held Pamela responsible for the deaths of her husband, a son, and three of her grandchildren. Pamela's life history was similar to Machi Jorge's in that both had belonged to poor, marginal families but became wealthy as adults. Both were initiated suddenly during earthquakes, became popular among non-Mapuche, and were viewed as witches.

Pamela did not change her behavior. "I'm too old to care what they say about me," she explained. But she advised her daughters, her female patients, and me to abide by gender norms in order to gain acceptance. She argued that women should be quiet and hard-working and should remain at home: "I don't like women who go to town to have fun and who leave their house abandoned." She praised her daughter Beatriz for waiting until she was married to have children and criticized her daughters Manuela and Emilia for having children out of wedlock. "When women are pregnant, when they are fooling around, men don't marry them," she explained.

Pamela and Rocío transgressed traditional gender roles for different reasons—Rocío because she believed female *machi* were superior to ordinary women, and Pamela because she believed widows were freed from gender norms and the demands of their husband's patrilineage. While she was married, Pamela conformed to gender norms and behaviors, but as a widow she openly challenged them and was impervious to the labels the community used to try to control her. Rocío and Pamela both saw female *machi* and widows as exceptions to the gender norms they reinforced in their dealings with ordinary women. Other Mapuche saw Pamela's gender transgressions as more serious than Rocío's because she openly challenged the patrilineal social order. In a society governed by men, Pamela was a powerful, independent women who was feared as a sorceress.[6]

Fresia: Domestic Desires and Rejection of *Machi*-hood

Fresia, twenty years old when I met her in 1991, wore full female *machi* attire and had a seven-step *rewe* planted in front of her kitchen door. She, her parents, and her brother shared a small plot of land with her paternal aunt, Clara. Fresia had lived with Clara as a child and, according to Fresia's mother, had been "spoiled" and become "picky." Fresia spoke Spanish at home but had inherited both her maternal grandmother's *machi* spirit and her paternal grandfather's *ngenpin* spirit and was therefore expected to heal and perform as a *machi* moon priestess in the community's collective *ngillatun* rituals.

As a teenager Fresia experienced inexplicable chills, dizziness, pain, and loss of appetite, which she interpreted as her shamanic illness. But she did not want to be a *machi*—she very much wanted a husband and children, whereas her mother pressured her to live at home and become an unmarried, celibate *machi*. Machi Sergio tried to exorcise Fresia's *machi* spirit: "We tried to reject the spirit, but he couldn't. I continued to be ill. The spirit was born with me. So I just had to become a *machi*." There was no other culturally acceptable explanation for her illnesses and dreams.

Fresia went to live with Sergio, her teacher, for a year of formal training in preparing herbal remedies, playing the *kultrun*, attending to patients, and generally behaving. Fresia explained: "Sergio said I could not ride my bike, play ball, or talk with my friends. He told me I had to talk in Mapudungu, speak to more adults, and take things more seriously. I had to ask my *rewe* for permission to leave, and wear traditional clothing. This was a big change for me."

Fresia was initiated at the age of sixteen. She enjoyed the attention, but when she returned home after her *machi* training, she became depressed. She was now expected to behave according to traditional norms into which she had not been socialized, and she was subject to the will of her spirit. Her social position changed: "My friends think being a *machi* is something terrible or they treat me with too much respect. I didn't sleep thinking about what I was going to do, how I was going to lose all my friends. I almost went crazy."

Fresia's mother, Dominga, drew on Chilean Catholic notions that "good" unmarried women should be controlled and remain at home. She had restricted Fresia's social interactions throughout her adolescence: "Fresia loved to dance and sing, but I never let her go out on her own or dance more than two pieces. Then she had to come home." Fresia, however, saw herself in terms of an urban Chilean model of domesticity. She fantasized about being an urban housewife and housemaid. Even though she was a *machi*, she performed domestic chores, which, unlike most other female *machi*, she prioritized over her healing practices. "I make the food, clean the house, and wash the dishes, like any other woman," she said.

By remaining at home with her parents, Fresia was unable to develop the self-confidence and skills she needed to become a successful *machi* and thereby to repay the money her parents had invested in her initiation. She lacked faith in her healing powers, so nobody came to her for treatment. Nor could she marry or have a family. "Imagine what my life is going to be like," she lamented. "I can't heal. I can't make money. I can't leave the house or have a boyfriend."

When Fresia turned twenty-one, she took off her *machi* attire, cut her hair (Mapuche associate long hair with rural womanliness and short hair with non-Mapuche urbanity), and abandoned her *machi* role. She went to live with an aunt in Santiago and found work as a housemaid. Sergio believed that Fresia's *machi* spirit would avenge itself, but she experienced no further shamanic dreams, illnesses, or trance states.

Unlike Rocío and Pamela, Fresia did not accept the paradigms of shamanic practice. She felt pressured to conform to cultural and *machi* norms only to avoid social disapproval and spiritual punishment; she did not internalize shamanic beliefs and practices as her own. Several anthropologists have shown how individual behavior and experience may run counter to ideal or normative cultural representations (Hollan and Wellenkamp 1994; Howard 1985; Spiro 1984). Fresia's case demonstrates that, in order for shamans to be convinced of their powers to heal others, they must have personal experiences that enact and reinforce cultural traditions they have learned formally. Shamans' individual thoughts, motivations, and emotions are closely tied to their professional performance. They need to participate in the discursive process of cultural maintenance and change in what Gannanath Obeyesekere (1981:77) calls "objectification," the expression of private emotions in a public idiom.[7]

In July 1992 Fresia returned to her community to uproot her *rewe* and bury her drum and *machi* attire, something normally done only when a *machi* dies. She wore her hair short, a miniskirt, and makeup to stress that she was an urban woman. She prayed to her spirit for the last time, asking it to allow her to continue with her life: "When the *rewe* came out of the ground, a part of me was pulled out from the depth of my chest. It was like a dead person. I cried. But it was difficult working as a *machi*. I didn't want to be a *machi*. Now I feel calm."

In 2001 Fresia married, but she continued to work as a live-in maid in Santiago, seeing her husband on her days off. She had reconciled with her parents after the rift caused by her leaving home, and she compensated them for the money they had spent on her *machi* initiation by buying them gifts: "I bought them a washing machine, a refrigerator, and a cellular phone," she told me.

Fresia, unlike Rocío and Pamela, valued urban women's domestic and family roles over rural *machi* practice and rural women's roles. She rejected her mother's interpretation of Catholic discourses that demanded she remain a celibate, unmarried *machi*. She refused to be ruled by a demanding spirit. She embraced the roles of married housewife and paid housemaid. Like other migrant Mapuche women, she reinforced traditional gender roles by embracing domesticity yet challenged gender norms by marketing her domestic skills in a paid job that granted her financial independence.

In December 2001 she reflected on her *machi* practice: "I don't know what happened to me at that time, because once I came to Santiago I never got the spirit anymore. I don't know if it was because of the pressure to do things they thought that I should do. Being a *machi* was what my mother and the community chose for me, not God. No one was ever worried about what I felt and wanted. I never felt I had the power to become a *machi*. I am happy now that I have my own money, that I can have friends and go out."

Marriage, Motherhood, and the Demands of Spirits

Susan Sered (1994:71–72) has argued that female-dominated religions around the world define women's identity mainly according to their role as mother, grandmother, and sister, whereas male-dominated religions cast women as daughters and wives. Female *machi* pose a challenge to this dichotomy because they negotiate their *machi* practice in relationship to all such roles—daughters and wives, mothers and grandmothers—and they combine female-dominant *machi* practice with male-dominant Catholicism.

Whereas male *machi* legitimate their sexuality as celibate priests, most female *machi* gain status and virtue by marrying and having children. Longko Daniel explained: "There is no chastity vote among female *machi*. Mapuche look down upon priests who have girlfriends, but not on female *machi* with husbands." Female *machi* who remain single identify themselves as pure "nuns" or "angels" to protect themselves against the "*bruja*" and "*mujer de la calle*" labels. These identities, however, do not grant them the power and agency they gain as traditional healers and *machi* moon priestesses.

Mapuche women's social identity depends on marriage and their relationship with the husband's family. Mapuche principles of patrilineal descent, inheritance, and succession were strengthened with the imposition of the reservation system in 1884. The status of Mapuche male lineage heads increased as they gained land titles (Faron 1956) and as Chilean Catholic values enforced male dominance. Mapuche had a preference for a man's marriage to a woman on his mother's side (Faron 1962). Today, Mapuche choose their partners either within or outside of this system and inherit land through the parents of either the wife or the husband (Bengoa 1992:141). Marriage influences the way female *machi* are perceived. Widowed *machi* who live in their husband's home are accused of witchcraft if they do not have the support of the community. Single *machi* who live in their natal homes with their patrilineal kin and have their support are rarely accused of witchcraft.

Despite the efforts of the Catholic Church and the Chilean government to eradicate polygyny, it remains an ideal for many Mapuche men, although only a few, such as Longko Edmundo—husband of Marcela and Carolina—can afford it. Female *machi* do not share their husbands with other women in polygynous marriages. Rather, husbands of *machi* adjust their lives to their wives' needs. Mapuche often view female *machi* as masculine and their husbands as feminine. Anthropologists have observed *machi*'s husbands treating their wives with greater consideration than other wives receive, listening to their opinions in a subservient manner, and remaining largely in the background (Eliade 1974; Faron 1986:32; Métraux 1942). Jaime, Machi Nora's son, explained:

JAIME: *Machi* husbands make a contract when they marry *machi*. When people came to get my mother *machi* for healing, my father stayed at home with the kids. He wouldn't get angry. Some people get jealous because they are taking away their *machi* wife.
MARIELLA: Would you like to marry a *machi*?
JAIME: No, *machi* have too much work. It involves a lot of sacrifice.
MARIELLA: Is it bad to have too much work?
JAIME: Yes, because finally the man gets tired, too. The woman may have a child and at night she has to go and heal other people.

More female *machi* marry than do male *machi,* but fewer of them marry than do ordinary Mapuche women. A female *machi*'s spiritual marriage to her jealous *machi* spirit takes precedence over her marriage to her husband. Abstinence allows the spirit to feed on the *machi*'s sexual energy. *Machi* spirits punish female *machi* with illness when they have sex with their husbands. Machi Pamela explained: "Ngünechen and the *machi filew* do not like the smell of husband and wife together [having sex], so I have to ask them for forgiveness."

Mapuche tend to perceive female *machi* as masculine because they transgress ordinary Mapuche women's gender roles, and this "masculinity" is sometimes paired with suspicions of same-sex behavior. Machi Javiera told me: "There is a *machi* who likes women. They say she falls in love with young girls, like men" (interview, December 27, 2001). Fabián told me that a female *machi* he knew "wears a man's hat during the full moon and then looks for women to be with" (interview, December 13,

2005). Mapuche speak of female *machi* who act "like men," but they do not recognize lesbian social identities.

Anthropologists, too, have characterized female *machi* as masculine and occasionally homosexual (Faron 1964:152; Métraux 1967) or have claimed that there is no Mapuche female homosexuality (Cooper 1946). Mischa Titiev's suggestion that there might be same-sex relationships between female neophytes and their female *machi* teachers (1951:115–117) is unfounded. Some female *machi* have romantic or sexual relationships with ordinary women, but sexual relationships between *machi* of any sex are taboo, because they share a co-gendered ritual identity. Machi Ana was horrified when I suggested that Machi Celia's husband become initiated as a *machi*: "No, God does not want that. A *machi* cannot be married to a *machi*. They are the same thing."

Mapuche do not stigmatize female *machi*'s same-sex practices to the same extent as those of male *machi,* for several reasons. First, female *machi* are not transvestite, and female *machi* who engage in same-sex relationships do not participate in the sexual economy of power represented by the active-passive, male-male penetration paradigm. Mapuche rarely speak of women's same-sex practices because they have no place in the Mapuche patrilineal social system and reproductive order. Second, female *machi*'s same-sex practices are less visible than those of male *machi*. Friendships among Mapuche women typically involve emotional intimacy and physical closeness. They are difficult to distinguish from romantic or sexual relationships between women. Mapuche women often share beds with women relatives, friends, and patients.

Mapuche's lack of interest in same-sex acts by female *machi* contrasts with their careful scrutiny of female *machi*'s relationships with men. In the past, Mapuche norms allowed women to have lovers or children out of wedlock. Although the number of single mothers remains high, Mapuche now subscribe to the ideology of Marianism. Women are expected to marry as virgins, and married women are to be chaste, morally superior, and loyal to their families. Female *machi* who challenge Marianism by having lovers are often viewed as witches or street women.

Marrying is one route to legitimation for female *machi,* and having children within marriage reinforces that legitimacy in Mapuche eyes. Feminists have debated the relationship between women, motherhood, and spiritual power. Some argue that women can gain power only if they break away from patriarchal religions (Eck and Jain 1987), overcome their unilateral symbolic association with birth and mothering, and assume formal positions of power (Atkinson, Buchanan, and Miles 1987; Christ

1980; Gilligan 1982; King 1989). Others have linked biological mother-hood to the ritual use of motherhood metaphors. They view female sha-manism as centered on menarche and birth (Tedlock 2005:202–206) and idealize motherhood as a path toward enlightenment (Ochs 1983) or a model for healing (Glass-Coffin 1998:189). Both models accept patriar-chal assumptions that the female body is somehow more engaged with the natural world than are male bodies (Grosz 1994:15).

For female *machi,* motherhood is neither a path toward enlighten-ment nor an instrument of subjugation. Their relationship to fertility and motherhood is complex and contradictory. On one hand, Mapuche value motherhood and believe that all women, including female *machi,* want to be mothers. Machi Sergio argued that "women *machi* marry more [than male *machi*] because they have an irresistible call to motherhood." Most married or widowed female *machi* are either biological or adop-tive mothers. Rural Mapuche have high birth rates and high infant mor-tality rates (Chiriguini and Vitello 2001), and Mapuche value children as company and laborers. Furthermore, female *machi* draw on mother-hood metaphors in *ngillatun* rituals to ensure agricultural fertility, and they claim insight into patients' problems because of their experiences as mothers.

On the other hand, Mapuche see marriage, sexuality, and mothering as interfering with female *machi*'s healing practices and as lessening their healing powers. In some shamanic traditions, menstrual blood grants spiritual power and can be used for healing (Tedlock 2005:184–185, 196–200). Mapuche, in contrast, view sexual fluids and blood from men-struation or birth as dangerous, polluting, and interfering with spiritual power. Mapuche use these substances to control the will of others or to perform witchcraft. Female *machi* who receive a shamanic calling before menarche and those who are older and no longer fertile or sexually active are considered the most powerful. Single female *machi,* those who are not mothers, and those who have older children hold an advantage over fertile female *machi* with young children who distract them from their healing endeavors.

Mapuche think women have natural maternal feelings that men lack, but this does not always hold true in practice. Motherly love is neither natural nor universal but represents a series of meanings, feelings, and practices that are socially and culturally produced in specific political, economic, and social conditions (Scheper-Hughes 1994). Some Mapuche women choose to be sterilized or use IUDs, effectively reducing the number of unwanted births (Mendenhall 2004:73–74). Others have more children than they can rear and "give" children to family members or friends. Mapuche mothering practices challenge cultural feminists' notions, as characterized by Nancy Scheper-Hughes (1994), that "women have common interests, goals and moral visions" and that there is "an essential womanly ethic and ethos of maternal responsiveness, attentiveness and caring labor." Female *machi* balance their marriages and motherhood against their shamanic practices in different ways. Again, the lives of Rocío, Pamela, and Fresia illustrate some of the diversity.

Machi Rocío accepted her spiritual calling only after marriage and motherhood, and with her family's support she was able to fulfill her *machi* role successfully. When Rocío was sixteen, her aunt arranged for her to marry her mother's forty-year-old cousin, Rubén. He gave Rocío's parents a cow as bride-price, and they lived on Rubén's reservation in accordance with the Mapuche patrilocal residence system. Rubén and Rocío had thirteen children, three of whom died before the age of five. Although she had resisted becoming a *machi* as a child, she now experienced *machi* dreams once again: "They [the spirits] gave me my *machi* name, Foye Likan [remedy], the power of my grandmother *machi*. They threw herbal remedies into my apron. They gave me two silver knives to scare the devil. They gave me a horse. 'Ride that horse,' they told me, and 'go around with your knives.'" She became ill again, too: "They punished me because I didn't want to become a *machi*."

This time, Rocío capitulated. She did not go through *machi* training but gained her knowledge through dreams. Rubén thought that his community of evangelical Christians would laugh at her, but she acquired patients within the community and performed as a *machi* moon priestess in *ngillatun* rituals in the area. Her grown children helped her with her *machi* practice. Rocío did not view marriage or motherhood as having detracted from her *machi* practice: "I am as you see me," she said, "mother, wife, grandmother, and *machi*. I cannot separate one thing from another."

When Rocío was widowed in 1985 she continued living in her husband's house. She remained free of accusations of witchcraft because she had a good relationship with the community. Her sons Leo and Hernán legitimated her in the patrilineal household after Rubén's death.

In contrast, Machi Pamela found that her healing practice conflicted with marriage and motherhood in ways that she could not fully reconcile. She had married Horacio according to the Mapuche tradition of bride abduction: "I liked him straight away, but I didn't say anything. One day he came to steal me." Horacio paid Pamela's mother, Teresa, two horses, three sheep, and money as bride-price, and they lived with his parents.

Pamela had six children with the help of a midwife and a bottle of wine. She gave her son Mario to her mother-in-law, Mónica. Pamela struggled to rear her daughters while healing: "My babies cried because I couldn't attend to them." Mónica cared for Pamela's daughters when she was away, but Horacio was jealous of the time Pamela spent healing. Pamela told me: "He said: 'I don't like *machi*. They wander like beggars. They are never at home. *Machi* are bossy, and the *chamal* stinks.'" Horacio had sex with other women because he claimed that "*machi* are not real wives."

When Horacio died, his family tried to expel Pamela from his house. She saw Horacio's land as her own, however, and refused to leave. Pamela drew parallels between her attachment to her *rewe* and men's ties to the land: "I am like a man. I cannot get married and leave. My spirit is here in this *rewe*. In this land. When I go away, my *rewe* calls me back in dreams." Pamela's brother-in-law, Tomás, allowed her to stay and lived with her. The community pressured Pamela to marry Tomás, but she refused: "Some husbands are jealous and bad tempered. I prefer to be alone. Chaw Dios is the one who bosses me around, not a husband." Her community then labeled Pamela a "*mujer de la calle*" and a witch.

Fresia, as we saw earlier, found it impossible to accommodate her *machi* calling to her desire for domesticity and rejected her *machi* practice altogether. Her mother, Dominga, believed that Fresia could not both be a *machi* and keep a husband and household: "A *machi* whose destiny is to be single will never do well if she marries later on. If God chooses a young woman, then he always wants to see her as a young woman." Dominga argued that Fresia was like an angel or a nun who should remain a virgin to keep God's favor: "Sergio taught her to act just like in a nun's school. A young *machi* is like an angel by God's side. If she sins with a man, God turns his back on her." Dominga believed Fresia should emulate Machi Leonor, who had remained single and lived in her natal home. Leonor explained: "I am strong, I don't need a man. First comes my profession, and then my feelings and the company of men."

After she abandoned her *machi* practice in 1994, Fresia married a non-Mapuche man and had two children. She worked as a housemaid, and her children lived with Dominga in the south and visited her periodically. Fresia paid for the children's expenses, food, school, and clothing. Domestic and maternal values remained central to her identity.

Rocío, Pamela, and Fresia experienced the tensions between marriage, motherhood, and *machi* practice in different ways. Because Rocío was initiated later in life and had the support of her husband and grown children, she saw marriage, motherhood, and *machi* practice as compatible. She did not have to care for young children or perform domestic roles while she was a *machi,* and her husband accepted her need to travel. Pamela and Fresia, in contrast, encountered conflict between the expectations of marriage and motherhood and *machi* practice. Pamela struggled to rear her children and heal while her husband rejected her *machi* practice; she reacted by giving precedence to her *machi* spirit over her husband and children. Fresia had the opposite reaction. Because her family expected her to remain an unmarried, celibate *machi* living at home, her *machi* practice was, in effect, incompatible with marriage and motherhood. Fresia chose to break away from *machi*-hood in order to become a wife and mother.

Traditional Healers, Traveling Doctors, and Ambivalent Love Magic

Just as female *machi*'s negotiations of gender roles and domestic norms are complex and diverse, so are their relationships with traditional healing and biomedicine. Female *machi* use their experiences as wives and mothers to gain insight into their patients' suffering. They also gain symbolic capital by construing themselves as independent, authentic, traditional healers who use processual, empathetic, and involved techniques or who possess the authority of God's word. Their healing strategies vary widely and depend on factors such as the type of initiation and their specific powers and spirits.

Female *machi* claim not to be interested in being "like doctors," in using biomedicine, or in working at intercultural hospitals, as male *machi* do. Machi Javiera said: "When Minister Krauss came to Temuco to meet with Mapuche authorities, we asked her to allow us to collect herbal remedies because that is where our wisdom is. We told her that we are *machi,* not doctors, and that we want to work by ourselves, not with doctors in intercultural health hospitals."

Some female *machi,* however, seek the prestige and mobility associated with the doctor image or incorporate elements of biomedicine into their practices, as long as these do not challenge their image as traditional healers. Machi Rocío, for example, viewed herself as a "woman doctor," although she rejected biomedicine. Machi Berta was a certified nurse,

Machi María Cecilia had a "doctor's" consulting room in Santiago, and Machi Myriam worked twice a week at an intercultural health hospital.

At the same time, nontraditional practices such as love and luck magic and midwifery are exclusive to female *machi,* though not all female *machi* practice them. Machi Pamela, for instance, practiced all three, and Machi Rocío, none of them. A closer look at the practices of Rocío and Pamela illustrates much of the range of approaches.

Rocío: Premonitions, Altruism, and Rejection of Biomedicine

Rocío was an altruistic *machi* who viewed her vocation to heal as a gift. "You have to be a *machi* to help others," she said in a prayer in 2001. "Now I know my *machi* spirit. It gives me the power to see and serve others." Her powers were strongest on Tuesdays and Fridays, when she divined people's illnesses, prayed in Mapudungu, and gave patients herbal remedies for the small price of 5,000 pesos (US$8.00). Although Chileans believe that women should be more empathetic and altruistic than men, Rocío argued that all *machi* should possess these traits, regardless of their gender, and that *machi* who became too commercialized lost their powers. She relied heavily on premonitory dreams about her patients, their illnesses, and the appropriate cures: "In a dream they told me: 'A patient who is very sick is going to arrive. He went to three *machi.* They told him he was going to die. But he is not going to die. You know how to make herbal remedies. Give him this remedy first. This remedy is good against evil, this other one for this, this other one for that.' And I had to find those herbal remedies. My patient cried. My son asked me: 'Will this patient get better?' 'Yes,' I said, 'because they told me.' And he got better."

She also diagnosed patients' illnesses through urine samples or clothing they had worn or simply by looking at their faces: "You can tell what intentions a person has by looking at their eyes, their mouth." Twenty-year-old Guacolda came to Rocío for depression and pain in her ovaries. Guacolda placed her blouse and her 5,000 peso fee on the table, and Rocío drummed over the blouse until her spirit possessed her. The spirit described Guacolda's illness as "a ball of clotted blood and tissue in the ovary" and warned her: "If you don't get treated you will get cancer." Rocío prepared medicine from laurel and *boldo* herbs to soothe the stomach and ovaries, and *foye* and *fulcon* medicine to expel evil and give Guacolda courage.

The heart, the locus of emotion, and the head, the locus of thought, were inextricably linked in Rocío's practice. She connected my then husband, Anthony's, heart arrhythmia and chest pains with depression. She put his sunglasses on top of her silver pendant and crossed knives over them to expel his illness while she prayed for him: "Father creator, take out the illness he has in his heart. Make his heart, his head, and his blood strong. May they be in their place again. Let your son come back to life. Lift this son who is so weak. Support him in all things, I am supplicating." Anthony had an angioplasty to unblock his arteries, and his depression subsided a week later.

Rocío upheld a Catholic morality according to which she expelled evil spirits during *datun* rituals through spiritual warfare but did not reveal the names of evildoers or practice ritual revenge. "It is dangerous for a *machi* to say who sent evil to the person. If you say: 'This person did evil to you,' then people fight, and the *machi* is on bad terms with the witch."

Although Rocío identified herself as a "woman doctor" to gain status and legitimate her traveling, she rejected biomedicine because doctors were unable to heal her shamanic illness when it struck. Her son Leo explained: "No number of doctors will really be able to tell what illness she has. That has to come through ritual treatment and belief." Rocío, like Machi José, focused on the power of God to heal others rather than on the patient's self-betterment. Her healing methodologies were more authoritarian than Machi Pamela's, but less so than Machi Jorge's. Rocío earned legitimacy in the eyes of other Mapuche by presenting herself as a traditional, altruistic *machi* who prayed exclusively in Mapudungu and connected thought, emotion, and spirit with physical ailments. She also gained status in terms of dominant Chilean discourses as a mobile doctor with God's authority to heal and as a Catholic *machi* who refused to practice ritual revenge.

Pamela: Psychic Sight, Love, and Luck

Machi Pamela treated a large number of Mapuche and *wingka* patients, speaking either Mapudungu or Spanish as appropriate. Unlike Rocío, she made her patients take responsibility for their actions and participate actively in the healing process, adapting her rituals to their needs. Like Machi Sergio, she stressed courage, faith, and forgiveness as requirements for healing to work. Pamela, too, charged 5,000 pesos for a divination; she also charged 40,000 pesos (US$60.00) for a *datun* healing ritual and 30,000 pesos (US$45.00) for an *ulutun*. She had no knowledge of biomedicine but believed that pharmaceutical remedies were effective. For example, she attributed the swelling of her feet to witchcraft and treated them with both laurel leaves and Calorub, an ointment for muscle pain that she bought at a pharmacy.

Pamela was known for her ability to exorcise evil spirits through spiritual warfare. She treated Luz, whom she described as an epileptic "possessed by an evil spirit who wanted her to kill herself." Pamela exorcised the evil *witranalwe* or *añchümalleñ* spirits from Luz's body by giving her herbal remedies that made her vomit what Pamela saw as frogs or worms. She rubbed Luz's body with firewater, performed a *sahumerio* of her house, and prayed to expel the evil spirit: "Leave my patient alone. We don't want your company, because you are bad for people's health. Go somewhere else. Take your business where we will never see you again. You filthy dog, you will not get what you want." Pamela then cleansed Luz with an enema and gave her calming herbs. She told Luz to paint crosses on the doors to protect herself against evil and to get pills from the doctor.

In her *machi* practice Pamela drew on several traditional healing therapies. According to her, patients must have *küme piuke* (a good heart), *küme rakiduam* (good thoughts and intentions), and faith in order for the cure to work. "If we think with the heart, there will be something, it will work. If we don't think with the heart, there will be nothing." Pamela diagnosed people holistically using *vista* (psychic sight) and special powers in her right arm. Her *vista* allowed her to see the patient's illness, thoughts, and feelings. It gave her an intuitive comprehension of the client's situation and how to solve it: "With my sight I know people. I know their thoughts [*rakiduam*], what illnesses they have. My arm tells me when the ill person is going to arrive, when people speak the truth, when the patient will get well. When it pulls this way [to the right], people have faith, the healing will come out well. My hand swells when the patient will get better. When it pulls that way [to the left], he has no faith, it is not good."

Pamela also incorporated nontraditional love and luck magic into her healing practice in order to improve the status of women within the constraints of hierarchical gender norms. She advised her patients not to be jealous or argue with their husbands. She told Aracely: "You must not be bitter toward your man, even if he is sleeping with another woman. It is bad to get angry. You won't change anything that way." She told Frida not to confront her husband about his infidelities or to demand money, but to win him back with sweet words. In helping her clients,

Pamela used what Don Joralemon and Douglas Sharon (1993:265, 268) call "disguised means of manipulation," by which she simultaneously articulated and redressed women's experiences of domination.

But Pamela also attempted to change men's behavior to improve the lives of the women they affected. She chided Mapuche men for being womanizers and performed rituals to make them faithful and hard working. She stopped Frida's husband, Rafael, from spending money on drink and other women by wrapping his photograph with sweet-smelling *nulawen* flowers and praying for Frida's well-being: "Chaw Dios, Chaw Ngünechen, give good luck to this poor woman who has worked so hard. Give her strength to deal with her hardships. May her husband give up women, treat her well, and her children help her when she is old. May her husband stop drinking and give her more money to care for the house."

Pamela also performed rituals to give people good luck and money. To treat Holdenis, a fifty-year-old Chilean woman with ten children, she first cleansed the patient's house and then pressed a concoction of pink flowers, vinegar, and coins onto Holdenis's arms and chest to grant the family good luck and wealth. She prayed loudly, alternating between Spanish and Mapudungu: "Chaw Dios, take pity on this poor woman. Give them good luck. Let them be rich and happy." That night Pamela dreamed that evil and poverty had left the house in the form of an old woman. She told Holdenis to carry the herbs and coins in a cloth in her purse to ensure good luck.

Machi such as Pamela who practice midwifery compete with hospitals in delivering babies and with ordinary midwives in positioning the fetus for birth. But only *machi* midwives can use spiritual power to ensure a pregnancy, bless the fetus, and grant mother and child good luck in childbirth and later. Pamela dreamed about rituals "to make God bring babies down" (from the sky). She told a non-Mapuche woman to cuddle a doll in bed every night to get pregnant. She treated some pregnant women with herbal remedies and massage and gave others contraceptive remedies made from the *rayin* herb. Like most other Catholic female *machi*, Pamela refused to perform abortions or to give her patients medicine that would cause an abortion.

Pamela held a humanized conception of witchcraft in which death was caused by the hate and envy of others. She attributed the deaths of her family members to her bad relationships with the community. She believed they had killed her sister through *illeluwün*, and her mother, her in-laws, and her husband through *infitun*. "The neighbors put poison in some bread they gave to my sister María; she died. My mother picked up some hexed coins and she died. My in-laws were wealthy, so they buried a dead snake to hex [them] . . . My in-laws died. They buried a dead buzzard and my husband died. They buried a dog's leg so that I would be poor like a dog. My spirit protects me, though." Pamela attempted to gain control over the community's antagonism by shooting and stabbing *añchümalleñ* and *witranalwe* spirits that made noises on her roof at night.

Pamela was ambivalent about her ethnicity. On one hand, she believed that if Mapuche became like non-Mapuche there would be less witchcraft. She also said that *wingka* enabled Mapuche to have zinc roofs, medical posts, and pensions for elders and widows. On the other hand, she argued that Chaw Dios "did not like Mapuche *awingkados*," and therefore they got fewer favors from him. She saw *awingkamiento* as decreasing her patients' faith in her healing practices, and *wingka* individualism as destroying collective solidarity.

Pamela's focus on the need for good hearts and thoughts in order for her healing to work, her rejection of the authoritarian doctor's model, and her empathetic relational healing model all legitimated her as a traditional *machi*. Her incorporation of pharmaceutical remedies into her practice did not challenge this. Pamela's love and luck rituals and midwifery, however, marked her as ambivalent. Some Mapuche view love and luck rituals as witchcraft because they involve "manipulating a person's will or destiny," and Mapuche criticize midwives for providing herbal contraceptives to women and therefore interfering with "God's plan." Furthermore, Pamela's humanized concept of evil as associated with specific people in the community and her ambivalence about her own ethnicity marked her as something of an outsider and possibly a witch.

Pamela and Rocío both used the discourse of tradition and the insights gained through their experiences as wives and mothers to legitimate their healing practices. They emphasized forgiveness, which was associated with both the priestly and the mothering models, and reinforced the connection between thought, emotion, and body. Other Mapuche considered Rocío to be more traditional and "authentic" than Pamela because she rejected biomedicine, refused to practice ritual revenge, and prayed exclusively in Mapudungu.

Although Mapuche favor the processual, empathetic, and involved healing techniques Pamela used, they respect *machi* like Rocío who speak the word of God and have the prestige ascribed to doctors without being authoritarian. Mapuche accepted Pamela's incorporation of pharmaceutical remedies as typical *machi* practice. They rejected her love and luck rituals as ambiguous, non-Mapuche practices to gain control over the will and destiny of others, although they secretly requested them.

Traditional Beliefs, Catholicism, and the New Age

Regardless of their varied approaches to healing, biomedicine, and love or luck magic, prestigious female *machi* appropriate the role of priestess in *ngillatun* rituals to become *machi* moon priestesses, gain recognition, and legitimate their role as public ritual leaders. They invoke the powers of the moon, the Virgin Mary, and Old Woman Ngünechen to petition for good crops and the fertility of animals and humans. Marian worship is particularly important to female *machi* because they associate Mary with the fertility powers controlled by the moon and Old Woman Ngünechen. Female *machi* claim spiritual kinship with the mother of God and grant her shamanic powers over life, fertility, and death. The Marian colors, blue and white, also represent the sky and the moon, and some female *machi* identify with Mater Dolorosa, who is morally superior and grieves for her Mapuche children who are ill.

Mapuche, regardless of their age or whether they are mothers in their everyday lives, symbolically associate female *machi* with the motherhood, fertility, and abundance granted by the Virgin and the moon. Mapuche associate the full moon with a pregnant woman, fertility, and a plentiful harvest and with Küyen-Kushe, the elder and more powerful of two Mapuche fertility goddesses. *Machi* perform rituals on full-moon nights, when they think the moon is most receptive to human petitions. Jaime, Machi Nora's son, explained that "the full moon fills the grain and makes the crops grow." Mapuche associate the new moon with Küyen-Ulcha Domo, the younger moon goddess. They seed their crops with the new moon and believe that seeds germinate and fetuses develop when the moon grows. Machi Ana said: "The moon helps [women] get pregnant. When the moon grows, then the baby grows in the belly." Female *machi* often depict the moon on their *kultrun* and ritual flags and use the powers of the moon and the Virgin Mary in diverse ways.

Machi Pamela represents the more typical pattern among female *machi:* she professed a belief in Catholicism and blended traditional beliefs with Catholic concepts in her *machi* practice. Pamela was initiated by prestigious Machi Nora and belonged to the same *machi* school of practice as Nora's other initiates, Ana and Leonor. Nora's *machi* school was ruled by the moon, and its initiates painted their *rewe* and *kultrun* in blue and white, the colors of the sky, the moon, and the Virgin Mary. Pamela gained power from the moon to enhance fertility, and she associated the phases of the moon with different gender identities: "The moon gives me power. Because of the moon I have voice. The moon is life, and it defends people. In the full moon is Jesus Christ, our saviour. The new moon is the woman. It has sheep, pigs, horses, beans. The good people, when they die, they go to the moon" (interview, February 1, 1992).

Pamela also identified as Catholic and baptized her children so that the holy water would protect them from evil spirits. She espoused a Catholic morality in which good predominated over evil. She communicated directly with Ngünechen, whom she associated with the Christian God and the Virgin: "I have to ask Ngünechen and the Virgin for help. I have to have faith." Nuns visited Machi Pamela and gave her an image of the Virgin Mary and a Bible in an attempt to convert her more fully to Catholicism.

Pamela drew on the powers of the Virgin Mary in her healing and in her everyday life. She hung a poster of the pope and another of the Virgin that read: "This is the house of God." She hung a statue of the Virgin in her bedroom beside her *kultrun,* because it gave her power and helped her exorcise evil spirits: "The Virgin takes care of you. The Virgin is good to heal people, to take out the filth. I don't like the cross, Jesus Christ dies, there are crosses in the cemetery. To dream about the cross and flowers is bad. It means someone is going to die." Pamela painted her *rewe* and house blue and white. When she died in 1996 her daughters painted her tombstone blue, hung a crucifix on it, and planted a *foye* tree at her feet.

According to Pamela, the Virgin Mary, the moon, and Jesus were inextricably linked. She gained her ability to enhance agricultural fertility directly from them. But since Pamela's powers had not been legitimated through formal *machi* training (despite her initiation by Nora), her community did not recognize her as a *machi* moon priestess, and her *machi* school could not protect her against accusations of witchcraft. Pamela saw herself as a suffering Virgin who granted fertility and happiness to those who believed in her.

Machi Rocío, atypically, kept Mapuche and Catholic beliefs separate and used only the former in her healing rituals. Rocío supported Catholicism in general, because it was more tolerant of *machi* practice than was evangelicalism, although she rarely went to church. "The evangelicals don't believe in *machi* rituals. They say it is witchcraft. I like the Catholics better because they allow *machi* to pray. All those years [when she lived in her husband's evangelical community], I was hiding my patients, healing far away where the evangelicals wouldn't hear me" (interview, February 2, 1993). She even described her *machi* moon priestess role as being like that of a Catholic priest leading Mass: "The *ngillatun* is like a church. I ask for good harvests, good health for everyone. The *machi* prays because they cannot pray."

Yet, unlike most other *machi*, Rocío believed that Ngünechen was unrelated to the Virgin Mary and the Christian God, and she did not use Catholic symbols in her healing. When she performed as a *machi* moon priestess, she wore her black woolen wrap, colored hair ribbons, and blue-and-pink-dyed chicken feathers. The stars and the moon gave her the power to heal and ensure agricultural fertility: "The moon and the old star give me power. All rituals must be performed on the full moon so that they will turn out properly." She painted red and blue stars on her *kultrun* and sewed blue and white moons and stars on her ritual flags. Rocío believed that, if she prayed, Old Woman Ngünechen would grant the community fertility, abundance, and well-being: "In the sky there was an old woman, Kuse, with gray hair, who looks down to see the people on earth. 'I'm going to give them this harvest,' she says. 'What do you want?' she asked me. I said: 'I want barley.' She got a basket and she filled it with barley, beans, potatoes, hazelnuts, chile peppers, cilantro, onions, and wheat. 'Give her all that she wants,' this voice told the old lady. She said: 'You have so many children, I will pray for you. All your children will be well and working.'" According to Rocío, it was Old Woman Ngünechen, not the Virgin Mary, who granted fertility.

A relatively new trend associated with the so-called New Age ignores the Catholic and Marian elements so common in *machi* practice. This trend is one in which non-Mapuche women use *machi* methods, linked to metaphors of motherhood, outside of Mapuche ritual contexts. Mapuche generally oppose it.

A feminist woman poet who went by the name of Rayen Küyen (Flower of the Moon), for example, expressed women's power and Mapuche identity through images of the moon: "The moon controls women and the fertility of the earth. We [women] are the earth, the moon, and life. We have our Mapuche identity inside us. The moon is also associated with identity. The new moon was the first [Mapuche] resistance, the moon's ash is the time of [Spanish and Chilean] domination, and now the full moon is the new identity that young Mapuche are creating, in which women play a central role" (interview, April 23, 1995).

Rayen supported a number of Mapuche artists and writers and was claimed by some as a "Mapuche literary mother." Other Mapuche believed that she faked Mapuche ancestry and sold the image of the fertile *machi* mother to American and German women in order to gain fame and fortune. Abel, who was training to be a *machi,* claimed: "Rayen is not Mapuche, but she learned Mapudungu and is treating people with her herbs. The Mapuche don't want to be *machi,* and now the *wingka* want to take their place. Rayen invents rituals for groups of Mapuche, Chilean women, and gringas. That's wrong. She does it to get money. Mapuche women don't have anything in common with gringas and Chilean women" (interview, April 21, 1995).

A Chilean woman who goes by the name of Luzclara (Clear Light) constructs herself as a "white *machi.*" She has a *rewe* in her house in El Cajón del Maipo, near Santiago, and uses the knowledge she has acquired from *machi* to hold New Age workshops for American and upper-class Chilean women. She takes them to "ride in the Andes Mountains and connect with Mother Earth," and she runs women's healing circles in which, as she describes it, "everybody comes together from the heart and connects with the shaman within."[8] Luzclara also holds weekend retreats in North Carolina to encourage American women to "find their feminine guides." During the workshops the women obtain their own *kultrun* as well as a Mapuche spirit name.[9]

Machi Ana was angry about Luzclara's activities because she invoked Mapuche spirits for tourists rather than on behalf of a ritual community, as *machi* do: "She's not Mapuche. She's not a *machi* and she is exploiting Mapuche spirits and culture. The spirits are going to punish her. Only *machi* can know certain things. This knowledge is not for gringas to play with."

Mapuche Catholicism and Marianism are fundamental to female *machi*'s healing and their performances as *machi* moon priestesses, but New Age practitioners disregard them in search of the "authentic" indigenous other. Female *machi* may claim priestly roles to gain legitimacy (Rocío); they may gain fertility powers from the Virgin Mary and experience her suffering (Pamela). Female *machi* associate the powers of fertility granted by the moon with Old Woman Ngünechen and the Virgin Mary and petition for the well-being of an entire ritual community. New Age women stress the universal association between women, the moon, and fertility for individual tourist consumption, ignoring the ethnic communal dimensions of these rituals and the existence of Mapuche Catholicism. These New Age manipulations of the feminine aspects of *machi* practice are beginning to affect the practices of female *machi*. *Machi* capitalize on the increasing feminization of spiritual practice to bolster their own power but claim that the fertility powers of the moon are available only to their own clients, not to New Age women.

The Pragmatic Political Negotiations of Female *Machi*

So far we have looked at female *machi*'s beliefs and practices solely in the context of their personal lives and healing careers. But some female *machi*, contrary to stereotype, also play roles in larger, political arenas. The Mapuche perception that female *machi* and Mapuche women in general do not participate in community, pan-Mapuche, or national politics is belied by actual practice.

Mapuche usually understand the term *politics* as meaning participation in national political ideologies. Because these ideologies are determined by the dominant Chilean culture, Mapuche believe that by participating in national politics they lose some of their traditional culture. And because Mapuche view female *machi* as more closely associated with tradition, they think it should be men who take on leadership roles and participate in politics (Bacigalupo 1994b, 1996a; Degarrod 1998; Faron 1964; Stuchlik 1976; Titiev 1951). Many Mapuche men and women claim that, when women participate in politics, they do so under the guidance of their fathers or husbands (Bacigalupo 1994b; Bengoa 1983; Montecino 1984). This attitude is shared by members of the male-dominant Chilean culture, who view women first and foremost in their family role and see men mainly in terms of their public role. Chilean men predominate over women in all positions of political and economic authority.

Anthropologists, too, have portrayed female shamans from around the world in terms of deprivation relative to male-dominant state apparatuses. Female possession has been seen as peripheral (Lewis 1971) and as a form of resistance to the power of men (Boddy 1989; Lambek 1981). Female shamanism is often depicted as the product of women's motherhood and fertility (Glass-Coffin 1998; Sered 1994). Women are portrayed as having become shamans in order to compensate for their marginalization from the state bureaucracy and institutionalized religion (Basilov 1997; Lewis 1971) or because of their peripheral social status or sexual deprivation (Obeyesekere 1981; Spiro 1967).

In practice, both Mapuche men and women have gained prestige by holding positions of power external to their communities and by acting as intermediaries between Mapuche communities and the government,

heads of NGOs, and politicians. Certainly, Mapuche men greatly out-
number women in such positions. Isolde Reuque (2002:227, 232–235)
argues that male Mapuche leaders do not want Mapuche women to hold
positions of political authority, to be involved in decision making, or to
speak in public. But sex role segregation is not as rigid among Mapuche
as it is in the Chilean dominant culture (Zambrano 1987). Mapuche
women have less representation in decision-making positions than do
Mapuche men, but more than non-Mapuche Chilean women. "Mapuche
women are more likely than their non-Mapuche counterparts to participate in all types of organizations (cultural and political organizations,
community development groups, unions) and are also more likely than
non-Mapuche women to achieve positions of authority in these organizations" (Richards 2004:184).

Some Mapuche think female *machi*'s participation in community, pan-
Mapuche, and national politics is problematic, because they see politics
as conflicting with the spiritual role. Chile's presidents and members
of Mapuche resistance movements, however, use female *machi* as symbols for their own political agendas, and *machi* themselves have devised
unique ways of participating in politics. Their relationships with political
authorities may support, transform, or contest the images of them deployed by the Mapuche resistance and Chilean politicians. In what follows, the experiences of female *machi*—not only Pamela and Rocío but
also Ana, Tegualda, Hortensia, and Javiera—reveal the variety of female
machi's modes of political participation: nonpartisan pragmatic politics;
spiritual negotiations of power; and increasing politicization.

Nonpartisan Pragmatic Politics

Despite popular stereotypes, few female *machi* are passive, apolitical retainers of tradition or political symbols of resistance; they are pragmatic
negotiators of power who use the opportunities presented to them by
politicians—at least, by those who follow the same protocols that *longko*
use to invite *machi* to rituals and events. Longko Daniel explained: "You
have to follow a strict protocol to invite *machi* to *ngillatun*. One has to tell
her at least fifteen to twenty days ahead of time. And know how to speak
to the *machi* with respect."

Political mobility and situational engagement with political actors are
common among Mapuche and other indigenous people. The novelty
of female *machi*'s pragmatic political negotiations lies in the way these
women play up their ostensible conformity to national stereotypes of

female *machi* as peasant, traditional, and apolitical while in fact transcending traditional norms by engaging with national and Mapuche authorities. In order to legitimate their spiritual practices in national and Mapuche discourses, female *machi* often reinforce the idea that spirituality and womanhood conflict with politics. Machi Pamela told me: "*Machi* don't get involved in politics. God doesn't want that." In reality, many of them do engage in politics, on their own terms. They draw on gender stereotypes but stretch and reinvent them for their own ends.

Like other Mapuche women, female *machi* take a personalized approach to politics. They support the political figures they believe will benefit them most or offer support to return favors to family and friends, not because of their political views. Machi Rocío, for example, played her drum at a rally for President Lagos in 2000 because her son Domingo belonged to his Socialist Party. "Domingo is working with Lagos. One has to give them votes, support. 'I like *machi* when they pray,' Lagos told me. 'How well you prayed, thank you,' he said."

Male *machi* define themselves partly in terms of political ideology. Female *machi*, in contrast, exercise their power independently of the political parties, agendas, and ideologies of Mapuche resistance movements and Chilean politicians.[10] Their unpredictable, nonpartisan, situational politics allows them to negotiate, for pragmatic ends, with a wider range of political authorities than male *machi* have available, without being perceived as disloyal to a political party. "Female *machi* go to different authorities because they are invited with the correct protocol. *Machi* want to meet and talk with the authorities. This does not mean that the *machi* support the political party and ideology of that authority but that they want to be known and negotiate with them," Machi Javiera's husband explained in December 2001. Machi Rocío supported any political candidate who invited her with the correct protocol:

> ROCÍO: He [the candidate for mayor] spoke to me in Mapudungu.
>   "Okay," I said, "I give you my vote."
> MARIELLA: You go with anyone who speaks to you in Mapudungu?
> ROCÍO: Yes, one has to go and support them. When one is invited, one
>   has to go.

Similarly, female *machi* participate in Mapuche resistance movements because the recovery of ancestral land, ancient forests, and traditions is central to their livelihood and spiritual practices. But they do not always support Mapuche ideologies of resistance against the Chilean state. Machi

Javiera became ill in 2001 when the construction of a highway bypass destroyed sacred places where spirits of rivers and waterfalls lived: "They destroyed the source of my spirit, my herbal remedies. I cannot diagnose patients and heal with the noise of the machines. I no longer have any strength," said Javiera. She sometimes participated in resistance movements, but in this instance she sought the support of CONADI to recover the sacred places from the government rather than promoting resistance against it.

Female *machi* often complain that Mapuche movements have manipulated them by politicizing their role as icons of tradition and failing to treat them with the correct protocol. Machi Javiera recalled: "The Consejo de Todas las Tierras invited me to perform a prayer, but it was really a protest. They used me. I asked them for a new drum, but they brought me nothing." In 1990 the Consejo de Todas las Tierras took *machi* and *longko* to the city of Valdivia, where King Juan Carlos of Spain was visiting, and asked to meet with him to discuss land treaties dating from colonial days. Chilean officials prevented the meeting from taking place. Machi Hortensia felt misled and disrespected: "The leader asked me to support Mapuche traditions. He said we were going to meet the king of Spain to talk about Mapuche problems, but we never saw the king. He nearly killed us from hunger. We marched through the whole town. We shouted, we played our drums, but there was no food. Is that the way to treat a *machi*?"

Machi Rocío, too, resented leaders' neglect of protocol and their inability to protect *machi* from police violence: "The older people treated *machi* with respect. They had good conversation, good manners. Today there are not these words. I don't go with the Consejo de Todas las Tierras because they don't take care of *machi*. *Machi* who went to the march in Temuco with their drums were wet and beaten by the police. Is that how you respect your *machi*?"

Gendered power and resistance in societies with polarized gender roles has been shown to be especially complicated. Women both resist and support existing systems of power, but their experiences and motivations should not be misattributed to false consciousness, feminist consciousness, or feminist politics (Abu-Lughod 1990:47). The practices of female *machi* are not strategies intended to empower women, nor are female *machi* conscious of how their actions reinforce or challenge dominant ideologies. What, then, is the relationship between the agency of female *machi* and the various gendered structures that shape their world?

Chilean national and Mapuche gendered discourses objectify *machi* and constrain their lives and actions. Neither Mapuche nor Chilean politicians expect female *machi* to be "modernized" by their participation in political events. Mapuche's traditional understandings of masculine political and feminine spiritual power shape *machi*'s interactions with authorities. Yet, *machi* do not let these images determine them completely, but use them to their advantage to promote their own understanding of power based on their relationships with spirits.

Spiritual Negotiations of Power

The knowledge of *machi* and their ability to heal with the help of spirits offer powerful symbolic tools for pursuing political goals without committing to the ideologies of political parties. The spiritual approach of *machi* to politics is concerned with interpersonal power, recognition, and identity. Female *machi* project Mapuche's personalized, reciprocal relationships with authorities and spirit beings onto their interactions with representatives of the Chilean state, taking advantage of the diverse possibilities that politicians and political parties offer them. In their rituals, *machi* greet spirits and deities using the honorary titles "king," "queen," and "chief" and shower them with offerings and prayers. In turn, the spirits recognize *machi* as powerful and worthy of the knowledge they give them. In the same manner, *machi* forge relationships with Mapuche and national figures of authority, honoring them with rituals to bolster the *machi*'s own power and gain recognition.

Machi Pamela, for example, boasted that she had met President Pinochet and healed his niece, which enhanced her prestige. In 1993, to gain public recognition, Pamela drummed at an event to celebrate the passing of the Indigenous Law under President Aylwin: "He greeted me and shook my hand. He knew I was an important *machi*." Some female *machi* believe these associations with political authorities will help them regain land, protect their community, and increase their powers. In 1986 Pinochet legitimated *machi* and *longko* from the city of Nueva Imperial, and they in turn legitimated him as "*ülmen, füta longko*," or powerful elder and chief. They hoped Pinochet would return the land he had usurped and believed they were more powerful after the encounter.[11]

Female *machi*, replicating national gendered kinship tropes and mirroring the relationship between the Mapuche deity Ngünechen and the ritual community, view the state in the role of father and donor to the Mapuche. Just as Ngünechen grants blessings, good crops, and remedies to *machi* who perform rituals, so association with the state, *machi* think, will bring them social and economic benefits. Machi Javiera said: "We pray to Ngünechen, we do *ngillatun* rituals; there we give him wheat, sheep's blood, and he gives us good harvests, animals, rain. If we don't do *ngillatun,* then he punishes us. We will have drought and frost. We also stand beside the president, we play *kultrun* for him, and we give him gifts so that his government will be good to us. Then maybe he gives us fertilizers, zinc roofs, good laws, and money before Christmas. If we don't support him, then we will be poorer than before and other people will be benefited."

Female *machi* use their spiritual approach to politics to propitiate, honor, and manipulate politicians for good, evil, or pragmatic ends. Machi Ana, for example, viewed Pinochet as a hypermasculine figure of military power and propitiated him to exorcise evil spirits: "Since Lagos has been president there has been a lot of disorder. People are insolent and don't respect the police. I have less power. In the time of Pinochet people did not rebel because Pinochet would kill them. People need to respect authority. They need to respect me like they need to respect Pinochet. He has strength and I admire him. I need that kind of power to chase the devil away." Female *machi* view democratic presidents as less masculine and less powerful than Pinochet but as easier to negotiate with for pragmatic ends. The democratic government promises them practical gains through government projects, legal recognition, and respect for their traditions and healing practices. In December 2001 Machi Javiera said: "I meet with the people in the government because I want to demonstrate that our culture is valuable and that they should take *machi* into consideration. We go so that people understand what *machi* are and learn that they are not witches but people who are central to Mapuche culture and traditions."

Through their pragmatic spiritual negotiations with political authorities, female *machi* try to transform a hierarchical relationship with the state, in which the masculine state stands over them, into one of mutual recognition. Although female *machi* do not assume formal political positions and tend to avoid discussions of political ideology, their engagement with political authorities in itself can be read as a political act.

Not all Mapuche agree with female *machi*'s need to be recognized by political authorities and with their spiritual, nonpartisan negotiations. Some Mapuche interpret *machi*'s engagement with authorities as their subordination to state powers. When a female *machi* gave President Frei a poncho in recognition of his authority in 1999, Julia Rulepan, a Mapuche woman, screamed: "You don't have to give them anything. They have to give us our land, you dumb Indian!" (*Las Últimas Noticias,* August 6, 1999).

Power and resistance have been recurring themes in scholars' understanding of spiritual experiences of domination. On one hand, spirit possession has often been viewed as a form of resistance to political, gender, race, or age domination (Boddy 1989; Comaroff 1985; Stoller 1995). Local expressions and idioms of spirituality have been seen to destabilize the assumptions on which state or Western logics of control are founded and to have become historically sensitive local modes of cultural resistance (Steedly 1993; Taussig 1987, 1993; Tsing 1993). On the other hand, anthropologists have argued that resistance theory has been overused (Abu-Lughod 1990; Brown 1996; Ortner 1995), that indigenous culture is not a site for spontaneous resistance to dominant cultural forms (Hall 1986; R. Williams 1977), and that hegemonic perspectives fail to address "the profound ambiguity and tension of living agents as they wrestle morally and socially with the inequities of change" (Knauft 1998:207). Female *machi*'s engagement with different discourses of authority demonstrates that the interworkings of power and resistance are complex. Mapuche, national, and *machi* forms of power sometimes work together and sometimes contradict one another. *Machi*'s simultaneous reiteration of and resistance to national and Mapuche gendered discourses illustrate the way new forms of power are created.

Work on resistance influenced by Antonio Gramsci (1971) theorizes ideological practices in terms of an opposition between hegemonic ideologies—secured by the construction of political and ideological consensus between dominant and subordinate groups—and counterhegemonic ideologies, which resist through transformation of consciousness (Burke 1999; Gramsci 1971:323; Strinati 1995:165). Contrarily, the ambivalences and contradictions that exist in female *machi*'s spiritual understandings of power, which conform to the ideologies of neither political parties nor resistance movements, demonstrate that ideologies are, instead, fluid and ambiguous. By resisting the ideological associations that Chilean politicians and members of Mapuche resistance movements ascribe to *machi* practice, female *machi* partake of national notions in which *machi* are apolitical. At the same time, by supporting the Mapuche resistance movements' ideals of tradition, which are associated with ancestral spirits of the forest and the recovery of Mapuche territory, self-determination, and sovereignty, *machi* resist the Chilean government's neoliberal policies and national notions that *machi* are apolitical.

Female *machi*'s ambiguous relationships with political authorities offer a new spiritual reading of the discourse of power and resistance. Female *machi* use their shamanic beliefs, in which political ideology does not prevail, to redefine power for their own ends. Not only do they read politicians through the lens of spiritual power, but they use the spiritual power gained from encounters with politicians to influence the thoughts (*rakiduam*) and hearts (*piuke*) of Chile's presidents to gain support for Mapuche traditions and to regain ancestral land. The purpose of female *machi*'s pragmatic relationship with authorities is not to resist the state but to bolster their spiritual power to benefit themselves and other Mapuche.

Female *machi*'s nonpartisan, pragmatic, and shamanic reinterpretations of political authorities offer a new understanding of the workings of power itself and the ways in which it can be manipulated for multiple ends. Their spiritual reading of politicians, which Mapuche view as a feminine mode of power, is a radical departure from the gendered discourses of the Chilean nation-state, in which female *machi* are seen as subordinate, folkloric symbols of indigenousness. The effectiveness of female *machi*'s nonpartisan strategies for negotiating with political authorities in democratic Chile, where identity is increasingly politicized, remains uncertain. Whereas male *machi* define themselves in political terms, work in intercultural hospitals, and speak to the media, female *machi* minister to their presidents by claiming the authenticity of tradition. Yet, they have a political stake in maintaining their practices. How much longer will female *machi* be able, without politicizing their identities, to wrap themselves in the veil of tradition without identifying with the Mapuche and national authorities who grant them benefits and support their practices?

The Increasing Politicization of Female *Machi*

The spiritual knowledge of *machi* offers new possibilities for rethinking indigenous identities in which shamans serve as icons of traditional knowledge used for purposes of pan-Mapuche resistance. Female *machi* do not gain legitimacy by associating themselves with male military authorities, as male *machi* do. But Mapuche activists have militarized female *machi* in creative ways to further their own goals. They have combined the spiritual role of *machi,* traditionally the feminine domain, with political activities and tropes of warfare, traditionally associated with masculinity. Instead of linking epic masculine warriors solely with contemporary male Mapuche leaders, resistance movements have masculinized female *machi* as political agents and spiritual warriors acting against forestry companies and the modern state. These hybrid images of the feminine, spiritual, but warlike political *machi* are used to gain support for resistance movements among native and non-native citizens alike.

Some female *machi* have begun to identify with the ideologies of Mapuche resistance movements, willingly adopting and enthusiastically enacting the images assigned to them. On December 21, 1997, I participated in a *weichan ngillatun,* or collective warring ritual, performed by forty-two-year-old Machi Tegualda in one of the communities whose land had been exploited by Forestal Mininco. The *ngillatun,* traditionally performed by *machi* to request fertility and well-being, has acquired political implications. It expresses a sense of community and a spiritual relationship to the homeland, and it helps create a boundary between what is traditionally Mapuche and a perceived outside world of non-Mapuche. Even though *machi*'s performances of *ngillatun* rituals have become increasingly generic in order to address the needs of a Mapuche nation rather those of a particular community, they are tailored to specific conflicts with forestry companies and the government. During the ritual, Tegualda propitiated ancestral spirits and Ngünechen in order to battle Forestal Mininco and President Frei. She and the male *longko* exhorted the community to be brave warriors:

TEGUALDA: Lift your *chuecas* every time you scream "Marichiweu" [We will win ten times over], as if you were winning. You are brave men. You are Mapuche; before, you always won.

LONGKO: You will win. You are a warring woman, a warring *machi.* Give us your wisdom, your words, your advice. With your help we will have strength. We will unite to continue our struggle. Marichiweu, Marichiweu!

TEGUALDA: That's right. You should scream "Marichiweu" all the time. It is the cry of our ancestors, which you should not forget. We are in the struggle. We are a united people and we should recover what is ours. Our land, our ancient forests. We have done this before. We will not be afraid. We will not forget our language. We will remember our ancestral laws. *Machi* should meet and combine their wisdom.

LONGKO: That's right. That way, we will have strength and we will not be shamed. Marichiweu—all of you scream Marichiweu!

TEGUALDA: We have started our warring *ngillatun.* We are visible. We are making news. Many will think we are right and will be happy because of what we are doing. The *kona* [young warriors] will explain what we are doing. We are brave people. People of struggle. Cry Marichiweu!

Tegualda beat her drum above her head and demanded that the participants echo her cry. She recast traditional rituals in political terms, gaining the support of ancient warriors to battle the spirit of neoliberalism.

Mapuche resistance movements have fostered an increasing "shamanization of indigenous identities" (Conklin 2002:1058) and a politicization of shamanic roles that offer a new understanding of power. During Pinochet's dictatorship, militant Mapuche such as Santos Millao drew on the icon of the Mapuche warrior of the past and brandished spears to assert their demands and oppose the government. Since the advent of democracy in 1990, some female *machi* have worked side by side with Mapuche chiefs in resistance movements, opening new possibilities of interaction with the government and other Mapuche groups. Unlike *longko,* female *machi* do not have to prove themselves to gain local Mapuche support.

Female *machi* have become symbols of Mapuche identity because their legitimacy stems from their links to ancestor and nature spirits, their knowledge and spiritual powers, and their symbolic value as representatives of the land, tradition, and forests. When Forestal Mininco eroded the land of the community of Lukutunmapu, Machi Tegualda said: "The *ngenko* [spirit owners of the water] and *ngenlawen* [spirit owners of herbal remedies] from around here have all left. There are only pine trees. No herbal remedies, no water. I cannot heal anymore, and I'm very ill. We will fight the forestry companies with our lives because without our forests there is no life."

Shamanism itself is being redefined as shamans become politically active. Shamans have always mediated between the human and the spirit worlds. They now use their skills, perspectives, knowledge, and imagery in the realm of interethnic politics and in mediating relations with the state (Conklin 2002:1050–1051).

Female *machi* are also beginning to subscribe to national political ideologies. Rocío explained that she would not support Pinochet or the military even if they asked her with the correct protocol: "I do not give my vote to Pinochet. He killed so many people. The military were looking for people over here. He asked me if I knew certain people."

The increasing politicization of *machi* and the shamanization of Mapuche politics illustrate how indigenous strategies are being creatively reformulated in response to the need to negotiate among multiple political discourses, ideologies, and values. The effects that the growing politicization of female *machi*'s identity will have on their perceptions and practices of power remains to be seen.

Conclusion

The micropolitics practiced by female *machi* illustrate Michel Foucault's notion that power is not just a repressive system but a productive network that runs through the whole social body. This power exercises itself through social production, social service, knowledge, discourse, and pleasure (Foucault 1980:119, 125). By incorporating Mapuche cultural norms, which are heavily influenced by male-dominant, Catholic national discourses, female *machi* enable these dominant ideologies to gain access to their bodies, acts, attitudes, and modes of everyday behavior. These "relations of power which permeate, characterize, and constitute the social body are established, consolidated, and implemented through discourse" (Foucault 1980:93). In turn, female *machi* transform these discourses and systems of power by finding alternative ways of practicing micropolitics within the parameters of the systems of power. Like everyone else, female *machi* are in the position of simultaneously feeling the effects of and exercising power. "The individual which power has constituted is at the same time its vehicle" (Foucault 1980:98).

As symbols of tradition and domesticity, female *machi* can sustain spiritual readings of power independently from male-dominant political ideologies and can legitimate a variety of gender-transgressive practices. But they are always constrained by Mapuche gender roles and Marian values in their everyday lives. They struggle to maintain their legitimacy as they are faced with the demands of the spirits and the *machi* profession, on one hand, and contradictory social expectations of Mapuche women, on the other. Although Mapuche claim that spirituality, dominated by female *machi,* is separate from social norms and politics, this is belied by the tension that exists between the social and spiritual orders in *machi*'s lives and by the increasing politicization of female *machi* by Mapuche resistance movements, national politicians, and female *machi* themselves. The ambiguity of female *machi* lies in their ability to straddle different worlds—to use the paradigm of spirituality to gain prestige in social and political contexts while allowing their spiritual practices to be constrained by gender norms.

Female *machi* illustrate how relations of power are interwoven with kinship, family, and sexual relations. In social contexts, the reputations of female *machi* are determined largely by the prestige of their natal families, their marital status, their relationship to their husband's family, their modesty and Catholic morality, and the gender roles they perform. Female *machi* are allowed gender transgressions in their everyday lives because their spiritual practices do not challenge the patrilineal social order or propose new roles for women. The key to a female *machi*'s success is to distinguish between the domestic role played by ordinary women and the female *machi*'s role as a symbol of domesticity who must transgress domestic roles in order to travel to heal others and to benefit the community. The symbolic effect that Michelle Bachelet will have on the legitimation of female *machi*'s public roles remains to be seen.

The mechanisms of power in Mapuche and Chilean society become effective through dominant discourses about bodies, health, reproduction, morality, and spirituality that constrain female *machi*'s lives. Marriage and motherhood link *machi*'s social, spiritual, and biological selves in complex and contradictory ways. They grant female *machi* social status and prestige and legitimate their sexuality within the patrilineage and Catholic discourses. But expectations of female *machi* as wives and mothers often conflict with their ritual roles. Mapuche celebrate spiritual wifeliness and motherhood. *Machi*'s spirit spouses are granted precedence over their husbands, and all female *machi* are symbolic mothers and Virgin Marys who draw on the powers of the moon to grant fertility. The biological side of *machi* wifeliness and motherhood is ambiguous, because the patrilineage claims control over women's sexuality and reproduction. Female *machi* who are sexually active and fertile biological mothers lose some of their autonomy in the spiritual realm, because their spiritual powers might override patrilineal control of sexuality and reproduction. Mapuche see menstrual blood, birth blood, and sexual fluids as instruments of witchcraft because they symbolize the power of uncontrolled sexuality and reproduction, challenges to the patrilineal social order. Female *machi* who are no longer fertile or who are celibate gain prominence because their spiritual powers pose no threat.

Female *machi* have developed different ways to think about Mapuche notions of body, health, reproduction, and the spiritual within the constraints of the Mapuche-Chilean system. Mapuche feminists and activists often reject female *machi*'s alternatives as furthering the domination of women, but rural women embrace these narratives because it grants them a place as guardians of tradition within the system. Catholicism restricts female *machi*'s behavior, but female *machi* embrace it as part of their "traditional practice" because it allows them to promote their own interests and transform their rituals. As priestesses who are legitimated by the Virgin Mary, female *machi* can perform public ritual roles without threatening the image of the domestic *machi* or the virtuous woman. Catholicism also serves as an alternative paradigm to the requirement of *machi* training, as it did for Pamela, and creates alternative forms of legitimacy for female *machi*.

Female *machi* use micropolitics as a "strategy for coordinating and directing relations of force" (Foucault 1980:189). They have capitalized on the separation between men's politics and women's spirituality in Mapuche discourses in order to promote a spiritual, nonpartisan reading of power that is viewed as unthreatening by both Chilean politicians and members of Mapuche resistance movements.

The recognition and interpersonal power that female *machi* gain from their pragmatic negotiations with political authorities have political and cosmic consequences. As possessors of spiritual power and traditional knowledge and as representatives of Mapuche identity, female *machi* gain political authority and begin to identify with political ideologies. The balance between clearly defined political and spiritual realms is challenged as *machi* gain power in the political realm and Mapuche and national politicians increasingly draw on the spiritual powers of *machi* to legitimate their discourses.

CHAPTER 9

Representing the Gendered Identities of *Machi*: Paradoxes and Conflicts

ABEL: You said in the small print that male machi *changed with the moon. You said that, when the moon was full,* machi *had penises, and when the moon was waning, then they were women. You said that sometimes they liked women and sometimes they liked men. You said that* machi *were witches.*

MARIELLA: I didn't say male machi *were witches and homosexuals, but that people accuse them of being homosexuals and witches. The small print you read is a quote where Machi Pamela states that Machi Jorge's sex and sexuality change with the moon . . .*

ABEL: Why don't you just say that all male machi *are good and traditional? That none of them are homosexuals? That none of them are witches? The Chileans look down on us. We need good publicity.*

MARIELLA: Do you believe that all machi *are good?*

ABEL: No, there are good and bad machi. *Some may be homosexual. What do you believe?*

MARIELLA: I have never seen anything that leads me to believe that any machi *is a witch. I don't know whether they are homosexual or not. The modern notion of homosexuality was introduced by non-Mapuche. I am trying to understand the reasons why people in the community and other* machi *use these terms to make accusations.*

ABEL: Yes, it is the wingka's fault. They are to blame.

—CONVERSATION, DECEMBER 19, 2001

Machi Abel was acutely aware of the power that Chilean majority discourses hold over *machi*'s gender identities and sexualities. He argued that Chilean national discourses used the labels "homosexual" and "witch" as political tools to denigrate *machi* and Mapuche and to mold them to the gendered expectations of the Catholic state. He pointed to the unequal power dynamics that allowed national discourses to represent *machi* rather than letting *machi* speak for themselves.

For political purposes he also created a false dichotomy between Chilean colonialist discourses and Mapuche traditional discourses. He failed to acknowledge that Mapuche—including himself—used the terms *homosexual* and *witch* to describe *machi*. Abel did not want me to deconstruct those terms or to legitimate *machi*'s co-gendered roles. Instead, he asked me to acquiesce to these labels by describing all male *machi* as traditional, good, heterosexual men, ignoring the complexity of Mapuche perceptions and *machi* practices.

His conversation with me reveals the paradoxical relationship *machi* have with colonial and older Mapuche gendered discourses. As a *machi,* Abel could not use the terms *homosexual* and *witch* without furthering the state's colonial project. But neither could he resist colonization and claim a permanent co-gendered role without challenging contemporary Mapuche perceptions and subjecting himself to accusations of sorcery and homosexuality by fellow Mapuche.

Abel tried to deflect attention from male *machi*'s quandary by depicting the United States as the source of immoral forms of homosexuality:

ABEL: There are many immoral people in the United States. They say that San Francisco is a whole town of homosexuals and that the priests have little boys as lovers.

MARIELLA: But there are also homosexuals who have their own partners and don't harm anyone. I have friends who are homosexuals.

ABEL: If they don't bother anyone, then that's fine. Here people don't talk much about homosexuality because people look down on it. (Conversation, December 13, 2005)

Machi held different notions about the meaning of my ethnography and the authority of my text. Machi José argued that the text reflected the perspectives of *machi*, not my own: "You see things, *machi* tell you things, and you write their words, whether they are right or wrong." Machi Abel, in contrast, focused on my power as author to represent *machi*. He knew I was opposed to gender and ethnic inequality, and that these perspectives, my subjective experiences with *machi,* and my choice of materials shaped my ethnography. But he was unable to distinguish between my words and the quotations of words spoken by other *machi,* and he did not understand the concept of critique. According to Abel: "If it appears in your book, they are your words."

Machi Rocío furthered Abel's argument by explaining that the weight and meaning accorded to labels of homosexuality and witchcraft differed according to who used them and in what context. She became angry in January 1991 when she heard that anthropologists had depicted *machi* as homosexuals and witches on television, although she used the same labels for other *machi*:

> ROCÍO: My son said that on television anthropologists said that *machi* are *brujas* and that male *machi* are like women . . . Why do anthropologists always say who we are? Why don't they ask us?
>
> MARIELLA: I have asked you. Sometimes you say *machi* are complete like Ngünechen—masculine, feminine, old, and new. But you also said that Marta [a *machi* who was genitally male but had adopted the gender role of a woman] was a witch and a *maricón*. So how is that different from what he told you the anthropologists said?
>
> ROCÍO: It is different because I said it against him [Marta], and we are both Mapuche. But if a *wingka* anthropologist says it, then people say it's true and that all Mapuche are like that.
>
> MARIELLA: Not all *wingka* anthropologists are the same. What if I write that the words *maricón* and *witch* do not represent *machi*'s co-gendered identities? That they are misused by *wingka* and Mapuche, too? What if I write that *machi*'s special gender identities like Ngünechen need to be recognized by Mapuche and *wingka*?
>
> ROCÍO: Then it would be good for Mapuche. But *wingka* are still going to say we are witches and *maricones*.

Rocío argued that when Mapuche used the terms *maricón* and *bruja*, those terms reflected local politics, conflicts, and dynamics, but when *wingka* anthropologists used them, they represented *machi* and Mapuche as a whole to others. She believed *wingka* anthropologists could speak of *machi*'s gender identities and sexualities only by using homophobic discourses, because we represented *wingka* ideologies and reflected the power that *wingka*'s gendered discourses held over Mapuche identities. She understood that I was not creating a generic text but was interested in gaining a deeper understanding of *machi*'s gender identities through various lenses and in different contexts. She knew that I was questioning the assumptions of gendered majority discourses and casting *machi*'s co-gendered roles in a positive light. But she did not believe my ethnography would change *wingka*'s perceptions about *machi*. And if Chilean colonialist gendered perceptions remained the same, then *machi* would have to continue to use these labels to protect themselves and slander others.

Rocío's, José's, and Abel's comments raised the question of how I should write about the gender identity and sexuality of *machi* when my responsibility for writing an honest ethnography conflicted with *machi*'s images of how they should be represented to others. Should my ethnography reflect the many contradictory ways in which knowledge by and about *machi*'s gendered identities is created and reproduced through testimony, gossip, storytelling, labeling, and ritual performances? Should it reflect the ambivalence of *machi* toward their gender identity, their complex roles in traditionalist and colonialist projects, and the complex intersection of gender, modernization, and witchcraft? Or should I write a political text that idealized *machi* as positive, heterosexual gender conformists—a text that would serve as publicity to promote the image and careers of particular *machi*? Doing so would perpetuate homophobic majority readings of gender variation and Chilean Catholic rejection of the ambivalence inherent in shamanism.

I chose to write about *machi*'s practices and perceptions and to analyze and critique the ways in which *machi* have been represented in majority discourses and by Mapuche themselves, rather than about how *machi* wish to be represented by others. Like Roger Lancaster (1997a:10–11), I believe that misrepresenting the critical capacities of social theory in the name of the politics of speech produces no useful analysis of the contraptions of power, nor does it improve the lives of the oppressed. *Machi*'s relational personhood and shifting gender identity are controversial for Mapuche because they are both a source of spiritual power, on which the cosmic and social order is based, and fodder for denigrating *machi* as homosexuals and witches. The complex intersections of gender, personhood, and power in the everyday lives of *machi* and their ritual and political practices show that they do not fit neatly into Chilean gender roles or categories. Male and female *machi* use these contradictory discourses to legitimate themselves as they negotiate between the gendered demands of spiritual and human worlds. Their conformity to and transgression of a variety of gender roles express Mapuche's need to negotiate with different languages, parameters, and discourses in order to survive in the contemporary Chilean world. *Machi*-hood is a site for gender differentiation and gender fusing. *Machi* practice marks the difference between the feminine and the masculine in cosmology, society, and politics, but it also fuses genders to gain control over the world and transform illness into health, scarcity into abundance, and marginality into participation.

In asking me to write a propagandistic text that would publicize *machi* as good, traditional, heterosexual healers, Abel was responding to the expectations that Chilean scholars and politicians have of Mapuche people, and particularly of *machi*. Non-Mapuche force *machi*'s gender identity and performances into gendered categories of homosexuality, heterosexuality, transvestism, transgenderism, and normality, and they expect *machi* to emulate the gendered roles of priests and nuns, doctors and nurses, Jesus and the Virgin Mary. At the same time, they demand that *machi* remain exotic, unchanged people of the past, and they construe those who do not match this ideal as having "lost their culture."

For example, when Machi Fresia decided to abandon her *machi* practice and move to Santiago, a Chilean scholar, advocating for "culture as tradition," tried to convince her to go back to her community. Fresia explained: "The teacher came to see me in Santiago. She told me that I had to go back [to the community] because Mapuche culture was disappearing, and that I was being irresponsible to the community by leaving" (interview, July 29, 1992). Some years later Fresia told me: "Those teachers should have . . . not gotten involved, because that was my problem with my family and community. But they thought I was wrong. She didn't think about me—how I was going to be a *machi* if that was not my destiny or what I wanted. She wanted to study Mapuche tradition" (interview, December 10, 2001). I believe anthropologists have an ethical obligation to inform their consultants about the possible consequences of their actions and then allow them to make their own decisions about their lives, even if those decisions conflict with their community's desires and the anthropologist's research agenda (Joralemon 1990:116–117).

Abel's search for legitimacy must also be understood within the context of the majority gendered discourses scholars use to define knowledge and the way it should be created and reproduced. Women scholars of Mapuche are increasingly recognizing the importance of attending to the ways Mapuche women and gender variants create and reproduce knowledge and meanings, and they are writing poststructural narratives and dialogical ethnographies that enable us to witness this process of knowledge making (Montecino 1999; Reuque 2002; Richards 2004). But not all scholars of Mapuche have been reflective about the gendered biases in discourses about knowledge. Some still draw on older, colonialist gendered discourses that marginalize women, gender variants, and spiritual practices from the making of Mapuche culture and history.

French historian Guillaume Boccara, for example, characterized my ethnography of the gendered lives and practices of *machi,* their struggles with evil and illness, and their interactions with their families, patients, and communities as a *"telenovela"* — a Latin American soap opera (Boccara 2003; Bacigalupo 2004b). Academic elites perceive *telenovelas* as superficial, melodramatic narratives about domestic issues, made for women, that have little to contribute to higher knowledge. Similarly, subscribers to Chilean majority discourses view *machi* as traditional, superstitious women or partially transvestite men who gossip and heal domestic strife but have little to contribute to medicine, religion, politics, or history. According to this perspective, knowledge is the prerogative of European or Chilean men, who make history and culture by writing authoritarian, generic, and positivistic texts. Women ethnographers; testimony by indigenous people, women, and gender variants; and subjective, dialogical ethnographies are gossip and *telenovelas*.

These perceptions trivialize the role that both *telenovelas* and *machi* play in reflecting and interpreting issues of common concern. *Telenovelas* and *machi* practices are cultural commentaries on gender, race, class, ethnic, religious, and political issues that help men and women make sense of the struggles they face in their everyday lives.[1] *Machi* are active agents in a complex constellation of knowledge and relations, and they play a central role in the creation and reproduction of culture and the making of Mapuche history in a variety of everyday, ritual, and political contexts. They struggle against illness, jealousy, envy, and fear and draw on older Mapuche notions as well as colonial and modern paradigms to forge a place for themselves in contemporary Chile. They revive the co-gendered and masculine roles of the spiritual warrior to build Mapuche consciousness; they develop gendered ideological and spiritual paradigms in order to practice politics. They use images of priests, doctors, generals, mothers, priestesses, nuns, and angels to legitimate themselves in Catholic, biomedical, and military contexts. They engage with the human, spirit, and animal worlds through relational personhood and draw on metaphors of kinship, marriage, and mastery to explain the hierarchical relationships Mapuche struggle with in their daily lives. *Machi* also make sense of modernization, capitalism, and the commodification of culture through witchcraft narratives.

Ironically, *machi* themselves watch soap operas to gain knowledge about the Chilean elites, not about Chilean popular culture. In December 2002 Machi María Cecilia told me: "In *telenovelas* you see the lives of the rich people. You see what they think, what they do. I have many rich *wingka* patients, so I have to know what they want."

Mapuche and *machi* have responded to the majority's demands for tradition and male-centered learning by creating two types of knowledge:

that which is acceptable to the Chilean majority and is expressed in public and political discourses; and public secrets—knowledge held and articulated by Mapuche in private, but not face to face in public settings, and rarely in front of outsiders. The shifting gender identities of *machi* are one of these public secrets. Although *machi*'s knowledge is diverse and contextual, they represent themselves to outsiders publicly in generic, ideal terms, to ensure their legitimacy. Knowing the public secret but being unable to say anything about it is testimony to the coercive power that gendered majority discourses hold over the Mapuche imagination. As Michel Foucault (1990) points out, secrecy is indispensable to the operation of the abuse of power, and those who maintain public secrets are manipulated and disempowered.

In this book I have written about the public secret of *machi*'s gendered identity from the perspectives of various Mapuche and have deconstructed majority gendered discourses. I agree with Michael Taussig (1999:8, 64) that, if we keep public secrets secret, we run the risk of falsifying a profound reality and eliminating much of what would make an ethnographic study worth doing in the first place. I believe the disclosure of public secrets can be positive as long as they are explicated in a way that does them justice. I hope my ethnography does justice to the complex knowledges reflected in *machi*'s shifting gender identities and performances.

My Mapuche intellectual friends dispute the value of making public secrets into public knowledge. Ramiro, whom other Mapuche criticized for telling me about *machi*'s gender identities, argued that revealing public secrets would not have the effect I desired: "Even though your intention is a good one, it won't produce what you want. Mapuche pointed a finger at me for speaking to you about this, and they will keep pointing fingers without paying attention to the value of what is being said."

Fabián disagreed: "You have to write about *machi*'s gender identities as you saw them. We Mapuche will never move ahead if we don't pay attention to *machi*'s gender identity and how we are using the words *homosexual* and *witch* against our own *machi,* against ourselves. When you write it, it will no longer be hidden. And we will have to think about this more."

Reading, like knowing, is a highly interpretive and political act. How people read depends on their situation and needs, but I believe that all readers of this text are responsible for the way they read it and what they do with the information it offers. Its many possible readings are deeply intertwined through unequal power relationships. *Machi* are connected to the United States through museums, writers' desire for "traditional indigenous knowledge," and *machi*'s desire for individual success, as well as through my writing about them in English. And modernization, the commodification of culture, and witchcraft narratives connect majority discourses in the United States and Chile with the collective interests of Mapuche communities. Images of mounted masculine warriors, brides, kin, priests, priestesses, doctors, politicians, Jesus, and the Virgin Mary bind Mapuche and *wingka* in a common colonial and national history, but their diverse readings of these images and the uses they make of them mark differences in power and authority. Euro-American categories of heterosexuality, homosexuality, transvestism, gender norms, and gender deviance have shaped some Chilean Catholic majority discourses, and other Latin American constructs, such as the penetration paradigm, have influenced American homosexuality. Both of these discourses have been appropriated and transformed by Mapuche, who combine them with older notions of co-gendered identity to create *machi*'s shifting gender identity. Perhaps Mapuche understandings of gender will, in turn, affect the ways in which Euro-Americans and Chileans think about gender, power, and personhood.

I hope that Euro-American and Chilean readers of this book will recognize that their own gendered constructs, while different from those of *machi,* are not separate from them. We are collectively responsible for allowing *machi* to negotiate a better place for themselves in the sea of gendered contradictions and asymmetries. I hope this book will help give both Mapuche and Chileans a deeper understanding of themselves today. And, no doubt, *machi*'s gendered identity and practices will continue to be reshaped.

I am interested in the effects my interpretations will have on Mapuche's representations and in the responses that Mapuche, Chileans, and Euro-Americans will have to these new representations. Like the elusive *foye* tree, *machi*'s gendered identities and practices can be experienced and interpreted endlessly along different paths and for different purposes that simultaneously bind people together and draw them apart.

Notes

I: Introduction

1. Diego de Rosales documented three types of *foye* (*voike*) trees in the seventeenth century. One type was used by *machi* to cure many illnesses. Priests called *boquibuye* (*foquiweye*) used another type as a symbol of peace during *parlamentos* (parleys). They used the third type of *foye* to create a mock peace parley when they were actually planning an ambush (Rosales 1989:209). The three types of *Drimys winteri* found in southern Chile today—*D. winteri punctata, D. winteri chilensis,* and *D. winteri andina*—are probably the same ones described by Rosales. All have white hermaphrodite flowers and leaves that are green on one side and whitish green or blue green on the other (Rodríguez, Matthei, and Quezada 1983:134).

2. Barbara Tedlock introduced the term *co-gendered* to refer to a partly feminine and partly masculine personality (Tedlock 2003:303).

3. A number of scholars have argued that the distinction between gender as culturally constructed and sex as natural and intractable is unsustainable because sex, too, is culturally constructed (e.g., Butler 1990; Foucault 1990:7). In this book I have chosen to use the distinction between sex and gender because Mapuche distinguish between what it means to be born with a penis or a vagina and what it takes to become a woman or a man.

4. The benefits of this approach are discussed by Handelman (1994:369), Hastrup (1987:292–294), Poewe (1996), and many others.

2: The Ambiguous Powers of *Machi*

1. E. E. Evans-Pritchard (1937:387) distinguishes between witches, who engage in conscious and deliberate acts of manipulation to cause harm through magic and medicines, and sorcerers, who engage in unconscious psychic acts that cause harm and who use hereditary psychophysical powers to attain their ends. *Kalku* do not fit into this classification.

2. Plants can operate on both sides of what Juan Carlos Gumucio (1999:128) calls "the social management of fear"; that is, they can create fear and suspicion in

their role as hidden poisons, but they can also cement trust and friendship when visibly displayed and shared.

3. Recorded by Juan Ñanculef.

4. For the laws that permitted the usurping of Mapuche land between 1883 and 1989, see "Tierras mapuches: Des pojo por Ley," *Revista Análisis,* November 30, 1987.

5. Some studies have explored witchcraft as the accepted processes of the state, as an idiom of expression for transnational capitalist ideology in local contexts (Comaroff and Comaroff 1993; Coronil 1997; Taussig 1997) and as an idiom of expression for the postcolonial political condition (Vidal and Whitehead 2004).

6. The high market value of *machi* practice has led some Mapuche to steal and sell sacred objects on the black market. Machi José said: "In Santiago there were eight old *rewe* that had been stolen from some communities in the south, and they brought them to sell them for eight hundred dollars each. I stood the *rewe* up and prayed to them so that they would not punish the people involved, and we left them at the Centro de Investigaciones until they found out which communities the *rewe* belonged to" (December 17, 2001).

3: Gendered Rituals for Cosmic Order

1. Nancy Scheper-Hughes and Margaret Lock (1987:15) argue that, in societies lacking in highly individualized notions of body and self, sickness is attributed to malevolent social relations.

2. *Machi* also perform a variety of other rituals, such as the *wetripantu,* or Mapuche New Year, held during the winter solstice and coinciding with the Catholic celebration of Saint John; the *ñellipun,* or thanking action, performed without the *kultrun;* the *pillamtun,* a prayer the *machi* performs to the *rewe;* and the *metrem longkon,* a penitential ritual performed when the *machi* has transgressed *machi* lore.

3. The Mapuche creation myth tells of a powerful spirit who controlled everything and possessed all possibilities and meanings within it. This spirit appeared under different names: Füta Newen (Big Spirit; Bacigalupo 1997, 1998a); Elmapun (Creator of the Earth; Marileo 1995); and Ngenmapun (Sustainer of the World; H. Carrasco 1996).

4. Ngünechen has taken the place of the historical warring spirit Epunamun in resisting and resignifying gendered majority discourses in terms of cogenderism and ritual gender fluidity.

5. See Catrileo (1995) for Mapuche kinship terms.

6. Gumucio argues that *relmu* are semantically equivalent to *rewe* (1999: 165).

7. In the Pewenche, the *pewen* (*Araucaria araucana,* or monkey-puzzletree) is planted in the middle of the sacred field and serves as the *ngillatuwe.*

8. Stewart and Strathern (2001:16) also describe bones in this way.

9. Guevara (1908) and Manquilef (1914) both associate this *choyke* dance with a totemic cult.

10. Similarly, the Zar cult in northern Sudan includes complementary and politically asymmetrical gender relations, although women alone ensure fertility. In the Zar cult, women are possessed by spirits, make provocative comments about village issues, and metaphorically reformulate everyday discourse to express consciousness of their own subordination. Women are responsible for ceremonies and practices ensuring the continuity of social life, whereas men are responsible for those that extend beyond the village to other groups and places (Boddy 1994:417).

11. Some authors have written that *machi* did not officiate in *ngillatun* ceremonies at the beginning of the twentieth century but that *ngenpin* performed as ritual priests on such occasions (Augusta 1934; Housse 1938:145; Latcham 1922:677; Moesbach 1936). Contrarily, others have written that *machi* played a fundamental role in the *ngillatun* (Titiev 1951) and held the status of ritual priests and mystic ambassadors in these rituals (Métraux 1942). Guevara (1925) takes the middle road by stating that *machi* sometimes performed in *ngillatun* rituals. These contradictory observations illustrate regional variations in who officiates at collective *ngillatun* (Bacigalupo 1995, 2001a).

12. *Machi* and other practitioners also propitiate mythical ancestors (*antü-painko*) and ancestors proper (*kuifiche*) in funerals and healing rituals (Dillehay 1990:81); more generalized regional deities and Ngünechen are invoked in *ngillatun* rituals (Faron 1964:63). Military chiefs and *machi* who played important roles in the struggle between the Mapuche and the Spanish or Chileans are also invoked in *ngillatun* rituals (Bacigalupo 1998b).

13. In September 2002 groups of *machi*, *longko*, and elders from Argentina and Chile visited each other to develop a petition to UNESCO requesting that *ngillatun* rituals be declared the cultural patrimony of humanity, in order to protect the *ngillatun* and "recover some of its original meaning" (telephone interview with Juan Ñanculef, September 10, 2002).

14. When a *machi* performs a *datun* at a patient's home, helpers make a temporary *rewe* by planting two dried canes (*coligüe*) from the *ringi* plant (bamboo) fifty centimeters apart outside the door.

15. Juan Ñanculef (Ñanculef and Gumucio 1991) finds references to the twelve apostles, twelve warriors, and twelve chiefs to be frequent in *machi* healing rituals.

16. Peruvian *curanderos* use similar categories for illness and healing (Glass-Coffin 1998; Joralemon and Sharon 1993).

17. In shamanic ceremonies in which the main purpose is to exorcise evil beings or materials, the patient's altered state of consciousness is the peak moment at which the demon enters into direct communion with the subject (Kapferer 1983:195) or subjects commune with their inner nature (Laderman 1992: 195).

18. Taussig (1993:2, 19) argues that the image affects the thing it is an image of; the representation shares in or takes power from the represented. The ability to mime is the capacity to "other."

19. Mischa Titiev argues that "there is often an element of bisexualism in a *machi*'s dealings with the other world" (1968:303), and Alfred Métraux states that, when *machi* are healing, "they may address various supernatural beings, one

of whom is likely to be a female-male personage" (1942:333). What these authors fail to notice is that the *machi* actually becomes these different gendered beings in healing, and that these ritual gendered performances do not necessarily translate into bisexualism in the *machi*'s everyday life.

20. The ritual performance of sacred co-genderism is not erotically charged among *machi* as it sometimes is among the Siberian Chukchi (Balzer 1996) and American channelers (Brown 1997), but Mapuche helping spirits who are enticed with music and gifts are often jealous of *machi*'s sexual partners.

21. William Roscoe (1998:209) notes that, among Native American people, gender fluidity leads to the diversification of identity, not to its elimination.

22. This phenomenon is also common among American channelers (Brown 1997:114) and Siberian shamans (Balzer 1996:172).

23. This pattern, too, is common in Siberian shamanic practices. Among the Chukchi, male shamans take on a female identity for particular shamanic séances, and female shamans may take on male identity (Balzer 1996:165, 169).

4: Ritual Gendered Relationships

1. Alfred Métraux (1942) and Robles Rodríguez (1911, 1912) describe *machi* initiation and renewal rituals.

2. *Machi* such as María Cecilia, who belong to a *machi* school of practice, invite their cohorts to heal them and grant them blessings. *Machi* who do not belong to a school of practice hire other *machi* to perform these functions in their rituals. *Machi*'s initiation and renewal rituals are grouped under the generic term *machi purrun* or *baile de machi* (dance of the *machi*).

3. Photographing María Cecilia's ritual, I reasoned, could be particularly dangerous. Her relationship with her spirit was new and tenuous, and I was uncertain which soul would be captured on film while she was in an altered state of consciousness and her personal soul might be traveling or displaced by a possessing spirit. I expressed my concerns to her, but she responded: "We know you. You are not a Mapuche and you have no power or bad intentions . . . The photo captures the soul when the photo is taken close up and the eyes are open. Take photos when the *machi*'s heads are covered with the head scarf, from behind, from far away, or when the eyes are closed . . . If someone else tells you to stop taking photos, don't stop. If the *machi* tell you to stop, then stop." I followed her instructions and took photographs during the first day of the ritual.

4. Some *machi* transfer power to their initiates by cutting crosses into the palms of their hands and rubbing them together in order to mix their blood. Juana and Elena considered the ritual exchange of animal blood and breath to be sufficient.

5. *Llankalawen*, the male counterpart of the *kopiwe*, is often associated with the *filew*. It serves as the masculine complement to the *machi*, who is perceived as feminine when seducing the filew (Bacigalupo 1998a).

6. Studies that have explored the ways in which gender identities are negotiated in various Latin American contexts have centered on male transgendered

prostitutes (Kulick 1998; Prieur 1998; Schifter 1998) or ordinary men (Lancaster 1992) but not on male and female shamans.

7. The kind of involuntary and uncontrolled possession common to voodoo and Oyo-Yoruba priests occurs only among Mapuche neophytes who experience a calling or among Mapuche who are possessed by evil spirits.

8. Carol Laderman (1992:191) describes a similar phenomenon among Malay shamans who mobilize their inner resources, personified as the Four Sultans, the Four Heroes, the Four Guardians, and the Four Nobles.

9. Prayer collected by Juan Ñanculef. Traditional Mapuche norms dictate that ritual objects, deities, and ritual actions be referred to in sets of twos and fours, but the Catholic notion of the twelve apostles has also been incorporated into Mapuche sacred numerology.

10. Don Pollock (1996:330) notes a similar process among the Kulina of Brazil, for whom the term *dzupinahe* refers to the physical embodiment of the spirit by either humans or animals.

11. Prayer collected by Juan Ñanculef.

12. Since the 1980s anthropologists have focused on the phenomenology of the body and used the paradigm of embodiment in an effort to compensate for previous mentalistic perspectives and transcend the Cartesian mind-body dualism (Csordas 1999; Lock 1993; Roseman 1991; Scheper-Hughes and Lock 1987; Stewart and Strathern 2001; Stoller 1989). These phenomenological perspectives often view non-Western people as grounding their experience in the body and not distinguishing between mind and body (Low 1994; Pandolfi 1993; Scheper-Hughes 1992; Scheper-Hughes and Lock 1987; A. Strathern 1996), whereas nonmarginal Euro-American groups are depicted as unaware of their bodies and distinguishing between mind and body. Many anthropologists interested in the relationship between personhood and spirits have drawn on the paradigm of embodiment to focus on the relationship between bodies and persons (Lambek and Strathern 1998), the personification of bodies (Lamb 2000; Lambek and Strathern 1998; Scheper-Hughes 1992), and the relationship between bodies and spirits (Boddy 1998; Corin 1998:89; Rasmussen 1995:155).

13. Mastery of control is viewed as the central element of shamanism and is described as "voluntary" by Oesterreich (1966), "solicited" by Lewis (1969), and "desired" by Bourguignon (1968).

14. These two forms of possession are easily confused. Machi Marta, for example, began training a young woman who she thought would become a *machi.* Marta gradually realized the young woman was possessed by an evil spirit because she danced like a *meulen.*

15. Some anthropologists have argued that there are culturally specific masculine and feminine healing strategies and symbols but that these may be performed by both male and female shamans (Bacigalupo 1998a, 1998b; Feinberg 1997; Munn 1973; Tedlock 2003).

16. Lambek (2003:48) points out that "agency" is a naïve or romanticized concept because it implies that acts are transparent to their agents and are always the product of deliberate plans; that agents fully understand the consequences of their actions or the relationship between act and consequence; that agents' inten-

tions are seldom dense, complex, and possibly even contradictory; that agents can fully and objectively recognize what constitutes their interests; that agency is a capacity of fully autonomous individuals rather than relationally constituted persons; and that action occurs irrespective of binding social commitments.

17. I disagree with other researchers who have claimed that *machi* share personhood with the spirit that possesses them (Alonqueo 1979; Kuramochi 1990; Métraux 1973).

18. Machi Ana argued that Pamela's instruments had to be broken and buried; otherwise, the *machi* spirit would not leave. Machi José disagreed with the way Ana performed the *amulpüllün:* "No *machi* instrument should be buried. It brings bad luck. The family has a bad time and is eventually exterminated because the *machi* spirit finds a way to play them in the cemetery and becomes a witch. Burying *machi* instruments brings huge calamities."

5: The Struggle for *Machi* Masculinity

1. The Spaniards labeled *machi weye "putos,"* but the term meant that the man was a male gender invert and passive sodomite rather than a male prostitute, the usual meaning in modern Spanish (Corominas 1954:701).

2. The conquistador Cabeza de Vaca was enslaved by Indians in Florida and became recognized as a powerful shaman because of his intermediate status as neither Spanish nor Indian and because of his ambivalent gender status as a male who performed a woman's role as go-between (Goldberg 1992:206–217).

3. For details on the significance of the horse in Mapuche spirituality and warfare, see Alvarado, de Ramón, and Peñaloza (1991).

4. The Jesuits claimed that the devil was responsible for the Mapuche's resistance to colonization and evangelization and insisted that the Spaniards practice "defensive warfare." The Franciscans blamed the Mapuche for this resistance and argued that the Indians could be "saved" only through violence, punishment, and slavery (Pinto 1991: 68–69).

5. The contact-period Maya, too, had a dance of the warriors in which penis perforation and bloodletting were dramatized (Landa 1941; Taube 2000).

6. The "dual sexual qualities" of Epunamun are mentioned by Ercilla y Zúñiga (1933:34), Gómez de Vidaurre (1889:432), González de Nájera (1889:99), Núñez (1863:361), Ovalle (1888:47), and Rosales (1989:162–163).

7. Many Native American societies also saw a close connection between co-gendered practitioners, hermaphroditic beings, and successful warfare. Some berdaches are known to have fought alongside warriors, accompanying them to battle or carrying the dead (Callender and Kochems 1983; Katz 1976; Roscoe 1998:17). In Chile, references to Epunamun disappeared at the beginning of the twentieth century, although Ricardo Latcham (1922:363) and Grete Mostny (1960) each mention Mapuche invocations of ancestral spirits who have a "dual sexual nature" and who are represented as either opposite-sex twins or hermaphrodites.

8. For discussions of how sexual ideologies are challenged by sexual performances and behaviors in Latin America, see Kulick (1998), Lancaster (1997b), and Prieur (1998).

9. Bernal Díaz del Castillo (1963:19), on the basis of some idols that represented Indians performing "sodomitical acts," claimed that all the natives of Mexico were sodomites. Jonathan Goldberg (1992:195) cites the same phenomenon.

10. When North American berdaches assumed the occupation of a woman or a man, they often followed the dress of that gender, and their intermediate gender status was signified either by combining the dress of women and men or by using a mode of dress associated with neither (Callender and Kochems 1983:447). The intermediate status of the Zuni berdache, for example, is illustrated by the practice of burying male berdaches in women's dress and men's trousers on the men's side of the graveyard (Parsons 1916:528). *Xaniths,* third-gendered male prostitutes in Oman, dress like women but do not behave like Omani women. They maintain the legal status of men while mingling freely with women in a gender-segregated society (Wikan 1991). The specific association between *machi weye*'s occupation and dress is less clear because it is heavily colored by Spanish notions of what constituted women's and men's dress and occupations.

11. See Ercilla y Zúñiga (1933:34), Gómez de Vidaurre (1889:432), González de Nájera (1889:99), Núñez (1863:361), Ovalle (1888:347), Rosales (1989:162–163).

12. Some Native Americans, such as the Omaha, distinguish between berdaches and hermaphrodites, whereas others, such as the Navajo, use the same term for both, although most berdaches are "anatomically normal" and are culturally defined as intersexed (Callender and Kochems 1983:444).

13. Portuguese planter Gabriel Soares da Sousa describes Brazilian Indians in Bahia in similar terms: "Many of them are addicted to the nefarious sin, and among them it is no affront. And the one who serves as the male is considered valiant, and they tell of this bestiality as of a feat" (in Parker 1991:13).

14. In contrast, Jordan (1997:163) argues that it is because Latin theologians thought of sodomites as having an identity—men who engage in same-sex acts—that American homosexuals can think of themselves as a separate people having a gay or a lesbian identity. His reading makes sense in a mainstream white, middle-class American context, in which both same-sex partners are labeled "homosexual," regardless of the acts they perform, and are equally stigmatized in relationship to heterosexuals. However, American mainstream homosexuality lacks the power dynamics that the Latin American penetration paradigm has in the construction of Chilean sodomy and homosexuality.

15. Because the Jesuits were unable to convert the Mapuche to Christian religious dogma, they baptized them and found Christian equivalents for Mapuche spirits and ritual practices, hoping that, through syncretism, the Mapuche would finally convert. *Machi,* however, did not see Christianity and Mapuche beliefs as mutually exclusive. They reversed the power dynamics of conversion by asking to be baptized and invoking the Christian God to increase their powers. They also incorporated images of the saints, the Virgin Mary, and Jesus into their healing epistemologies and practices.

16. The perception that women are the vehicle through which the devil operates on earth is presented in the *Malleus Malleficarum,* or *Witch's Hammer,* published in 1486 (Kramer and Sprenger 1970).

17. Kate Weston (1998:167) points out that scholars are unclear about what

makes a particular classification qualify as a discrete gender identity. At what point, she asks, does berdache stop being an instance of gender ambiguity or a variant of masculinity or femininity and start becoming a gender in its own right?

18. The most prominent female berdaches were Slave Woman (Chipewyan), Pine Leaf (Crow), Running Eagle (Blackfoot), Qánqon (Kutenai), Kuiliy (Kalispel), and Kwisai (Mohave). Outside observers did not recognize female Plains Indian berdache roles (Blackwood 1984), and it is possible that a similar situation held for the Mapuche.

19. Some Native American examples include the Lakota *winkete*, who had auspicious powers in relation to childbirth and child rearing (Powers 1977); the Cheyenne *he'emane'o,* who embodied the principles of balance and synthesis (Coleman in Roscoe 1998:14); the Inuit third-gender shamans (Saladin D'Anglure 1992:147); the Ingalik berdache shamans; the Bella Coola supernatural berdache portrayed in masked dances (McIlwraith 1948:45–46); and the Flathead and Klamath berdache shamans (Spier 1930; Teit 1930:384). Third- and fourth-gender persons in California often had ceremonial roles associated with death and burial (Roscoe 1998:16), man-woman *katsinas* were portrayed in Pueblo masked dances, and the Zuni *ihamana we'wha* was a religious specialist who regularly participated in ceremonies (Roscoe 1991).

20. See Augusta (1934), Cooper (1946:750), Faron (1964), Guevara (1908:245), Hilger (1957:112), Latcham (1922:630), Moesbach (1936:330–349), Olivares (1864–1901:54), E. Smith (1855:234–236).

21. See Robles (2001) for a political history of the homosexual movement in Chile.

22. The current modified law criminalizes only nonconsensual anal intercourse between adult men and anal intercourse with male minors (Article 365, Penal Code, Book II, Title VII).

6: *Machi* as Gendered Symbols of Tradition

1. When Mapuche protests against forestry companies began in 1997, Frei imposed the Ley de Seguridad del Estado (Martial Law of Internal Security) and had Mapuche protesters arrested. He threatened to keep the Mapuche in line "by reason or by force," as the Chilean coat of arms reads. For a description of the results in one community, see J. Marimán (1998).

2. Until the nineteenth century, voting rights were restricted to literate, tax-paying men, which effectively excluded Mapuche. The notion of political rights for all of Chile's citizens was developed in the twentieth century.

3. The most notable resistance movements were those of Indians in Ecuador, Brazil, Colombia, Panama, and Chiapas, Mexico (Bengoa 2000:333).

4. Chile is one of the few Latin American countries that has not ratified the International Treaty on Indigenous Peoples in Independent States, passed in Geneva in 1989. This treaty states that "indigenous people should "exercise control over their own institutions, ways of life and economic development and to maintain and develop their identities, languages and religions, within the framework of the States in which they live" (International Labour Organisation Con-

vention [No. 169] Concerning Indigenous and Tribal Peoples in Independent Countries; adopted June 27, 1989, by the General Conference of the International Labour Organization at its 76th session; entered into force September 5, 1991; http://vedda.org/ilo169.htm, accessed November 4, 2004.

5. CONADI was created as an organization co-managed by indigenous people and the government, but in practice it is a state organization that implements governmental policies and in which the opinion of the indigenous minority does not prevail.

6. The role of Mapuche shamans in the dichotomy of male and female spheres is similar to that of Korean shamans; see Kendall (1998:62).

7. Although the Chilean state constructs itself as urban, it has assimilated traditional rural images of masculinity, combining images of the Spanish conquistador with those of the criollo landowner, or *huaso,* who becomes feudal lord and father through sexual and social exploitation of indigenous workers (Bengoa 1999; Valdés, Rebolledo, and Wilson 1995). Chileans may celebrate Mapuche men who participate in the project of the nation-state; for example, the public statue Roto Chileno glorifies blue-collar Chilean soldiers who protected the nation against the Peruvian-Bolivian Confederation in 1839. But, ultimately, it is the *huaso,* not the Mapuche *roto,* who is celebrated as a model of masculinity on Chilean Independence Day.

8. Among those detained have been the leaders of the resistance movement Coordinadora Malleko-Arauco. Leaders Víctor Ancalf and Mireya Figueroa and *longkos* Pichun and Norin have remained political prisoners for over a year without trial. There have also been documented cases of torture of Mapuche, secret investigations, the use of anonymous witnesses in trials against Mapuche, and sentences that are disproportionate to the alleged delinquent acts. Meanwhile, the policeman who killed the Mapuche Alex Lemun at a peaceful protest was set free (Cayuqueo and Painemal 2003; J. Marimán 2004; Muga 2004).

9. National ideologies reflect not the social organization of gender but the ideological needs of the state. Male-female relations are often used to express power relationships between nation-states and indigenous subjects (Joan Scott 1997:48). Nationalism and citizenship have traditionally been linked to heterosexual men and masculinity, whereas women, indigenous people, and effeminate homosexual men are marginalized. Theorists of nationalism have often used maleness and femaleness to distinguish between insiders and outsiders, respectively. In the same way that men and women are defined reciprocally (though never symmetrically), national identity is determined on the basis of what it (presumably) is not. With historical regularity, men tend to stand for national agents who determine the fate of nations in a metonymic relation to the nation as a whole. They are often imagined as rulers who claim the prerogatives of nation building (Mayer 2000:2). In contrast, women and indigenous people are seen to function only symbolically or metaphorically—as signifiers of ethnic and national difference, marking the margins of nations—and as vehicles for male agency (Schein 2000:107; B. Williams 1996:6, 12).

10. Eighty percent of Chileans have some Indian blood, but racially or culturally mixed persons identify themselves as either Chilean or Mapuche and not as mestizo. For a contrasting situation in Peru, see de la Cadena (2000:323).

11. Contrary to Chilean national images of *machi* as static cultural artifacts, the interrelations between nationalism and shamanism are multifaceted, multidirectional, and dynamic (Hill and Staats 2002:13; Thomas and Humphrey 1994:4). Latin American shamans have shaped their own relationships with nation-states, just as shamanic traditions have helped shape local indigenous histories—which range from open resistance to state authorities to covert resistance through syncretic mergings with state-sponsored religions and even conversion of entire indigenous societies (Brown 1991; Conklin 2002; Hill 1988; Langdon and Baer 1992). Anthropologists have explored how shamanism has often been the target of institutionalized religions and state powers (Anagnost 1987; Atkinson 1992:315; Balzer 1990; Taussig 1987) and how it becomes marginalized, fragmented, and feminized in relation to the state (Hamayon 1990). They have addressed the transformation of indigenous systems under colonialism, the relations between shamanic activities and state cults, and the ways shamanic powers may be used as forms of political agency to mediate resistance or operate as markers of ethnic difference (Thomas and Humphrey 1994).

12. For discussions of Mapuche resistance movements and proposals for autonomy, see Campos (2002), Foerster and Vergara (2003), Saavedra (2002), and Vergara (2000).

13. Isolde Reuque (2002:113, 115, 148) argues that the strength of the Mapuche movement comes from the fact that communities use their cultural practices in political ways to rebuild solidarity and participation and to stress the importance of development and unity, although some Mapuche movements have involved confrontation and class conflict, not cultural strategies.

14. Aucan Huilcaman says that there are conflicts among Mapuche who look indigenous but have Chilean minds, those who are Mapuche both racially and culturally, and those who neither look nor act like Mapuche but feel Mapuche because their grandfathers belonged to an indigenous community (Morin 1999).

15. Saavedra (2002) argues that the Mapuche do not propose to be an independent nation, but the discourses of the Mapuche resistance movements themselves and the work of other academics such as Campos (2002), Foerster and Vergara (2003), and Vergara (2000) prove the contrary.

16. Mapuche intellectuals Rosamel Millamán and José Quidel argue that traditional political alliances between Mapuche lineages should be revitalized and made permanent in order to create large, independent Mapuche political organizations.

17. Some researchers, such as Alejandro Saavedra, have drawn on notions of tradition as static and immutable to argue that Mapuche culture and identity are being lost (2002:208–211, 263) and that the Mapuche problem is not primarily an ethnic one but one of poverty and social class (111, 143, 190). Saavedra argues that Mapuche have multiple social identities but draws on the ideological categories of Chilean national society to construct the Mapuche mainly as rural wage workers and peasants (2002:37–45). Such preconceived notions have made it difficult for researchers to comprehend the dynamics of Mapuche culture and the emergence of Mapuche urban identities. Andrea Aravena (2002) demonstrates that migration and distancing from rural community life do not do away with Mapuche identity but create new identities centered on different Mapuche orga-

nizations. In the urban context, ritual plays an important role in the affirmation of Mapuche identity and the recovery of their cultural and political systems.

18. Anthropologists have argued that autonomy exercised within a defined territory does not meet the needs of native peoples in the contemporary world and ignores the political consequences of indigenous economic and social dispersion. The assumption of a unitary identity for intercommunity political action contradicts the promise of a plurinational system with alternative political values and the application of indigenous power in ever-wider settings of state, market, and civil society (Colloredo-Mansfeld 2002; Legaré 1995). Mapuche essentialist notions of a traditional, utopian homeland also conflict with Mapuche proposals of "development with identity," which combine ecological interests with technological innovation (Ancan 1997; Chihuailaf 1999:123) and the development of Mapuche industry. Members of Mapuche resistance movements, however, are interested not in accounting for the diverse ideals, values, and realities of the predominantly migrant, urban Mapuche but in creating a homogeneous image based on tradition and a utopian homeland for the purpose of political mobilization. This preoccupation with territorial enclaves and unifying identities can become a form of "nested nationalism" in which the autonomy and diversity of indigenous people are carefully organized and simplified by the national categories that created the indigenous problem in the first place (Colloredo-Mansfeld 2002; James Scott 1999:4). Mapuche cultural revitalization through essentialist discourses should be read as a strategic process of political articulation and cultural hybridization, not as a nostalgic escape to the past (Clifford 1988; Warren 1998:171).

19. Anthropologists have argued that, in places where a rural land base has come to stand for indigenous society, native communities have been forced to recover the territorial base usurped by colonizers (Keesing 1989:29; Rappaport and Dover 1996:30).

20. *Diario Austral* (December 21, 2000; June 1, March 15, March 21, 2001; January 17, 2002).

21. This image recalls the Gary Larson cartoon of "natives" stowing the TV and VCR as figures in pith helmets come up the path, over the caption, "Anthropologists! Anthropologists!"

7: The Responses of Male *Machi* to Homophobia

1. The Chilean media and general public view Mapuche men as virile, "uncivilized" *huasos*—hard-drinking, violent, womanizing, criollo horsemen, landowners, or animal herders (Cardemil 2000; X. Valdés 2000). Mapuche, however, have developed their own versions of homophobic, heterosexual masculinity. Edmundo Llaima, a wealthy, forty-five-year-old *longko* with two wives, argued that being macho meant being responsible and caring toward his family, and he characterized non-Mapuche men as violent, irresponsible *maricones:* "I am macho. I have many animals, much land, two wives who care for me. The priests criticize me for having two wives, but I take care of them both and all my children. Not like the Chilean men who are *maricones,* cowards because they have a wife and then several lovers they don't care for. They don't recognize their children. I don't

272 Notes to Pages 174–176

beat my wives. That is something the people in the city do, the *wingka*." Longko Daniel promoted the idea of a "civilized" Mapuche masculinity, in opposition to the dominant images of the macho and the *maricón:* "Before, Mapuche men were very macho; they had several wives as servants in the house, they beat them and dominated them. Now we are more civilized. I let my wife work in Santiago because she doesn't like the countryside. She's Chilean and says she doesn't want to live like an Indian. I'm Indian but a civilized Indian. I respect her but I still wear the pants around the house. I'm not a dominant macho. I'm a manly man [*hombre hombre*], not a *maricón.*"

2. Some therapists and scholars have constructed shamanic behavior as being a result of mental disorder, because shamans' experiences with altered states of consciousness differ from those of most Westerners. Shamans enter into altered states of consciousness, experience extraordinary illnesses, have visions, are possessed by spirits, and are often solitary, taciturn, and fantasy-prone. Anthropologists have equated shamans with schizophrenics (J. Silverman 1967), epileptics (Radin 1937), and people of abnormal psychology (Ohnuki-Tierney 1980); they have labeled their personality formation as "controlled hysterical dissociation" (Wallace 1966:150) and "neurosis" (Deveraux 1961). *Machi* have been described as "slightly psycho-pathological" (Barría 1984) and as "individuals who are strangely sick, morbidly sensitive with weak hearts, disordered digestion and subject to vertigo" (Housse 1938:98). Contemporary research has demonstrated that shamans have great powers of concentration, superior intelligence, and the ability to control their altered states of consciousness. Therefore, there is no reason to consider shamans as a group either deranged or abnormal (Peters and Price-Williams 1980:398). Researchers have found that neurotics lack the altruistic and ministerial qualities that are important in shamanic healing (Jilek 1978:132–139) and the sharp lucidity and spontaneous imagery needed to accomplish healing and divination tasks (Noll 1983). Because shamanism is both a corporal technique and a spiritual exercise (Rouget 1985:219), "the comparative understanding of the physiological and psychological processes employed by shamans in different traditions can be useful, but only insofar as these processes are taken to be elements of shamanic practice and not shamanism itself" (Atkinson 1992:312). *Machi* as a group are not ordinarily considered psychotic by Mapuche, because their experiences are meaningful in Mapuche cultural terms. Many neophytes are considered to be temporarily ill and "crazy" just before they become initiated, because "self" is challenged by an intruding spirit. But once they heal themselves and are initiated, they are considered to have more foresight than ordinary Mapuche.

3. Harriet Whitehead (1981:97) comes to a similar conclusion in her study of Native American berdaches. Callender and Kochems (1986) and Levy (1973) document cases in which co-gendered males were not just receptors during sexual intercourse but performed mutual fellatio and masturbation with their male partners.

4. Holders of Euro-American biologically reductionist views of homosexuality refuse to encompass the variety of cultural specifics that structure sexual behaviors cross-culturally. Callender and Kochems (1986) acknowledge that male berdaches do not have a homosexual identity, but they still refer to the genitally organized activities between male berdaches and men as homosexual acts. Lesbi-

ans and gay men in the West draw on biological explanations as a culturally authorized and politically potent justification (Blackwood 1986; Weston 1991), but anthropologists should see such claims as a Euro-American folk exegesis on the meaning of homosexuality that speaks to, and through, Euro-American cultural contexts and political dynamics (Elliston 1995).

5. "Entregan fundo a comunidad Mapuche Antonio Ñirripil" (*Diario Austral,* April 7, 2001); "Convocan a ngillatun para reestablecer confianzas" (*Diario Austral,* April 19, 2001).

6. As Taussig points out: "There is a synergism between rulers and those who may sustain them magically as well as through more material labor" (1987: 217).

7. José was unlike Machi Ignacio in this regard: "Machi Ignacio went to meet the president. I think the president said a few things. But then Ignacio asked to speak and he became the star with the press. He appeared beside the president in photographs and interviews" (Fabián, interview, December 19, 2001).

8. Marie Trigona, www.petroleumworld.com; accessed November 2, 2003.

8: Female *Machi*

1. I initially met the family in November 1991 through Reinaldo, who made María Cecilia's first *kultrun* drum in preparation for her initiation as a shaman in April 1992.

2. Spanish chroniclers noted that Mapuche women were forcefully abducted by men (Quiroga 1979:25; Rosales 1989:133) and that men had many wives who served them, performed the most arduous tasks, and stood behind them silently in public meetings (González de Nájera 1889:44; Núñez 1863:193, 453–454; Rosales 1989:152). Men often used violence against wives and could return them to their fathers if they did not produce offspring (Quiroga 1692:234).

3. Mapuche intellectuals and professionals use the idea of domains corresponding to Mapuche women's and men's worlds (as articulated by the anthropological-feminist critique) as a way of mapping or reflecting on external worlds. "Domaining" for rural Mapuche, on the other hand, corresponds to local models.

4. Degarrod (1998:345–346) argues that contemporary Mapuche men who perform agricultural tasks have been "feminized." I found no evidence for this argument. In the seventeenth century, men and women worked together in the gardens. Men plowed the land, and women sowed it (Núñez 1863:278). Today, work in the gardens is considered "women's work," but the practice of intensive agriculture has been considered men's work since it was introduced in the post-reservation era. Women who plow the land when their husbands are absent are considered "masculine." Male *machi,* who are often perceived as "feminized," are barred from performing agricultural tasks, especially plowing, because this is considered to be "men's work."

5. This phenomenon is common among indigenous women in South America (Brown 2001) and Melanesia. As Marilyn Strathern (1988:77) observes, in such circumstances, "it looks almost as though women now come to stand for [rural traditional] society itself."

6. Paul Stoller and Cheryl Olkes (1987:191–192) observed similar character-istics in Kassey, a powerful Songhay woman.

7. Fresia's case also demonstrates John Roberts's (1984) point that lack of commitment, conflict, and tension are the main reasons for voluntary disengage-ment from a certain role. Fresia was not committed to her *machi* role and was anx-ious about expectations she could not fulfill. She felt an internal conflict between wanting to please her parents and act out *machi* cultural ideals and wanting to satisfy her own desire to be a housemaid. She also had an ongoing conflict with her mother, Dominga.

8. Interview, December 17, 2006.

9. Electronic document, www.luzclara.com/Quinturray02.html, accessed November 4, 2002.

10. Some Mapuche feminist movements have also used this strategy. Isolde Reuque (2002:216–217) avoided becoming involved with political parties for many years because they divide Mapuche social organizations and movements. Mapuche organizations, however, often run by men, prefer to engage with Ma-puche who have the backing of specific political parties. Reuque finally joined the Christian Democratic Party in order to have weight and influence in Mapuche social organizations and political systems.

11. Historically, the Mapuche's relationship with the order established by the state was also nonideological, their resistance, contextual. Although today they resist state neoliberal policies and control of their territories, at the same time, Mapuche believe that their autonomous position is marginal to the state and will have little effect. Consequently, they participate actively in the space made avail-able to them by civil society (Foerster and Lavanchy 1999; R. Millamán 2001:12). Resistance in the eighteenth century incorporated new social forms and devel-oped new identities. Institutions of colonial power were transformed into local Mapuche political mechanisms and became part of Mapuche consciousness. The concentration of power in the hands of a few representatives and parleys became the local way of practicing politics (Boccara 1998). Mapuche today want their autonomy but also seek associations with representatives of the state and military who hold national political power and who, they believe, will grant them bene-fits (P. Marimán 1990:26–27). They often vote for right-wing candidates who promise order, progress, and jobs (*El Mercurio,* December 30, 2001). In Decem-ber 2001 a Mapuche man stated: "I voted for the Right because it is the party of the rich people. If I vote for the rich people who have money, there will be jobs. Lagos works for the poor people, but he is also poor."

9: Representing the Gendered Identities of *Machi*

1. Thomas Tufte (2003), Giovanna Del Negro (2003), and Gustavo Geirola (2003) all offer excellent examples of the role soap operas play in constituting the myriad faces of Latin American modernity.

Glossary

añchümalleñ — wife of *witranalwe* spirit

admapu — traditional religious or social norms

amulpüllün — a special funerary ritual

awingkamiento — any action, practice, or belief associated with becoming like a *wingka*

awün — an event in which mounted Mapuche warriors, carrying flags and lances and shouting war cries, gallop counterclockwise around an altar

boquibuye — celibate "*weye* of the *foye* tree"; also called *foyeweye*

bruja(o) — witch

champurrea — mestizo, mestiza

cherrufe — fireballs

chiripa — breeches

chon-chon — evil bird or flying *kalku*'s head

choyke — Patagonian ostrich

chueca — sticks used in games associated with masculinity and warfare

coligüe — bamboo; also called *koliu*

contra — counterhex

cuel — mounds under which *machi* and *longko* are publicly buried

datun — healing ritual

dungumachife — ritual interpreter

epeu — Mapuche creation myth

filew — generic ancestral spirit of all *machi*, literally, "the knowledgeable one"

foki — vines

foye tree — winter's bark, *Drimys winteri;* symbol of office for both male and female *machi* and the place where the *machi*'s spirit resides

foyeweye — see *boquibuye*

fuñapue — a substance composed of nails; hair; pieces of lizards, frogs, or worms; earth from the cemetery; poisonous herbs; or parts of the decomposing cadavers of animals

huaso — criollo landowner

illeluwün — the act of poisoning with food

infitun — the act of contaminating
kalkutun — witchcraft or illness caused by *kalku*
kalku — witch
kastikutran — punishment illness
killa — woman's shawl
klon — *maqui*, or *Aristotelia chilensis*
koliu — see *coligüe*
konpapüllü — an ecstatic state experienced by *machi* at the end of *datun* healing
  rituals
kopiwe — Chilean bellflower, *Lapageria rosa*
kultrun — painted shallow drum
kurewen — the coupling of *machi* bride and spirit husband
kutran — illness
küymi — an altered state of consciousness
llang-llang — an arch made from vines in the form of a rainbow
longko — a community chief
machi — Mapuche shamans
machikutran — a shamanic or spiritual illness
machil — a person called to *machi*-hood
machiluwün —
machi-pewma — *machi* dreams
machi püllü — the specific spirit that guides a *machi*'s actions
machi purun — an initiation or renewal ritual
machi weye — a male shaman
makuñ — poncho
mapu — the earth
maricón — a passive, anal-receptive, feminized man
Meli Küyen — the four moon spirits
meli-ko-lawen — marsh marigold, *Caltha sagittata*
Meli Wangülen — the four spirits of the stars
metawe — a ceramic vessel used in rituals
metrumtun — calling of the spirits
meulen — whirlwinds
munche mapu — underworld, where the *wekufe* spirits are believed to reside
naturista — natural healing practitioner
nervios — nerves
ngen — spirit owners of various ecosystems
ngenpin — orators
ngeykurewen — a renewal ritual
ngillatucar — to pray, sing, speak in ritual language
ngillatuwe — collective *rewe;* also called *la cruz* (the cross)
ngillatun — collective rituals to bind ritual congregations together
nünkün — emotion
nulawen — plant used for sweet-smelling flowers and love magic powers
perimontun — shamanic visions
pewma — dreams
pillamtun — rogation to the spirits

piuke—heart

piwichen—winged serpent

püllomeñ—green fly

püllü—living soul or spirit

püllüam—first male warrior spirits

punon-namun—scrapings from a victim's footsteps or a place where she has sat

puto—male invert

rakiduam—thought

rewe—a step-notched pole with branches tied to its side, which serves as an axis mundi, or tree of life; also "the purest"

sahumerio—smoke exorcism

trabajo—witchcraft job

trawa—body

triwe—laurel

ulutun—diagnostic ritual

waki—spears

wedakutran—negative spiritual illnesses

wekufe—evil spirit

wekufetun—witchcraft or illness caused by *wekufe*

wenukutran—spiritual illness

wenu mapu—upper skies

wenu püllüam—ancestral spirits that live in the sky

Wünyelfe—morning star

wingka—non-Mapuche Chilean

witranalwe—mounted conquistador spirit

yerbatera—herbalist

zuam—consciousness

References

Abu-Lughod, Lila
    1990 The Romance of Resistance: Tracing Transformations of Power through Bedouin Women. *American Ethnologist* 17(1):41–55.
    1991 Writing against Culture. In *Recapturing Anthropology: Working in the Present*, edited by Richard G. Fox, pp. 137–162. Santa Fe, N.M.: School of American Research Press.

Acosta, José de
    1894 [1590] *Historia natural y moral de las Indias.* Madrid: R. Anglés.

Alcoff, Linda
    1994 Cultural Feminism versus Poststructuralism: The Identity Crisis in Feminist Theory. In *Culture/Power/History: A Reader in Contemporary Social Theory,* edited by Nicholas B. Dirks, Geoff Eley, and Sherry B. Ortner, pp. 96–122. Princeton, N.J.: Princeton University Press.

Alonqueo, Martín
    1979 *Instituciones religiosas del pueblo mapuche.* Santiago: Ediciones Nueva Universidad.

Alonso, Ana
    1994 The Politics of Space, Time, and Substance: State Formation, Nationalism, and Ethnicity. *Annual Review of Anthropology* 23:379–405.

Alvarado, Margarita; Ema de Ramón; and Cecilia Peñaloza
    1991 Weichan, la guerra de Arauco: Una mirada desde la estética 1536–1656. Unpublished. Santiago.

Anagnost, Ann S.
    1987 Politics and Magic in Contemporary China. *Modern China* 13(1): 40–61.

Ancan, José
    1997 Urban Mapuches: Reflections on a Modern Reality in Chile. *Abya-Yala News* 10(3):1–3.

Anonymous
1890 *Memoire inedite del FFMM Capuccini nel Chili.* Rome: The Vatican.

Appadurai, Arjun
1990 Topographies of the Self: Praise and Emotion in Hindu India. In *Language and the Politics of Emotion,* edited by Catherine Lutz and Lila Abu-Lughod, pp. 92–112. Cambridge: Cambridge University Press.

Apples for Health
2001 Mapuche Medicine Enters Mainstream. *Apples for Health* 3(15) (September 7, 2001). http://www.applesforhealth.com.

Aravena, Andrea
2002 Los Mapuche-Warriache: Migración e identidad mapuche urbana en el siglo XX. In *Colonización, resistencia y mestizaje en las Américas, siglos XVI–XX,* edited by Guillaume Boccara, pp. 359–385. Quito: Ediciones Abya-Yala.

Ashforth, Adam
2000 *Madumo: A Man Bewitched.* Chicago: University of Chicago Press.

Atkinson, Clarissa; Constance Buchanan; and Margaret Miles
1987 *Shaping New Vision: Gender and Values in American Culture.* Ann Arbor: University of Michigan Press.

Atkinson, Jane
1992 Shamanisms Today. *Annual Review of Anthropology* 21:307–330.

Augusta, Félix José
1934 [1910] *Lecturas araucanas.* Padre de las Casas, Chile: Editorial San Francisco.
1966 *Diccionario araucano,* vol. 1, *Araucano-Español.* Padre de las Casas, Chile: Editorial San Francisco.

Auslander, Mark
1993 "Open the Wombs!": The Symbolic Politics of Modern Ngoni Witch-finding. In *Modernity and Its Malcontents: Ritual and Power in Postcolonial Africa,* edited by Jean Comaroff and John Comaroff, pp. 167–192. Chicago: University of Chicago Press.

Bacigalupo, Ana Mariella
1994a Variación de rol de machi en la cultura mapuche: Tipología geográfica, adaptiva e iniciática. *Revista de Antropología Universidad de Chile* 12: 19–43.
1994b The Power of the Machi: The Rise of Female Shaman/Healers and Priestesses in Mapuche Society. PhD diss., University of California, Los Angeles.
1995 El rol sacerdotal de la machi en los valles centrales de la Araucanía. In *¿Modernización o sabiduría en tierra mapuche?* edited by Cristián Parker and Ricardo Salas, pp. 51–98. Santiago: Ediciones San Pablo.
1996a Mapuche Women's Empowerment as Shaman/Healers. *Annual Review of Women in World Religions* 4:57–129
1996b Imágenes de diversidad y consenso: La cosmovisión mapuche a través de trés machi. *Aisthesis* 28:120–141.

1996c Identidad, espacio y dualidad en los *perimontun* (visiones) de machi mapuche. *Scripta Ethnológica* 18:37–63.
1997 Las múltiples máscaras de Ngünechen: Las batallas ontológicas y semánticas del ser supremo mapuche en Chile. *Journal of Latin American Lore* 20(1):173–204.
1998a Chamanes mapuche et le experience religieuses masculine et féminine. *Anthropologie et Sociétés* 22(2):123–143.
1998b The Exorcising Sounds of Warfare: Shamanic Healing and the Struggle to Remain Mapuche. *Anthropology of Consciousness* 9(5):1–16.
2000 Shamanism as Reflexive Discourse: Gender, Sexuality and Power in the Mapuche Religious Experience. In *Gender, Bodies, Religions,* edited by Sylvia Marcos, pp. 275–295. Cuernavaca: ALER Publications.
2001a The Mapuche Moon Priestess. *Annual Review of Women in World Religions* 6:208–259.
2001b *La voz del kultrun en la modernidad: Tradición y cambio en la terapeútica de siete machi.* Santiago: Editorial Universidad Católica.
2003 Rethinking Identity and Feminism: Contributions of Mapuche Women and Machi from Southern Chile. *Hypatia* 18(2):32–57.
2004a The Mapuche Man Who Became a Woman Shaman: Selfhood, Gender Transgression, and Competing Cultural Norms. *American Ethnologist* 31(3):440–457.
2004b Local Shamanic Knowledges: A Response to Guillaume Boccara. *L'homme* 169:219–224.
2005 The Creation of a Mapuche Sorcerer: Sexual Ambivalence, the Commodification of Knowledge, and the Coveting of Wealth. *Journal of Anthropological Research* 61(3):317–336.

Bakhtin, Mikhail
1981 *The Dialogical Imagination.* Translated by Caryl Emerson and Michael Holquist. Austin: University of Texas Press.
1986 *Speeches, Genres, and Other Late Essays.* Translated by Vern W. McGee; edited by Caryl Emerson and Michael Holquist. Austin: University of Texas Press.

Balzer, Marjorie Mandelstam
1996 Sacred Genders in Siberia: Shamans, Bear Festivals, and Androgyny. In *Gender Reversals and Gender Cultures,* edited by Sabrina Ramet, pp. 164–182. London: Routledge.

Balzer, Marjorie Mandelstam, ed.
1990 *Shamanism: Soviet Studies of Traditional Religion in Siberia and Central Asia.* London: M. E. Sharp.

Barrera, Aníbal
1999 *El grito mapuche (una historia inconclusa).* Santiago: Editorial Grijalbo.

Barría, Cristián
1984 Cultura mágica: Medicina indígena y tradicional. *Revista de Psiquiatría* 1:174–179.

Basilov, Vladimir
1976 Shamanism in Central Asia. In *The Realm of the Extra-Human: Agents*

and Audiences, edited by Agehananda Bharati, pp. 149–157. The Hague: Mouton.

1990 Chosen by the Spirits. In *Shamanism: Soviet Studies of Traditional Religion in Siberian Central Asia,* edited by Marjorie Mandelstam Balzer, pp. 3–48. Armonk, N.Y.: Sharpe.

Behar, Ruth

1993 *Translated Woman: Crossing the Border with Esperanza's Story.* Boston: Beacon Press.

1996 *The Vulnerable Observer: Anthropology That Breaks Your Heart.* Boston: Beacon Press.

Bem, Sandra

1993 *The Lenses of Gender: Transforming the Debate on Sexual Inequality.* New Haven, Conn.: Yale University Press.

Bengoa, José

1983 *Economía mapuche: Pobreza y subsistencia en la sociedad mapuche contemporánea.* Santiago: Pas.

1992 Mujer, tradición y shamanismo: Relato de una machi mapuche. *Proposiciones* 21:132–155.

1999 *Historia de un conflicto: El estado y los Mapuches en el siglo XX.* Santiago: Editorial Planeta.

2000 Políticas públicas y comunidades mapuches: Del indigenismo a la autogestión. *Revista Perspectivas* 3(2):331–365.

Blackwood, Evelyn

1984 Sexuality and Gender in Certain Native American Tribes: The Case of Cross-Gender Females. *Signs: Journal of Women in Culture and Society* 10(1):27–42.

1986 Breaking the Mirror: The Construction of Lesbianism and the Anthropological Discourse on Homosexuality. In *The Many Faces of Homosexuality: Anthropological Approaches to Homosexual Behavior,* edited by Evelyn Blackwood, pp. 1–7. New York: Harrington Park Press.

Blest Gana, Alberto

1968 [1862] *Mariluán.* Santiago: Zig-zag.

Boccara, Guillaume

1998 *Guerre et ethnogenese mapuche dans le Chili colonial: L'invention du soi.* Paris: L'Harmattan.

2003 Review of *La voz del Kultrun en la modernidad: Tradición y cambio en la terapeútica de siete machi. L'homme* 166:263–266.

Boddy, Janice

1989 *Wombs and Alien Spirits: Women, Men, and the Zar Cult in Northern Sudan.* Madison: University of Wisconsin Press.

1994 Spirit Possession Revisited: Beyond Instrumentality. *Annual Review of Anthropology* 23:407–434.

Bolin, Anne

1996 Traversing Gender: Cultural Context and Gender Practice. In *Gender Reversals and Gender Cultures,* edited by Sabrina Ramet, pp. 22–51. London: Routledge.

Bourdieu, Pierre
1977 *Outline of a Theory of Practice.* Translated by Richard Nice. Cambridge: Cambridge University Press.

Bourguignon, Erika
1965 The Self, the Behavioural Environment, and the Theory of Spirit Possession. In *Context and Meaning in Cultural Anthropology,* edited by Milford Spiro, pp. 39–60. London: Macmillan.
1968 *Cross-Cultural Study on Dissociational States.* Columbus: Ohio State University Press.
1976 *Possession.* San Francisco: Chandler and Sharp.

Boyle, Catherine
1993 Touching the Air: The Cultural Force of Women in Chile. In *Viva Women and Popular Protest in Latin America,* edited by Sarah Radcliff and Sallie Westwood, pp. 156–172. London: Routledge.

Brown, Michael F.
1991 Beyond Resistance: Utopian Renewal in Amazonia. *Ethnohistory* 38(4): 363–387.
1996 On Resisting Resistance. *American Anthropologist* 98(4):729–749.
1997 *The Channeling Zone: American Spirituality in an Anxious Age.* Cambridge, Mass.: Harvard University Press.
2001 Worlds Overturned: Gender-Inflected Religious Movements in Melanesia and the Amazon. In *Gender in Amazonia and Melanesia: An Exploration of the Comparative Method,* edited by Thomas Gregor and Donald Tuzin, pp. 207–220. Berkeley & Los Angeles: University of California Press.

Burke, Barry
1999 Antonio Gramsci and Informal Education. *The Encyclopedia of Informal Education,* http://www.infed.org/thinkers/et-gram.htm.

Butler, Judith
1990 *Gender Trouble: Feminism and the Subversion of Identity.* New York: Routledge.
1993 *Bodies That Matter: On the Discursive Limits of Sex.* New York: Routledge.

Bynum, Caroline
1986 Introduction: The Complexity of Religious Symbols. In *Gender and Religion: On the Complexity of Symbols,* edited by Caroline Bynum, Steven Harrell, and Paula Richman, pp. 1–20. Boston, Mass.: Beacon Press.

Callender, Charles, and Lee Kochems
1983 The North American Berdache. *Current Anthropology* 24(4):443–456.

Campos, Luis
2002 La problemática indígena en Chile: De las políticas indigenistas a la autonomía cultural. *Revista de la Academia* 7:39–58.

Cardemil, Alberto
2000 *El huaso chileno.* Santiago: Editorial Andrés Bello.

Carrasco, Hugo

1986 Trentren y Kaikai: Segundo nacimiento de la cultura mapuche. *Estudios Filológicos* 21:23–24.

1996 *Reviviendo historias antiguas.* Temuco, Chile: Instituto de Estudios Indígenas, Universidad de la Frontera.

Carrasco, Rafael

1986 *Inquisición y represión sexual en Valencia: Historia de los sodomitas (1565–1785).* Barcelona: Laertes.

Casanova, Holdenis

1994 *Diablos, bujos y espíritus maléficos: Chillán, un proceso judicial del siglo XVIII.* Temuco, Chile: Editorial Universidad de la Frontera.

Catrileo, María

1995 *Diccionario lingüístico-etnográfico de la lengua mapuche.* Santiago: Editorial Andrés Bello.

Cayuqueo, Pedro, and Wladimir Painemal

2003 Análisis político mapuche: Hacia un imaginario de nación. *Azkintuwe: Periódico Nacional Mapuche* (www.nodo50.org/azkintuwe/), no. 1 (October).

Chaumeil, Jean-Pierre

1992 Varieties of Amazonian Shamanism. *Diogenes* 158:101–113.

Chihuailaf, Elicura

1999 *Recado confidencial a los chilenos.* Santiago: Lom Ediciones.

Chiriguini, María Christina, and María Elina Vitello

2001 Reproductive Health and Culture among the Mapuche and Tehuelche of South America. *Mankind Quarterly* 42(2):117–131.

Christ, Carol

1980 *Diving Deep and Surfacing: Women Writers on a Spiritual Quest.* Boston: Beacon Press.

Citarella, Luca; Ana María Conejeros; Bernarda Espinosa; Ivonne Jelves; Armando Marileo; Ana María Oyarce; and Aldo Vidal

1995 *Medicinas y culturas en la Araucanía.* Santiago: Editorial Sudamericana.

Clifford, James

1988 *The Predicament of Culture: Twentieth-Century Ethnography, Literature, and Art.* Cambridge, Mass.: Harvard University Press.

2000 Taking Identity Politics Seriously: "The Contradictory Stony Ground." In *Without Guarantees: In Honor of Stuart Hall,* edited by Paul Gilroy, Lawrence Grossberg, and Angela McRobbie, pp. 94–112. New York: Verso.

Colloredo-Mansfeld, Rudi

2002 Autonomy and Interdependence in Native Movements: Towards a Pragmatic Politics in the Ecuadorian Andes. *Identities: Global Studies in Culture and Power* 9:173–195.

Comaroff, Jean

1985 *Body of Power, Spirit of Resistance.* Chicago: University of Chicago Press.

Comaroff, Jean, and John Comaroff
  1999 Occult Economies and the Violence of Abstraction: Notes from South African Postcolony. *American Ethnologist* 26(2):279–303.

Comaroff, Jean, and John Comaroff, eds.
  1993 *Modernity and Its Malcontents: Ritual and Power in Postcolonial Africa.* Chicago: University of Chicago Press.

Conklin, Beth
  1997 Body Paint, Feathers, and VCRs: Aesthetics and Authenticity in Amazonian Activism. *American Ethnologist* 24(4):711–737.
  2002 Shamans versus Pirates in the Amazonian Treasure Chest. *American Anthropologist* 104(4):1050–1061.

Cooper, Johan
  1946 *Handbook of South American Indians.* Bureau of American Ethnology 2(143). Washington, D.C.: Smithsonian Institution.

Corin, Ellen
  1998 Refiguring the Person: The Dynamics of Affects and Symbols in an African Spirit Possession Cult. In *Bodies and Persons: Comparative Perspectives from Africa and Melanesia,* edited by Michael Lambek and Andrew Strathern, pp. 80–102. Cambridge: Cambridge University Press.

Corominas, Juan
  1954 *Diccionario crítico etimológico de la lengua castellana,* vol. 4. Berne: Francke.

Coronil, Fernando
  1997 *The Magical State.* Chicago: University of Chicago Press.

Crapanzano, Vincent, and V. Garrison, eds.
  1977 *Case Studies in Spirit Possession.* New York: Wiley.
  1980 *Tuhami: Portrait of a Moroccan.* Chicago: University of Chicago Press.

Csordas, Thomas
  1990 Embodiment as a Paradigm for Anthropology. *Ethos* 18:5–47.
  1999 Ritual Healing and the Politics of Identity in Contemporary Navajo Society. *American Ethnologist* 26(1):3–23.

Darío, Rubén
  1941 *Obras poéticas completas.* Madrid: Aguilar.

Davis, D. L., and R. G. Whitten
  1987 Cross-Cultural Study of Human Sexuality. *Annual Review of Anthropology* 16:69–98.

Degarrod, Lydia
  1998 Female Shamanism and the Mapuche Transformation into Christian Chilean Farmers. *Religion* 28:339–350.

de la Cadena, Marisol
  2000 *Indigenous Mestizos: The Politics of Race and Culture in Cuzco, Peru, 1919–1991.* Durham, N.C.: Duke University Press.

Del Negro, Giovanna
  2003 Gender, Class and Suffering in the Argentinean Telenovela *Milagros:* An Italian Perspective. *Global Media Journal* 2(2).

Del Solar, Alberto
1888 *Huincahual*. Paris: Ediciones Pedro Roselli.

Desjarlais, Robert
1997 *Shelter Blues: Sanity and Selfhood among the Homeless*. Philadelphia: University of Pennsylvania Press.
2000 The Makings of Personhood in a Shelter for People Considered Homeless and Mentally Ill. *Ethos* 27(4):466–489.

Deveraux, George
1961 Shamans as Neurotics. *American Anthropologist* 63:1088–1090.

Díaz del Castillo, Bernal
1963 *The Conquest of New Spain*. Translated by J. M. Cohen. Baltimore, Md.: Penguin.

Dillehay, Tom
1985 La influencia política de los chamanes mapuches. *CUHSO* 2(2): 141–157.
1990 *Araucanía, presente y pasado*. Santiago: Editorial Andrés Bello.
1995 Mounds of Social Death: Araucanian Funerary Rites and Political Succession. In *Tombs for the Living: Andean Mortuary Practices*, edited by Tom Dillehay, pp. 87–106. Washington, D.C.: Dumbarton Oaks Research Library and Collection.

Douglas, Mary, ed.
1970 *Witchcraft Confessions and Accusations*. London: Tavistock.

Dougnac, Antonio
1981 El delito de la hechicería en Chile indiano. *Revista Chilena de Historia del Derecho* 8:97–107.

Dubisch, Jill
1995 Lovers in the Field: Sex, Dominance, and the Female Anthropologist. In *Taboo: Sex, Identity, and Erotic Subjectivity in Anthropological Fieldwork*, edited by Don Kulick and Margaret Wilson, pp. 29–50. London: Routledge.

Eck, Diana, and Devaki Jain, eds.
1987 *Speaking of Faith: Global Perspectives on Women, Religion, and Social Change*. Philadelphia: New Society.

Eliade, Mircea
1974 [1964] *Shamanism: Archaic Techniques of Ecstasy*. Princeton, N.J.: Princeton University Press.

Elliston, Deborah
1995 Erotic Anthropology: Ritualized Homosexuality in Melanesia and Beyond. *American Ethnologist* 22(4):848–867.

Encuentro Nacional de Mujeres Indígenas
1995 *Memoria: Encuentro Nacional de Mujeres Indígenas*. Temuco, Chile: Coordinadora de Mujeres de Organizaciones e Instituciones Mapuches.

Epple, Carolyn
1998 Coming to Terms with Navajo *Nádleehí:* A Critique of Berdache,

Gay, Alternate Gender, and Two-Spirit. *American Ethnologist* 25(2): 267–290.

Ercilla y Zúñiga, Alonso de
1933 [1569] *La Araucana*. Santiago: Editorial Nacimiento.

Evans-Pritchard, E. E.
1937 *Witchcraft, Oracles and Magic among the Azande*. Oxford: Clarendon Press.

Ewing, Katherine
1990 The Illusion of Wholeness: Culture, Self, and the Experience of Inconsistency. *Ethos* 18:251–278.

Falkner, Thomas
1774 *A Description of Patagonia and the Adjoining Parts of South America*. London: C. Pugh.

Faron, Louis
1956 Araucanian Patri-Organization and the Omaha System. *American Anthropologist* 58(3):435–456.
1962 Matrilateral Marriage among the Mapuche (Araucanians) of Central Chile. *Sociologus* 12(1):54–66.
1963 Death and Fertility Rites of the Mapuche (Araucanian) Indians of Central Chile. *Ethnology* 2:135–156.
1964 *Hawks of the Sun: Mapuche Morality and Its Ritual Attributes*. Pittsburgh: University of Pittsburgh Press.
1986 [1968] *The Mapuche Indians of Chile*. Prospect Heights, Ill.: Waveland Press.

Febres, Andrés
1846 *Diccionario hispano chileno*. Santiago: Imprenta del Progreso.
1882 [1765] *Diccionario araucano-español*. Buenos Aires: Juan A. Alsina.

Feinberg, Leslie
1996 *Transgender Warriors: Making History from Joan of Ark to RuPaul*. Boston: Beacon Press.

Flax, Jane
1990 *Thinking Fragments: Psychoanalysis, Feminism, and Postmodernism in the Contemporary West*. Berkeley and Los Angeles: University of California Press.

Foerster, Rolf
1993 *Introducción a la religiosidad mapuche*. Santiago: Editorial Universitaria.
1996 *Jesuitas y mapuches 1593–1767*. Santiago: Editorial Universitaria.

Foerster, Rolf, and Javier Lavanchy
1999 La problemática mapuche. In *Análisis del año 1999: Sociedad-política-economía*, edited by Departamento de Sociología, pp. 65–102. Santiago: Universidad de Chile.

Foerster, Rolf, and Sonia Montecino
1988 *Organizaciones, líderes y contiendas mapuches (1900–1970)*. Santiago: Centro de Estudios de la Mujer.

Foerster, Rolf, and Jorge Iván Vergara

2003 Etnia y nación en la lucha por el reconocimiento: Los Mapuches en la sociedad chilena. In *Mapuches y Aymaras: El debate en torno al reconocimiento y los derechos ciudadanos,* edited by Hans Gundermann, Rolf Foerster, and Jorge Vergara, pp. 105–178. Santiago: Universidad Católica de Chile.

Foucault, Michel

1977 *Discipline and Punishment: The Birth of the Prison.* Translated by Alan Sheridan. London: Allen Lane.

1980 *Power/Knowledge: Selected Interviews and Other Writings.* Edited by Colin Gordon. New York: Pantheon.

1990 [1978] *The History of Sexuality: An Introduction,* vol. 1. New York: Vintage.

Frigerio, Alejandro

1988 Faking: Possession Trance Behavior and Afro-Brazilian Religions in Argentina. Paper presented at the meeting of the Southwestern Anthropological Association, March. Monterey, Calif.

Garber, M.

1992 *Vested Interests: Cross-Dressing and Cultural Anxiety.* New York: Routledge.

Gay, Claudio

1846 *Historia física y política de Chile,* vol. 1. Paris: Imprenta de Maulde y Renos.

Geertz, Clifford

1966 Religion as a Cultural System. In *A Reader in the Anthropology of Religion,* edited by Michael Lambek, pp. 61–82. Oxford: Blackwell.

1973 *The Interpretation of Cultures.* New York: Basic Books.

1983 *Local Knowledge: Further Essays in Interpretive Anthropology.* New York: Basic Books.

Geirola, Gustavo

2000 *Teatralidad y experiencia política en América Latina.* Irvine, Calif.: Gestos.

2003 From AIDS to Gender and Vice Versa: Cultural Representations of Homosexuals in Latin American *Telenovelas.* In *Homosexualités hispaniques,* edited by Nicolás Balutet, pp. 135–151. Paris: L'Harmattan.

Geschiere, Peter

1997 *The Modernity of Witchcraft: Politics and the Occult in Postcolonial Africa.* Charlottesville: University Press of Virginia.

Giddens, Anthony

1997 *Sociology.* 3rd ed. Cambridge: Polity Press.

Gilligan, Carol

1982 *In a Different Voice: Psychological Theory and Women's Development.* Cambridge, Mass: Harvard University Press.

Glass-Coffin, Bonnie
1998 *The Gift of Life: Female Spirituality and Healing in Northern Peru.* Albuquerque: University of New Mexico Press.

Gluckman, Max
1955 *Custom and Conflict in Africa.* Oxford: Blackwell.

Goldberg, Jonathan
1992 *Sodometries: Renaissance Texts and Modern Sexualities.* Stanford, Calif.: Stanford University Press.

Gómara, Francisco López de
1554 *La historia general de las Indias.* Anvers, Belgium: Casa de Iuan Steelsio.

Gómez de Vidaurre
1889 [1789] *Historia geográfica, natural y civil del reino de Chile,* vols. 14, 15. Santiago: Imprenta Ercilla.

Góngora Marmolejo, Alonso de
1862 [1575] *Historia de las cosas que han acaecido en el reino de Chile y de los que lo han gobernado.* Colección de Historiadores de Chile, vol. 2. Santiago: Imprenta del Ferrocarril.

González de Nájera, Alonso
1889 [1614] *Desengaño y reparo de la guerra del reino de Chile.* Colección de Historiadores de Chile, vol. 16. Santiago: Imprenta del Ferrocarril.

Gramsci, Antonio
1971 [1925–1935] *Selections from the Prison Notebooks.* New York: International.

Grebe, María Ester
1973 El *kultrun:* Un microcosmos simbólico. *Revista Musical Chilena* 123–124:3–42.
1975 Taxonomía de enfermedades mapuches. *Nueva Época* 2. Santiago: Universidad de Chile.

Grebe, María Ester; Sergio Pacheco; and Jorge Segura
1972 Cosmovisión mapuche. *Cuadernos de la Realidad Nacional* 14:46–73.

Greenberg, David
1988 *The Construction of Homosexuality.* Chicago: University of Chicago Press.

Grosz, Elizabeth
1994 *Volatile Bodies: Towards a Corporeal Feminism.* Bloomington: Indiana University Press.

Guajardo, Gabriel
2000 Homosexualidad masculina y opinión pública chilena en los noventa. In *Masculinidades: Identidad, sexualidad y familia,* pp. 123–140. Santiago: Facultad Latinoamericana de Ciencias Sociales (FLACSO).

Guerra, Armaldo
2003 ¿Nuevo trato o nuevo teatro con Mapuches? *Opinión* (November 17, 2003).

Guevara, Tomás
1908 *Psicología del pueblo araucano.* Santiago: Imprenta Cervantes.
1913 *Las últimas familias y costumbres araucanas.* Santiago: Imprenta Cervantes.
1925 *Historia de Chile: Chile pre-hispano.* Santiago: Barcells.

Gumucio, Juan Carlos
1999 *Hierarchy, Utility and Metaphor in Mapuche Botany.* Uppsala Studies in Cultural Anthropology, 27. Uppsala: Acta Universitatis Upsaliensis.

Gupta, Akhil, and James Ferguson
1997 *Culture, Power, Place: Explorations in Critical Anthropology.* Durham, N.C.: Duke University Press.

Gusinde, Martín
1917 Medicina e higiene de los antiguos Araucanos. *Revista Chilena de Historia y Geografía* 26:382–415.

Guss, David
2000 *The Festive State: Race, Ethnicity, and Nationalism as Cultural Performance.* Berkeley and Los Angeles: University of California Press.

Halberstam, Judith
1998 *Female Masculinity.* Durham, N.C.: Duke University Press.

Hall, Stuart
1986 Gramsci's Relevance for the Study of Race and Ethnicity. *Journal of Communication Inquiry* 10(2):5–27.

Halliburton, Murphy
2002 Rethinking Anthropological Studies of the Body: Manas and Bôdham in Kerala. *American Anthropologist* 104(4):1123–1134.

Halperin, David M.
2000 How to Do the History of Male Homosexuality. *GLQ* 6(1):87–124.

Hamayon, Roberte
1990 *La chasse à l'âme: Esquisse d'une théorie du shamanisme sibérien.* Nanterre: Société d'Etnologie.

Handelman, Don
1994 Critiques of Anthropology: Literary Turns, Slippery Bends. *Poetics Today* 15(3):341–381.

Haraway, Donna
1991 *Simians, Cyborgs, and Women: The Re-invention of Nature.* New York: Routledge.

Harvey, Youngsook Kim
1979 *Six Korean Women: The Socialization of Shamans.* Saint Paul, Minn.: West Publishing.

Hastrup, Kirsten
1987 The Reality of Anthropology. *Ethnos* 52(3–4):287–300.

Hausman, Bernice
1995 *Changing Sex: Transsexualism, Technology, and the Idea of Gender.* Durham, N.C.: Duke University Press.

Havestadt, Bernardo
1882 [1777]   *Chilidugu, Sive Tractus Linguae Chilensis.* Leipzig: Teubner.

Herdt, Gilbert
1984   Ritualized Homosexual Behavior in Male Cults of Melanesia, 1862–1983: An Introduction. In *Ritualized Homosexuality in Melanesia,* edited by Gilbert Herdt, pp. 1–82. Berkeley and Los Angeles: University of California Press.

Hilger, María Inez
1957   *Araucanian Child Life and Its Cultural Background.* Smithsonian Miscellaneous Collection, vol. 133. Washington, D.C.: Smithsonian Institution.

Hill, Jonathan, ed.
1988   *Rethinking History and Myth: Indigenous South American Perspectives on the Past.* Urbana: University of Illinois Press.

Hill, Jonathan, and Susan Staats
2002   Redelineando el curso de la historia: Estados Euro-americanos y las culturas sin pueblos. In *Colonización, resistencia y mestizaje en las Américas,* edited by Guillaume Boccara, pp. 13–26. Lima: Instituto Francés de Estudios Andinos Abya-Ayala.

Hobsbawm, Eric, and Terence Ranger
1983   *The Invention of Tradition.* Cambridge: Cambridge University Press.

Hollan, Douglas, and Jane Wellenkamp
1994   *Contentment and Suffering: Culture and Experience in Toraja.* New York. Columbia University Press.

Horswell, Michael
1997   *Third Gender, Tropes of Sexuality, and Transculturation in Colonial Andean Historiography.* Ann Arbor, Mich.: University Microfilms International.

Housse, Émile
1938   *Une epopée indienne: Les Araucans du Chili.* Paris: Plon.

Houston, Stephen, and David Stuart
1989   *The Way Glyph: Evidence for Co-Essences among the Classic Maya.* Washington, D.C.: Center for Maya Research.

Howard, Alan
1985   *Ethnopsychology and Prospects for a Cultural Psychology.* Berkeley and Los Angeles: University of California Press.

Hultkrantz, Ake
1973   A Definition of Shamanism. *Temeneos* 9:25–37.

Humphrey, Caroline, and Urgunge Onon
1996   *Shamans and Elders: Experience, Knowledge, and Power among the Daur Mongols.* Oxford: Oxford University Press.

Instituto de Estudios Indígenas, Universidad de la Frontera
2003   *Los derechos de los pueblos indígenas en Chile.* Santiago: LOM Ediciones.

Jilek, Wolfgang
　1978　Native Renaissance: The Survival and Revival of Indigenous Therapeutic Ceremonials among North American Indians. *Transcultural Psychiatric Research Review* 15:117–147.

Joralemon, Don
　1990　The Selling of the Shaman and the Problem of Informant Legitimacy. *Journal of Anthropological Research* 46(2):105–117.

Joralemon, Don, and Douglas Sharon
　1993　*Sorcery and Shamanism: Curanderos and Clients in Northern Peru.* Salt Lake City: University of Utah Press.

Jordan, Mark
　1997　*The Invention of Sodomy in Christian Theology.* Chicago: University of Chicago Press.

Kapferer, Bruce
　1983　*A Celebration of Demons: Exorcism and the Aesthetics of Healing in Sri Lanka.* Bloomington: Indiana University Press.

Karlsen, Carol
　1987　*The Devil in the Shape of a Woman: Witchcraft in Colonial New England.* New York: W. W. Norton.

Katz, Jonathan
　1976　*Gay American History: Lesbians and Gay Men in the U.S.A.* New York: Cromwell.

Keesing, Roger
　1989　Creating the Past: Custom and Identity in the Contemporary Pacific. *Contemporary Pacific* 1(1–2):19–42.

Kendall, Laurel
　1985　*Shamans, Housewives, and Other Restless Spirits: Women in Korean Ritual Life.* Honolulu: University of Hawaii Press.
　1998　Who Speaks for Korean Shamans When Shamans Speak of the Nation? In *Making Majorities: Constituting the Nation in Japan, Korea, China, Malaysia, Fiji, Turkey, and the United States,* edited by Dru C. Gladney, pp. 55–72. Stanford, Calif.: Stanford University Press.
　1999　Shamans. In *Encyclopedia of Women and World Religions,* edited by Serenity Young, pp. 892–895. New York: Macmillan.

King, Ursula
　1989　*Women and Spirituality: Voices of Protest and Promise.* New York: New Amsterdam.

Klaits, Joseph
　1985　*Servants of Satan: The Age of the Witch Hunts.* Bloomington: Indiana University Press.

Knauft, Bruce
　1998　Creative Possessions: Spirit Mediumship and Millennial Economy among Gebusi of Papua, New Guinea. In *Bodies and Persons: Comparative Perspectives from Africa and Melanesia,* edited by Michael Lambek

and Andrew Strathern, pp. 197–209. Cambridge: Cambridge University Press.

Kramer, Heinreich, and James Sprenger

1970 [1486] *Malleus Maleficarum.* New York: Benjamin Blom.

Kulick, Don

1998 *Travestí: Sex, Gender and Culture among Brazilian Transgendered Prostitutes.* Chicago: University of Chicago Press.

Kulick, Don, and Margaret Wilson

1995 *Taboo: Sex, Identity, and Erotic Subjectivity in Anthropological Fieldwork.* London: Routledge.

Kuramochi, Yosuke

1990 Contribuciones etnográficas al estudio del machitun. Paper presented at the Cuartas Jornadas de Lengua y Literatura Mapuche, Temuco, Chile.

Laderman, Carol

1991 *Taming the Wind of Desire: Psychology, Medicine, and Aesthetics in Malay Shamanistic Performance.* Berkeley and Los Angeles: University of California Press.

1992 Malay Medicine, Malay Person. In *Anthropological Approaches to the Study of Ethnomedicine,* edited by M. Nichter, pp. 191–206. Amsterdam: Gordon and Breach.

1994 The Embodiment of Symbols and the Acculturation of the Anthropologist. In *Embodiment and Experience: The Existential Ground of Culture and Self,* edited by Thomas Csordas, pp. 183–197. Cambridge: Cambridge University Press.

Lakoff, George, and Mark Johnson

1980 *Metaphors We Live By.* Chicago: University of Chicago Press.

Lamb, Sarah

2000 *White Saris and Sweet Mangoes: Aging, Gender, and Body in North India.* Berkeley and Los Angeles: University of California Press.

Lambek, Michael

1980 Spirits and Spouses: Possession as a System of Communication among Malagasy Speakers of Mayotte. *American Ethnologist* 7(2):318–331.

1981 *Human Spirits: A Cultural Account of Trance in Mayotte.* Cambridge: Cambridge University Press.

Lambek, Michael, and Andrew Strathern, eds.

1998 *Bodies and Persons: Comparative Perspectives from Africa and Melanesia.* Cambridge: Cambridge University Press.

Lancaster, Roger

1992 *Life Is Hard: Machismo, Danger, and the Intimacy of Power in Nicaragua.* Berkeley and Los Angeles: University of California Press.

1997a Sexual Positions: Caveats and Second Thoughts on Categories. *Americas* 54:1–16.

1997b Guto's Performance: Notes on the Transvestism of Everyday Life. In *The Gender and Sexuality Reader: Culture, History, Political Economy,* edited by Roger N. Lancaster and Micaela di Leonardo, pp. 559–574. New York: Routledge.

2001 Tolerance and Intolerance in Sexual Cultures in Latin America. Paper presented at the seminar "Sex, Art, and the Body Politic in Latin America," Ohio University, May 16–18.

Landa, Diego de
1941 *Relación de las Cosas de Yucatán: A Translation*. Cambridge, Mass.: Peabody Museum of American Archaeology and Ethnology.

Landry, Donna, and Gerald MacLean, eds.
1996 *The Spivak Reader*. New York: Routledge.

Langdon, Jean
2004 Commentary. In *In Darkness and Secrecy: The Anthropology of Assault Sorcery and Witchcraft in Amazonia*, edited by Neil Whitehead and Robin Wright, pp. 306–313. Durham, N.C.: Duke University Press.

Langdon, E. Jean, and Gerhard Baer, eds.
1992 *Portals of Power: Shamanism in South America*. Albuquerque: University of New Mexico Press.

Langness, Lewis
1987 *The Study of Culture*. Rev. ed. San Francisco, Calif.: Chandler and Sharp.

Larraín, Raimundo
1870 *Cailloma*. Santiago: Imprenta El Independiente.

Latcham, Ricardo
1915 *Conferencias sobre antropología, etnología y arqueología*. Santiago: Imprenta Universitaria.
1922 *La organización social y las creencias religiosas de los antiguos araucanos*. Santiago: Publicaciones del Museo de Etnología y Antropología de Chile.

Legaré, Evelyn
1995 The Otavalo Trade Diaspora: Social Capital and Transnational Entrepreneurship. *Ethnic and Racial Studies* 22(2):422–426.

Leiva, Arturo
1982 El otro cautiverio: El relato de fray Juan Falcón y su oposición a la doctrina del padre Luis de Valdivia. *Revista Frontera*. Temuco, Chile: Universidad de la Frontera.

Levy, Robert
1973 *Tahitians: Mind and Experience in the Society Islands*. Chicago: University of Chicago Press.

Lewis, I. M.
1966 Spirit Possession and Deprivation Cults. *Man* 1(3):306–329.
1969 Spirit Possession in Northern Somaliland. In *Spirit Mediumship and Society in Africa*, edited by J. Beattie and J. Middleton, pp. 188–219. London: Routledge.
1971 *Ecstatic Religion: An Anthropological Study of Spirit Possession and Shamanism*. Baltimore, Md.: Penguin.

Lira, Máximo
1867 *A orillas del Bio-Bio.* Santiago: Imprenta El Independiente.
1870 *Gualda.* Santiago: Imprenta El Independiente.

Lock, Margaret
1993 Cultivating the Body: Anthropology and the Epistemologies of Bodily Practice and Knowledge. *Annual Review of Anthropology* 22:133–155.

Low, Setha
1994 Embodied Metaphors: Nerves as Lived Experience. In *Embodiment and Experience: The Existential Ground of Culture and Self,* edited by Thomas Csordas, pp. 139–162. Cambridge: Cambridge University Press.

Manquilef, Luis
1914 *Las misiones franciscanas y el importantísimo rol que han desempeñado en la civilización y pacificación de la Araucanía.* Ancud, Chile: Imprenta Asilo de Huérfanas.

Marileo, Armando
1995 Mundo mapuche. In *Medicinas y culturas en la Araucanía,* edited by Luca Citarella, pp. 91–108. Santiago: Editorial Sudamericana.

Marimán, José
1998 Lumaco y el movimiento mapuche. Electronic document, http://www .xs4all.nl/~rehue/art/jmar6.html, accessed March 30, 2001.
2003 Análisis político mapuche: Identidad fragmentada. *Azkintuwe: Periódico Nacional Mapuche* 2 (December) (www.nodo50.org/azkintuwe/).
2004 El gigante silenciado. *Azkintuwe: Periódico Nacional Mapuche* 4 (March) (www.nodo50.org/azkintuwe/).

Marimán, Pablo
1990 Algunas consideraciones entorno al voto mapuche. *Liwen* 2:25–35.

Matory, Lorand
1994 *Sex and the Empire That Is No More: Gender and Politics of Metaphor in Oyo Yoruba Religion.* Minneapolis: University of Minnesota Press.

Matus, Zapata Leotardo
1912 Vida y costumbres de los indios araucanos. *Revista Chilena de Historia y Geografía* 8(4):47–68.

Mayer, Tamar
2000 *Gender Ironies of Nationalism: Sexing the Nation.* London: Routledge.

McIlwraith, Thomas F.
1948 *The Bella Coola Indians.* Toronto: University of Toronto Press.

McKee Irwin, Robert
2000 The Famous 41: The Scandalous Birth of Modern Mexican Homosexuality. *GLQ* 6(3):353–376.

Medina, José Toribio
1882 *Los aborígenes de Chile.* Santiago: Guttemberg.

Mege, Pedro
1997 Louis Faron en el Espejismo de la Pulcritud: Hawks of the Sun, Revisited. *Liwen* 4:129–142.

Mendenhall, Emily
2004 Contraception, Community, and Control: A Global Analysis of Reproductive Autonomy. MA thesis, Davidson College.

Mentore, George
2004 The Glorious Tyranny of Silence and the Resonance of Shamanic Breath. In *In Darkness and Secrecy: The Anthropology of Assault Sorcery and Witchcraft in Amazonia,* edited by Neil Whitehead and Robin Wright, pp. 132–156. Durham, N.C.: Duke University Press.

Merleau-Ponty, Maurice
1962 *Phenomenology of Perception.* Translated by James Edie. Evanston, Ill.: Northwestern University Press.

Métraux, Alfred
1942 Le shamanisme araucan. *Revista del Instituto de Antropología de la Universidad Nacional de Tucumán* 2(10):309–362.
1967 *Réligions et magies indiennes d'Amerique du Sud.* Paris: Gallimard.
1973 *Religión y magias indígenas de América del Sur.* Ediciones Madrid: Aguilar.

Millamán, Rosamel
2001 Mapuches Press for Autonomy. *NACLA Report of the Americas* 35(2): 10–12.

Miller, Francesca
1991 *Latin American Women and the Search for Social Justice.* Hanover, N.H.: University Press of New England.

Moesbach, Wilhelm de
1936 [1929–1931] *Vida y costumbres de los indígenas araucanos en la segunda mitad del siglo XIX.* Santiago: Imprenta Universitaria.
1992 *Botánica indígena de Chile.* Santiago: Editorial Andrés Bello.

Mohanty, Chandra; Ann Russo; and Lourdes Torres, eds.
1991 *Third World Women and the Politics of Feminism.* Bloomington: Indiana University Press.

Molina, Juan Ignacio
1901 [1787] *Compendio de la historia civil del reino de Chile.* Colección de Historiadores de Chile, vol. 24. Santiago: Imprenta del Ferrocarril.

Montecino, Sonia
1984 *Mujeres de la tierra.* Santiago: CEM-PEMCI.
1995 *Sol viejo, sol vieja: Lo feminino en las representaciones mapuche.* Santiago: Servicio Nacional de la Mujer (SERNAM).
1999 *Sueño con menguante: Biografía de una machi.* Santiago: Editorial Sudamericana.

Monter, William
1990 *Frontiers of Heresy: The Spanish Inquisition from the Basque Lands to Sicily.* Cambridge: Cambridge University Press.

Morin, Françoise
1999 La Ley Indígena es una ley nociva: Entrevista a Aucan Huilcaman. *L'Ordinaire Latino-Americain* 177:25–28.

Mostny, Grete
 1960 *Culturas pre-colombinas de Chile.* Santiago: Editorial del Pacífico.

Muehlebach, Andrea
 2003 What Self in Self-Determination? Notes from the Frontiers of Transnational Indigenous Activism. *Identities: Global Studies in Culture and
 Power* 10:241–268.

Muga, Ana
 2004 A 10 años de la promulgación de la Ley Indígena: Las contradicciones
 de Lagos. *Azkintuwe: Periódico Nacional Mapuche* 3 (January) (http://
 www.nodo50.org/azkintuwe).

Munn, Henry
 1973 The Mushrooms of Language. In *Hallucinogens and Shamanism,* edited
 by Michael Harner, pp. 86–122. Oxford: Oxford University Press.

Murray, Stephen, ed.
 1995 *Latin American Male Homosexualities.* Albuquerque: University of New
 Mexico Press.

Ñanculef, Juan, and Juan Carlos Gumucio
 1991 El trabajo de la machi: Contenido y expresividad. *Nütram* 25:3–12.

Nanda, Serena
 1985 The Hijras of India: Cultural and Individual Dimensions of an Institutionalized Third Gender Role. *Journal of Homosexuality* 11(3–4):35–54.

Narayan, Kirin
 1993 How Native Is the Native Anthropologist? *American Anthropologist*
 95(3):671–686.

Neruda, Pablo
 1951 *Poesías completas.* Buenos Aires: Editorial Losada.

Noll, Richard
 1983 Shamanism and Schizophrenia: A State Specific Approach to the
 Schizophrenia Metaphor of Shamanic States. *American Ethnologist*
 10(3):443–459.

Núñez de Pineda y Bascuñán, Francisco
 1863 [1673] *Cautiverio felíz y razón de las guerras dilatadas de Chile.* Santiago:
 Imprenta el Ferrocarril.

Obeyesekere, Gannanath
 1981 *Medusa's Hair: An Essay on Personal Symbols and Religious Experience.*
 Chicago: University Of Chicago Press.

Ochs, Carol
 1983 *Women and Spirituality.* Totowa, N.J.: Rowman and Allanheld.

Oesterreich, T. K.
 1966 *Possession: Demoniacal and Other.* Secaucus, N.J.: Citadel Press.

Ohnuki-Tierney, Emiko
 1980 Shamans and the Imu among Two Ainu Groups: Toward a Cross-
 Cultural Model of Interpretation. *Ethos* 8(3):204–228.

Olivares, Miguel de
1864–1901   *Historia militar, civil y sagrada de Chile.* Colección de Historiadores de Chile, vol. 4. Santiago: Imprenta del Ferrocarril.

Oña, Pedro de
1975 [1596]   *Arauco domado.* Santiago: Editorial Universitaria.

Ortner, Sherry
1995   Resistance and the Problem of Ethnographic Representation. *Comparative Studies in Society and History* 37(1):173–193.

Ovalle, Alonso de
1888 [1646]   *Histórica relación del reino de Chile y de las misiones que ejercita en
el la Compañía de Jesús.* Santiago: Imprenta Ercilla.

Oyarce, Ana María
1988   *Sistemas médicos que coexisten en la novena región de Chile: Una descripción
general.* Santiago: Enfoques en Atención Primaria, year 3, no. 3.
1989   *Conocimientos, creencias y prácticas en torno al ciclo vital en una comunidad
mapuche de la IX región de Chile.* Documentos de Trabajo series, no. 2
(May). Temuco: Programa de Apoyo y Extensión en Salud Materno
Infantil (PAESMI).

Pandolfi, Mariella
1993   Le self, le corps, la crise de la présence. *Anthropologie et Sociétés* 17(1–2):
57–78.

Parker, Richard
1991   *Bodies, Pleasures, and Passions: Sexual Culture in Contemporary Brazil.*
Boston: Beacon Press.
1999   *Beneath the Equator: Culture of Desire, Male Homosexuality, and Emerging
Gay Communities in Brazil.* New York: Routledge.

Parsons, Elsie Clews
1916   The Zuni *la'mana. American Anthropologist* 18:521–528.

Perry, Mary Elizabeth
1990   *Gender Disorders in Early Modern Seville.* Princeton, N.J.: Princeton University Press.

Peters, Larry
1981   *Ecstasy and Healing in Nepal: An Ethnopsychiatric Study of Tamang Shamanism.* Malibu, Calif.: Undena Publications.

Peters, Larry, and Douglas Price-Williams
1980   Towards an Experiential Analysis of Shamanism. *American Ethnologist*
7(3):397–448.

Pinto, Jorge
1991   *Misticismo y violencia en la temprana evangelización de Chile.* Temuco,
Chile: Ediciones Universidad de la Frontera.
2002   Las heridas no cicatrizadas: La exclusión del Mapuche en Chile en la
segunda mitad del siglo XIX. In *Colonización, resistencia y mestizaje en las
Americas, siglos XVI–XX,* edited by Guillaume Boccara, pp. 329–358.
Quito: Ediciones Abya-Yala.

Poewe, Karla
  1996 Writing Culture and Writing Fieldwork: The Proliferation of Experimental and Experiential Ethnographies. *Ethnos* 61(3–4):177–206.

Pollock, Don
  1996 Personhood and Illness among the Kulina. *Medical Anthropology Quarterly* 10(3):319–341.

Powers, William K.
  1977 *Oglala Religion*. Lincoln: University of Nebraska Press.

Prieur, Annick
  1998 *Mema's House, Mexico City: On Transvestites, Queens, and Machos*. Chicago: University of Chicago Press.

Quidel, José
  1998 Machi Zugu: Ser machi. *CUHSO* 4(1):30–37.

Quiroga, Jerónimo de
  1979 [1692] *Memoria de los sucesos de la guerra de Chile*. Santiago: Editorial Andrés Bello.

Radin, Paul
  1937 *Primitive Religion*. New York: Viking.

Ramos, Alcida Rita
  1998 *Indigenism: Ethnic Politics in Brazil*. Madison: University of Wisconsin Press.

Rappaport, Joanne, and Robert Dover
  1996 The Construction of Difference by Native Legislators: Assessing the Impact of the Colombian Constitution of 1991. *Journal of Latin American Anthropology* 1(2):22–45.

Rasmussen, Susan
  1995 *Spirit Possession and Personhood among the Kel Ewey Tuareg*. Cambridge: Cambridge University Press.

Reuque, Paillalef Rosa Isolde
  2002 *When a Flower Is Reborn: The Life and Times of a Mapuche Feminist*. Edited, translated, and with an introduction by Florencia Mallon. Durham, N.C.: Duke University Press.

Richards, Patricia
  2004 *Pobladoras, Indígenas, and the State: Difference, Equality, and Women's Rights in Chile*. Piscataway, N.J.: Rutgers University Press.

Roberts, John M.
  1984 Quitting the Game: Covert Disengagement from the Butler County Eight Ball. *American Anthropologist* 86:549–567.

Robertson–De Carbo, Carol
  1977 *Lukutun: Text and Context in Mapuche Rogations*. Latin American Literatures, vol. 1, no 2. Pittsburgh: University of Pittsburgh.

Robles, Víctor Hugo
  2001 Historia política del movimiento homosexual chileno. MA thesis, ARCIS University.

Robles Rodríguez, Eulogio
1911 Costumbres y creencias araucanas: *Neigurehuen,* baile de machi. *Revista de Folklore Chileno* 3:113–136.
1912 Costumbres y creencias araucanas: *Machiluhun,* iniciación de machi. *Revista de Folklore Chileno* 4:155–181.
1942 *Costumbre y creencias araucanas.* Santiago: Ediciones Universidad de Chile.

Rodríguez, Roberto; Óscar Matthei; and Max Quezada
1983 *Flora arbórea de Chile.* Concepción, Chile: Editorial de la Universidad de Concepción.

Rosaldo, Michelle Zimbalist
1974 Women, Culture, and Society: A Theoretical Overview. In *Women, Culture, and Society,* edited by Michelle Rosaldo and Louise Lamphere, pp. 17–42. Stanford, Calif.: Stanford University Press.

Rosaldo, Renato
1989 *Culture and Truth: The Re-Making of Social Analysis.* Boston: Beacon Press.

Rosales, Diego de
1989 [1674] *Historia general del reino de Chile,* vol. 1. Santiago: Editorial Andrés Bello.

Roscoe, William
1991 *The Zuni Man-Woman.* Albuquerque: University of New Mexico Press.
1998 *Third and Fourth Genders in Native North America.* New York: Saint Martin's.

Roseman, Marina
1991 *Healing Sounds from the Malaysian Forest: Temiar Music and Medicine.* Berkeley and Los Angeles: University of California Press.

Rouget, Gilbert
1985 *Music and Trance: A Theory of Relations between Music and Possession.* Chicago: University of Chicago Press.

Rubenstein, Steven
2002 *Alejandro Tsakimp: A Shuar Healer in the Margins of History.* Lincoln: University of Nebraska Press.

Ruether, Rosemary Radford
1987 Spirit and Matter, Public and Private: The Challenge of Feminism to Traditional Dualisms. In *Embodied Love: Sensuality and Relationship as Feminist Values,* edited by Paula M. Cooey, Sharon A. Farmer, and Mary Ellen Ross, pp. 65–76. San Francisco: Harper and Row.

Saavedra, Alejandro
2002 *Los Mapuche en la sociedad chilena actual.* Santiago: LOM Ediciones.

Saint-Saëns, Alain
1996 *Sex and Love in Golden Age Spain.* New Orleans: University Press of the South.

Saladin D'Anglure, Bernard
1992 Re-Thinking Inuit Shamanism through the Concept of the Third Gender. In *Northern Religions and Shamanism,* edited by Mihaly Hoppal and Juha Pentikainen, pp. 146–150. Budapest: Akademiai Kiado.

San Martín, René
1976 Machitun: Una ceremonia mapuche. In *Estudios antropológicos sobre los Mapuches de Chile sur-central,* edited by Tom Dillehay, pp. 83–97. Temuco, Chile: Universidad Católica.

Santos-Granero, Fernando
2004 The Enemy Within: Child Sorcery, Revolution, and the Evils of Modernization in Eastern Peru. In *In Darkness and Secrecy: The Anthropology of Assault Sorcery and Witchcraft in Amazonia,* edited by Neil Whitehead and Robin Wright, pp. 272–305. Durham, N.C.: Duke University Press.

Schein, Louisa
2000 *Minority Rules: The Miao and the Feminine in China's Cultural Politics.* Durham, N.C.: Duke University Press.

Scheper-Hughes, Nancy
1992 *Death without Weeping: The Violence of Everyday Life in Brazil.* Berkeley and Los Angeles: University of California Press.
1994 Mother Love. *New Internationalist* 254 (April) (http://www.newint .org/issue254/mother.htm).
2001 *Saints, Scholars, and Schizophrenics: Mental Illness in Rural Ireland.* Berkeley and Los Angeles: University of California Press.

Scheper-Hughes, Nancy, and Margaret Lock
1987 The Mindful Body: A Prolegomenon to Future Work in Medical Anthropology. *Medical Anthropology Quarterly* 1:6–41.

Schifter, Jacobo
1998 *Lila's House: Male Prostitution in Latin America.* Translated by Irene Artavia Fernández and Sharon Mulhern. New York: Haworth.

Schindler, Helmut
1989 Con reverencia nombreys al Pillan y Huecuvoe. (Sermón IV, Luis de Valdivia, 1621). Budapest. *Revindi,* no. 1:15–27.

Scott, James
1999 *Seeing Like a State: How Certain Schemes to Improve the Human Condition Have Failed.* New Haven, Conn.: Yale University Press.

Scott, Joan
1997 *Gender and the Politics of History.* New York: Columbia University Press.

Sered, Susan
1994 *Priestess Mother, Sacred Sister: Religions Dominated by Women.* New York: Oxford University Press.

Servicio Nacional de la Mujer (SERNAM)
1997 *Propuestas de políticas de igualdad de oportunidades para las mujeres rurales.* Santiago: SERNAM.

Sider, Gerald
1987 When Parrots Learn to Talk, and Why They Can't: Domination, Deception, and Self-Deception in Indian-White Relations. *Comparative Studies in Society and History* 29:3–23.

Silverblatt, Irene
1987 *Moon, Sun, and Witches: Gender Ideologies and Class in Inca and Colonial Peru.* Princeton, N.J.: Princeton University Press.

Silverman, Julian
1967 Shamanism and Acute Schizophrenia. *American Anthropologist* 69: 21–31.

Silverman, Kaja
1992 *Male Subjectivity at the Margins.* New York: Routledge.

Smith, A. C.
1941 American Species of *Drimys. Journal of the Arnold Arboretum* 24(1): 1–20.

Smith, Edmund Reul
1855 *The Araucanians, or Notes of a Tour among the Indian Tribes of Southern Chili.* New York: Harper and Brothers.

Sosa, Pedro de
1966 [1616] *Memorial del peligroso estado espiritual y temporal del reino de Chile.* Santiago: Fondo Histórico y Bibliográfico José Toribio Medina.

Spier, Leslie
1930 Klamath Ethnography. *University of California Publications in American Archaeology and Ethnology* 30:51–53.

Spiro, Milford
1967 *Burmese Supernaturalism: A Study in the Explanation and Reduction of Suffering.* Englewood Cliffs, N.J.: Prentice-Hall.
1984 Some Reflections on Cultural Determinism and Relativism with Special Reference to Emotion and Reason. In *Culture Theory: Essays on Mind, Self, and Emotion,* edited by R. Shweder and R. Levine, pp. 323–346. Cambridge: Cambridge University Press.

Steedly, Mary
1993 *Hanging without a Rope: Narrative Experience in Colonial and Post-Colonial Karoland.* Princeton, N.J.: Princeton University Press.

Stewart, Pamela, and Andrew Strathern
2001 *Humors and Substances: Ideas of the Body in New Guinea.* Westport, Conn.: Bergin and Garvey.

Stoler, Ann Laura
1995 *Race and the Education of Desire: Foucault's History of Sexuality and the Colonial Order of Things.* Durham, N.C.: Duke University Press.

Stoller, Paul
1989 *The Taste of Ethnographic Things: The Senses in Anthropology.* Philadelphia: University of Pennsylvania Press.

1995 *Embodying Colonial Memories: Spirit Possession, Power, and the Hauka in West Africa.* New York: Routledge.

Stoller, Paul, and Cheryl Olkes
1987 *In Sorcerer's Shadow: A Memoir of Apprenticeship among the Songhay of Niger.* Chicago: University of Chicago Press.

Strathern, Andrew
1996 *Body Thoughts.* Ann Arbor: University of Michigan Press.

Strathern, Marilyn
1988 *The Gender of the Gift.* Berkeley and Los Angeles: University of California Press.

Strinati, Dominic
1995 *An Introduction to Theories of Popular Culture.* London: Routledge.

Stuchlik, Milan
1976 *Life on a Half Share.* London: C. Hurst.

Tarifa, Fatos
2001 *Culture, Ideology and Society.* The Hague: Smiet.

Taube, Karl
2000 Dance. In *The Oxford Encyclopedia of Mesoamerican Cultures: The Civilizations of Mexico and Central America,* edited by David Carrasco, pp. 305–308. New York: Oxford University Press.

Taussig, Michael
1987 *Shamanism, Colonialism, and the Wild Man: A Study in Terror and Healing.* Chicago: University of Chicago Press.
1993 *Mimesis and Alterity: A Particular History of the Senses.* New York: Routledge.
1997 *The Magic of the State.* New York: Routledge.
1999 *Defacement: Public Secrecy and the Labor of the Negative.* Stanford, Calif.: Stanford University Press.

Tedlock, Barbara
2000 Ethnography and Ethnographic Representation. In *Handbook of Qualitative Research,* 2nd ed., edited by Norman Denzin and Yvonne Lincoln, pp. 455–486. Thousand Oaks, Calif.: Sage Publications.
2003 Recognizing and Celebrating the Feminine in Shamanic Heritage. In *Rediscovery of Shamanic Heritage,* edited by Mihaly Hoppal, pp. 297–316. Budapest: Akademiai Kiado.
2005 *The Woman in the Shaman's Body: Reclaiming the Feminine in Religion and Medicine.* New York: Bantam.

Tedlock, Dennis, and Bruce Manheim
1995 *The Dialogical Emergence of Culture.* Urbana: University of Illinois Press.

Teit, James
1930 The Salish Tribes of the Western Plateau. *Annual Report of the Bureau of American Ethnology* 45:384.

Teixeira Pinto, Márnio

2004 Being Alone amid Others: Sorcery and Morality amongst the Arara (Carib Brazil). In *In Darkness and Secrecy: The Anthropology of Assault Sorcery and Witchcraft in Amazonia*, edited by Neil Whitehead and Robin Wright, pp. 215–243. Durham, N.C.: Duke University Press.

Thomas, Nicolas, and Caroline Humphrey

1994 *Shamanism, History, and the State*. Ann Arbor: University of Michigan Press.

Titiev, Mischa

1951 *Araucanian Culture in Transition*. Ann Arbor: University of Michigan Press.

1968 Araucanian Shamanism. *Boletín del Museo Nacional de Historia Natural de Chile* 30:299–312.

Torres, Ricardo

1997 Percepción del SIDA y de las campañas de prevención en la población homosexual: Estudio cualitativo exploratorio. Unedited document. Santiago: Consejo Nacional para la Prevención y Control del Síndrome de la Inmunodeficiencia Adquirida/Ministerio de Salud.

Tsing, Anna Lowenhaupt

1993 *In the Realm of the Diamond Queen*. Princeton, N.J.: Princeton University Press.

Tufte, Thomas

2003 *Living with the Rubbish Queen: Telenovelas, Culture and Modernity in Brazil*. Luton, U.K.: University of Luton Press.

Valdés, Marcos

2000 Entre la integración y la autonomía: La mirada intelectual del conflicto mapuche. http://www.mapuche.cl.

Valdés, Teresa; Marisa Weinstein; Isabel Toledo; and Lily Letelier

1989 *Centros de madres, 1973–1989. ¿Sólo disciplinamiento?* Documento de Trabajo, no. 416. Santiago: Facultad Latinoamericana de Ciencias Sociales (FLACSO)-Chile.

Valdés, Ximena

2000 Masculinidad en el mundo rural: Realidades que cambian, símbolos que permanecen. In *Masculinidad/es: Identidad, sexualidad y familia*, edited by José Olavarría y Rodrigo Parrini, pp. 29–46. Santiago: Facultad Latinoamericana de Ciencias Sociales (FLACSO)-Chile.

Valdés, Ximena; Loreto Rebolledo; and Angélica Wilson

1995 *Masculino y femenino en la hacienda chilena del siglo XX*. Santiago: Fondart-CEDEM.

Valdivia, Luis de

1887 [1606] *Arte, vocabulario y confesionario de la lengua de Chile*. Leipzig: Teubner.

Vergara, Jorge

2000 La cuestión nacional y el rol del estado en los procesos de integración étnica en el debate latinoamericano y chileno. *Revista de la Academia de Humanismo Cristiano* 5:127–170.

Vergara, Jorge; Andrea Aravena; Martín Correa; and Raúl Molina
1999 Las tierras de la ira: Los sucesos de Traiguén y los conflictos entre comunidades mapuches, empresas forestales y el estado. *Praxis, Subjetividad y Cambio; Revista de Psicología y Ciencias Humanas* 1(1):112–128.

Vidal, Sylvia, and Neil Whitehead
2004 Dark Shamans and the Shamanic State: Sorcery and Witchcraft as Political Process in Guyana and the Venezuelan Amazon. In *In Darkness and Secrecy: The Anthropology of Assault Sorcery and Witchcraft in Amazonia,* edited by Neil Whitehead and Robin Wright, pp. 51–81. Durham, N.C.: Duke University Press.

Villalobos, Sergio
2000 Araucanía, errores ancestrales. *El Mercurio* (May 14, 2000).

Vivar, Gerónimo de
1966 [1558] *Crónica y relación copiosa y verdadera.* Santiago: Fondo.

Wallace, Anthony
1966 *Religion: An Anthropological View.* New York: Random House.

Warren, Kay
1998 *Indigenous Movements and Their Critics: Pan-Maya Activism in Guatemala.* Princeton, N.J.: Princeton University Press.

Weston, Kate
1991 *Families We Chose: Lesbians, Gays, Kinship.* New York: Columbia University Press.
1998 *Longslowburn: Sexuality and Social Science.* London: Routledge.

Whitehead, Harriet
1981 The Bow and the Burden Strap: A New Look at Institutionalized Homosexuality in Native North America. In *Sexual Meanings: The Cultural Construction of Gender and Sexuality,* edited by Sherry Ortner and Harriet Whitehead, pp. 80–115. Cambridge: Cambridge University Press.

Whitehead, Neil
1999 *Dark Shamans: Kanaima and the Poetics of Violent Death.* Durham, N.C.: Duke University Press.

Whitehead, Neil, and Robin Wright
2004 Anthropology of Assault Sorcery and Witchcraft. In *In Darkness and Secrecy: The Anthropology of Assault Sorcery and Witchcraft in Amazonia,* edited by Neil Whitehead and Robin Wright, pp. 1–19. Durham, N.C.: Duke University Press.

Whiting, Beatrice
1950 *Paiute Sorcery.* New York: Viking Fund.

Wikan, Unni
1991 *Behind the Veil in Arabia: Women in Oman.* Chicago: University of Chicago Press.

Wilbert, Johannes

2004 The Order of Dark Shamans among the Warao. In *In Darkness and Secrecy: The Anthropology of Assault Sorcery and Witchcraft in Amazonia,* edited by Neil Whitehead and Robin Wright, pp. 21–50. Durham, N.C.: Duke University Press.

Williams, Brackette

1996 Introduction: Mannish Women and Gender after the Act. In *Women Out of Place: The Gender of Agency and the Race of Nationality,* edited by Brackette Williams, pp. 1–33. New York: Routledge.

Williams, Raymond

1977 *Marxism and Literature.* Oxford: Oxford University Press.

Williams, Walter

1986 *The Spirit and the Flesh: Sexual Diversity in American Indian Culture.* Boston: Beacon Press.

Wolf, Margery

1974 Chinese Women: Old Skills in a New Context. In *Women, Culture, and Society,* edited by Michelle Rosaldo and Louise Lamphere, pp. 157–172. Stanford, Calif.: Stanford University Press.

Zambrano, Mireya

1987 Mujer mapuche: Organización y participación. Serie *Agricultura y Sociedad* 5:85–104.

Index

Page numbers in italics refer to photographs.